NOORDHUIS, KLAAS
THE GARDEN P PLANTS

ENCYCLOPEDIA

| JUN 27 | DATE DUE | |
|---|---|---|
| SEP 30 | | |
| 6-24-02 | | |
| 9/17/08 | | |
| 3-30-11 | | |
| | | |
| | | |
| | | |
| | | |
| | | |
| | | |
| | | |

# THE GARDEN PLANTS ENCYCLOPEDIA

KLAAS T. NOORDHUIS WITH DAVID TOMLINSON

# THE GARDEN PLANTS ENCYCLOPEDIA

FIREFLY BOOKS

# A FIREFLY BOOK

Cataloguing in Publication Data
Noordhuis, Klaas T.
    The garden plants encyclopedia
Includes index.
ISBN 1-55209-206-2

1. Plants, Ornamental—Encyclopedias.
2. Plants, Ornamental—Pictorial works.
3. Gardening—Encyclopedias. 4. Gardening–
Pictorial Works I. Tomlinson, David, 1934- .
II. Title.
SB403.2.N66              1998
635.9'03                 C97-932268-5


Published in the United States in 1998
by Firefly Books (U.S.) Inc.
P.O. Box 1338
Ellicot Station
Buffalo, NY USA
14205

Printed and bound in Slovenia.

98 99 00 01 6 5 4 3 2 1

*Thanks to:*
The organization 'Het Tuinpad Op'/'In Nach-bar's Garten' for their unselfish encouragement of so many people's interest in gardening.

Cover design: *Ton Wienbelt*
Editorial: *Gerda Leegsma*
Production: *TextCase*
Translation: *Mary Charles for First Edition Translations Ltd.*
Typesetting: *Computech for First Edition Translations Ltd.*
Typesetting and updating: *Playne Books Limited*

*Explanation of the symbols and abbreviations referring to plant descriptions:*

| | |
|---|---|
| * | This plant is not usually stocked, but can be ordered by garden centers. |
| ** | This plant is only obtainable from highly specialized nurseries. |
| ! | A plant much admired by the author. |

| | |
|---|---|
| (d) | double-flowered |
| (sd) | semi-double-flowered |

| | |
|---|---|
| bl. | blue |
| blue. | blueish |
| bri. | bright |
| carm. | carmine |
| cr. | cream |

| | | | |
|---|---|---|---|
| cr. | crimson | pur. | purple |
| d. | dark | purpl. | purplish |
| flu. | fluorescent | red. | reddish |
| g. | gold | sal. | salmon |
| gold. | golden | tricol. | tricolor |
| gr. | green | varieg. | variegated |
| gray. | grayish | viol. | violet |
| l. | light | w. | white |
| lav. | lavender | yel. | yellow |
| lem. | lemon | yell. | yellowish |
| lil. | lilac | | |

| | |
|---|---|
| mauv. | mauvish |
| or. | orange |
| p. | pink |
| pom. | pomegranate |
| pu. | pure |

## Hardiness Zones
These are given as a general guide. As there are usually several species given for each genera, the range of zones cover all the species listed. The complete range may not apply to each individual species. Consult your local nursery or an experienced gardener in your area on the particular hardiness of a plant before purchasing.

# Contents

# Preface

Gardening is the most rapidly expanding leisure pursuit in North America and every year more and more young and old people discover the joy and the spiritual and physical satisfaction of gardening.

Traditionally most gardeners begin their gardens by planting tall growing trees to shade the house during the heat of summer. A selection of low-growing evergreen shrubs, often junipers, dwarf spruce or yew, are grouped around the foundations of the house. To complete the design, a colorful edging of spring flowering bulbs is added; these are replaced with annual flowering box plants in summer.

In recent years there has been a marked change in gardening style which has resulted from gardeners becoming better educated as their interest develops; consequently they have become more sophisticated in their selection of garden plants. Their knowledge of hardy trees, flowering shrubs and particularly perennial plants has increased and this has resulted in a wider selection of plants being stocked by nurseries and garden centers.

In a garden which relies on hardy plants to ensure constant color, texture and year-round interest, it is vital to grow as wide a variety of plants as practicable. To achieve this in our continental climate with its mild winters and scorching hot summers in the south and the hot summers and frequently bitterly cold winters in the north, it is necessary to utilize the various microclimates which can be found in all gardens. In northern gardens these can be the warmest spots in the garden which are frequently located close to the house foundation where the snow melts first. In these locations, some plants which will normally only survive in one or two zones to the south can, with some protection, be wintered and flower successfully. Equally, to grow northern plants which need cool conditions in the south, you need to select the coolest location in your garden.

To grow some plants you will also need to modify your soil. If you wish to grow plants which like dry conditions, on a heavy clay, you will need to add coarse sand to improve drainage, or on a lime-rich soil add large quantities of acid peat moss if rhododendrons or other acid-soil-loving plants are desired.

Whatever your needs or gardening ambitions, this encyclopedia of garden plants should be of assistance to both experienced and inexperienced gardeners in helping to select the bext possible plants to suit your climate and the growing conditions within your garden.

David Tomlinson

Left: *Sedum kamtschaticum*

# 1. Trees

## Trees for large gardens

*Choosing a large tree, which can obviously be grown only in a large garden, is no simple matter. Only a few trees are suitable for any particular spot, regardless of the preferences of the owner of the property. The life expectation of an average tree is 100 years. In far less time too large a tree can become a problem in a garden and may need to be cut down prematurely. There are other reasons why such drastic action may unfortunately be necessary: the roots of the tree may have dislodged paving; the type of soil may be unsuitable for the species; or a tree sensitive to wind may have been planted in a coastal area and exposed to gales. A lot of money can be wasted through such mistakes. The aim of this chapter is to help you to make a preliminary selection from the huge variety available. Good professional advice, however, in making the final decision is almost indispensable. Trees have a major effect on the character of a garden and fully justify time being spent in choosing them carefully. If the flowers have no decorative value, their color and the month in which they appear are not mentioned. In this chapter, the height of the trees is indicated in meters, with an approximate equivalent in feet.*

## The Grove

Free-standing trees are often planted in large open spaces, and in some instances it is also possible to create a grove or a shrubbery

Left: *Aesculus hippocastanum*

featuring a variety of species. Suitable examples are listed below and may be combined in different ways, depending on the type of soil. Ask a local expert to work out a suitable combination: he or she will be familiar with the soil type and the water table. Allowance should also be made for height: some trees grow really tall, while 3m (10ft) is the maximum for others. There should, however, be a variety of heights, so that the grove gradually acquires a layered effect. If you have too many trees, it will be impossible for underplanting to survive, and if you have too many shrubs, the trees will lack volume. Details of the various species, which are generally supplied as potted saplings or shrubs, are given in the descriptions of the trees and shrubs.

| | |
|---|---|
| *Acer campestre* | Hedge maple |
| *A. saccharum* | Sugar maple |
| *Alnus glutinosa* | Black alder |
| *A. incana* | Green alder |
| *Amelanchier laevis* | Service berry |
| *Betula papyrifera* | Paperbark birch |
| *B. pendula* | European white birch |
| *Carpinus betulus* | European hornbeam |
| *Catalpa speciosa* | Northern catalpa |
| *Cornus alba* | Tatarian dogwood |
| *C. florida* | Flowering dogwood |
| *C. mas* | Cornelian cherry |
| *C. sanguinea* | Bloodtwig dogwood |
| *Corylius avellana* | European filbert |
| *Crataegus crus-gallii* | Cockspur thorn |
| *C. laevigata* | English hawthorn |
| *Eleaynus angustifolia* | Russian olive |
| *Euonymus alatus* | Burning bush |
| *Fagus sylvatica* | European beech |
| *Fraxinus americana* | White ash |
| *Ilex verticillata* | Winterberry |
| *Larix kaempferi* | Japanese larch |
| *Ligustrum vulgare* | Common privet |
| *Picea abies* | Norway spruce |
| *P. sitchensis* | Sitka spruce |
| *Pinus nigra* | Austrian pine |
| *P. strobus* | White pine |
| *Populus alba* | White poplar |
| *P. tremuloides* | Aspen |
| *Prunus avium* | Mazzard, sweet cherry |
| *P. padus* | European bird cherry |
| *P. sargentii* | Sargent's cherry |
| *Pseudotsuga menziesii* | Douglas fir |
| *Quercus robur* | English oak |
| *Q. rubra* | Red oak |
| *Rhamnus frangula* | Buckthorn |
| *Rhus typhina* | Sumac |
| *Ribes alpinum* | Alpine currant |

| | |
|---|---|
| *Rosa setigera* | Prairie rose |
| *R. virginiana* | Virginia rose |
| *Salix alba* | White willow |
| *S. capres* | Goat willow, Pussy willow |
| *S. cinerea* | Gray willow |
| *S. pentandra* | Bay willow |
| *S. purpurea* | Purple willow |
| *S. repens* | Creeping willow |
| *Sambucus canadensis* | American elder |
| *S. nigra* | European elder |
| *Sorlous ancuparia* | European mountain ash |
| *Taxus cuspidata* | Japanese yew |
| *Tsuga canadensis* | Eastern hemlock |
| *Viburnum opulus* | Guelder rose |

*Acer campestre*

# *Acer*

**MAPLE**

The *A. campestre* (hedge maple) is decorative, has a fantastic shape, and therefore looks splendid in a landscape setting. The named cultivars are more regular in shape (see also: Hedging plants). *A. platanoides* (Norway maple) is suitable for inland sites, partly because of its beautiful fall colors. *A. pseudoplatanus* (sycamore maple) thrives in coastal regions. Its leaves often suffer from maple tar spot (*Rhytisma acerinum*). This disease can only be fought by the removal of its fallen leaves. *A. rubrum* (red maple) is well known for its bright red fall color. *A. sac-harinum* (silver maple) is a good tree for parks and large gardens, with slightly pendulous branches. *A. (x) zoech-ense* is a hybrid reminiscent of the field maple.
**Hardiness: US Zone 5-2, Canadian Zone 5-2.**

| | |
|---|---|
| *A. campestre* | decorative, 8–10m (26–33ft) |
| *A. c.* 'Queen Elizabeth' | broadly pyramidal, 8–10m (26–33ft) |
| *A. negundo* | broadly pendulous, 15m (50ft) |
| *A. platanoides* | ovoid, 15m (50ft) |
| *A. p.* 'Cleveland' | compactly round, 8–15m (26–50ft) |

| | |
|---|---|
| *A. p.* 'Crimson King' | dark brownish-red leaves, 8–15m (26–50ft) |
| *A. p.* 'Drummondii' | white–edged leaves, 15m (50ft) |
| *A. p.* 'Emerald Queen' | good grower, 15m (50ft) |
| *A. p.* 'Globosum' | flat, round, 8–15 (26–50ft) |
| *A. p.* 'Olmsted' | broadly columnar, 8–15m (26–50ft) |
| *A. p.* 'Royal Red' | conical, dark brown leaves, 8–15m (26–50ft) |
| *A. p.* 'Schwedleri' | broadly pyramidal, 15m (50ft) |
| *A. pseudoplatanus* | broad crown, 30m (100ft) |
| *A. p.* 'Atropurpureum' | underside leaves purple, 15m+ (50ft+) |
| *A. p.* 'Erectum' | broadly pyramidal, 15m+ (50ft+) |
| *A. p.* 'Leopoldii' | yellow–spotted leaves, 8–15m (26–50ft) |
| *A. p.* 'Red Sunset' | pyramid, 15m+ (50ft) |
| *A. p.* 'Scarlet Sentinel' | fast growing, 14m (45ft) |
| *A. p.* 'Worlei' | yellow leaves, 8–15m (26–50ft) |
| *A. rubrum* | open crown, 15m (50ft) |
| *A. r.* 'Scanion' | dense, broad column, 15m (50ft) |
| *A. r.* 'Tilford' | broadly upright, 15m (50ft) |
| *A. rufinerve* | bushy growth, 10m (33ft) |
| *A. saccharum* | upright oval, 20m (65ft) |
| *A. saccharinum* | pendulous branches, 20m+ (65ft+) |
| *A. s.* 'Laciniatum Wieri' | deeply lobed leaves, 15m+ (50ft+) |
| *A. s.* 'Pyramidale' | broadly columnar, 15m+ (50ft+) |
| *A,s* 'Silver Queen' | upright, 15m (50ft) |

*Acer negundo*

## Aesculus

### HORSE-CHESTNUT, BUCKEYE

Horse-chestnuts are undemanding. The leaf bud scales are the first to fall; then come the petals, followed by small chestnuts in summer and large chestnuts in fall, until the tree finally sheds its leaves.
**Hardiness: US Zone 3, Canadian Zone 3.**

| | |
|---|---|
| A. carnea | red, May, 15m+ (50ft+) |
| A. c. 'Briotii' | dark red, compact round crown, 8–15m (26–50ft) |
| A. c. glabra | broad rounded, yellow, May-June, 6-12m (20-40ft) |
| A. flava | pale yellow, May-June, 8-15m (26-50ft) |
| A. hippocastanum | white, reddish–yellow spotted, May–June, 20m+ (65ft+) |
| A. h. 'Baumannii' | white, double, broad, 15m+(50ft+) |

*Aesculus carnea* 'Briotti'

## Ailanthus

### TREE OF HEAVEN

This tree with its pinnate leaves resembles the maple and has an open crown. Underplanting is possible. The tree is tolerant of polluted atmosphere and is therefore suitable for industrial areas. The female trees bear large panicles of reddish fruit. It requires ordinary soil.
**Hardiness: US Zone 4, Canadian Zone 3.**

| | |
|---|---|
| A. altissima | broad open crown, 15m (50ft+) |

## Alnus

### ALDER

The alder is suitable for wet gardens. *A. incana* is the sole species to require drier soil. Its cultivar 'Laciniata' has a more beautiful shape and, like *A. g.* 'Imperialis', lobed leaves. (For the cultivars of *A. incana*, see: Trees for small gardens). *A. cordata*, more tolerant of wind, has shiny dark green leaves which are less sticky than those of *A. glutinosa*. *A. g.* 'Imperialis' is a slow grower and bushier.
**Hardiness: US Zone 5-2, Canadian Zone 5-2.**

| | |
|---|---|
| A. cordata | 15m (50ft) |
| A. glutinosa | Mar–Apr, 15m+ (50ft+) |
| A. g. 'Imperialis' | pendulous branches, 10m (33ft) |
| A. g. 'Incisa' | small leaves, 10m (33ft) |
| A. g. 'Laciniata' | broad crown, 10–15m (33–50ft) |
| A. incana | 15m+ (50ft+) |

*Alnus glutinosa* 'Incisa'

*Ailanthus altissima*

## Betula

### BIRCH

The common wild birch is the *B. papyrifera* which has few garden varieties, but the European wild birch (*B. pendula*) has many. There is a curly-leafed cultivar (*B. p.*'Cris-pa'), a very upright one (*B. p.* 'Fastigiata'), one with pendulous branches (*B. p.*'Tristis'), and a dome-shaped cultivar (*B. p.* 'Youngii'). Birches thrive in all kinds of soil but do not tolerate offshore winds.

**Hardiness: US Zone 7-2, Canadian Zone 6-1.**

| | |
|---|---|
| *B. costata* | cream bark, 12–20m (40–65ft) |
| *B. ermannii* | pink–white trunk, 8–15m (26–50ft) |
| *B. nigra* | rough bark, 8–15m (26–50ft) |
| *B. papyrifera* | white, paper–like bark, 15m (50ft+) |
| *B. pendula* | dusty–white trunk, 15m+ (50ft+) |
| *B. p.* 'Crispa'** | curly leaves, 8–15m (26–50ft) |
| *B. p.* 'Fastigiata' | very upright, 8–15m (26–50ft) |
| *B. p.* 'Tristis' | pendulous, 8–15m (26–50ft) |
| *B. p.* 'Youngii' | broadly pendulous, 5m (16ft) |
| *B. utilis* ssp. *jackemontii* | copper–col. bark, 8–15m (26–50ft) |

*Betula utilis*

## Carpinus

### HORNBEAM

These have a large round head and ascending branches. The American hornbeam, also known as (Blue beach), does best when naturalized. Hornbeams can be used for hedges (see: Hedging plants).

**Hardiness: US Zone 7-5, Canadian Zone 6-4.**

| | |
|---|---|
| *C. betulus* | light green leaves, 8–15m (26–50ft) |
| *C. b.* 'Fastigiata' | dark green leaves, 8–15m (26–50ft) |
| *C. b.* 'Purpurea'** | dark leaves, 8–15m (26–50ft) |
| *C. b.* 'Quercifolia'** | oak–shaped leaves, 8–15m (26–50ft) |
| *C. caroliniana* | dark green leaves, gray bark, 6-9m (20-30ft) |

## Castanea

### CHESTNUT

This undemanding tree is tolerant of dry conditions. In the USA chestnut bark disease is prevalent and has spread into southern Canada. The Chinese chestnut (*C. mollissima*) is a good replacement for the native American chestnut.

**Hardiness: US Zone 5, Canadian Zone 5.**

| | |
|---|---|
| *C. mollissima* | yellow creamy, June, 15m (50ft) |
| *C. sativa* | yellowish green, June, 20m (65ft) |

*Castanea sativa*

## Catalpa

### INDIAN BEAN TREE, NORTHERN CATALPA

The trees have large light green leaves and large trumpet-shaped flowers. It has a broad crown and prefers a moisture-retentive, but not excessively wet soil.

**Hardiness: US Zone 4, Canadian Zone 4.**

| | |
|---|---|
| *C. bignonioides* | whitish, June–July, 15m (50ft) |
| *C. speciosa* | whitish, July, 15m (50ft) |

*Catalpa bignonioides*

## Cercis

### JUDAS TREE, REDBUD

Though it does not grow tall, this is a spreading tree and therefore better suited for large gardens. Plant in a sheltered spot.

**Hardiness: US Zone 7-5, Canadian Zone 6-5.**

| | |
|---|---|
| *C. siliquastrum*** | pinkish–lilac, May, 8m (26ft) |
| *C. canadensis* | rosy pink, May, 8m (20ft) |

*Cercis siliquastrum*

## Corylus

### HAZEL

This tree is suitable for dry soils. It has a regular-shaped crown. *C. avellana* produces edible cobnuts.

**Hardiness: US Zone 5, Canadian Zone 5.**

| | |
|---|---|
| *C. avellana* 'Pendula'** | broad, 1.5m (5ft) |
| *C. colurna* | regular crown, 15m (50ft) |

*Corylus avellana* 'Pendula'

## Fagus

### BEECH

The European beech grows well in moderately damp as well as moderately dry soils, but it dislikes varying water tables. Do not cut off branches at random: beeches do not tolerate sudden sunshine on their bark, which may result in death. American beech (*F. grandifolia*) does not have these problems. Beeches are suitable for both sandy and clay soils.

**Hardiness: US Zone 6, Canadian Zone 6.**

| | |
|---|---|
| *F. grandifolia* | large green leaves, 30m (100ft) |
| *F. sylvatica* | dark green leaves, 30m (100ft) |
| *F. s.* 'Asplenifolia' | deeply lobed leaves, 20m (65ft) |
| *F. s.* 'Pendula' | weeping shape, 25m (80ft) |

*Fagus sylvatica* 'Pendula'

| | |
|---|---|
| F. s. 'Purpurea' | brown–leafed, 20m (65ft) |
| F. s. 'Purpurea Pendula' | weeping shape, red, 20m (65ft) |
| F. s. 'Purpurea Tricolor' | brown leaves, pink-edged, 10m (33ft) |

## Fraxinus

### ASH

The ash is an adaptable tree which tolerates a variety of soil types but grows best in a clay soil. *A.americana* (white ash) in old age forms a broad rounded crown. *F.pennsylvanica* (green ash) has a more irregular crown. Both have many cultivars of which 'Marshall's Seedless' is a male form with a good yellow fall color.
**Hardiness: US Zone 5-4, Canadian Zone 5-3.**

| | |
|---|---|
| F.americana | round spreading, 15m (50ft) |
| F.a. 'Fall purple' | purple fall color, 15m (50ft) |
| F.a. 'Rose Hill' | dull red fall color, 15m (50ft) |
| F.a. 'Skyline' | oval, orange red fall color, 15m (50ft) |
| F. excelsior | irregular, 15m (50ft) |
| F.pennsylvanica | upright spreading, 18m (60ft) |
| F.p. 'Dakota ('Centennial') | very hardy, 15m (50ft) |
| F.p. 'Marshall's Seedless; | seedless variety, 15m (50ft) |
| F.p. 'Summit' | upright pyramidal, 14m (45ft) |
| F.p. 'Urbanite' | bronze fall color, 15m (50ft) |

*Fraxinus excelsior*

*Gleditsia triacanthos*

## Ginkgo

### MAIDENHAIR TREE

The ginkgo, which turns a beautiful color in the fall, has a tendency to be many-stemmed. Remove the double tops from the trees regularly to ensure that you have a handsome single bole later on. There is a difference between male and female plants: the latter spread wider and bear edible fruits. Pollination by a male tree is not always required for seed production. The ginkgo is in a class of its own and difficult to fit into the botanical system. Although the tree is a gymnosperm and therefore a conifer, it has ordinary leaves. In floras, the tree is therefore always classified separately, in between conifers and deciduous trees. The cultivars 'Mayfield' (narrow), 'Aurea' (yellow leaves), 'Variegata' (white variegations), and 'Laciniata' (deeply lobed leaves) are rare.
**Hardiness: US Zone 3, Canadian Zone 4.**

| | |
|---|---|
| G. biloba | 15–20m (50–65ft) |
| G. b. 'Fastigiata'* | columnar, 20m (65ft) |

## Gleditsia

### HONEY LOCUST

The large thorns on the bark of this tree are remarkable, but the cultivars 'Inermis', 'Shademaster', and 'Moraine' are thornless. Like the robinia, this is a tree for fairly poor soil. Branches may break off if the tree's growth is too rapid. The delicate pinnate leaves and light structure of the branches make underplanting a possibility. Gleditsias do not require any special kind of soil.
**Hardiness: US Zone 5, Canadian Zone 5.**

| | |
|---|---|
| G. triacanthos | cream, June, 20m (65ft) |
| G. t. 'Inermis' | thornless, 15m (50ft) |
| G. t. 'Shademaster' | broadly upright, thornless, 15–20m (50–65ft) |
| G. t. 'Skyline' | pyramidal, 8–15m (26–50ft) |
| G. t. 'Sunburst' | yellow leaves, slow-growing, 15m (50ft) |

## Gymnocladus

### KENTUCKY COFFEE TREE

The leaves are reminiscent of the ash. Don't plant these slow–growing trees in very dry soil. They are sensitive to wind.
**Hardiness: US Zone 7, Canadian Zone 6.**

| | |
|---|---|
| G. dioicus | greenish white, May–June, 20m (65ft) |

*Juglans cordiformis*

## Juglans

### WALNUT

Although *J. nigra* (black walnut) is less frost-tender, *J. regia*, which produces better nuts, is grown more frequently. At one time, the tree was planted close to kitchen windows to keep out flies. The fall leaves are toxic to some plants which makes underplanting difficult.
**Hardiness: US Zone 6-3, Canadian Zone 5-3.**

| | |
|---|---|
| J. cinerea | broadly spreading, slow-growing, 15m (50ft) |
| J. cordiformis | |
| J. nigra | pyramidal, spreading later, 20m+ (65ft+) |
| J. regia | rounder crown, 15–20m (50–65ft) |

## Liquidambar

### SWEET GUM

This slender handsome tree with ivy-shaped leaves is suitable for any position. It develops an open domed crown. The leaves turn purple, yellow, and red in the fall. The bark has attractive corky ridges.
**Hardiness: US Zone 5, Canadian Zone 5.**

| | |
|---|---|
| L. styracyflua! | fall colors, 15m (50ft) |
| L.s. 'Varietgata' | leaves marked yellow, 15m (50ft) |

*Liquidambar styracyflua*

## Liriodendron

**TULIP TREE**
This park tree has a large broad crown. The flowers are tulip-shaped, hence the name.
**Hardiness: US Zone 5, Canadian Zone 5.**

| | |
|---|---|
| *L. tulipifera* | yellowish-green, 20+m (65ft+) |
| *L. t.* 'Aureomarginatum'* | yellowish-green, 20m (65ft) |
| *L. t.* 'Fastigiatum'* | columnar, 20m (65ft) |

*Liriodendron tulipifera*

## Magnolia

When planning to plant a magnolia, don't just think in terms of deciduous or evergreen shrubs, but consider these trees as well. The 10cm (4in) flowers of M.kobus appear just before the leaves. This means that late night frosts will sometimes kill the flowers.
**Hardiness: US Zone 5, Canadian Zone 5.**

| | |
|---|---|
| *M. kobus*! | white, Apr–May, 10m (33ft) |
| *M. acuminata* | greenish yellow, June, 20m (65ft) |

## Metasequoia

See: Conifers.

## Morus

**MULBERRY**
This medium-sized tree has light green leaves, deeply lobed when older. The trunks of older trees become gnarled. The fruits make stains: so don't plant near steps or patios (see also: Trees for small gardens and Vines and wall plants).
**Hardiness: US Zone 5, Canadian Zone 5.**

| | |
|---|---|
| *M. alba* | white or red fruits, 8–15m (26–50ft) |

*Magnolia kobus*

## Ostrya

**HOP HORNBEAM**
The leaves and growth of this tree resemble those of the hornbeam. It bears yellowish green catkins in early spring. Hop-like fruits are formed later. This is an undemanding tree as far as position is concerned.
**Hardiness: US Zone 3, Canadian Zone 3.**

| | |
|---|---|
| *O. virginiana* | broad round crown, 8–15m (26-50ft) |

## Paulownia

**FOXGLOVE TREE, PRINCESS TREE**
The paulownia is popular because of its pale mauve trumpet-shaped flowers. The tree is not so suitable for small gardens. Young trees in particular are subject to frostbite; when they are older it is the flower buds that tend to be damaged by late night frosts. A sheltered position is desirable.
**Hardiness: US Zone 7, Canadian Zone 7.**

| | |
|---|---|
| *P. tomentosa* | pale mauve, May–June 10m (33ft) |

*Paulownia tomentosa*

## *Phellodendron*

**AMUR CORK TREE**
This medium-sized tree with pinnate leaves resembling those of an alder has a low spreading crown, inconspicuous flowers but a magnificent fall color. The tree is sensitive to late night frosts and needs fairly dry, humus-rich soil.
**Hardiness: US Zone 4, Canadian Zone 4.**

| | |
|---|---|
| *P. amurense* | greenish yellow, June, 8–15m (26–50ft) |

## *Platanus*

**SYCAMORE**
Sycamore trees are suitable for large parks only. As the tree ages, its bark flakes off. The trunk then resembles a jigsaw puzzle with missing pieces: the bark in such places is pale in color. The leaves closely resemble those of the maple, but compare the base and you will never confuse them again.
**Hardiness: US Zone 5, Canadian Zone 5.**

| | |
|---|---|
| *P.* x *acerifolia* | green, May, 20–30m (65–100ft) |
| *P. occidentalis* | green, May, 20-30m (65-100ft) |

## *Populus*

**POPLAR**
The poplar is unsuitable for gardens. Its disadvantages include roots that push up paving, extremely fast growth, and the stickiness of fallen leaves. The branches of older trees are inclined to break off, causing much damage to the garden. Planting poplars may appear to be cheap, but the essential lopping after only a short while is expensive. *P. tremuloides* is the aspen. This tree develops a tire-some amount of suckers from its roots. *P.*

*Populus* x *canescens* 'Honthorpa'

*Platanus occidentalis*

*trichocarpa** (black cottonwood, western balsam poplar) is sensitive to wind and exudes a sweet, balsamic scent (see also: Hedging plants).
**Hardiness: US Zone 4-1, Canadian Zone 3-1.**

| | |
|---|---|
| *P. alba* 'Nivea' | white underside to leaves, 15–30m (50–65ft) |
| *P.* x *canescens* 'Hunthorpe' | upright, 20m (65ft) |
| *P.* x *canadensis* 'Eugenei' | canker resistant, 15m (50ft) |
| *P. deltoides* | irregular habit, 20-30m (65-100ft) |
| *P. d.* 'Siouxland' | fast grower, 23m (75ft+) |
| *P. nigra* 'Thevestina' | narrow, 15-20m+ (50-65ft) |
| *P. tremula* 'Erecta' | upright, 15m (50ft) |
| *P. tremuloides* | rounded, 12m (40ft) |
| *P. trichocarpa* | columnar, 30m (100ft) |

# Prunus

## CHERRY

*P. avium* (European wild cherry) is a large tree with a round open crown and a purplish-brown bark, which produces almost black cherries; *P. padus* (bird cherry) is tolerant of shade. Plant in moisture-retentive soil. *P. maackii* (Amur choke cherry is a good all year-round tree with white flowers and attractive golden brown flaking bark.
**Hardiness: US Zone 5-3, Canadian Zone 5-3.**

| | |
|---|---|
| *P. avium* | white, 10–15m+ (33–50ft+) |
| *P. a.* 'Plena'! | white, double, 8–15m (26–50ft) |
| *P. padus* | white, 8–12m (26–40ft) |
| *P. maackii* | white, 10m (35ft) |
| *P. sargentii* | pink, 9m (30ft) |
| *P.s.* 'Columnaris' | narrow crown, 9m (30ft) |

*Prunus avium*

# Pterocarya

## WING NUT

This park tree's pendulous, yellowish-green catkins are highly decorative. The leaves resemble those of the ash. They are also larger. The tree thrives in clay soil.
**Hardiness: US Zone 7, Canadian Zone 6.**

| | |
|---|---|
| *P. fraxinifolia* | broad crown, 15–20m (50–65ft) |

*Pterocarya fraxinifolia*

# Quercus

## OAK

Oaks grow very slowly and are great trees for parks and avenues. Because of their deep roots, it is totally impossible for the wind to blow them down. *Q. palustris* (Pin oak) and *Q. bicolor* (Swamp white oak) grow in wet as well as drier soils, and will tolerate acid conditions. *Q. robur* (English oak), the largest native tree in western Europe, grows best on a rich fertile soil. *Q. rubra* (Red oak) and *Q. coccinea* (Scarlet oak) have the best fall color, growing quickly when young, and can be planted in poor sandy acid or alkaline soils. *Q. velutina* (Black oak), also found on dry acid soils. *Q. macrocarpa* (Bur oak) grows best on an alkaline clay soil, and is often more tolerant of city conditions.

**Hardiness: US Zone 5-3, Canadian Zone 5-3.**

| | |
|---|---|
| *Quercus alba* | pyramidal, 15-25m (50-80ft) |
| *Q. bicolor* | broad rounded, 15-20m (50-65ft) |
| *Q. coccinea* | rounded open, 22-25m (70-80ft) |
| *Q. macrocarpa* | broad, spreading, 22-25m (70-80ft) |
| *Q. palustris* | pyramidal, 18-20m (60-70ft) |
| *Q. robur* | broad rounded, 24-30m (75-100ft) |
| *Q. r.fastigiata* | narrow, 15-18m (50-60ft) |
| *Q. rubra* | round, symmetrical, 20-25m (65-80ft) |
| *Q. velutina* | irregular, 15-20m (50-65ft) |

*Quercus palustris*

# Robinia

**BLACK LOCUST**

Although tall trees, they can often be grown in medium-sized gardens. Their crowns are open and airy, thus allowing underplanting. In rich soil, the tree grows so fast that branches remain weak and break off in the wind. Therefore, do not give them any fertilizer (see also: Trees for small gardens).

**Hardiness: US Zone 5, Canadian Zone 4.**

| | |
|---|---|
| *R. x ambigua* 'Decaisneana' | pale pink, June–Aug, 8–10m (26–33ft) |
| *R. pseudoacacia* | cream, July, 20m (65ft) |
| *R. p.* 'Appalachia' | richly flowering, 25m (80ft) |
| *R. p.* 'Bessoniana' | few thorns, 20m (65ft) |
| *R.p.* 'Frisia' | yellow leaves, July, 20m (65ft) |
| *R. p.* 'Unifoliola' | thornless, simple leaves, 20m (65ft) |

# Salix

**WILLOW**

Like poplars, willows are unsuitable for gardens. If the garden already contains one overgrown

*Salix matsudamna* 'Tortuosa'

willow, pollarding is a possible solution. The *S. pentandra* (Bay willow) is a medium-sized tree which is suitable for large, wet gardens. The large weeping willow, with its beautiful pale green shoots in spring, is listed below under its new name *S. x sepulcralis* 'Tristis'. This cultivar is suitable for wet soil by a large pond. The Dragon's claw willow grows taller than most people anticipate at the time of purchase.

**Hardiness: US Zone 4, Canadian Zone 4.**

| | |
|---|---|
| *S. alba* | broadly oval crown, 25m (80ft) |
| *S. a.* 'Belders' | narrow crown, 20m (65ft) |
| *S. a.* 'Chermesina' | pyramidal crown, 20m (65ft) |
| *S. matsudamna* 'Tortuosa' | twisted branches, 12m (40ft) |

*Robinia pseudoacacia*

| | |
|---|---|
| *S.* x *sepulcralis* 'Tristis' | weeping, 15m+ (50ft+) |
| *S. pentandra* | fast-growing, 10m (33ft) |

## *Sophora*

**PAGODA TREE**

This tree has a broad round crown and beautiful pinnate leaves. They do not change color in fall, but remain on the tree for a long time. Young trees are frost-tender, and do not tolerate much wind. The Pagoda tree thrives in any kind of soil.
Hardiness: US Zone 5, Canadian Zone 5.

| | |
|---|---|
| *S. japonica* | white, Aug–Sept, 10–15m (33–50ft) |

## *Sorbus*

These slender medium–sized trees have striking flowers and large clusters of berries. They dislike clay and wet soils. *S. aria* (whitebeam) has reddish-orange fruits; the leaves, white-felted beneath, are not pinnate. *S. intermedia* (Swedish whitebeam) prefers lime-rich soil. Its leaves are pinnate at the base only (see also: Trees for small gardens).
Hardiness: US Zone 6-4, Canadian Zone 5-4.

*Sorbus intermedia*

| | |
|---|---|
| *S. americana* | rapid grower, 6m (20ft) |
| *S. aria* | creamy white, June, 8–12m (26–40ft) |
| *S. a.* 'Magnifica'** | broad, ovoid crown |
| *S.* x *arnoldiana*** | oval crown, 6–8m (20–26ft) |
| *S. aucuparia* | white, May–June, 10m (33ft) |
| *S. a.* 'Edulis' | open crown, 10m (33ft) |
| *S.a.* 'Rossica' | upright, May, 6m (20ft) |
| *S. intermedia* | cream, May, 8–10m (26–33ft) |
| *S. i.* 'Brouwers' | regular crown, 10m (33ft) |
| *S. latifolia* | creamy white, May, 10m (33ft) |

## *Taxodium*

See: Conifers.

## *Tilia!*

**LINDEN**

The leaf of the linden is recognizable by its oblique base; the tree itself by the shoots produced at its foot by most species. Lime trees can live for 1500 years, whereas the maximum age for oaks is "merely" 500 years. Aphids on limes secrete honeydew, a sticky substance which soils anything placed under the tree. Do not therefore plant a

*Tilia tomentosa* 'Brabant'

lime tree near a patio or parking area. Espaliered limes, which are trained along fencing when they are young, were at one time intended to keep out the sun. *T. cordata* (small leaf lime) has scented yellowish-white flowers in July. *T.* x *euchlora* (Caucasian lime, Crimean lime) is a large tree with a fairly narrow crown. *T. petiolaris* (silver pendent lime) has many pendulous branches. Although this tree is less frequently affected by aphids than other species, it is not planted very often. *T. platyphyllos* (broad-leafed lime, large-leafed lime) has large leaves, with soft hairs underneath. *T.* x *vulgaris* (common lime) has most wildshoots. *T.* x *vulgaris* 'Pallida' is a large wind-resistant lime. The cultivar 'Zwarte Linde' owes its name to its dark bark.

**Hardiness: US Zone 6-4, Canadian Zone 5-4.**

| | |
|---|---|
| *T. americana* 'Redmond' | broad ovoid crown, 25m (80ft) |
| *T. cordata* 'Erecta' | conical, subsequently ovoid, 20m (65ft) |
| *T. c.* 'Greenspire' | ovoid, upright, 20m (65ft) |
| *T. c.* 'Rancho'** | ovoid, upright, 20m (65ft) |
| *T.* x *euchlora* | narrower crown, 20m (65ft) |
| *T. flavescens* 'Glenleven' | 20m (65ft) |
| *T. mongolica* | compact, 10m (33ft) |
| *T. petiolaris** | many pendulous branches, 25m (80ft) |
| *T. platyphyllos* | broad round crown, 25m (80ft) |
| *T. p.* 'Fastigiata'** | upright, 25m (80ft) |
| *T. tomentosa* | broadly ovoid, 20m (65ft) |
| *T.t.* 'Sterling Silver' | broad pyramidal, 20m (65ft) |

# Ulmus

**ELM**

Elm disease (*Ceratocystus ulmi*), first diagnosed in the Netherlands, has felled so many trees that the countryside throughout North America has suffered. The disease is spread by the elm bark beetle (*Scolytus scolytus*), harmless in itself. Affected trees need to be removed rapidly, which means in practical terms that they are immediately stripped of their bark, placed under water or burned. Most of the beetle's breeding places are found in firewood that has not been debarked and is stacked up outside private dwellings. Don't grow this one-time favorite any more: Dutch elm disease may then disappear sometime in the future. The following species and cultivars are less risky.

**Hardiness: US Zone 5, Canadian Zone 5.**

| | |
|---|---|
| *U. carpinifolia* 'Dampieri' | broadly columnar, 15m (50ft) |
| *U. c.* 'Wredei' | pyramidal, golden yellow leaves, 8m (26ft) |
| *U. glabra* 'Camperdownii'! | weeping form, 3m (10ft) |
| *U. g.* 'Exoniensis' | narrowly upright, 15m (50ft) |
| *U.* x *hollandica* | tall, irregular, 20m (65ft) |
| *U. h.* 'Clusius' | new, 15m (50ft) |
| *U. h.* 'Dodoens' | severely upright, 20m (65ft) |
| *U. h.* 'Groeneveld' | straight, regular, 20m (65ft) |
| *U. h.* 'Lobel' | narrowly upright, 15m (50ft) |
| *U. h.* 'Plantijn' | broadly upright, dense, 20m (65ft) |

# Zelkova

This medium-sized tree with its flat spherical crown has spreading horizontal branches and thrives in any soil that is fertile and well drained. This tree is the sole non-elm to be susceptible to Dutch elm disease. It can be propagated by seed or layering.

**Hardiness: US Zone 6, Canadian Zone 5.**

| | |
|---|---|
| *Z. serrata* | broad, flat crown, 15m (50ft) |

*Ulmus carpinifolia* 'Dampieri'

# Trees for small gardens

*When choosing trees for small gardens, it is necessary to consider the type of growth; the density of the crown and its effect on underplanting; the color of the leaves and berries; special fall colors; and the rate of growth. This chapter will provide you with the kind of information about trees that will help you to make an initial choice, though you will also need some professional advice. The list will show you how much choice there is if you wish to grow a tree in a small garden, where they are needed to create a visual impression of depth. A shady spot is also very attractive in mid-summer. The height of the trees is indicated in metres and feet; flowers and flowering season are mentioned only if the flowers are sufficiently decorative.*

## Acer

**MAPLE**

Some maples are suitable for small gardens in spite of their size. Their foliage is not dense, so that underplanting with many kinds of small shrubs is possible. The green flowers are inconspicuous; the maple's beauty is in its leaves, trunk or shoots. There are many varieties. Maples are undemanding: they like moist soil in a sunny or shady position (see also: Trees for large gardens and Deciduous shrubs).
**Hardiness: US Zone 5-3, Canadian Zone 5-2b.**

| | |
|---|---|
| A.negundo 'Aureovariegatum' | golden yellow leaves, 8m (26ft) |
| A. palmatum | green, 8m (26ft) |
| A. p. 'Atropurpureum' | brownish-red leaves, 8m (26ft) |
| A. p. 'Bloodgood' | red leaves, 8m (26ft) |
| A. pensylvanicum | striped green and white trunk, 8m (26ft) |
| A. rufinerve | green and white trunk, 10m (33ft) |

## Aesculus

**BOTTLE BRUSH BUCKEYE**

The many species of this magnificent small tree with its 15cm (6in) panicles include large-sized trees (15m/50ft and over), medium-sized trees (8–15m/26–50ft), and smaller-sized trees (under 8m/26ft). The genus also includes low and very low shrubs (see also: Deciduous shrubs and Trees for large gardens.)
**Hardiness: US Zone 5, Canadian Zone 5.**

| | |
|---|---|
| A. pavia | reddish, May–June, 6–8m (20–26ft) |
| A. p. 'Splendens' | scarlet, May–June, 6–8m (20–26ft) |

## Alnus

**ALDER**

The alder is unisexual, with small red female catkins (the subsequent alder-cones) and long yellow male catkins on a single tree. The tree can be a handsome sight, but in the garden it is subject to attack by alder leaf beetle (*Agelastica alni*), which eats into the leaves. These are subsequently skeletized by the beetles' larvae. *A. incana*, the gray alder, thrives in moist as well as dry habitats, and is very hardy.
**Hardiness: US Zone 3, Canadian Zone 3.**

| | |
|---|---|
| A. incana 'Aurea' | golden-yellow leaves, 5–8m (16–26ft) |
| A. i. 'Laciniata' | deeply lobed leaves, 5–8m (16–26ft) |

*Acer palmatum* 'Atropurpureum'

*Aesculus pavia*

| *A. arborea* 'Robin Hill' | white ascending branches, May–June, 5–8m (16–26ft) |
| *A. lamarckii* 'Ballerina' | large white leaves, May–June, 5–8m (16–26ft) |

# Betula

### BIRCH
Although most birches grow tall, they remain slender. This enables sufficient light to penetrate and permits good underplanting; the trees are therefore suitable for small gardens.
**Hardiness: US Zone 2, Canadian Zone 2.**

| *B. pendula* | grayish-white trunk, narrow, 15m (50ft) |
| *B. p.* 'Youngii' | dome-shaped, pendulous, 3m (10ft) |

*Betula pendula*

# Amelanchier

### JUNEBERRY, SERVICEBERRY, SHADBERRY
The American amelanchier (*A. lamarckii*) was imported into Europe in the nineteenth century and rapidly became established there. Several cultivars are grown as trees suitable for small gardens. The tree's white flower sprays, reddish purple berries which attract birds, and red and orange colors in fall are highly decorative. Amelanchiers are suitable for any kind of moist or dry soil, and like full sun or half-shade (see also: Deciduous shrubs).
**Hardiness: US Zone 3, Canadian Zone 3.**

*Amelanchier lamarckii*

# Cercidiphyllum

### KATSURA
The flowers of this spreading tree are insignificant; the fall colors are its main at-traction. Katsuras are affected by late night frosts.
**Hardiness: US Zone 5, Canadian Zone 5.**

| *C. japonicum* | pale green, 8–15m (26–50ft) |

*Cercidiphyllum japonicum*

## Cornus

**CORNELIAN CHERRY, FLOWERING DOGWOOD**
These species of dogwood usually form large bushes or small trees. Both can be grown with a single stem. They are highly suitable for small gardens.
**Hardiness: US Zone 6-5, Canadian Zone 6-5.**

| | |
|---|---|
| *C. mas* | yellow, Feb–Apr, 5m (16ft) |
| *C. florida* | white, April-May, 6m (20ft) |
| *C.f.* 'Rubra' | red, April-May, 6m (20ft) |

*Cornus mas*

## Corylus

**EUROPEAN HAZEL**
Although the hazel, like the *cornus*, is usually cultivated as a bush, it is quite possible to grow it with a single stem, which gives it a tree shape. Remove all the stems from the bush except for the straightest and most upright one. This tree is suitable for a shady position. The pendent yellow catkins herald the spring.
**Hardiness: US Zone 5, Canadian Zone 5.**

| | |
|---|---|
| *C. avellana* | yellow, Mar, 4m (13ft) |
| *C. maxima* 'Purpurea' | purple leaves, 4m (13ft) |

## Crataegus

**HAWTHORN**
Hawthorns are suitable for urban streets and show up well in the countryside and in suburban gardens, either as hedges or as trees. The trees flower in May, just as the leaves appear; they are followed in fall by red berries. The shiny red berries of the *C.* x *prunifolia* remain on the tree for a very long time.
**Hardiness: US Zone 5, Canadian Zone 5.**

| | |
|---|---|
| *C. crus galli* | white, 5m (16ft) |
| *C. laevigata* | white, 5m (16ft) |
| *C. l.* 'Paul's Scarlet' | pinkish red (d), 5m (16ft) |
| *C. l.* 'Plena' | white (d), 5m (16ft) |
| *C. monogyna* 'Rosea Plena' | pink (d), 6m (20ft) |
| *C.* x *prunifolia* | shiny dark green leaves, 6m (20ft) |

*Crataegus monogyna*

## Cydonia

**QUINCE**
Depending on their shape, quinces may resemble either apples or pears. The quince is a small broad tree with large flowers, and requires a sunny position.
**Hardiness: US Zone 5, Canadian Zone 5.**

| | |
|---|---|
| *C. oblonga* | pear-shaped, 3m (10ft) |

## Davidia

**DOVE-TREE, HANDKERCHIEF TREE**
This medium-sized tree has large leaves. The English name "handkerchief tree" refers to the large white bracts of the flowers. These "handkerchiefs" can usually be seen in late spring.
**Hardiness: US Zone 7, Canadian Zone 7.**

| | |
|---|---|
| *D. involucrata* | white, May–June, 10m (33ft) |

*Cydonia oblonga*

*Fagus sylvatica* 'Dawyck'

*Davidia involucrata*

## *Fagus*

**BEECH**
Don't even think of planting a native beech *F. grandifolia* as it can grow up to 30m (100ft) tall. The columnar *F. sylvatica* is just about suitable for medium-sized gardens. The leaves rot slowly and therefore need to be raked up in a small garden.
**Hardiness: US Zone 6, Canadian Zone 6.**

| | |
|---|---|
| *F. sylvatica* 'Dawyck'* | upright, 15m (50ft) |

## *Fraxinus*

**FLOWERING ASH**
The ash is relatively undemanding as far as position is concerned, but it does require light. Fallen leaves cause few problems in a garden, as they shrivel into minute proportions.
**Hardiness: US Zone 6, Canadian Zone 6.**

| | |
|---|---|
| *F. ornus* | round crown, 8m (26ft) |
| *F. o.* 'Arie Peters'** | round, 6–8m (20–26ft) |
| *F.* 'Obelisk'** | upright, 6–10m (20–33ft) |

## *Ginkgo*

**MAIDENHAIR TREE**
Male trees are narrow and upright; female trees are widely spreading. The problem is that these trees are grown from seed and it is impossible to distinguish between male and female plants at an early stage. Because of its shape, the male version is suitable for small gardens, whereas the female tree is not. Why not take a chance? (see also: Trees for large gardens).
**Hardiness: US Zone 3, Canadian Zone 4.**

| | |
|---|---|
| *G. biloba* | 15–20m (50–65ft) |

*Fraxinus ornus*

# Gleditsia

## HONEY LOCUST

Although gleditsias grow tall, it is possible to plant one in a small garden. This is because of its loose open crown, which lets a great deal of light penetrate to good underplanting. It also makes the tree look less massive. It has fine fall colors. The tree is tolerant of air pollution and thrives on well-drained soil.

**Hardiness: US Zone 5, Canadian Zone 5.**

| | |
|---|---|
| *G. triacanthos* | fresh green, 8–15m (26–50ft) |
| *G. t.* 'Moraine' | vase-shaped, 15m (50ft) |
| *G. t.* 'Sunburst' | golden-yellow leaves, 10m (33ft) |

*Gleditsia triacanthos*

# Koelreuteria

## PRIDE OF INDIA, GOLDEN RAIN TREE

This tree is slightly frost-tender when it is young. It is an ideal undemanding urban tree which flowers better in hot summers. Branches may be inclined to break off in open ground. The tree is suitable for most soils.

**Hardiness: US Zone 6, Canadian Zone 6.**

| | |
|---|---|
| *K. paniculata* | yellow, July–Aug, 10m (33ft) |

# Laburnum

## LABURNUM

Laburnums are usually supplied as shrubs, but there are also standard trees. The shrubs will also grow into trees, but will remain many-stemmed from the ground upwards. A laburnum is one of the best trees for a small garden, especially because of its striking yellow flowers. Don't plant them in excessively moist soil. The common laburnum has short racemes; those of the 'Vossii' cultivar, which, unfortunately, is considerably more expensive, are much longer.

**Hardiness: US Zone 6, Canadian Zone 6.**

| | |
|---|---|
| *L.* x *watereri* 'Vossii' | yellow, May–June, 5–7m (16–23ft) |

*Laburnum* x *watereri* 'Vossii'

*Koelreuteria paniculata*

# Magnolia

Even in a sheltered position, the 10cm (4in) flowers of this lovely regular-shaped tree may be ruined by a late night frost. In that case: better luck next year. Magnolias need moisture-retentive soil, but it should not be excessively wet.
**Hardiness: US Zone 7-6, Canadian Zone 6-5.**

| | |
|---|---|
| *M. kobus!* | white, May, 10m (33ft) |
| *M. salicifolia* | white, May, 8m (25ft) |
| *M.x. Soulangeana* | white/pink, May, 8m (25ft) |

*Magnolia kobus*

# Malus

**CRAB APPLE**

These graceful trees provide interest throughout the year. Plant them in a sunny spot, in soil which is not too moist in view of the risk of canker. This disease causes ugly growths to develop on the branches, and then slowly kills the tree. Trees are usually available as standards. The lowest branches of a standard malus are at least 2m (6ft) above the ground. This makes them convenient trees for small gardens.
**Hardiness: US Zone 5-4, Canadian Zone 5-4.**

*Malus* 'Prof Sprenger'

| Malus | color of flower | color of fruit | height | details |
|---|---|---|---|---|
| *M.* 'Adams' | pinkish red | carmine red | 6m (20ft) | round crown |
| *M.* 'Aldenhamensis' | purplish red | purplish brown | 6m (20ft) | reddish–brown leaves |
| *M.* 'Almey' | lilac red | red | 6m (20ft) | purple leaves |
| *M.* 'Butterball' | white | golden yellow | 5–8m (16–26ft) | broadly upright |
| *M. floribunda* | reddish pink | yellowish green | 5–8m (16–26ft) | pendulous |
| *M.* 'Georgeus' | pale pink | red | 5m (16ft) | pendulous branches |
| *M.* 'Golden Hornet' | white | yellow | 6m (20ft) | upright |
| *M.* 'Hopa' | pale lilac red | bright red | 6m (20ft) | green leaves |
| *M.* 'John Downie' | white | orange | 8m (26ft) | upright |
| *M.* 'Liset' | pinkish red | red | 6-7m (20–23ft) | red leaves, compact |
| *M.* 'Makamik' | lilac pink | bright red | 6m (20ft) | |
| *M.* 'Prof Sprenger' | white | orange yellow | 5-6m (16–20ft) | fall color |
| *M.* 'Radiant' | deep pink | carmine red | 6m (20ft) | disease-free |
| *M.* 'Red Jade' | white | red | 6m (20ft) | weeping form |
| *M.* 'Red Sentinal' | pink | bright red | 6m (20ft) | green leaves |
| *M.* 'Rudolf' | dark red | dark orange red | 5–8m (16–26ft) | red leaves |
| *M.* 'Wintergold' | white | bright yellow | 8m (26ft) | round crown |

## Mespilus

### MEDLAR

In the Netherlands, these small old-fashioned trees were often planted on the banks of canals. They have low broad crowns. Medlars are attractive to look at, but not many people are able to make good use of them in the kitchen. The trees like sun or semi-shade, and are usually supplied as half-standards.
**Hardiness: US Zone 6, Canadian Zone 5.**

| | |
|---|---|
| *M. germanica* | white, Apr–May, 3m (10ft) |

*Mespilus germanica*

## Morus

### MULBERRY

The black mulberry (*M. nigra*) is a large shrub or a small tree, depending on the height at which it is grafted. The leaves are hardly lobed. The white weeping mulberry is suitable for even the smallest garden (see also: Trees for large gardens and vines and wall plants).
**Hardiness: US Zone 5, Canadian Zone 5.**

| | |
|---|---|
| *M. alba* 'Pendula' | white or red fruits, 3m (10ft) |
| *M. nigra* | red/black fruits, 5–10m (16–33ft) |

*Morus alba* 'Pendula'

## Nothofagus

### SOUTHERN BEECH

The nothofagus is often many-stemmed and has beautiful spreading branches and small flowers. The white lenticils on the bark present a striking appearance.
**Hardiness: US Zone 7, Canadian Zone 7.**

| | |
|---|---|
| *N. antarctica* | small dark green leaves, 5–8m (16–26ft) |

*Nothofagus antarctica*

## Parrotia

The parrotia is usually grown as a shrub. If it is not available as a tree, then train it yourself and make it into a broad tree. It has magnificent, perhaps unsurpassed fall colors and is tolerant of acid as well as limy soils.
**Hardiness: US Zone 5, Canadian Zone 5.**

| | |
|---|---|
| *P. persica*\*! | red stamens, Mar, 6m (20ft) |

*Parrotia persica*

## Phellodendron

### AMUR CORK-TREE
This cork-tree from Manchuria is medium-sized, with a broad open domed crown. It has pinnate leaves up to 35cm (14in) long. The stem has a thick corky bark.
**Hardiness: US Zone 4, Canadian Zone 3.**

| | |
|---|---|
| *P. amurense* | greenish yellow, June, 8–15m, (26–50ft) |

*Phellodendron amurense*

## Photinia

This small tree has oval leaves which turn red in fall. The scarlet fruits remain on the widely spreading branches for a long time.
**Hardiness: US Zone 5, Canadian Zone 5.**

| | |
|---|---|
| *P. villosa*! | scarlet fruits, 5–8m (16–26ft) |

*Photinia villosa*

## Prunus

### ORNAMENTAL CHERRY
Some of these flowering trees produce berries. In view of the many species of prunus, *P. serrulata* (Japanese cherry) in the form of *P.* 'Kanzan', and *P. pramus* 'Amanogawa,' which grows with its very fastigiate habit, may be unjustifiably overrated. But there are many beautiful hybrids, even though the flowering period is short. *P. cerasifera* 'Trailblazer' (syn. *P. c.* 'Hollywood') produces large red edible fruits in addition to small pink flowers.
**Hardiness: US Zone 5-3, Canadian Zone 5-3.**

| | |
|---|---|
| *P. avium* 'Plena'! | white (d), May–June, 8m (26ft) |
| *P. cerasifera* 'Nigra' | brownish–red leaves, April–May, 8m (26ft) |
| *P. c.* 'Trailblazer' | brownish-red leaves, Apr–May, 8m (26ft) |
| *P. maackii* 'Amber Beauty' | white, Apr |
| *P. padus* 'Wateri' | white, May, 10m (33ft) |
| *P. serrulata* 'Amanogawa' | pale pink, Apr, 8m (26ft) |
| *P. s.* 'Kiku–shidare–zakura' | deep pink, weeping form, full, 4–6m (13–20ft) |
| *P. subhirtella* 'Autumnalis' | white, Nov–Apr, 6m (20ft) |
| *P. s.* 'Autumnalis Rosea'* | pink, Nov–Apr, 6m (20ft) |

*Prunus subhirtella*

## Prunus

### PLUM, DAMSON
Of all the common fruit trees, plums are most suitable for flower gardens. A florescence no less exuberant than that of ornamental cherries is followed by a crop of plums. The following cultivars are self–pollinating: only one tree is needed. This does not mean that cross–pollination will not give slightly better results. 'R. Cl. d'Althan' (reddish purple) and 'R. Cl. Verte' (green) are not self-pollinating. Plum trees grow to 6m (20ft) tall. The color of the fruit and time of ripening is given in the list below after the names of the cultivars.
**Hardiness: US Zone 5, Canadian Zone 5.**

| | |
|---|---|
| *P. domestica* | blue, Aug–Sept |
| *P.* 'Czar' | red/blue, Aug |
| *P.* 'Mirabelle de Nancy' | greenish yellow, Aug–Sept |
| *P.* 'Ontario' | yellow, Aug |
| *P.* 'Opal' | pinkish red, July–Aug |
| *P.* 'Victoria' | red, Aug–Sept |

*Prunus domestica*

## Pyrus

**ORNAMENTAL PEAR**
Unlike the fruit tree (the common pear also belongs to the genus *Pyrus*), these trees are not very susceptible to pear blight, a bacterial disease common among members of the rose family. *P. salicifolia* 'Pendula' has willow-shaped leaves. The branches are very pendulous, which makes it look like a weeping tree. Once planted, the tree seems to have difficulty in taking root. Take extra care during transportation (drying out) and planting. Although these trees grow tall, they are narrowly pyramidal in shape and therefore suitable for smaller gardens. They like a fairly dry position in full sun.
**Hardiness: US Zone 6, Canadian Zone 5.**

| | |
|---|---|
| *P. callereyana* 'Chanticleer' | white, Apr, 8–12m (26–40ft) |
| *P. c.* 'Redspire' | shiny green, 8–12m (26–40ft) |
| *P. communis* | white, Apr, 8–15m (26–50ft) |
| *P. salicifolia* 'Pendula' | gray leaves, white, Apr–May, 6–8m (20–26ft) |

## Robinia

**BLACK LOCUST**
The short laburnum-like flowers are suspended in between the light green, delicate pinnate leaves. There is not enough light for under-planting beneath the trees. Branches tend to break off if the tree is planted in very rich soil or in a windy location. They make ideal urban trees, requiring a light soil that is not excessively moist.
**Hardiness: US Zone 5, Canadian Zone 4.**

| | |
|---|---|
| *R. ambigua* 'Decaisneana' | pale pink, June–Aug, 8–10m (26–33ft) |
| *R.pseudoacacia* 'Umbraculifera' | fully round, thornless, 5m (16ft) |
| *R. viscosa* | pale pink, 5–8m (16–26 ft) |

## Salix

**WILLOW**
This medium-sized tree grows rapidly in moist soil, and is recommended if other trees fail to thrive. Poplars and willows do not, in my opinion, belong in gardens. They are suitable for parks and countryside. Two small trees which produce yellow catkins in spring are listed below.
**Hardiness: US Zone 7, Canadian Zone 8-2.**

| | |
|---|---|
| *S. magnifica!*** | large leaves, 6m (20ft) |
| *S. pentandra* | dark green leaves, 8–15m (26–50ft) |

*Salix magnifica*

*Robinia pseudoacacia*

Right: *Sorbus* x *thurigiaca* 'Fastigiata'

## Sophora

### PAGODA TREE

This "Japanese pagoda" tree is medium-sized and has a rounded shape. The trees do not start flowering until they are older. The light green foliage casts beautiful reflections in water. Plant these acacia-like trees in sheltered spots in full sun; location apart, they are easy to grow and will thrive in any kind of soil.

**Hardiness: US Zone 5, Canadian Zone 5.**

| | |
|---|---|
| *S. japonica* | cream, Aug–Sept, 5–15m (16–50ft) |
| *S. j.* 'Pendula' | cream, Aug–Sept, 5m (16ft) |

## Sorbus

### WHITEBEAMS, ROWANS

Rowans are suitable trees for small areas. Plant them in full sun to show up the white umbels and the color of the berries. The berries may cause stains, so do not plant them near a door or a patio. The color of the berries is listed below (see also: Trees for large gardens).

**Hardiness: US Zone 6-4, Canadian Zone 5-4.**

| | |
|---|---|
| *S. aria* 'Majestica'** | orange red, 5–8m (16–26ft) |
| *S. aucuparia* 'Fastigiata' | orange, 10m (33ft) |
| *S. decora* | red, 10m (33ft) |
| *S. hybr.* 'Gibbsii'** | dark carmine red, 6–8m (20–26ft) |
| *S.* 'Joseph Rock'** | cream, 5–8m (16–26ft) |
| *S. latifolia* 'Atrovirens** | brownish orange, 8–10m (26–33ft) |
| *S. x thurigiaca* 'Fastigiata' | deep red, large, 10m (33ft) |

## Tilia

### LINDEN

There is good reason for referring to the color of many plants as "lime green." During the summer flowering period, swarms of insects make their way to the tree, which then seems to hum with music. The greenish-white flowers have a strong scent. Don't plant them next to a patio or a parking area: the trees "drip", and there is often a sticky layer of honeydew beneath them. The fall color is bright yellow (see also: Trees for large gardens).

**Hardiness: US Zone 4, Canadian Zone 3.**

| | |
|---|---|
| *T. mongolica* | greenish white, round crown, 8m (26ft) |

## Ulmus

### ELM

The *U. glabra* 'Camperdownii' which, like the

*Betula youngii*, lets its branches droop from a single point, can serve as a bower in a corner of the garden. An elm may be needed for a specific planting scheme because of its shape or color, but beware of the risks: these trees may also be affected by Dutch elm disease, after which all you can do is to uproot them (see also: Trees for large gardens).

**Hardiness: US Zone 5, Canadian Zone 5.**

| | |
|---|---|
| *U. carpinifolia* 'Wredei'** | golden elm, 5–8m (16–26ft) |
| *U. glabra* 'Camperdownii' | pendular shape, 5m (16ft) |

*Tilia mongolica*

*Ulmus glabra* 'Camperdownii'

# 2. Shrubs

## Evergreen shrubs

*It is worth noting first of all that several species of evergreen shrubs require acid soil. As a rule, evergreen plants cannot tolerate morning sunshine: the leaves thaw out too quickly after a night frost, and this causes damage. Evergreen shrubs usually do quite well in semi-shade.*

*Like most deciduous shrubs, evergreen varieties are sold potted which enables them to be planted throughout the summer. Evaporation by way of the leaves continues throughout the winter; as the roots have to ensure the absorption of moisture, it is important for them not to be damaged. When it is frosty, the leaves often begin to droop as a result of stagnating moisture absorption. When you design your garden, make sure that you create a pleasing mixture of evergreen and deciduous shrubs, especially where something – the garbage bin, for instance – needs to be concealed. Conifers are often what comes to people's minds first when they are thinking about evergreen shrubs, but this chapter will show you that there is an equally large choice of evergreen foliage plants.*

*The height of the shrubs is given in metres or centimetres as specified in the lists of cultivars, with the approximate number of feet or inches in brackets.*

*In the case of shrubs with insignificant flowers, information is provided about their width, the color of their berries, leaves, and so on.*

## *Andromeda*

**BOG ROSEMARY**
This small creeping shrub for damp acid soil is not attractive in itself, so the sudden appearance of large flowers is all the more surprising. Plant bog rosemary in full sun. The shrub is usually sold only when it is in flower.
**Hardiness: US Zone 5, Canadian Zone 5.**

| | |
|---|---|
| A. glaucophylla | pink, May–June, 1m (3ft) |
| A. polifolia | pink, May–June, 1m (3ft) |

*Andromeda polifolia*

## *Arctostaphylos*

**BEARBERRY, BEAR'S GRAPE**
This small trailing shrub has flowers resembling bell heather, and blooms in May. It has attractive red berries and requires acid soil.
**Hardiness: US Zone 1, Canadian Zone 1.**

| | |
|---|---|
| A. uva–ursi | pink, May–June, 30cm (12in) |

## *Aucuba*

In sheltered spots, aucubas are among the finest evergreen shrubs. *A. japonica* 'variegata' is also supplied as an indoor plant (for cool rooms). In ideal positions, aucubas grow up to 3m (10ft) tall. They are fully hardy in sheltered spots only. Remember: no morning sunshine! The shrubs usually on sale have yellow-speckled leaves, but do try to get hold of a green-leafed one, which would blend in more with the other plants in the garden. The flowers (May–August) are inconspicuous: the shrub's beauty is in its shiny leaves and red berries. More berries will appear if you

also grow a male plant. The cultivar 'Rozannie' is dioecious. If you just ask for an Aucuba, you will always be sold a "variegata." In many garden centers, it is not even known that there may well be others! Depending on its position, the shrub will grow up to 2–3m (6–10ft) tall.
**Hardiness: US Zone 7, Canadian Zone 7.**

**Green–leafed cultivars:**

| | |
|---|---|
| A. japonica 'Borealis'* | |
| A. j. 'Longifolia'** | male, no berries |
| A. j. 'Dentata'** | |
| A. j. 'Rozannie'! | |
| A. j. 'Hillieri' | |

**Cultivars with speckled leaves:**

| | |
|---|---|
| A. j. 'Crassifolia'* | male, no berries |
| A. j. 'Crotonifolia'* | male, no berries |
| A. j. 'Variegata' | |

*Aucuba japonica* 'Variegata'

# Azalea

See: *Rhododendron*.

# Berberis

**BARBERRY**

The genus *Berberis* includes over 200 species, some of which are evergreen. *B.* x *media* 'Park Jewel' is semi-evergreen. The thorns make pruning difficult and, as the leaves are also prickly, maintenance jobs like weeding under and near the shrubs are rather unpleasant tasks. The same problems arise in the case of holly which, however, includes cultivars with leaves that have very few spines or none at all. Prevent leaf burn after a night frost in early spring by planting berberis where it does not catch the early morning sun. The growing of berberis has been restricted or banned in Canada and some parts of the USA because some species are an alternative host to a rust fungus on wheat. Check with local County Agent or Department of Agriculture before selecting and planting any berberis.
**Hardiness: US Zone 7-4, Canadian Zone 6-3.**

| | |
|---|---|
| B. candidula** | bright yellow, Apr–May, 0.75m (30in) |
| B. darwinii | yellowish orange, red spots, May, 2m (6ft) |
| B. gagnepainii** | pruinose blue fruits, May, 1.5m (5ft) |
| B. g. var. lanceifolia** | pruinose blue fruits, narrow leaves |
| B. julianae | yellow, pruinose blue fruits, May, 2m (6ft) |
| B. linearifolia | orange, Apr–May, 1.25m (4ft 2in) |
| B. l. 'Orange Beauty' | orange, Apr–May, 1m (3ft) |
| B. x media 'Park Jewel' | dark green leaves, 1m (3ft) |

*Berberis darwinii*

| | |
|---|---|
| B. m. 'Red Jewel' | red leaves, 1m (3ft) |
| B. stenophylla | orange yellow, Apr–May, 2.5m (8ft) |
| B.s. 'Corallina Compacta' | organge yellow, 30cm (1ft) |
| B. thunbergii 'Green Ornament' | red berries, 1.5m (5ft) |
| B.t. 'Rose Glow' | silver pink leaves in spring, 1.5m (5ft) |
| B. verruculosa | yellow, large, May, 1.25m (4ft 2in) |

## *Buxus*

### BOX

It is not always realized that this evergreen shrub, so often used for hedges or topiary, will grow up to 5m (16ft) tall. There are also many cultivars which differ in growth patterns as well as in the size, shape, and color of their leaves. Taking cuttings is simple, though it will take a year for the first rootlets to develop. Plant the cuttings close together in a shady spot, and don't forget to water them regularly in the summer (see also: Hedging plants). The following plants are the most suitable cultivars to grow as free-standing bushes.
**Hardiness: US Zone 6, Canadian Zone 5.**

| | |
|---|---|
| B. microphylla 'Asiatica' | |
| B. m. var. koreana | spreading, 1m (3ft) |
| B. sempervirens | small leaves, 4m (13ft) |
| B. s. 'Suffruticosa' | small leaves, 0.5m (20in) |

*Buxus sempervirens*

## *Calluna*

### LING HEATHER

Like bell heather (Erica), ling heather is suitable for sandy and peaty soils with high acidity. To create a long-flowering heather garden, it will be necessary to combine ling and bell heathers and, of course, to add other shrubs and perennials. Don't forget to plant a few deciduous shrubs as well as evergreens, as this will add a sense of the changing seasons. If, however, a garden contains nothing but heathers and conifers, it will remain virtually the same throughout the year, and there will be no more looking forward to spring.
**Hardiness: US Zone 4, Canadian Zone 5.**

| | |
|---|---|
| C. vulgaris | pale mauve, July–Aug, 40cm (16in) |
| C. v. 'Alba Dumosa' | white, July–Aug, 40cm (16in), spreading |
| C. v. 'Alba Erecta' | white, bright green foliage, Aug–Sept, 50cm (20in) |
| C. v. 'Alba Plena' | white, Aug–Oct, 40cm (16in), spreading |
| C. v. 'Alba Rigida' | white, Aug–Sept, 15cm (6in), low, spreading |
| C. v. 'Alportii' | mauve, Aug–Sept, 70cm (28in), upright |
| C. v. 'Aurea' | purplish pink, golden yellow foliage, July–Sept, 40cm (16in) |
| C. v. 'Barnett Anley' | purple, Aug–Sept, 50cm (20in), broad |
| C. v. 'Beoley Gold' | white, yellow foliage, Aug–Sept, 40cm (16in) |

*Calluna vulgaris* 'Alba Erecta'

| | |
|---|---|
| *C. v.* 'Blazeaway' | violet, yellowish-green leaves, 45cm (18in) |
| *C. v.* 'Carmen' | purplish red, Aug–Sept, 45cm (18in), broadly upright |
| *C. v.* 'Cramond' | pink, Sept–Nov, 50cm (20in), broadly upright |
| *C. v.* 'Cuprea' | purple, bronze-colored foliage, Aug–Sept, 45cm (18in) |
| *C. v.* 'C.W. Nix' | red, Aug–Sept, 80cm (32in), upright |
| *C. v.* 'Dainty Bess' | pink, blueish-gray foliage, Aug–Oct, 10cm (4in) |
| *C. v.* 'Darkness' | purplish pink, Aug–Sept, 40cm (16in), upright |
| *C. v.* 'Dark Beauty' | purplish pink, Aug–Sept, 35cm (14in), upright |
| *C. v.* 'Dark Star' | dark red, July–Sept |
| *C. v.* 'Egelantissima' | white, grayish-green foliage, Sept–Dec, 55cm (22in) |
| *C. v.* 'Elegant Pearl' | white, July–Sept |
| *C. v.* 'Elsie Purnell' | silvery pink, grayish-green foliage, Aug–Sept |
| *C. v.* 'Flore Pleno' | pink, Sept–Oct, 45cm (18in), broadly upright |
| *C. v.* 'Golden Carpet' | pink, golden-yellow foliage, Aug–Sept, 10cm (4in) |
| *C. v.* 'Golden Feather' | purple, yellow foliage, Aug–Sept, 30cm (12in), spreading |
| *C. v.* 'Gold Haze' | white, bright yellow foliage, Aug–Sept, 50cm (20in) |
| *C. v.* 'Hamondii' | white, dark foliage, Aug–Sept, 60cm (24in), upright |
| *C. v.* 'H.E. Beale' | pink, Aug–Nov, 60cm (24in), flowers suitable for cutting |
| *C. v.* 'J.H. Hamilton' | deep pink, Aug–Sept, 25cm (10in), spreading |

| | |
|---|---|
| *C. v.* 'Joan Sparkes' | pale mauve (d), 20cm (8in) |
| *C. v.* 'Hookstone' | purplish pink, July–Sept |
| *C. v.* 'Long White' | white, Sept–Oct, upright |
| *C. v.* 'Marleen' | white and purple, dark foliage, Sept–Nov, 35cm (14in) |
| *C. v.* 'Mountain Snow' | white, July–Sept, 50cm (20in) |
| *C. v.* 'Peter Sparkes' | pink, Sept–Nov, 60cm (24in), flowers suitable for cutting |
| *C. v.* 'Ralph Purnell' | purple, Aug–Sept, 40cm (16in), broadly upright |
| *C. v.* 'Red Star' | red, July–Sept |
| *C. v.* 'Robert Chapman' | pink, Aug–Sept, 40cm (16in), broadly upright |
| *C. v.* 'Silver Knight' | lilac, July–Sept, 45cm (18in), upright |
| *C. v.* 'Silver Queen' | mauve, gray foliage, Aug–Sept, 45cm (18in) |
| *C. v.* 'Sister Anne' | lilac, grayish-green foliage, Aug–Sept, 10cm (4in) |
| *C. v.* 'Sunset' | purplish pink, bronze-colored foliage, Aug–Sept, 30cm (12in) |
| *C. v.* 'Tenuis' | pink, July–Nov, 30cm (12in), spreading |
| *C. v.* 'Tib' | purple, June–Oct, 40cm (16in), |
| *C. v.* 'Underwoodii' | purple, Oct–Nov, 45cm (18in) |
| *C. v.* 'Wickwar Flame' | purplish pink, July–Sept |

# *Camellia*

### CAMELLIA

Although there are more (almost) hardy cultivars available nowadays, it is still not advisable to plant camellias in an exposed position out of doors in more northerly regions. As well as producing flowers in every pastel shade, the shrubs have attractive shiny leaves. They cannot tolerate morning sunshine after a frost. Preferably plant them in acid soil in an unheated greenhouse. In the park at Pillnitz near Dresden in Germany, a 200-year-old camellia, 6m (20ft) tall, has a purpose-built mobile greenhouse, so that the temperature can be kept at 5°C (41°F) and the humidity at 60%.
**Hardiness: US Zone 8, Canadian Zone 7.**

*Calluna vulgaris* 'Tib'

*Camellia japonica*

| *C. japonica* | gray, white, pink, yellow, red, Apr, 2m (6ft) |
|---|---|

## Ceanothus

This late-flowering shrub is semi-evergreen and cannot tolerate much frost. Grow it only as a container plant, though it may do well against a west-facing wall, protected from cold east winds.
**Hardiness: US Zone 8, Canadian Zone 7.**

| *C.* x *delilianus* | |
|---|---|
| 'Gloire de Versailles' | blue, July–Oct, 2m (6ft) |
| *C. d.* 'Henri Desfossé' | blue, Aug–Oct |
| *C. d.* 'Indigo'** | blue, Aug–Sept |
| *C. d. pallidus* | |
| 'Marie Simon' | pink, Aug–Sept |
| *C. p.* 'Pearl Rose'** | pink, Aug–Sept |
| *C. thirsiflorus* var. *repens* | blue, Aug–Sept |

## Cotoneaster

Pay attention to the height: some make good ground cover; others are large shrubs. They all have striking white flowers and gleaming red berries. The plant thrives in all kinds of soil, in full sun or half-shade (see also: Deciduous shrubs).

*Ceanothus* x *delilianus* 'Gloire de Versailles'

**Hardiness: US Zone 7-6, Canadian Zone 8-5.**

| *C. conspicuus* | white, May, 0.5m (20in) |
|---|---|
| *C. c.* 'Decorus' | white, May |
| *C. d.* 'Flameburst' | white, May |
| *C. dammeri*! | white, May, 0.15m (6in) |
| *C. d.* 'Mooncreeper' | white, 0.15m (6in) |
| *C. microphyllus* | white, May–June, 0.4m (16in) |
| *C. m.* var. *cochleatus* | white, May–June, 0.8m (32in) |
| *C. m.* var. *melanotrichus* | white, May–June, 1m (3ft) |
| *C. salicifolius* | white, May–June, 2m (6ft) |
| *C.* x *watereri* 'Winter Jewel' | white, May, 3.5m (11ft) |

**Hybrid cultivars:**

| *C.* 'Coral Beauty' | white, May, 0.5m (20in) |
|---|---|
| *C.* 'Skogholm' | white, May, 0.5m (20in) |
| *C.* 'Queen of Carpet' | white, May, 0.3m (12in) |

## Daboecia

### IRISH BELL HEATHER
This heather is in every respect larger than ordinary bell heather. As the plant is frost tender, it requires acid soil in a sheltered position.
**Hardiness: US Zone 9, Canadian Zone 8.**

| *D. cantabrica* 'Alba' | white, July–Sept, 30cm (12in) |
|---|---|

*Cotoneaster* x *watereri* 'Winter Jewel'

| | |
|---|---|
| *D. c.* 'Atropurpurea' | deep purple, 25cm (10in) |
| *D. c.* 'Pragerae' | purple, July–Sept, 15cm (6in) |
| *D. c.* 'William Buchanan' | carm. red, June–Nov, 30cm (12in) |

*Daboecia cantabrica* 'Atropurpurea'

## Daphne

This small shrub is quite different from its spring-flowering relative which is not evergreen. It thrives in a rock garden, in a position without morning sunlight. This applies to all evergreens, though these small shrubs are in fact semi-evergreen.
**Hardiness: US Zone 7-5, Canadian Zone 6-4.**

| | |
|---|---|
| *D.* x *burkwoodii* | dusty pink, May–June, 1.5m (5ft) |
| *D. cneorum*! | pink, red, July–Sept, 50cm (20in) |
| *D. laureola* | yellow, May–June, 50cm (20in) |
| *D. odora* | pink, Mar–Apr, 1.5m (5ft) |
| *D. tangutica*** | lilac pink, May, 50cm (20in) |

## Deutzia

This semi-evergreen, moderately tall shrub has finely serrated leaves and slender racemes of flowers (see also: Deciduous shrubs).
**Hardiness: US Zone 9, Canadian Zone 8.**

| | |
|---|---|
| *D. taiwanensis*** | white, June-July 1.5m (5ft) |

## Elaeagnus!

The elaeagnus is one of the strongest evergreen shrubs. The leaves are highly decorative; the flowers and berries are insignificant. The underside of the leaves is gray. *E. pungens* has spines. Plant cultivars with variegated leaves in the sun, as this helps the leaves retain their color; the green-leafed shrubs can tolerate some shade.
**Hardiness: US Zone 8, Canadian Zone 7.**

| | |
|---|---|
| *E.* x *ebbingei* | gray beneath, 3m (10ft) |
| *E. e.* 'Gilt Edge' | golden yellow edge, 3m (10ft) |
| *E. glabra*** | white flowers, orange berries, Sept–Oct, 3m (10ft) |
| *E. pungens* | cream flowers, dark green leaves, May, 3m (10ft) |
| *E. p.* 'Maculata' | large yellow spots, 2.5m (8ft) |

*Eleagnus* x *ebbingei*

*Daphne cneorum*

# Empetrum

This handsome evergreen ground cover definitely requires moist acid soil in half-shade. The flowers are insignificant; the black berries give the plant its beauty.
**Hardiness: US Zone 1, Canadian Zone 1.**

| | |
|---|---|
| E. nigrum | reddish, Mar, 20cm (8in) |
| E. hermaphroditum | reddish, Apr, 30cm (12in) |

*Empetrum nigrum*

# Erica

**HEATHER**

Ericas have striking pendent flowers. The colors are more pronounced than those of the ling heathers, and their times of flowering are spread out over a longer period. The best-known species is *E. x darleyensis*, which flowers in the first four months of the year. About ten (unnamed) cultivars are cultivated. The plant is suitable for containers and, by way of exception, does not require acid soil: ordinary potting compost is satisfactory. *E. arborea*, tree heather, (height 2m/6ft), is suitable for very sheltered courtyards, but should be protected in the event of severe frost. It flowers from March until May. Other species and cultivars of bell heather are listed below.
**Hardiness: US Zone 7-5, Canadian Zone 6-4.**

**Erica carnea – alpine heath, winter heath:**

| | |
|---|---|
| E. c. 'Ann Sparkes' | deep purple, yellow foliage |
| E. c. 'Aurea' | purplish pink, yellow foliage, Feb–Apr, 20cm (8in) |
| E. c. 'Cecilia M. Beale' | white, Nov–Mar, 20cm (8in) |
| E. c. 'Challenger' | deep purple |
| E. c. 'Foxhollow Fairy' | pink, yellowish–green foliage, Jan–Mar, 20cm (8in) |
| E. c. 'Heathwood' | purplish pink, bright green foliage, Mar–Apr, 25cm (10in) |
| E. c. 'James Backhouse' | purplish pink, bright green leaves, Feb–Apr, 25cm (10in) |
| E. c. 'King George' | purplish pink, Dec–Mar, 15cm (6in) |
| E. c. 'Loughrigg' | purplish pink, bronze–colored foliage, Feb–Apr, 20cm (8in) |
| E. c. 'March Seedling' | pinkish mauve |
| E. c. 'Myreton Ruby' | wine red, Mar–Apr, 20cm (8in) |
| E. c. 'Pink Spangles' | pinkish red, Mar–Apr, 25cm (10in), spreading, open |
| E. c. 'Praecox Rubra' | purplish red, Dec–Mar, 20cm (8in), spreading |
| E. c. 'Rosy Gem' | pinkish red, Feb–Apr, 20cm (8in) |
| E. c. 'Ruby Glow' | purplish pink, Nov–Apr, 20cm (8in) |
| E. c. 'Snow Queen' | white, Jan–Mar, 15cm (6in) |
| E. c. 'Springwood Pink' | pale pink, Jan–Mar, 20cm (8in), trailing |
| E. c. 'Springwood White' | white, Jan–Mar, 20cm (8in), trailing |
| E. c. 'Thomas Kingscote' | purplish pink, Mar–Apr, 20cm (8in) |
| E. c. 'Vivelii' | carmine, bronze-colored foliage, Dec–Apr, 20cm (8in) |
| E. c. 'Winter Beauty' | deep purplish pink, Dec–Mar, 15cm (6in), compact |
| **E. ciliaris** | pinkish red, July–Oct, 30cm (12in), spreading |
| E. c. 'Corfe Castle' | red, Sept, 40cm (16in) |
| E. c. 'Globosa' | pink, Sept, 30cm (12in) |
| E. c. 'Stroborough' | pink or white, Sept, 50cm (20in), upright |

**E. cinerea – bell heather:**

| | |
|---|---|
| E. c. 'Alba' | white, July–Aug, 25cm (10in), broad growth |
| E. c. 'Alba Minor' | white, July–Oct, 15cm (6in), compact |
| E. c. 'Atropurpurea' | deep purple, Aug–Sept, 20cm (8in) |

*Erica cinerea* 'Alba'

| | |
|---|---|
| *E. c.* 'Atrorubens' | deep pink, July–Oct, 25cm (10in) |
| *E. c.* 'C.D. Eason' | bright red, dark foliage, June–Sept, 30cm (12in) |
| *E. c.* 'C.G. Best' | salmon pink, Aug–Sept, upright |
| *E. c.* 'Cevennes' | pink, July–Oct, 25cm (10in), upright |
| *E. c.* 'Coccinea' | carmine, June–Sept, 20cm (8in), trailing |
| *E. c.* 'Domino' | white, brown petals, July–Sept, 25cm (10in) |
| *E. c.* 'Eden Valley' | lilac white, July–Sept, 15cm (6in), dwarf |
| *E. c.* 'Golden Drop' | purplish pink, bronze-colored foliage, July–Aug, 15cm (6in) |
| *E. c.* 'Golden Hue' | lilac, yellow foliage, July–Aug, 35cm (14in) |
| *E. c.* 'G. Osmond' | lilac, July–Sept, 35cm (14in), upright |
| *E. c.* 'Katinka' | deep purple, June–Oct, 30cm (12in), upright |
| *E. c.* 'Knap Hill' | bright pink, July–Sept, 30cm (12in) |
| *E. c.* 'Mrs. Dill' | bright red, June–Aug, 15cm (6in) |
| *E. c.* 'Pallas' | purple, June–Sept, 35cm (14in), broadly upright |
| *E. c.* 'Pink Ice' | soft pink, June–Sept, 15cm (6in), compact |
| *E. c.* 'P.S. Patrick' | purple, Aug–Sept, 30cm (12in) |
| *E. c.* 'Pygmaea' | pinkish red, June–Aug, 15cm (6in), trailing |
| *E. c.* 'Rosea' | bright pink, July–Aug, 25cm (10in), compact |
| *E. c.* 'Velvet Knight' | deep purple, July–Aug, 30cm (12in) |

**E. x stuartii:**

| | |
|---|---|
| *E. s.* 'Irish Lemon' | light purplish mauve, 20cm (8in), broad |

**E. tetralix – cross–leafed heather:**

| | |
|---|---|
| *E. t.* 'Alba' | white, grayish-green foliage, June–Aug, 25cm (10in) |

*Erica vagans* 'Mrs. F.D. Maxwell'

| | |
|---|---|
| *E. t.* 'Alba Mollis' | white, June–Sept, 30cm (12in), bushy |
| *E. t.* 'Alba Praecox' | white, grayish-green foliage, June–Aug, 25cm (10in) |
| *E. t.* 'Con. Underwood' | carmine, grayish-green foliage, July–Sept, 35cm (14in) |
| *E. t.* 'Daphne Underwood' | salmon pink, June–Aug, 20cm (8in), weak growth |
| *E. t.* 'Helma' | pink, July–Aug, 30cm (12in), |
| *E. t.* 'Hookstone Pink' | salmon pink, grayish-green foliage, June–Oct, 25cm (10in) |
| *E. t.* 'Ken Underwood' | carmine, June–Oct, 25cm (10in), |
| *E. t.* 'L.E. Underwood' | apricot, June–Oct, 25cm (10in), |
| *E. t.* 'Pink Glow' | pink, July–Sept, 25cm (10in) |
| *E. t.* 'Pink Star' | purplish pink, June–Sept, 15cm (6in), low, broad |

**E. vagans – Cornish heath:**

| | |
|---|---|
| *E. v.* 'Alba' | white, July–Sept, 40cm (16cm), broadly upright |
| *E. v.* 'Diana Hornibrook' | red, July–Oct, 35cm (14in) |
| *E. v.* 'George Underwood' | salmon pink, July–Oct |
| *E. v.* 'Grandiflora' | soft pink, Aug–Oct, 60cm (24in) |
| *E. v.* 'Holden Pink' | pink, Aug–Oct, 35cm (14in), broadly upright |
| *E. v.* 'Lyonesse' | white, yellow anthers, Aug–Oct, 35cm (14in) |

*Erica vagans* 'Valerie Proudley'

*Escallonia* 'Victory'

| | |
|---|---|
| E. v. 'Mrs. F.D. Maxwell' | red, July–Oct, 35cm (14in), |
| E. v. 'Nana' | creamy white, Aug–Oct, 25cm (10in), compact |
| E. v. 'Pyrenees Pink' | salmon pink, red anthers, Aug–Oct, 35cm (14in) |
| E. v. 'St. Keverne' | salmon pink, Aug–Oct, 35cm (14in), compact |
| E. v. 'Valerie Proudley' | white, Aug–Oct, 20cm (8in), broadly upright |
| E. v. 'Willamsii' | purplish pink, July–Oct, 20cm (8in), broad |

## Escallonia!

Escallonias flower over a long period, but never exuberantly. The small flowers appear in between the shiny leaves of a dense bush. Plant in a sheltered position in any kind of well-drained soil.
**Hardiness: US Zone 9, Canadian Zone 8.**

| | |
|---|---|
| E. 'C.F. Ball' | carmine, 3m (10ft) |
| E. 'Dart's Rosyred' | pinkish red, 2m (6ft) |
| E. 'Donard Seedling' | soft pink, May–July, 2m (6ft) |
| E. 'Slieve Dunard' | white, pink spots, 2m (6ft) |
| E. 'Victory' | carmine pink, 2m (6ft) |

## Euonymus

Although these evergreen plants can be grown as climbers, they generally serve as ground cover. They can climb over low walls and are suitable for a heather or ground-cover garden. The color of the leaves shows up better in a sunny position, but they also do well in the shade. *E. fortunei* var. *radicans* and *E. f.* 'Vegetus' can also be trained up walls (or trees!); they then grow up to 6m (20ft) tall. *E. f.* 'Variegatus' can also do that, but does not grow so tall.
**Hardiness: US Zone 8-6, Canadian Zone 7-5.**

*Euonymus fortunei* 'Vegetus'

| | |
|---|---|
| E. fortunei 'Carrierei' | shiny dark green, 1.5m (5ft) |
| E. f. 'Coloratus' | semi-matt dark green, 50cm (20in) |
| E. f. 'Dart's Carpet' | dull dark green, 30cm (12in) |
| E. f. 'Green Carpet' | new |
| E. f. 'Emerald Gaiety' | grayish green, white edges, 1.25m (4ft 2in) |
| E. f. 'Emerald 'n Gold' | grayish green, yellow edges, 50cm (20in) |
| E. f. var. radicans | matt green, 1.5m (5ft) |
| E. f. 'Silver Queen' | creamy yellow, grayish green later on, 80cm (32in) |
| E. f. 'Variegatus' | green, narrow white edges, 40cm (16in) |
| E. f. 'Vegetus' | matt green, large, 1.5m (5ft) |

## x *Gaulnettya*

This dense shrub is a cross between *Gaultheria* and *Pernettya*; it has small, leatherish, dark green leaves. Red fruits ripen in late fall. Plant in moisture-retentive acid soil, but not in full sun.
**Hardiness: US Zone 9, Canadian Zone 8.**

| | |
|---|---|
| G. wisleyensis 'Ruby'* | white, May-June 1m (3ft) |

*Gaultheria procumbens* 'Coral'

## Gaultheria

Like the entire blueberry family, the *Gaultheria* requires acid soil which is rich in humus, well drained, and moisture-retentive. Shade tolerant.
**Hardiness: US Zone 5-3, Canadian Zone 4-2.**

| | |
|---|---|
| G. procumbens | white, red fruits, 15cm (6in) |
| G. p. 'Coral' | white, large red fruits, 20cm (8in) |
| G. shallon | white, black fruits, 75cm (30in) |

# Hebe

See: Container plants and some cold-greenhouse plants.

*Hedera helix* 'Arborescens'

# Hedera

**IVY**

These cultivars are the flower stems of the common climbing ivy. The flower stems themselves do not have adventitious rootlets. If cuttings can be taken from them, a non-climbing form is created which can be cultivated in full sun or

*Hypericum calycinum*

shade in any type of soil. It is suitable for planting under tall shrubs which are bare lower down.
**Hardiness: US Zone 7, Canadian Zone 6.**

| | |
|---|---|
| *H. colchica* 'Arborescens' | green, Dec–Feb, 1m (3ft) |
| *H. helix* 'Arborescens' | green, Dec–Feb, 1m (3ft) |

# Hypericum

*H. uralum* is semi-evergreen. Hypericums are sun lovers, ideal for ground cover; they thrive in any kind of soil.
**Hardiness: US Zone 7, Canadian Zone 6.**

| | |
|---|---|
| *H. calycinum* | large, yellow, 30cm (12in) |
| *H. uralum* | small-leafed, yellow, 1m (3ft) |

# Ilex

**HOLLY**

This genus of shrubs includes tall as well as low-growing species. The deciduous *I. verticillata* (see: Deciduous shrubs) is well known. All are relatively slow growing and require sun and half-shade. The 'Pyramidalis' cultivar has few spines on its leaves, which makes looking after the shrub more agreeable. *I. a.* 'Atlas' is a male form which may be needed for pollination, but does not produce berries. *I .a.* 'Ferox' is very spiny and does not produce berries either. Like 'Golden Queen' and 'Silver Queen'(!), it is a male plant.
**Hardiness: US Zone 7-6, Canadian Zone 6-5.**

**Green–leafed:**

| | |
|---|---|
| *I. aquifolium* | dark green, 12m (40ft) |
| *I. a.* 'Bacciflava' | yellow berries, 8m (26ft) |
| *I. a.* 'Ferox'! | densely spined, no berries, 8m (26ft) |
| *I. a.* 'Duc van Tol' | red berries, 8m (26ft) |
| *I. a.* 'J.C. van Tol'! | orange–red berries, 10m (33ft) |
| *I. a.* 'Pyramidalis' | red berries, 8m (26ft) |

**Variegated leaves:**

| | |
|---|---|
| *I. a.* 'Argenteomarginata' | silver-edged, 8m (26ft) |
| *I. a.* 'Aureomarginata' | yellow-edged, 8m (26ft) |

*Ilex* 'Duc van Tol'

| | |
|---|---|
| *I. a.* 'Ferox Argentea' | silvery variegated, 8m (26ft) |
| *I. a.* 'Golden Queen' | broad golden edges, 5m (16ft) |
| *I. a.* 'Golden van Tol' | yellow edged, 4m (13ft) |
| *I. a.* 'Madame Briot' | golden-yellow edges, 8m (26ft) |
| *I. a.* 'Rubricaulis Aurea' | slightly yellow edges, 8m (26ft) |
| *I. a.* 'Silver Queen' | creamy edges, 6m (20ft) |
| *I. crenata* | green, 1m (3ft) |
| *I. c.* 'Convexa' | convex leaves, 1m (3ft) |
| *I. c.* 'Golden Gem' | golden yellow, 50cm (20in) |
| *I. c.* 'Green Lustre' | compact, dark green, 1.5m (5ft) |
| *I. c.* 'Rotundifolia' | large leafed, 1.5m (5ft) |
| *I. meservae*! | |
| *I. m.* 'Blue Angel' | remains low, 1m (3ft) |
| *I. m.* 'Blue Girl' | new, 1.5m (5ft) |
| *I. m.* 'Blue Prince' | 2.5m (8ft) |
| *I. m.* 'Blue Princess' | remains low, 1.5m (5ft) |
| *I. m.* 'Dragon Lady' | upright, sharp leaves, 2.5m (8ft) |

*Kalmia latifolia*

# Kalmia

**MOUNTAIN LAUREL**
This shrub has incredible flowers. The bluish-green leaves look slightly withered. The plant requires humus-rich acid soil and full sun.
**Hardiness: US Zone 4, Canadian Zone5.**

| | |
|---|---|
| *K. angustifolia* | pinkish red, June, 1m (3ft) |
| *K. a.* 'Rubra' | pinkish red, May–July, 1m (3ft) |
| *K. latifolia* | carm. pink, May–June, 1.5m (5ft) |
| *K. l.* 'Red Crown' | red, June, 1m (3ft) |
| *K. polifolia* | bright pinkish mauve, Apr, 50cm (20in) |

*Ledum groenlandicum*

# Ledum

**LABRADOR TEA**
The ledum is a native of the swamps in northern regions. The racemes of flowers appear at the tips of the branches. The plant likes a wet peaty garden and, above all, acid soil and sun or half-shade.
**Hardiness: US Zone 2, Canadian Zone 1.**

| | |
|---|---|
| *L. groenlandicum* | white, Apr–June, 1m (3ft) |
| *L. g.* 'Compactum' | white, Apr–June, 50cm (20in) |

*Leucothoe walteri* 'Rainbow'

# Leucothoe

This low-growing shrub has graceful pendulous branches and a purple-brown fall color. Its former name was *L. fontanesiana*. There are only two species; the cultivar 'Rainbow' has yellowish-orange-pink spots on its leaves.
**Hardiness: US Zone 7, Canadian Zone 6.**

| | |
|---|---|
| *L. walteri* | white, May–June, 1m (3ft) |
| *L. w.* 'Rainbow' | variegated leaves, cream, yellow and pink |

# Ligustrum

**PRIVET**
Only *L. lucidum* and *L. ovalifolium* are evergreen. The others are not, but they do not drop their leaves after the very first night frost. They are therefore

classified as semi-evergreen. *L. vulgaris*, the common deciduous privet, includes three evergreen cultivars which can be grown as underplanting; the others are decorative shrubs. *L. lucidum* can be cultivated as a tree in a sheltered urban garden. The shrubs have decorative white flowers which do not appear when they are pruned as hedges.
**Hardiness: US Zone 9-7, Canadian Zone 8-6.**

| | |
|---|---|
| *L. japonicum* | olive green, dense, 2m (6ft) |
| *L. lucidum* | large shiny leaves, 5m (16ft) |

*Ligustrum lucidum*

| | |
|---|---|
| *L. obtusifolium* | |
| var. *regelianum* | broad, 2m (6ft) |
| *L. ovalifolium* | green leaves, 4m (13ft) |
| *L. o.* 'Argenteum'** | white-edged leaves, 3m (10ft) |
| *L. o.* 'Aureum' | yellow leaves, 3m (10ft) |
| *L. o.* 'Dart's Abundance'** | broad, black berries, 4m (13ft) |

*Lonicera fragrantissima*

| | |
|---|---|
| *L. quihui*! | white, Aug–Sept, 2m (6ft) |
| *L. x vicaryi* | upright, yellow leaves, 2m (6ft) |
| *L. vulgare* 'Lodense' | green leaves, 50cm (20in) |
| *L. v.* 'Liga'** | vigorous, strong, 2.5m (8ft) |
| *L. v.* 'Atrovirens'** | green leaves, 4m (13ft) |

## *Lonicera*

**HONEYSUCKLE**

This extensive genus includes climbers and deciduous shrubs. *L. fragrantissima* is semi-evergreen. This shrub has an open growth pattern and requires a sheltered position. The others may be planted in any position and in any kind of soil. They can also be clipped into all kinds of shapes. The flowers are insignificant.
**Hardiness: US Zone 7-6, Canadian Zone 6-5.**

| | |
|---|---|
| *L. fragrantissima* | creamy white, Mar–June, 2m (6ft) |
| *L. nitida* | broad, 1.25m (4ft 2in) |
| *L. n.* 'Baggeson's Gold' | yellowish green, 80cm (32in) |
| *L. n.* 'Elegant'** | coarse leaves, 1m (3ft) |
| *L. n.* 'Graziosa'** | frost tender, 80cm (32in) |
| *L. n.* 'Maygreen' | fresh green, 80cm (32in) |
| *L. pileata* | broad, 60cm (24in) |
| *L. p.* 'Mossgreen'** | fresh green, 50cm (20in) |

## x *Mahoberberis***

This ugly cross between *Mahonia* and *Berberis* is a botanical curiosity and therefore a collector's plant. It likes sun or semi-shade.
**Hardiness: US Zone 8, Canadian Zone 7.**

| | |
|---|---|
| *M. neubertii* 'Dart's Desire' | yellow, May–June, 2m (6ft) |
| *M. n.* 'Dart's Treasure' | yellow, 2m (6ft) |

## *Mahonia*

Compared with other evergreens, these undemanding and rewarding shrubs are relatively inexpensive. They prefer part shade. The leaves may be damaged by frost in winter.
**Hardiness: US Zone 6-8, Canadian Zone 7-5.**

*Mahonia bealii*

| | |
|---|---|
| M. aquifolium 'Apollo'** | golden yellow, Apr–May, 60cm (24in) |
| M. a. 'Atropurpurea' | yellow, Mar–Apr, 60cm (24in) |
| M. a. 'Emerald'** | yellow, Mar–Apr, 80cm (32in) |
| M. a. 'Undulata'* | deep yellow, Apr–May, 1.5m (5ft) |
| M. bealii | pale yellow, Dec–Apr, 1.5m (5ft) |
| M. japonica* | pale yellow, long racemes, Jan–Mar, 1m (3ft) |
| M. j. 'Hilvernant'** | new |
| M. x media 'Charity' | yellow, long racemes, Jan–Mar, 2m (6ft) |
| M. m. 'Winter Sun'** | bright yellow, long racemes, Jan–Mar, 1.5m (5ft) |
| M. nervosa | bright yellow, upright racemes, May–June, 40cm (16in) |
| M. n. 'Calypso'* | yellow, broad, 40cm (16in) |
| M. repens | yellow, dense racemes, Apr–May, 1m (3ft) |
| M. w. 'Moseri'** | yellowish pink leaves, Apr–May, 80cm (32in) |
| M.x. wagneri 'Kings Ransom' | yellow, Apr–May, 1.5m (5ft) |
| M. w. 'Pinnacle**'! | yellow, Mar–May, 1.5m (5ft) |

## Osmanthus

It is hard to distinguish this shrub from common holly. Its leaves are opposite, whereas holly has alternate leaves. The leaves are leathery with sharp spines; they are also slightly smaller and duller than those of holly. Osmanthus grows

*Osmanthus heterophyllus*

slowly and likes humus-rich soil in semi-shade.
**Hardiness: US Zone 8, Canadian Zone 7.**

| | |
|---|---|
| O. heterophyllus | white, 2m (6ft) |
| O. h. 'Variegatus' | creamy leaf edges, 2m (6ft) |

## Oxycoccus

See: *Vaccinium.*

## Pernettya*

This dense dioecious shrub produces large berries, but only on female plants. One male plant is enough to pollinate a number of female plants. The flowers are white but insignificant. Give them a sheltered position in acid soil. Also known as *Gaultheria mucronata.*
**Hardiness: US Zone 8, Canadian Zone 7.**

| | |
|---|---|
| P. mucronata | pink, red or white, 1m (3ft) |
| P. m. 'Crimsonia' | carmine, 1m (3ft) |
| P. m. 'Rosalind' | pink |
| P. m. 'Wintertime' | pure white, late |

## Photinia

The photinia produces white flowers in spring and red berries in fall. Flowers and berries appear only in favorable circumstances. Plant this large-leafed shrub in semi-shade in a shel-tered position (see also: Trees for small gardens).
**Hardiness: US Zone 9, Canadian Zone 8.**

| | |
|---|---|
| P. x fraseri 'Red Robin' | dark red young leaves, 2–3m (6–10ft) |

*Photinia* x *fraseri* 'Red Robin'

## Pieris

Only the shoots of this fully hardy shrub can be cut by a late night frost. The shoots, however, particularly those of the hybrid cultivars, are one of its charms. Plant in humus-rich, acid soil.
**Hardiness: US Zone 6, Canadian Zone 6.**

| | |
|---|---|
| *P. floribunda* | white, Apr–May, 2m (6ft) |
| *P. japonica* | white, pendulous, Mar–Apr, 2m (6ft) |
| *P. j.* 'Cupido' | creamy white, Apr–May, 80cm (32in) |
| *P. j.* 'Debutante'* | white, Mar–Apr, 80cm (32in) |
| *P. j.* 'Purity' | pure white, Apr–May, 1m (3ft) |
| *P. j.* 'Valley Rose' | pink, Mar, 1.5m (5ft) |
| *P. j.* 'Variegata' | cream, silvery variegated leaves, 1m (3ft) |
| *P. j.* 'White Cascade'! | white, long racemes, Apr–May, 2m (6ft) |
| **Hybrid cultivars:** | |
| *P.* 'Flaming Silver' | leaves with creamy white edges, 2m (6ft) |
| *P.* 'Forest Flame' | white leaves, red shoots, 2.5m (8ft) |

*Pieris japonica*

## Potentilla

This evergreen shrub has dark green, shiny, trifoliate leaves, and forms a dense mat. The new cultivar mentioned below flowers exuberantly but as yet this cultivar is a very rare plant (see also: Deciduous shrubs).
**Hardiness: US Zone 6, Canadian Zone 5.**

| | |
|---|---|
| *P. tridentata* 'Nuuk' | white, May–June, 30cm (12in) |

## Prunus

### CHERRY LAUREL

This most famous of evergreens includes a number of species. Choose the height to suit the conditions of the garden and to cut down on pruning! The cherry laurel is easy to grow in any soil, in sun or shade.
**Hardiness: US Zone 8, Canadian Zone 7.**

| | |
|---|---|
| *P. laurocerasus* 'Caucasica'!** | narrowly upright, very hardy, 3m (10ft) |

| | |
|---|---|
| P. l. 'Mischeana'** | very spreading, 1m (3ft) |
| P. l. 'Mount Vernon'* | very broad, 30cm (12in) |
| P. l. 'Otto Luyken' | compact, striking florescence, 1m (3ft) |
| P. l. 'Reynvaanii'** | upright, sinuate leaves, 1.75m (5ft) |
| P. l. 'Rudolf Billeter'** | broadly upright, 1.25m (4ft 2in) |
| P. l. 'Skipkaensis' | spreading, 2m (6ft) |
| P. l. 'Skipkaensis Macrophylla'** | strongly upright, broad, 2.5m (8ft) |
| P. l. 'Van Nes'** | broad, very dark green, 1.75m (5ft) |
| P. l. 'Zabeliana' | horizontal growth, 2.5m (8ft) |
| P. lusitanica | see: Container plants |

Prunus laurocerasus 'Reynvaanii'

# Pyracantha

**FIRETHORN**

Although pyracanthas are usually grown as climbers, they are also suitable to plant as free-standing trees in a sheltered position. The first one mentioned is a new cultivar which is suitable for ground cover (for the other cultivars see: Vines and wall plants). 'Orange Glow' with its orange red berries is known to be disease-free, and can also be grown as a free-standing shrub. Pyracanthas thrive in any kind of soil, provided it is not too limy.
**Hardiness: US Zone 6, Canadian Zone 5.**

| | |
|---|---|
| P. coccineum | |
| P.c. 'Kasan' | orange red, 3m (10ft) |
| P.c. 'Lalandei' | orange red, 3m (10ft) |
| P.c 'Red Column' | red, upright, 3m (10ft) |
| **Hybrids:** | |
| P. 'Golden Charmer'* | orange yellow |
| P. 'Mohave' | red, 1.5m (5ft) |
| P. 'Orange Charmer' | deep orange, 1.5m (5ft) |
| P. 'Orange Glow'* | orange red, 3m (10ft) |
| P. 'Soleil d'Or'* | yellow, 3m (10ft) |
| P. 'Teton' | orange yellow, 3m (10ft) |

# Rhododendron

**LARGE-FLOWERED HYBRIDS**

The commonest hybrids are readily available. You will find the large fully hardy cultivars which have already proved themselves on page 48. The more unusual ones are not usually stocked at garden centers, but can generally be ordered.
**Hardiness: US Zone 9-6, Canadian Zone 8-5.**

| | |
|---|---|
| R. 'A. Bedford' | lavender blue, blackish red spots |
| R. 'Album Novum' | white |
| R. 'Bernstein' | yellowish orange, orange red spots |
| R. 'Bismark' | faint lilac white, brownish red spots |
| R. 'Blue Peter' | lavender blue, brownish spots |
| R. 'Caractacus' | crimson |
| R. 'Carola' | bright pink and lilac, yellowish brown spots |
| R. 'Catharina van Tol' | pink, yellowish green markings |
| R. 'Constanze' | deep pink, wine red markings |

Pyracantha coccineum 'Red Column'

A large-flowering Rhododendron-hybrid

| | |
|---|---|
| R. 'Dr. H.C. Dresselhuys' | crimson |
| R. 'Duke of York' | bright pink |
| R. 'Edward S. Rand' | purple, greenish brown markings |
| R. 'Fastuosum Flore Pleno' | blueish violet, yellow markings |
| R. 'Gomer Waterer' | white, yellowish markings |
| R. 'Gudrin' | faint pinkish lilac to white |
| R. 'Holstein' | lilac pink, blackish red spots |
| R. 'Humboldt' | purple violet, dark red spots |
| R. 'Janet Blair' | pink |
| R. 'Lady A. de Trafford' | pink, dark reddish brown spots |
| R. 'Eleanor Cathcart' | pink, dark brownish red spots |
| R. 'Lee's Dark Purple'! | dark purplish violet, yellowish brown spots |
| R. 'Maharani' | creamy yellow, reddish-brown dots |
| R. 'Maria Stuart' | soft pinkish violet, dark spots |
| R. 'Marie Forty' | deep purple, blackish red spots |
| R. 'Mme Carvalho' | white, yellowish green markings |
| R. 'Mme Masson' | bright white, yellow spots |
| R. 'Mrs. G.M. Millais' | cream, golden-yellow spots |

| | |
|---|---|
| R. 'Mrs. P. den Ouden' | dark ruby red |
| R. 'Old Port' | dark purplish violet, light markings |
| R. 'Sammelglut' | dark red, white stamens |
| R. 'Simona' | soft pink, dark red markings |

## Rhododendron

### REPENS-HYBRIDS

These low early-flowering, large-flowered rhododendrons take many years to attain their maximum height of 1m (3ft). They are fully hardy, but the flowers sometimes need to be covered to protect them from a late night frost. They tolerate some shade, but may also be planted in full sun.

| | |
|---|---|
| R. 'Abentglut' | bright red |
| R. 'Baden-Baden' | bright scarlet |
| R. 'Carmen' | blood-red |
| R. 'Jewel' | deep scarlet |
| R. 'Red Carpet' | bright red |
| R. 'Scarlet Wonder' | scarlet |

*Rhododendron* 'Pink Pearl'

48

# Rhododendron

## EVERGREEN AZALEA

This group is often referred to as Japanese azaleas, but also as *Obtusum* hybrids. They have small flowers, small leaves, and are semi-evergreen. Find them a sheltered spot with acid soil out of the sun. The broad squat cultivar 'Diamant' (25cm/10in) in deep pink, purple, pink and red is new. They are ideal little shrubs for small urban gardens, where the low sun usually cannot reach the plants. Their heights are given below; allow for the fact that the width of the plants will often exceed their height. A selection from the current range:

| | |
|---|---|
| R. 'Addy Weri' | orange, 1m (3ft) |
| R. 'Adonis' | white, 50cm (20in) |

*Rhododendron* 'Baden-Baden'

| | |
|---|---|
| R. 'Aladdin' | orange red, small leafed, 50cm (20in) |
| R. 'Amoena' | carm. lilac, s. leafed, 75cm (30in) |
| R. 'Beethoven' | lilac, 1m (3ft) |
| R. 'Campfire' | red, 1m (3ft) |
| R. 'Favorite' | ruby red, large leafed, 1m (3ft) |
| R. 'Hatsugiri' | purplish violet, small leafed, 50cm (20in) |
| R. 'Hino–crimson' | carm. red, s. leafed, 40cm (16in) |
| R. 'Kermesina' | pinkish red, s. leafed, 50cm (20in) |
| R. 'Lilac Time' | lilac, 1m (3ft) |
| R. 'Moederkensdag' | red, large leafed, 40cm (16in) |
| R. 'Orange Beauty' | orange, large leafed, 1m (3ft) |
| R. 'Palestrina' | white, large leafed, 1m (3ft) |
| R. 'Schubert' | pink, 1m (3ft) |
| R. 'Silvester' | lilac, small leafed, 60cm (24in) |
| R. 'Stewartstown' | orange red, large leafed, 1m (3ft) |
| R. 'Vuyk's Rosyred' | pinkish red, large leafed, 1m (3ft) |
| R. 'Vuyk's Scarlet' | red, large leafed, 1m (3ft) |

# Rhododendron

## DWARF RHODODENDRON, EVERGREEN

These are the evergreen, small-flowered rhododendrons with small, scale-like leaves. With the exception of *R.* 'Praecox', they are all suitable for small gardens, especially rock gardens. They are readily available.

| | |
|---|---|
| R. 'Blue Diamant' | lilac, 1m (3ft) |
| R. 'Blue Tit' | grayish blue, 50cm (20in) |
| R. 'Intrifast' (*R. impeditum*) | lilac, 25cm (10in) |
| R. 'Laetevirens' | pink, 1m (3ft) |
| R. 'Moerheim' | lilac, 30cm (12in) |
| R. 'Oudijks Favorite' | lilac, 1m (3ft) |
| R. 'Pink Drift' | pinkish lilac, 25cm (10in) |

*Rhododendron* 'Amoena'

| | |
|---|---|
| R. 'Praecox' | lilac, 1.5m (5ft) |
| R. 'Purple Pillow' | purple, 2m (6ft) |
| R. 'Ramapo' | lilac purple, 50cm (20in) |

# Rhododendron**

## BOTANICAL SPECIES**

The genus *Rhododendron* includes about 1,000 natural species, most of which originally came from eastern Asia. Those listed here are ever-green and shallow-rooted; therefore they should not be planted in very dry soil. Instead, it is essential to grow them in humus-rich, moisture- retentive soil in a semi-shaded position. The large- leafed species in particular cannot tolerate winter sunshine! Growth patterns and flower shapes differ considerably, and it is advisable to consult specialist literature for all the following species. The shrubs are available only from highly specia-lized nurseries and the garden centers with which they are in touch. They are real collector's plants.

*Rhododendron* 'Praecox'

| | | | |
|---|---|---|---|
| R. adenogynum | pink/carmine, Apr, 1–2m (3–6ft) | R. litiense | yellow, foliage plant, 2m (6ft) |
| R. adenophorum | pink, spotted carmine, Apr, 1–2m (3–6ft) | R. lutescens | lemon yellow, Mar–Apr, 60cm (24in) |
| R. aechmophyllum | purplish pink, dark spots, May, 1.5m (5ft) | R. minus | lilac pink, May–June, 80cm (32in) |
| | | R. orbiculare | pink, May, 1m (3ft) |
| R. aeruginosum | pink to reddish purple, 1.5m (5ft) | R. peregrinum** | pinkish white, 3m (10ft) |
| R. ambiguum | yellow, spotted green, Apr–May, 1m (3ft) | R. puralbum | bright white, May, 3m (10ft) |
| R. argyrophyllum | white/pink, silver leaves, 2–3m (6–10ft) | R. radicans | purple, June, 10cm (4in) |
| | | R. triflorum | yellow, green markings, Apr–May, 2m (6ft) |
| R. astrocalyx | bright yellow, s. leaves, 1m (3ft) | R. wardii | yellow, May–June, 2m (6ft) |
| R. augustinii | blueish violet lilac, Apr, 2m (6ft) | R. williamsianum | pink, Apr, 1m (3ft) |
| R. auriculatum! | white, fragrant, Aug, 3m (10ft) | R. yakusianum | bright pink, May, 1m (3ft) |
| R. beesianum | pink, dark red spots, Apr–May, 4m (13ft) | | |
| R. brachycarpum | creamy white, green spots, June–July, 2m (6ft) | | |
| R. bureavii | pink and white to red, May, 1.5m (5ft) | | |

## Rhododendron

See: Hedging plants and Deciduous shrubs.

| | | | |
|---|---|---|---|
| R. calophytum | whitish pink and white, Mar–Apr, 3m (10ft) | | |
| R. calostrotum | purplish violet, 30cm (12in) | | |
| R. campanulatum | white and purplish pink, Apr–May, 2m (6ft) | | |

## Ribes

These remarkable dwarf shrubs with their leathery leaves need a sheltered position. The greenish-white flowers appear as early as February or March, followed later on by reddish black berries. The plant is not very frost tender, but be sure to put it in semi-shade in a sheltered spot.
**Hardiness: US Zone 9, Canadian Zone 8.**

| | | | |
|---|---|---|---|
| R. carolineanum | pale pink, May–June, 1.5m (5ft) | | |
| R. cyanocarpum | soft pink, Apr–May, 3m (10ft) | | |
| R. decorum | pink, Mar, 2.5m (8ft) | | |
| R. discolor | pinkish white, July, 2m (6ft) | R. henryi** | yellowish green, Feb–Mar, 30cm (12in) |
| R. ferrugineum | dark purplish red, June–July, 1m (3ft) | R. laurifolium** | greenish white, Feb–Mar, 50cm (20in) |
| R. floribundum | purplish pink, 3m (10ft) | | |
| R. forrestii | scarlet, Apr, 25cm (10in) | | |
| R. fortunei | light pink, May, 2m (6ft) | | |
| R. haemaleum | deep carmine, May–June, 75cm (30in) | | |

## Rosa

**R O S E**

Although roses are not evergreen, they do not shed their leaves after the first night frost. Several of them retain their leaves until February, especially when they are in a sheltered position (usually not the best place for roses).

| | |
|---|---|
| R. haematodes | dark scarlet, May, 2m (6ft) |
| R. hirsutum | pale pink, 1m (3ft) |
| R. hirtipes | white to pinkish red, 1.5m (5ft) |
| R. impeditum | see: R. 'Intrifast' |
| R. insigne | pinkish w., May–June, 1.5m (5ft) |
| Rhododendron 'Intrifast' | |

## Rubus

**BLACKBERRY, BRAMBLE**

This genus includes evergreen as well as deciduous shrubs and ground cover. *R. tricolor* even produces large edible fruits. They are not always as hardy as they appear to be, but the new cultivars 'Dutch Wintercover' and 'Kenneth Ashburner' are an exception to this. They make good ground cover for sunny positions as well as for semi-shade. Shelter them from the east wind.
**Hardiness: US Zone 7, Canadian Zone 6.**

| R. calycinoides | white, June–July, 30cm (12in) |
| **Hybrids:** | |
| R. 'Green Wave'** | white, compact, 20cm, (8in) |
| R. 'Kenneth Ashburner'** | white, 60cm (24in) |
| R. tricolor | white, July, 40cm (16in) |

## Ruscus

What is unknown tends to be unloved, and that is a pity in the case of this evergreen shrub which is suitable for semi-shade in a corner of the shrubbery. It is a dense plant, with branches emerging from humus-rich, moisture-retentive soil like those of a perennial. Ruscus is often dried and sometimes painted for dried-flower arrangements.
**Hardiness: US Zone 9, Canadian Zone 8.**

| R. aculeatus** | dark green, 60cm (24in) |

*Ruscus aculeatus*

## Sarcococca

In early spring, small white flowers with pink stamens appear on this dwarf shrub suitable for limy soil in a shady position. The female flowers are insignificant. The leaves are shiny dark green.
**Hardiness: US Zone 6, Canadian Zone 5.**

| S. humilis | white, Feb–Mar, 60cm (24in) |

*Sarcococca humilis*

## Skimmia

Plant this slow-growing shrub for shade and moisture-retentive acid soil in a sheltered spot. The result will be a dense, rounded plant. The flower buds are formed in the fall and adorn the shrub in winter. There are male and female plants, which is important for pollination. *S. reevesiana* is self-pollinating.
**Hardiness: US Zone 8, Canadian Zone 7.**

| S. japonica | white, Apr–May, 1m (3ft) |
| S. j. 'Foremanii'** | red berries (fem.), 1m (3ft) |
| S. j. 'Rubella'** | brownish-red clusters (male), 1m (3ft) |
| S. reevesiana | red berries, 90cm (36in) |

*Skimmia japonica* 'Foremanii'

## Stranvaesia

This is a very vigorous tall-growing shrub. However, this plant can be susceptible to fireblight.
**Hardiness: US Zone 7, Canadian Zone 6.**

| S. davidiana | white, red fall color, 4m (12ft) |

*Stranvaesia (Photinia)*

## Vaccinium

### BILBERRY, CRANBERRY

*V. macrocarpon* (American cranberry), frequently still referred to as *Oxycoccus*, is a low trailing plant with small pink flowers for damp, acid, humus-rich soil in shade or semi-shade. *V. vitisidaea* (cowberry) is evergreen, as opposed to *V. myrtillis* (blueberry). They do best in poor acid sandy soil under trees.
**Hardiness: US Zone 2, Canadian Zone 1.**

| | |
|---|---|
| *V. macrocarpon* | red berries, 10cm (4in) |
| *V. vitis-idaea* | white, red berries, June–Aug, 30cm (12in) |

*Vaccinium*

## Viburnum

### GUELDER ROSE

Several species of this extensive genus of tall as well as low-growing shrubs are evergreen. Both the berries and the flowers are important. They require some sun or semi-shade, protected from morning sunshine, and thrive in any kind of soil.
**Hardiness: US Zone 8-7, Canadian Zone 8-6.**

| | |
|---|---|
| *V. x burkwoodii* | soft pink, May, 2m (6ft) |
| *V. davidii* | w., blue berries, June, 50cm (20in) |
| *V. henryi** | white, May–June, 2m (6ft) |

| | |
|---|---|
| *V. rhitidophyllum* | cream, May, 4m (13ft) |
| *V. tinus* | see: Container plants |

*Viburnum* x *burkwoodii*

## Viscum

### EUROPEAN MISTLETOE

Mistletoe is a semi-parasite which needs another tree rather than soil to live on (not off). This evergreen plant, so popular as a Christmas decoration, can be sown by squeezing the slimy white berries into the bark of other trees. Most suitable for this purpose are fruit trees (especially apples), poplars, willows, and silver firs. Birds need to wipe the sticky substance round the pips off their beaks, and frequently do so against the bark of a tree. It is therefore an old wives' tale to believe that the seed will not germinate unless it has passed through a bird's stomach.
**Hardiness: US Zone 9, Canadian Zone 8.**

| | |
|---|---|
| *V. album* | white berries, Nov–Jan, 1m (3ft) |

*Viscum album*

## Deciduous shrubs

*Forsythia, philadelphus, currants, and lilac: they are found in every garden. Just take a look at these genera and see how much variety there is in the color of the flowers, shape of the leaves, height, single or double forms, and so on. It is hoped that this book will help to prevent far too big a lilac or mock orange being planted in every small front garden! Then there are all those thousands of species and cultivars of shrubs that are still planted all too rarely. Every nursery grows its own special selection. Computers at many garden centers and nurseries provide opportunities for improved communication, thus making it easier to track down which nurseries grow a specific kind of shrub. In addition, your list of requests can be stored and not forgotten as easily as it was formerly. If you place your order at the beginning of the planting season, you will be able to collect your shrub in time. In mild areas the planting season extends from mid-November to mid-April, but shrubs that have been heeled in can be planted out until mid-May – a little earlier in more southerly areas, and a little later further north. Plants grown in containers can also be planted out all summer. Where the soil is dry, it is always best to plant in fall. The height of the shrub is indicated in meters and feet, or in centimeters and inches if less than 1m (3 ft). If the flowers are insignificant, details about the leaves or the growth of the shrub are provided instead.*

## Acanthopanax

There are as many leaflets as there are syllables in the generic name; does that make it easier to remember? The palmate leaf is somewhat reminiscent of the chestnut. This prickly shrub produces small greenish-yellow flowers, but the light green leaves are its greatest attraction. The plant can be grown as an impenetrable hedge.
**Hardiness: US Zone 6, Canadian Zone 5.**

| | |
|---|---|
| A. sieboldianus | light green leaves, 3m (10ft) |

*Acanthopanax sieboldianus*

## Acer

**JAPANESE MAPLE**

The colors mentioned below refer to the leaves. The slow-growing *A. palmatum* is grafted and therefore expensive. The cultivars including the word 'Dissectum' all have delicate pinnate leaves (see also: Trees for large and small gardens).
**Hardiness: US Zone 7, Canadian Zone 6.**

| | |
|---|---|
| A. palmatum | |
|   'Atropurpureum' | red, 4m (13ft) |
| A. p. 'Bloodgood' | blackish red, 5m (16ft) |
| A. p. 'Dissectum' | green, finely pinnate, 1.5m (5ft) |
| A. p. 'Dissectum Nigrum' | dark reddish brown, 2.5m (8ft) |

*Acer palmatum* 'Atropurpureum'

## Aesculus

**BUCKEYE**
The common *Aesculus*, the white horse-chestnut, is a well-known tree. The reference here is to the Bottlebrush buckeye, which produces open, airy panicles of flowers later in the summer. The shrub may spread considerably. The species *pavia* is a small tree, with spineless fruits; its cultivars grow far less tall. Plant in a sunny position.
**Hardiness: US Zone 6, Canadian Zone 5.**

| | |
|---|---|
| *A. parviflora* | cream-colored, July–Aug, 2–4m (6–13ft) |
| *A. pavia* 'Humilis'** | pinkish red, May, 1m (3ft) |

*Aesculus parviflora*

## Amelanchier

**JUNEBERRY, SERVICEBERRY, SHADBERRY**
This shrub has an open structure. It is an ideal shrub for beginners learning how to prune, as each untidy branch is clearly visible. The leaves have a fine fall shade of bronze in early spring. White flowers are followed by small purplish-red berries. They are marketed in several different qualities: inexpensive shrubs with a single branch are suitable for planting in shrubberies, but a well-developed bushy shrub is better for a flower garden. *A. lamarckii* was imported into western Europe in the nineteenth century. *A. ovalis* originally came from Central Europe.

*Amelanchier ovalis* 'Helvetica'

| | |
|---|---|
| *A. lamarckii* | white, Apr–May, 4m (13ft) |
| *A. laevis* 'Cumulus' | white, Apr–May, 3m (10ft) |
| *A.l.* 'Snow Cloud' | white, Apr-May, 3m (10ft) |

## Aralia

In planting schemes with handwritten names of plants, the aralia is occasionally confused with azalea. So be careful! This is a tall narrow shrub with large white panicles of flowers at the top. The spiny branches are its greatest attraction in winter.
Hardiness: US Zone 6, Canadian Zone 5.

| | |
|---|---|
| *A. elata* | white, 5m (16ft) |
| *A. e.* 'Variegata' | white, leaves with silvery variegations |

*Aralia elata*

## Aronia

### CHOKEBERRY
When thinking of low garden shrubs, genistas or spiraeas are generally the first to come to mind. Aronia, so common and yet so rarely supplied, is usually overlooked. This is a very undemanding shrub for sun or shade, a small wood to attract birds, or a flower garden. The black berries and fine fall color add to its decorative appeal.
Hardiness: US Zone 6, Canadian Zone 5.

| | |
|---|---|
| *A. arbutifolia* | white, berries red, Apr–May, 2m (6ft) |
| *A. a.* 'Brilliant' | white, berries bright red, 2m (6ft) |
| *A. melanocarpa* | white, berries black, May–June, 2m (6ft) |
| *A. m.* 'Viking' | white, berries black, 4m (13ft) |

| | |
|---|---|
| *A. prunifolia* | white, berries blacking red, 4m (13ft) |

## Berberis

### BARBERRY
All cultivars of *berberis* have thorns. This makes pruning unpleasant, particularly because the thorns immediately cause minor infections. Make sure you wear strong gloves. The difference between *B. thunbergii* and *B. vulgaris* is apparent in the fruits: *B. thunbergii* has shiny red fruits; those of *B. vulgaris* are dull red (see also: Evergreen shrubs).
Hardiness: US Zone 6, Canadian Zone 5.

| | |
|---|---|
| *B. aggregata* | pale yellow, July–Aug, 1.75m (5ft) |
| *B. buxifolia*** | orange yellow, Apr–May, 3m (10ft) |
| *B. b.* 'Nana'** | non-flowering, 50cm (20in) |
| *B. koreana* | bright red fruits, 1.75m (5ft) |
| *B.* x *mentorensis* | fall colors, 1.5m (5ft) |
| *B.* x *ottawensis*** | yellowish red fruits, 2m (6ft) |
| *B. o.* 'Auricoma'** | purplish brown leaves, 2.25m (7ft) |
| *B. o.* 'Decora'** | blueish-purplish-red leaves, 1.75m (5ft) |
| *B. o.* 'Forescate'** | |
| *B. o.* 'Superba'** | dull purplish red leaves, 2m (6ft) |
| *B.* x *robrustilla*** | orange red fruits, 1m (3ft) |

*Aronia melanocarpa*

| | |
|---|---|
| B. r. 'Autumn Beauty'** | |
| B. r. 'Buccaneer'** | whitish-green and orange-red fruits, 1m (3ft) |
| B. r. 'Fireball'** | red fruits, 1m (3ft) |
| B. r. 'Pirate King'** | carmine-red fruits, pruinose, 1.5m (5ft) |
| B. r. 'Wisley'** | pinkish-orange-red fruits, 1m (3ft) |
| B. thunbergii | light yellow, fruits red, May, 1.5m (5ft) |
| B. t. 'Atropurpurea' | purplish-brownish-red leaves, 1.5m (5ft) |
| B. t. 'Nana' | dwarf, 50cm (20in) |
| B. t. 'Bagatelle' | brownish red leaves, 30cm (12in) |
| B. t. 'Dart's purple'* | brownish red leaves, 1m (3ft) |
| B. t. 'Green Carpet'* | green leaves, fall color, 1m (3ft) |
| B. t. 'Green Ornament'* | light green, dark green later on, 1.5m (5ft) |
| B. t. 'Kobold' | dark green leaves, 40cm (16in) |
| B. t. 'Red Chief' | purplish-brownish-red leaves, 2m (6ft) |
| B. wilsonae | golden yellow, fruits salmon red, 1m (3ft) |

**Hybrid cultivar:**

| | |
|---|---|
| B. 'Red Tears' | grayish green leaves, red fruits, 1.5m (5ft) |

*Buddleja davidii* 'Black Knight'

*Berberis koreana*

# Buddleia

## BUTTERFLY BUSH

Buddleias are popular because they attract butterflies. The fact that they are frost-tender is less well known. Earth up the soil all round them in fall to prevent their being cut down to the base by frost. The method of pruning differs from that for all other shrubs: in spring, prune all branches down to 50cm (20in) above ground after the final period of frost. Failure to do this will mean that the shrub will grow very tall and produce far fewer flowers. This is one of the few trees that are easy to propagate by taking cut-tings. Height (employing the customary method of pruning): 2m (6ft). Plant in full sun.

**Hardiness: US Zone 6, Canadian Zone 5.**

| | |
|---|---|
| B. *davidii* 'African Queen' | dark violet purple |
| B. *d.* 'Black Knight' | dark purple |
| B. *d.* 'Border Beauty' | deep lilac mauve |

*Buddleia weyeriana*

*Callicarpa bodinieri* var. *giraldii*

| | |
|---|---|
| B. *d.* 'Empire blue' | deep blue to mauvish blue |
| B. *d.* 'Ile de France' | deep mauve |
| B. *d.* 'Pink Delight' | pink |
| B. *d.* 'Royal Red' | mauvish red |
| B. *d.* 'White Profusion' | long pure white clusters |

# Callicarpa

## BEAUTY BERRY

This apparently simple shrub has an upright growth pattern. It produces mauve berries which remain on the shrub for a long time and can be dried. The flowers are insignificant. The cultivar 'Profusion' is self-pollinating. You always need two of the common species to produce berries.

**Hardiness: US Zone 7, Canadian Zone 6.**

| | |
|---|---|
| C. *bodinieri* var. *giraldii*** | mauve, Oct–Nov, 3m (10ft) |
| C. *b.* 'Profusion' | mauve, Oct–Nov, 3m (10ft) |
| C. *dichotoma** | deep mauve, Oct–Nov, 1.5m (5ft) |

# Calycanthus

## CAROLINA ALLSPICE

This native undemanding aromatic shrub is dense, medium-sized, and has very shiny leaves. It thrives in almost any soil.

**Hardiness: US Zone 6, Canadian Zone 5.**

| | |
|---|---|
| C. *fertilis* | brownish red, June–Aug, 2.5m (8ft) |
| C. *floridus* | brownish red, June-Aug, 2m (6ft) |

# Caragana

Fine, light green leaves and bright yellow flowers give this shrub great appeal. The cultivar 'Walker' is suitable for containers and as ground cover. The

*Calycanthus fertilis*

leaves of this cultivar are more deeply lobed and delicate. *C. maximowicziana* is a semi-trailing shrub. The caragana needs full sun or half-shade.
**Hardiness: US Zone 5-2, Canadian Zone 4.**

| | |
|---|---|
| *C. arborescens* | lemon yellow, May, 6m (20ft) |

*Caragana arborescens*

| | |
|---|---|
| *C. a.* 'Lorbergii' | lemon yellow, May, 4m (13ft) |
| *C. a.* 'Pendula'! | yel., weep., Apr–May, 1.5m (5ft) |
| *C. a.* 'Walker' | yel, weep., Apr–May, 50cm (20in) |
| *C. aurantiaca*** | orange yellow, May, 1m (3ft) |
| *C. maximowicziana*** | yellow, May, 1.5m (5ft) |

*Caryopteris clandonensis* 'Heavenly Blue'

## *Caryopteris*

The caryopteris is not very hardy. The flowers appear on one-year-old wood and the shrub may therefore be cut back to the base in spring. Plant in a warm sheltered spot in full sun and in soil that is not too moist.
**Hardiness: US Zone 7, Canadian Zone 6.**

| | |
|---|---|
| *C.* x *clandonensis* | light blue, Aug–Sept, 1.5m (5ft) |
| *C. c.* 'Heavenly Blue' | blue, Aug–Sept, 1.5m (5ft) |
| *C. incana* | dark blue, Aug–Sept, 1.5m (5ft) |

## *Chaenomeles*

### DWARF QUINCE
Flowers resembling apple blossom appear in May and are followed in fall by apple-like fruits in shades of yellow, yellowish green and green. This shrub prefers a position in full sun. It is frequently still sold under the name *Cydonia*.
**Hardiness: US Zone 6, Canadian Zone 5.**

| | |
|---|---|
| *C. japonica* 'Sargentii'** | orange, thorny, 75cm (30in) |
| *C. speciosa* | red, sometimes pink, 2m (6ft) |
| *C. s.* 'Brilliant'** | deep red, tall, 1.5m (5ft) |
| *C. s.* 'Rosea Plena'** | pink, bushily upright, 1.5m (5ft) |
| *C. s.* 'Simonii'** | blood red, trailing, 50cm (20in) |
| *C. s.* 'Umbilicata'** | pink, tall upright, 2m (6ft) |
| *C. Superba* 'Cameo' | peachy pink double, prolific, Mar-Apr 2-3m (6-10ft) |
| *C.s.* 'Nicoline' | scarlet, broad, Mar-April, 2-3m (6-10ft) |
| *C.s.* 'Nivalis' | pure white, upright, Mar-Apr, 2-3m (6-10ft) |
| *C.s.* 'Jet Trail' | white, floriferous, Mar-Apr, 2-3m (6-10ft) |

*Chaenomelis speciosa* 'Nicoline'

| | |
|---|---|
| _C.s._ 'Spitfire' | vivid red, upright, Mar-Apr, 2-3m (6-10ft) |
| _C.s._ 'Texas scarlet' | tomato red floriferous, Mar-Apr, 2-3m (6-10ft) |
| _C.s._ 'Toyo-Nishiki' | pink, white & red, upright, susceptible to fireblight, Mar-Apr, 2-3m (6-10ft) |

# Chimonanthus

This frost-tender shrub is suitable for growing

_Chimonanthus praecox_

_Chionanthus virginicus_

against sheltered south-facing walls on well-drained limy soil. The flowers appear in early spring on leafless branches.
**Hardiness: US Zone 9, Canadian Zone 8.**

| | |
|---|---|
| _C. praecox_ | creamy yellow and purple, Jan–Feb, 2m (6ft) |

# Chionanthus

**WHITE FRINGE TREE**
Earthing up is required for this summer-flowering upright shrub with yellow fall color: the shrub may be cut down to the ground by frost. It is suitable for a solitary position, and requires loamy soil in full sun.
**Hardiness: US Zone 7, Canadian Zone 6.**

| | |
|---|---|
| _C. virginicus_ | white, June–July, 3m (10ft) |

# Clerodendrum

Give this shrub a warm sheltered position. The fragrant flowers are followed by blue fruits. _C. t._ var. _fargesii_ is less frost-tender.
**Hardiness: US Zone 8, Canadian Zone 7.**

| | |
|---|---|
| _C. trichotomum_ | white, Aug–Sept, 2.5m (8ft) |

_Clerodendrum trichotomum_

# Clethra

One of the best late-flowering shrubs with fragrant blossom and fine fall colors. The spreading *C. barbinervis* is frost-tender. Clethras require acid moisture-retentive soil in half-shade; they cannot tolerate full sun.

**Hardiness: US Zone 6, Canadian Zone 5.**

*Clethra alnifolia*

| | |
|---|---|
| *C. alnifolia* | yel. white, July–Sept, 2.5m (8ft) |
| *C. a.* 'Rosea' | pink, July–Sept, 2m (6ft) |
| *C. barbinervis* | white, Aug, 1.5m (5ft) |

# Colutea

This upright shrub has light green rounded seed pods. Coluteas require poor dry sandy soil and full sun.

**Hardiness: US Zone 6, Canadian Zone 5.**

| | |
|---|---|
| *C. arborescens*! | yellow, May–Aug, 3.5m (11ft) |
| *C.* x *media*** | orange-brown spotted, May–Aug, 2.5m (8ft) |

# Cornus

**DOGWOOD**

*C. alba* bears white flowers in May, followed by white berries later on. The principal reason for planting it is the color of its stems. This also applies to *C. amonum*, a shrub for wetter soil. *C. controversa, florida* and *kousa* have large white flowers. These species are suitable only for quite large gardens and need acid soil; the others are less particular. All species can grow in the sun, or in full or half-shade.

**Hardiness: US Zone 6-2, Canadian Zone 6-2.**

| | |
|---|---|
| *C. alba* | reddish brown stems, 4m (13ft) |
| *C. a.* 'Elegantissima' | leaves with white variegations, 3m (10ft) |
| *C. a.* 'Gouchaultii' | yellow-spotted leaves, 1.5m (5ft) |
| *C. a.* 'Kesselringii*' | dark stems, 1.5m (5ft) |
| *C. a.* 'Sibirica' | bright red branches, 2.5m (8ft) |
| *C. a.* 'Sibirica Variegata'* | bright red branches, variegated leaves, 2m (6ft) |
| *C. alternifolia* | broadly upright, 6m (20ft) |
| *C. amonum* | purplish brown twigs, 4m (13ft) |
| *C. canadensis* | see: Perennials |
| *C. controversa* | creamy white flowers, 8m (26ft) |
| *C. florida* | white, red berries, 10m (33ft) |
| *C. kousa* | cream, May–June, 3.5m (11fift) |
| *C. mas* | yellow, Feb–Apr, 5–7m (16–23ft) |
| *C. sanguineum* | reddish-brown branches, 4m (13ft) |

*Colutea arborescens*

| | |
|---|---|
| C. s. 'Midwinter Fire'* | orange-red branches, 3m (10ft) |
| C. stolonifera 'Flaviramea' | yellowish-green branches, 3m (10ft) |
| C. s. 'Kelsey's Dwarf' | brownish-red branches, 75cm (30in) |

## Corylopsis!

This is a truly ideal yellow flowering shrub for spring, with light green leaves in summer. It is a handsome shrub to look at and its branch structure makes it attractive in winter as well. The corylopsis requires half-shade in any type of soil.
**Hardiness: US Zone 8, Canadian Zone 7.**

| | |
|---|---|
| C. pauciflora! | sulfur yellow, Mar–Apr, 1m (3ft) |
| C. spicata! | light yellow, Mar–Apr, 2m (6ft) |

## Corylus

**HAZEL**

The hazel is an easy upright shrub suitable for larger gardens. As for *C. a.* 'Contorta', don't let your choice be guided merely by its twisting branches; what is not apparent at the time of purchase is the fact that the leaves look curled and sickly, a less attractive aspect. Hazels thrive in any kind of soil in sun or shade.
**Hardiness: US Zone 6, Canadian Zone 5.**

*Corylopsis spicata*

*Corylus avellana* 'Contorta'

*Cornus kousa*

| | |
|---|---|
| *C. avellana* | yellow catkins, Mar–Apr, 4–5m (13–16ft) |
| *C. a.* 'Contorta' | yellow catkins, twisted branches, 3m (10ft) |

## Cotinus

This shrub has magnificent large and delicate flower plumes, but in winter you will see its ugly branch structure. Furthermore, the tips of branches tend to be cut by frost. Don't, therefore, plant *Cotinus* in the front row of a shrubbery. The shrubs produce flowers on two-year-old wood. Plant them out of the wind in full sun in any kind of soil.
**Hardiness: US Zone 6, Canadian Zone 5.**

*Cotinus coggygria*

| | |
|---|---|
| *C. coggyria*! | brownish yellowish, June–July, 3–5m (10–16ft) |
| *C. c.* 'Red Beauty' | dark red leaves, 3–5m (10–16ft) |
| *C. c.* 'Rubrifolius' | wine-red leaves, 3–5m (10–16ft) |

## Cotoneaster

You can grow cotoneasters for various purposes: the low ones for rock gardens and trailing over low walls, and also as ground cover and for parterres; the taller ones for shrubberies and groves for attracting birds. Nearly all species produce shiny red berries, much loved by birds.

But beware: they are hosts to fireblight. Plant the shrubs in full sun (see also: Evergreen shrubs).
**Hardiness: US Zone 7-5, Canadian Zone 6-4.**

| | |
|---|---|
| *C. adpressus* | reddish, June, 25cm (10in) |
| *C. apiculatus* | pink, pendulous, June, 2m (6ft) |
| *C. bullatus*\* | reddish, May–June, 4m (13ft) |
| *C. b.* 'Firebird'\*\* | white, fruits orange red, 4m (13ft) |
| *C. dielsianus* | pink or white, June, 3m (10ft) |
| *C. franchetti* | white/pink, June, 1.5m (5ft) |
| *C. horizontalis* | white or pinkish red, June, 1.5m (5ft) |
| *C. h.* 'Robustus'\*\* | white or pinkish red, 2m (6ft) |
| *C. praecox* | reddish, broad, May, 60cm (24in) |
| *C. p.* 'Copra'\*\* | red fruits, broad, 1m (3ft) |

*Cotoneaster horizontalis*

| | |
|---|---|
| *C. racemiflorus* var. *soongoricus*\*\* | leaves grayish white beneath, 2m (6ft) |
| *C. splendens*\*\* | grayish green, round leaves, 2m (6ft) |
| *C. sternianus* | reddish white, May–June, 2m (6ft) |
| *C. wardii* | upright, leaves white beneath, 2m (6ft) |
| *C.* x *watereri* 'Winter Jewel' | white, large, May, 3.5m (11ft) |

## Crataegus

**HAWTHORN, MAY**
These undemanding shrubs are suitable for shrubberies in large gardens; they require regular pruning. The flowers are followed in fall by berries, a treat for the birds. *C. laevigata* (two styles) is frequently still sold under the name *C. oxycantha*. The more common *C. monogyna* (one style) is also a native shrub in Europe. Hawthorn thrives in any soil, even in the strongest winds (see also: Hedging plants).
**Hardiness: US Zone 4, Canadian Zone 3.**

| | |
|---|---|
| *C.crus-gallii* | white, red fruit, 5m (16ft) |

| | |
|---|---|
| *C. laevigata* | white, 7m (23ft) |
| *C. l.* 'Paul's Scarlet' | red, double, 6m (20ft) |
| *C. lavallei* 'Carrieri' | white, orange-red fruits |
| *C. monogyna* | white, May, 8m (26ft) |
| *C. m.* 'Stricta' | more ascending branches |
| *C. prunifolia* 'Splendens' | shiny oval leaves, 6m (20ft) |

## Cydonia

See: Trees for small gardens, *Chaenomeles*.

## Cytisus

### BROOM

Only a handful of the many cultivars of *C. scoparius* (the *scoparius* hybrids) has been named. These shrubs dislike being transplanted after a few years; they are therefore always sold in a container. In severe winters, *C. scoparius* (common broom) may be killed by frost. Broom needs fairly dry soil in full sun (see also: *Genista* and *Spartium*).
**Hardiness: US Zone 6-8, Canadian Zone 5-7.**

| | |
|---|---|
| *C. decumbens* | gold. yel., May–June, 20cm (8in) |
| *C.* x *kewensis*** | white, slightly yellowish, May, 30cm (12in) |
| *C.* x *praecox* | creamy yellow, May, 2m (6ft) |
| *C. p.* 'Allgold' | golden yellow, May, 2m (6ft) |
| *C. p.* 'Boskoop Ruby'** | dark pinkish red, May–June, 1.5m (5ft) |
| *C. p.* 'Hollandia' | lilac red, May–June, 1.5m (5ft) |

*Crataegus monogyna*

| | |
|---|---|
| *C. p.* 'Zeelandia'* | pink, Apr–May, 1.5m (5ft) |
| *C. purpureus*** | lilac p., May–June, 50cm, (20in) |
| *C. p.* 'Atropurpureus'*** | lilac, May–June, 40cm (16in) |
| *C. scoparius* | br. yellow, May–June, 2m (6ft) |
| *C. s.* 'Burkwoodii' | red, May–June, 1.5m (5ft) |
| *C. s.* 'Lena' | red. yel., May–June, 1.5m (5ft) |

*Cytisus* x *praecox*

| | |
|---|---|
| *C. s.* 'Luna'** | wh. yellow, May–June, 1.5m (5ft) |
| *C. s.* 'Moonlight' | sulfur yellow, June, 1.5m (5ft) |
| *C. s.* 'Windlesham Ruby'* | creamy white & pale lilac, June, 2m (6ft) |

## Daphne

Light and dark mauve flowers are followed later in the year by poisonous red berries. The fleshy branches are upswept, unlike those of

*Daphne mezereum* 'Alba'

*D. cneorum* which have a more horizontal growth. Propagation is by layering: bend a few branches down on to the ground and put a stone on each of them. Cut off the branches after they have rooted.
**Hardiness: US Zone 4, Canadian Zone 3.**

| | |
|---|---|
| *D. mezereum* | mauve, Mar–Apr, 2m (6ft) |
| *D. m.* 'Alba'* | white, Mar–Apr, 2m (6ft) |
| *D. m.* 'Rubra' | red. mauve, Mar–Apr, 2m (6ft) |

## Decaisnea

This upright shrub with large pinnate leaves looks quite exotic. Its large, steel-blue, bean-shaped fruits are highly decorative. It is a tall and narrow shrub, which makes it suitable for small gardens. Decaisneas require a sunny position.
**Hardiness: US Zone 7, Canadian Zone 6.**

*Decaisnea fargesii*

| | |
|---|---|
| *D. fargesii* | green. yel., May–June, 5m (16ft) |

## Deutzia

This ideal upright garden shrub is suitable for planting in full sun in any soil. There is an appropriate one for every garden or other location. The growth pattern and leaves of some species resemble those of *Philadelphus*.
**Hardiness: US Zone 7-6, Canadian Zone 6-5.**

| | |
|---|---|
| *D. gracilis* | white, May–June, 6m (20ft) |
| *D.* x *kalmiiflora**! | pink, large, June, 1.5m (5ft) |
| *D. lemoinei* | white, June, 1.5m (5ft) |
| *D.* x *magnifica** | bright white (d), May–June, 3m (10ft) |
| *D. scabra** | white, June–July, 3m (10ft) |

| | |
|---|---|
| *D.s.* 'Codsall Pink' | pink, June–July, 2.5m (8ft) |
| *D. s.* 'Plena'* | white, pink (d), June–July, 2.5m (8ft) |
| *D. s.* 'Pride of Rochester' | white (d), 2.5m (8ft) |

## Diervilla

These low shrubs with flowers resembling those of weigelias bloom on one-year-old wood: cutting them down to the base does not affect their florescence the following season. Diervillas prefer dryish soil in sun or half-shade.

| | |
|---|---|
| *D. rivularis*** | lemon yellow, July–Aug, 1m (3ft) |
| *D. sessiflora* | sulfur yel., June–Aug, 1m (3ft) |

*Diervilla sessilifolia*

*Deutzia scabra* 'Pride of Rochester'

## Elaeagnus

Some species are evergreen, but the shrubs listed here are deciduous. It is a suitable shrub for a large, deceptively wild-looking garden. *E. angustifolia* (Russian Olive) is native in some parts of Europe. Its striking gray leaves resemble those of the willow. Plant this shrub in relatively dry soil in full sun.
**Hardiness: US Zone 6-3, Canadian Zone 5-2.**

| | |
|---|---|
| *E. angustifolia* | cream, July–Aug, 4m (13ft) |
| *E. commutata* | white, June–Aug, 3m (10ft) |
| *E. umbellata* | silvery leaves, 3m (10ft) |

*Elaeagnus angustifolia*

*Enkianthus campanulatus*

## Enkianthus

This is one of the few large shrubs that prefer acid humus-rich soil. It needs sun and half-shade. Cover the base to protect the plant from harsh sunlight. Its bright red fall color adds to the appeal of this broadly upright shrub.
**Hardiness: US Zone 6, Canadian Zone 5.**

| | |
|---|---|
| *E. campanulatus* | pinkish yellow, May, 3m (10ft) |

## Euonymus

The white flowers, the orange fruits in their red casing, and the unrivalled fall colors make up these splendid shrubs. Euonymus will thrive in full sun or half-shade in any soil (limy for preference).
**Hardiness: US Zone 5-3, Canadian Zone 4-3.**

| | |
|---|---|
| *E. alatus*! | corky wings on shoots, 2m (6ft) |
| *E. a.* 'Compactus'! | corky wings on shoots, compact, 1m (3ft) |
| *E. atropurpureus* | crimson fruits, 6m (20ft) |
| *E. europaeus* | red fruits, 4m (13ft) |
| *E. e.* 'Atrorubens'** | dark leaves, 4m (13ft) |
| *E. e.* 'Red Cascade'! | pinkish red fruits, 5m (16ft) |
| *E. phellomanes*** | pink fruits, 2.5m (8ft) |
| *E. sachalinensis***! | red fruits, 4m (13ft) |

*Euonymus alatus*

## Exochorda

This small shrub bears flowers resembling those of the philadelphus. *E. racemosa* produces a lot of shoots from the base and is therefore easy to propagate. The compact little *E.* x *macrantha* 'The Bride' produces a great many flowers. It thrives in any kind of soil in full sun.
**Hardiness: US Zone 5, Canadian Zone 5.**

| | |
|---|---|
| E. giraldii** | white, Apr–May, 4m (13ft) |
| E. x *macrantha* 'The Bride'! | white, May–June, 1m (3ft) |
| E. racemosa | white, May–June, 3m (10ft) |

*Exochorda* x *macrantha*

## Ficus

**FIG**

The fig is related to the rubber tree, a favorite indoor plant in the 1960s. It seems incredible that, like hops, this genus is classified as belonging to the stinging nettle family! Figs can be grown as shrubs in sheltered positions, but may also be trained up a south-facing wall. Don't give young plants too much fertilizer, or they will grow too fast and consequently develop weak branches. Take a few root cuttings if growth is too rapid. Although a severe winter will not kill the plant, northern regions are not warm enough for the fruits to ripen. Figs, however, are interesting shrubs even without fruits.
**Hardiness: US Zone 8, Canadian Zone 7.**

| | |
|---|---|
| F. carica | dark green leaves, 4m (13ft) |

## Forsythia

It is open to debate whether the forsythia is deservedly one the most popular shrubs. Its florescence is of course magnificent, but does that really outweigh the sight of the shrub's ugly structure during the fifty weeks of the year when it is not in flower? It therefore always makes sense to plant it in the second row of a shrub border, as the flowers appear before the leaves of other shrubs. The buds of these splendid flowers for cutting only develop when there has been a good period of frost. After a frostless winter, the plant occasionally does not flower at all. (If the temperature fails to drop below zero out of doors, put some branches in a plastic bag in the freezer, and you will have a vase of flowering forsythia indoors as early as January!). Enthusiasts will find that there are many more species and cultivars than are listed here (see also: Vines and wall plants).

**Hardiness: US Zone 6-5, Canadian Zone 5-4.**

| | |
|---|---|
| F. hybr. 'Northern Gold' | golden yellow, 2m (6ft) |
| F. x *intermedia* 'Lynwood' | golden yellow, 2.5m (8ft) |
| F. 'Arnold's Dwarf' | deep yellow, compact, 1m (3ft) |
| F. i. 'Spectabilis' | golden yellow, 2.5m (8ft) |
| F. i. 'Spring Glory' | light yellow, 2.5m (8ft) |
| F. ovata | yellow, early, 1m (3ft) |

*Forsythia intermedia* 'Spectabilis'

## Fothergilla

The fothergilla is closely related to the witch hazel, which has a similar early florescence and magnificent fall colors. The shrub is slow-growing and therefore expensive. The flowers are reminiscent of yellow catkins.
**Hardiness: US Zone 7-6, Canadian Zone 6-5.**

| | |
|---|---|
| F. gardenii | creamy pale yellow, Apr–May, 1m (3ft) |
| F. major | creamy pale yellow, Apr–May, 2m (6ft) |

## Fuchsia*

If planted in a sheltered position, these fuchsias will not be killed by frost, which makes them ideal shrubs for an urban garden. Cut the shrub back close to the

base after a severe winter, and it will start growing again in spring. This does not affect its florescence. The heights indicated are those reached in the year after pruning. Fuchsias flower from July to October.
**Hardiness: US Zone 9-8, Canadian Zone 8-7.**

| | |
|---|---|
| *F. magellanica* 'Corallina' | red and violet, 1.5m (5ft) |
| *F. m. 'Gracilis'* | red and violet, 1m (3ft) |
| *F. m.* 'Variegata' | reddish pink, variegated leaves, 1.2m (4ft) |

**Hybrid cultivars:**

| | |
|---|---|
| *F.* 'Chillerton Beauty' | pale p. a. viol. mauve, 75cm (30in) |
| *F.* 'Mme Cornelissen' | white and red, 75cm (30in) |
| *F.* 'Riccartonii' | red and violet, 1.2m (4ft) |

*Fuchsia* 'Riccartonii'

## Genista

**BROOM**

This is a low-growing broom for a dry sunny spot in the rock garden. The taller *G. tinctoria* (dyers' greenweed)

is native to Europe. The other species flower more profusely. You can extend the flowering period considerably by growing several species. Plant in well-drained soil in full sun.
**Hardiness: US Zone 6-4, Canadian Zone 5-3.**

| | |
|---|---|
| *G. hispanica* | gol. yellow, May–June, 1m (3ft) |
| *G. lydia* | gol. yellow, June–July, 60cm (24in) |
| *G. pilosa* 'Goldilocks' | gol. yellow, May–June, 40cm (16in) |
| *G. p.* 'Vancouver Gold' | yellow, May–Aug, 40cm (16in) |
| *G. sagittalis*! | bright yellow, May, 30cm (12in) |
| *G. tinctoria* | deep yellow, June–Aug, 1m (3ft) |

*Genista lydia*

| | |
|---|---|
| *G. t.* 'Royal Gold' | gol. yellow, June–Aug, 1m (3ft) |

## Halesia

**SNOWDROP TREE**

This tree-like shrub produces bell-shaped flowers followed by small fruits resembling pears. It is

*Halesia carolina*

large, broad, and suitable for only the very largest of gardens. The halesia prefers neutral or acid soil and full sun.
**Hardiness: US Zone 6, Canadian Zone 5.**

| | |
|---|---|
| *H. carolina* | white, May, 4m (13ft) |

## *Hamamelis*

**WITCH HAZEL**

This very early-flowering shrub is often planted in too small a garden. It grows up to 4m (13ft) tall, and is equally broad. Pruning is virtually impossible: the result would be a total loss of shape. Therefore let the witch hazel have plenty of space, preferably in a half-shady position. A period of frost may delay flowering.
**Hardiness: US Zone 7-5, Canadian Zone 6-4.**

| | |
|---|---|
| *H. intermedia* | |
| 'Arnold's Promise' | yellow, Feb-Mar |
| *H.i.* 'Diane' | wine red, Feb |
| *H. i.* 'Fire Charm' | brownish red, Feb |
| *H. i.* 'Jelena' | orange, Dec–Jan |
| *H. i.* 'Primavera'* | pale yellow, Jan–Feb |
| *H. i.* 'Westerstede' | pale yellow, Mar |

*Hibiscus syriacus*

*Hamamelis mollis* 'Pallida'

| | |
|---|---|
| *H. mollis* | yellow, Dec–Jan |
| *H. m.* 'Pallida' | pale yellow, Dec–Jan |

## *Hibiscus*

**ROSE OF SHARON**

The name hibiscus usually brings to mind indoor plants from China, but the garden hibiscus comes from Asia Minor. This strong, evenly shaped shrub grows up to 2.5m (8ft) tall. The severe shape of these

shrubs make them suitable for symmetrical layouts. Their flowering season is from August to October.
**Hardiness: US Zone 7-6, Canadian Zone 6-5.**

**Single–flowered cultivars:**

| | |
|---|---|
| *H. syriacus* 'Aphrodite' | dark pink |
| *H.s.* 'Blue Bird' | blue |
| *H.s.* 'Diana' | white |
| *H.s.* 'Helene' | white purple base |
| *H.s.* 'Minerva' | lavender |
| *H. s.* 'Red Heart' | pure white, brownish red center |
| *H. s.* 'Rubis'* | deep pink |
| *H. s.* 'Woodbridge' | deep pink, large |

**Double–flowered cultivars:**

| | |
|---|---|
| *H.* 'Ardens' | purplish blue |
| *H.* 'Boule de Feu' | dark red |
| *H.* 'Puniceus Plenus'** | red |
| *H.* 'Violet Clair Double'** | lilac |

# Hippophae

## SEA BUCKTHORN

The sea buckthorn is an ideal shrub for coastal regions as it can withstand even the severest gales. It will grow in any soil and can tolerate considerable drought. Its appeal is due to the narrow gray leaves and branches laden with bright orange berries. The shrub looks rather untidy and is therefore not recommended for every garden.
**Hardiness: US Zone 3, Canadian Zone 2.**

| | |
|---|---|
| *H. rhamnoides* | or. berries, Sept–Oct, 3m (10ft) |
| *H. r.* 'Leikora'** | orange berries, large fruits, 3m (10ft) |

*Hippophae rhamnoides*

# Hydrangea

The brightness of the hydrangea's flowers depends entirely on the acidity and iron content of the soil. The blue hydrangeas listed below are pink in limy soil. Plant them in half-shade in a spot that is not too dry, as they will otherwise droop. *H. macrophylla* has an even rounded shape suitable for a symmetrical layout. If the large buds at the tips are removed in spring, the flowers will be distributed evenly over the entire shrub. *H. paniculata* has very large panicles of flowers and very fragile branches, which makes the shrub unsuitable for a garden with small children. *H. aspera* has large pubescent leaves and grows much taller. *H. serrata* and its cultivars are hardier than *H. macrophylla*.
**Hardiness: US Zone 8-4, Canadian Zone 7-3.**

**'Lace–cap' species and cultivars:**

| | |
|---|---|
| *H. aspera* | mauve and white |
| *H. macrophylla* 'All Summer Beauty' | July-Aug |
| *H.m* 'Blue Wave' | blue, July-Aug |
| *H.m.* 'Nikko Blue' | blue, July-Aug |
| *H.m* 'Pink Beauty' | pink, July-Aug |
| *H. m.* 'White Wave** | white, June–Sept |
| *H. serrata* 'Acuminata'** | blueish, July |
| *H. s.* 'Bluebird' | bright blue, July |
| *H. s.* 'Peziosa' | pinkish red, Aug–Sept |

**Species and cultivars with domed heads:**

| | |
|---|---|
| *H. arborescens* 'Annabelle'! | cream, large bush |
| *H. macrophylla* 'Maculata'* | July–Sept |
| *H. m.* 'Pia'* | May–July |
| *H. m.* 'Tovelit'** | dwarf |

**Cultivars with large conical panicles of flowers:**

| | |
|---|---|
| *H. paniculata* 'Floribunda'* | white, July–Sept |
| *H. p.* 'Grandiflora' | white, Aug–Sept |
| *H. p.* 'Kiyushu' | white, Aug–Sept |
| *H. p.* 'Praecox'* | white, May–Sept |
| *H. p.* 'White Moth' | white, Aug–Sept |
| *H. quercifolia* | white, June-July |

*Hydrangea aspera*

# Hypericum

## ST. JOHN'S WORT

These low shrubs produce their large bright-yellow flowers on one-year-old wood, and may therefore be cut right down to the base every year. In fall, *H. androsaemum* bears brownish-black berries which remain on the bush throughout the winter. The hypericum likes fairly dry soil in full sun or half-shade. (Photograph of flower: p. 42).
Hardiness: US Zone 8-5, Canadian Zone 7-4.

| | |
|---|---|
| *H. androsaemum* | yellow, July–Sept, 1.2m (4ft) |
| *H. forrestii*\*\* | gol. yellow, June–Oct, 1m (3ft) |
| *H. hookerianum* 'Hidcote' | gol. yellow, July–Oct, 1.5m (5ft) |
| *H. inodorum*\*\* | yellow, July–Sept, 1m (3ft) |
| *H.* x *moserianum* | yellow, July–Oct, 50cm (20in) |
| *H. prolificum*\*\* | br. yel., July–Sept, 50cm (20in) |
| *H. Uralum*\*\* | gol. yel., Aug–Sept, 75cm (30in) |

*Hypericum androsaemum*

# Ilex

## HOLLY

Holly looks like an ordinary deciduous shrub. In fall, large bright shiny berries appear on every branch. There are male (without berries) and female shrubs; both are required for pollination (see also: Shrubs).

Hardiness: US Zone 4, Canadian Zone 3.

| | |
|---|---|
| *I. verticillata* | red berries, Nov–Dec, 3m (10ft) |

*Ilex verticillata*

# Indigofera

## INDIGO PLANT

This shrub was called *I. gerardiana* until recently. The bushes can be cut down quite low in spring as they flower on one-year-old wood. Plant in a warm sunny spot.
Hardiness: US Zone 7, Canadian Zone 6.

| | |
|---|---|
| *I. heterantha* | pink, July–Sept, 2m (6ft) |

*Indigofera heterantha*

## Kerria

This shrub has bright green branches and is one of the easiest to grow in either sun or shade. The least attractive cultivar, 'Pleniflora', is, unfortunately, the one most frequently on sale. Underground runners can be divided.
**Hardiness: US Zone 6, Canadian Zone 5.**

| | |
|---|---|
| K. japonica | yellow, May, 2.5m (8ft) |
| K. j. 'Picta' | white variegated leaves, May–July, 2.5m (8ft) |
| K. j. 'Pleniflora' | yel. (d), June–Aug, 2.5m (8ft) |

*Kerria japonica* 'Pleniflora'

## Kolkwitzia

The kolkwitzia resembles the weigelia but has more spectacular flowers, which appear just as

*Kolkwitzia amabilis*

those of the spring shrubs are over. The leaves turn yellow in fall; the shrub thrives in sun or half-shade in any soil.
**Hardiness: US Zone 6, Canadian Zone 5.**

| | |
|---|---|
| K. amabilis | light purplish pink, May–June, 2m (6ft) |
| K. a. 'Pink Cloud' | pink, June, 2m (6ft) |

## Laburnum

Regular pruning is needed to prevent the shrub's branches developing into those of a medium–sized tree. Plant in a sunny spot in soil that is not too dry. The seed pods are poisonous (see also: Trees for small gardens).
**Hardiness: US Zone 7, Canadian Zone 6.**

| | |
|---|---|
| L. alpinum | yellow, May, 5m (16ft) |
| L. a. 'Pendulum' | yellow, weeping form, May, 2m (6ft) |
| L. x *watereri* 'Vossii' | yellow, long racemes, May, 7m (23ft) |

*Laburnum anagyroides*

## Lespedeza!

This shrub has long pendulous branches and flowers on one-year-old wood: it is therefore safe to cut back to near the base in early spring. The shrub's late flowering period makes it a welcome addition to the shrub collection. Earthing up is desirable. *L. thunbergii* is rather frost tender: cover it during the winter. The long pliant branches hang down to the ground.
**Hardiness: US Zone 6-5, Canadian Zone 5-4.**

*L. bicolor* 'Summer Beauty'  deep pink, Aug–Oct, 1.5m (5ft)
*L. thunbergii*!  deep pink, Aug–Oct, 1m (3ft)

## Leycesteria

In a normal winter, the leycesteria dies down to the ground. This does not matter, as it flowers on one-year-old wood. The flowers appear between brownish-purple bracts. Plant in moisture-retentive, but porous soil in full sun.
**Hardiness: US Zone 8, Canadian Zone 7.**

*L. formosa*\*\*  pink. red, June–Aug, 1.5m (5ft)

## Ligustrum

**PRIVET**
The genus *Ligustrum* comprises evergreen, semi-evergreen and deciduous shrubs. *L. sinense* pro-duces a profusion of flowers. The flowers of the yellow-leafed species retain their color better in the sun (see also: Evergreen shrubs).
**Hardiness: US Zone 7-6, Canadian Zone 6-5.**

*L. obtusifolium*
   var. regelianum  white, July, 50cm (20in)
*L. quihoui*\*  white, Aug–Sept, 2m (6ft)
*L. sinense*\*!  white, July, 3m (10ft)
*L. vicaryi*  white, leaves yellow June–July, 2m (6ft)

*Ligustrum obtusifolium* var. *regelianum*

*Leycesteria formosa*

# Lonicera

These are well-known undemanding shrubs for sun or shade. They originally came from northern regions and are therefore fully hardy, even in the severest winters. The shrubs are quite unlike the honeysuckles described in other chapters. They are more or less spherical in shape and are not very striking. Because of their berries they are suitable for a grove of trees to attract birds (see also: Vines and wall plants and Evergreen shrubs).

**Hardiness: US Zone 6-3, Canadian Zone 5-2.**

| | |
|---|---|
| L. fragantissima | creamy white, Feb–Mar |
| L. korolkowii | pink, May, 3m (10ft) |
| L. maackii | white, June-July, 3m (10ft) |
| L. morrowii | yellowish, May–June, 2m (6ft) |
| L. tatarica | pink, Apr–May, 3m (10ft) |
| L. t. 'Arnold Red' | red, June, 2.5m (8ft) |
| L. t. 'Rosea' | pink, June, 2.5m (8ft) |
| L. xylosteum | yellowish white, May, 1m (3ft) |

# Magnolia

Unlike evergreen magnolias, the deciduous species are fully hardy. The flower buds may, however, be lost in the event of a late night frost. The early-flowering and smaller *M. stellata* (Star magnolia) is not troubled in this way. The others are suitable only for the very largest gardens. Magnolias prefer humus-rich acid soil. The best time to transplant them is early spring. Transplanting the shrubs when they are in flower does not matter: dehydration can occur only by evaporation through the leaves.

**Hardiness: US Zone 7-6, Canadian Zone 6-5.**

| | |
|---|---|
| M. liliflora 'Nigra' | deep purpl. red, Apr, 6m (20ft) |
| M. soulangeana | pinkish red and white, Apr–May, 6m (20ft) |
| M. s. 'Alba Superba'** | white, Apr, 5m (16ft) |
| M. s. 'Lennei' | wine red, Apr, 5m (16ft) |
| M. stellata! | pure white, Mar–Apr, 2m (6ft) |

*Magnolia stellata*

*Lonicera tatarica* 'Rosea'

# Malus

### CRAB APPLE

Crab apples can be bought as standard or half-standard trees, or as shrubs. Pruning them like other shrubs makes them suitable for medium-sized gardens. Some of the most popular species and cultivars of the very extensive and attractive *Malus* range are listed below. Crab apples can be used as a flowering garden divider which attracts many birds. The shrub is available in every form (see also: Trees for small gardens).
**Hardiness: US Zone 7-5, Canadian Zone 6-4.**

| | color of flower | height | color of fruit | details |
|---|---|---|---|---|
| M. floribunda | pink | 4m (13ft) | yellowish green | pendulous branches |
| M. 'Golden Hornet' | white | 4m (13ft) | deep yellow | round fruits |
| M. 'John Downie' | white | 6m (20ft) | orange red | upright |
| M. 'Liset' | pinkish red | 6m (20ft) | red | leaves red to green |
| M. 'Neville Copeman'** | lilac pink | 4m (13ft) | red to orange | broad |
| M. toringo var. sargentii | white | 4m (13ft) | bright red | dark green leaves |
| M. 'Wintergold'* | whitish pink | 4m (13ft) | bright yellow | shiny leaves |

# Myrica

### BOG MYRTLE

*M. gale* is low-growing and tolerates marshy soil in full sun. The second species prefers drier but acid soil in semi-shade. Both have strongly aromatic leaves.
**Hardiness: US Zone 3, Canadian Zone 2.**

| | |
|---|---|
| M. gale | red catkins, Feb–Mar, 1m (3ft) |
| M. pennsylvanica | grayish-white berries, 1.5m (5ft) |

*Myrica gale*

# Neillia!

### CHINESE NEILLIA

These shrubs are genuinely unknown and therefore unloved. They have small lime-green leaves, with delicate flowers appearing in between them.
**Hardiness: US Zone 6, Canadian Zone 5.**

| | |
|---|---|
| N. affinis* | pink, May–June, 2m (6ft) |
| N. sinensis | white, May–June, 1.5m (5ft) |

*Neillia racemosa*

## Paeonia

The flowers are like those of the ordinary plant, as are the lobed leaves. The name tree peony, *P. arborea*, is somewhat exaggerated: the tree will reach no more than a maximum height of 2m (6ft) in many parts of North America. There are Japanese, Chinese and European cultivars. Most of them are sold by color and not by the name of the cultivar. Most cultivars have inordinately large and full flowers, which often begin to droop because of their weight. Although they are entirely winter-hardy, a late night frost may cause serious damage. Tree peonies are usually grafted (for ordinary peonies see: Perennials).

**Hardiness: US Zone 6, Canadian Zone 5.**

| | |
|---|---|
| *P. delavayi** | red, June–July, 2m (6ft) |
| *P. lutea** | yellow, May–June, 2m (6ft) |
| *P. suffruticosa* | |
|   'Rock's Variety'** | w., br. spots (sd), May, 2m (6ft) |

*Paeonia* 'Rock's Variety'

## Parrotia

Any member of the *Hamamelis* family guarantees a beautiful fall color. This large, slow-growing shrub can even be cultivated to become a small tree. Young plants do not flower and are frost-tender.

**Hardiness: US Zone 8, Canadian Zone 7.**

| | |
|---|---|
| *P. persica* | reddish, Jan–Mar, 4m (13ft) |

## Perovskia

Like most late-flowering species, this small aromatic shrub blooms on one-year-old wood. You should earth it up in fall and cut it down to the base in March. It can be propagated by division.

**Hardiness: US Zone 7, Canadian Zone 6.**

| | |
|---|---|
| *P. atriplicifolia* | pale blue, Sept–Oct, 1m (3ft) |
| *P. a.* 'Blue Spire' | pale blue, Sept–Oct, 1m (3ft) |

*Perovskia atriplicifolia* 'Blue Spire'

*Parrotia persica*

## Philadelphus

Is there anyone who does not recognize a philadelphus? Its fragrance is an essential for any garden. There are so many species and cultivars that it must be possible to find a philadelphus for every situation, even for the smallest garden. Note the varied heights! They bear white flowers in May, unless stated otherwise. *P. coronarius* is the old-fashioned mock orange.

**Hardiness: US Zone 6-4, Canadian Zone 5-3.**

| | |
|---|---|
| P. 'Avalanche' | single, pendulous, 2m (6ft) |
| P. 'Belle Etoile' | white, brownish center, 2m (6ft) |
| P. 'Bouquet Blanc' | white, double, 1.5m (5ft) |
| P. 'Buckley Quill' | white, narrow petals, 1.2m (4ft) |
| P. coronarius | pure white, single, 3m (10ft) |
| P. c. 'Aureus' | yellow leaves, 3m (10ft) |
| P. c. 'Variegatus' | variegated leaves, 3m (10ft) |
| P. 'Innocence' | sing., leaf somet. varieg., 2m (6ft) |
| P. 'Lemoinii' | single, 2.5m (8ft) |
| P. microphyllus | single, fragrant, 1m (3ft) |
| P. 'Mont Blanc' | single, 2.5m (8ft) |
| P. 'Snow Goose' | single, 1.5m (5ft) |
| P. 'Snow Storm' | double, 2.5m (8ft) |
| P. virginalis | semi-double, May-June 2m (6ft) |
| P.v. 'Minnesota Snow Flake' | white double, 2.4m (8ft) |

*Philadelphus* 'Lemoinii'

## Physocarpus

The beauty of this rather inconspicuous shrub is due in part to its flaking branches. It is suitable for a shady position, for instance in a grove to attract birds. It thrives in any soil and in the severest of gales.

**Hardiness: US Zone 3, Canadian Zone 2.**

| | |
|---|---|
| P. opulifolius | white, June–July, 3m (10ft) |
| P. o. 'Dart's Gold' | white, yellow leaves, 2.5m (8ft) |

## Poncirus

The leaves of this small shrub resembling a lemon tree turn golden yellow in fall. The green branches with large spines look striking in winter. The shrub produces small non-edible lemons. In spite of its tropical appearance, it is frost-hardy and can simply be left in the garden. It is suitable for a container which, however, should be brought indoors when it is frosty. It prefers a sunny spot with well-drained soil.

**Hardiness: US Zone 7, Canadian Zone 6.**

| | |
|---|---|
| P. trifoliata | white, May–June, 1.5m (5ft) |

*Poncirus trifoliata*

## Potentilla

Potentillas flower on one-year-old wood: the shrubs may be cut down close to the soil if they have been neglected. It is better to cut off a third of the branches near the ground every year, which means that there will always be an attractive bush. Flowering begins in June and continues into September. The cultivars 'Princess' and 'Red Ace' are particularly early. They are suitable for planting in parterres and

*Physocarpus opulifolius*

for hedges; they thrive in full sun in any soil.
**Hardiness: US Zone 4-2, Canadian Zone 3-1.**

| | |
|---|---|
| P. 'Abbotswood' | white, broad, 75cm (30in) |
| P. 'Arbuscula'** | yel., ground cover, 30cm (12in) |
| P. 'Elizabeth' | golden yellow, flat growth, 30cm (12in) |
| P. 'Farreri' | bright yellow, low, 60cm (24in) |
| P. 'Goldfinger' | butter yellow, broadly upright, 70cm (28in) |
| P. 'Gold Carpet' | gol. yellow, broad, 30cm (12in) |
| P. 'Hachmann's Giant'* | golden yellow, broad bush |
| P. 'Jackman' | deep yellow, upright, 1m (3ft) |
| P. 'Katherine Dykes' | pale yellow, arching, 1m (3ft) |
| P. 'Klondyke'* | golden yellow, upright, 1m (3ft) |
| P. 'Longacre' | yel., low and broad, 50cm (20in) |
| P. 'Moonlight' | lemon yellow, 1.2m (4ft) |
| P. 'Pink Queen'* | whitish pink, upr., 80cm (32in) |
| P. 'Primrose Beauty' | creamy yel., pendulous. 1m (3ft) |
| P. 'Princess'* | pink, upright, 1m (3ft) |
| P. 'Red Ace' | reddish orange, broad, upright, 50cm (20in) |
| P. 'Snowflake'* | white, upright, 1m (3ft) |
| P. 'Sommerflor'* | yel., broadly upr., 70cm (28in) |
| P. 'Tangerine' | orange and bright yellow, open, 75cm (30in) |

*Potentilla* 'Moonlight'

# Prunus

This genus includes tall and low shrubs; fruit trees such as cherry, plum, peach, and nectarine; and Japanese as well as European trees. All those listed here can be grown as shrubs, they are very suitable for a grove to attract birds. The Japanese ornamental cherries are grafted low down and are suitable for medium-sized and large gardens. *P. triloba* is often grafted on to a short stem with the intention that the branches will be cut back annually immediately after flowering. If left to grow freely, this shrub will become much taller (see also: Trees for small gardens and Evergreen shrubs).
**Hardiness: US Zone 7-3, Canadian Zone 6-2.**

| | |
|---|---|
| P. americana | white, Mar–May, 6m (20ft) |
| P. ceracifera | white, Mar, 8m (26ft) |
| P. c. 'Thundercloud' | p., r. leaves, Mar–Apr, 6m (20ft) |
| P. c. 'Rosea' | salmon pink, bronze-colored leaves, Mar–Apr, 6m (20ft) |
| P. x cistena | white, red leaves, Apr, 2m (6ft) |
| P. glandulosa 'Alboplena' | white (d), May, 1.5m (5ft) |
| P. incisa | white, Mar, 4m (13ft) |
| P. padus | white, May, 6m (20ft) |
| P. pensylvanica | white, May-June, 9m (30ft) |
| P. serrulata 'Amanogawa' | Apr–May, 6m (20ft) |
| P. s. 'Kiku–shidare–zakura' | deep pink (d), weeping, 2m (6ft) |
| P. s. 'Kanzan' | deep pink (d), 6m (20ft) |
| P. s. 'Miyako'** | pink buds, white flowers (d), 6m (20ft) |
| P. s. 'Shirotae' | snow-white (sd), 6m (20ft) |
| P. subhirtella* | pale pink, Mar–Apr, 2m (6ft) |
| P. s. 'Autumnalis' | white (sd), Nov–Mar, 5m (16ft) |
| P. s. 'Autumnalis Rosea'* | pink (sd), Nov–Mar, 5m (16ft) |
| P. triloba 'Multiplex' | pink (d), 5m (16ft) |
| P. virginiana | white, Apr-May, 9m (30ft) |

*Prunus subhirtella* 'Autumnalis'

# Rhamnus

**ALDER BUCKTHORN**
This is a rather unspectacular shrub for the wild garden or grove to attract birds. It berries freely and in many locations can become a weed. The shrubs can tolerate shade and moist as well as dry conditions.

| | |
|---|---|
| R. frangula | red berries, 5m (16ft) |
| R. f. 'Asplenifolius'* | very narrow leaves, 4m (13ft) |

Rhamnus catharticus

# Rhododendron, Luteum-hybriden

### DECIDUOUS AZALEA

The deciduous azaleas are subdivided into several groups which are combined here for the sake of convenience. Together, they are sometimes called *Luteum* hybrids. For those growing the plants, it is simpler to classify them according to their speed of growth rather than botanical accuracy. The groups classified as *Luteum* hybrids are referred to as Knaphill–Exbury hybrids, Gent hybrids and *Pontica* hybrids. Their height and width are between 1.5 and 2m (5 and 6ft). The slow-growing cultivars are usually more expensive. The colors are often very bright and sometimes there is a second flowering. Like all *Rhododendrons*, these azaleas need a sheltered position which is not excessively dry, and humus-rich acid soil.
Hardiness: US Zone 7, Canadian Zone 6.

**Fast-growing:**

| | |
|---|---|
| R. 'Berryrose' | pink, yellow spots, broad |
| R. 'Cecile' | salmon pink, dense |
| R. 'Fireball' | orange red |
| R. 'Gibraltar' | orange, darker spots |
| R. 'Glowing Embers' | orange, lighter spots |
| R. 'Golden Eagle' | bright orange |
| R. 'Golden Sunset' | yellow, dark spots |
| R. 'Irene Koster' | pink, yellow spots, fragrant |
| R. 'Persil'! | white, yellow spots |
| R. 'Pink Delight' | bright pink |
| R. 'Royal Command' | copper red |
| R. 'Satan' | scarlet |
| R. 'Seville' | orange |
| R. 'Silver Slipper'! | cream, silvery leaves |
| R. 'Tunis' | red, small flowers |

**Slow–growing:**

| | |
|---|---|
| R. 'Coccinea Speciosa' | fluorescent orange |
| R. 'Corneille' | pink, full |
| R. 'Daviesii' | cream |
| R. 'Homebush'! | deep pink |
| R. 'Jos Baumann' | deep salmon pink |
| R. 'Josephine Klinger' | bright salmon pink |
| R. 'Klondike' | orange yellow |
| R. 'Möwe' | white, yellow spots |
| R. 'Nancy Waterer' | golden yellow |
| R. 'Narcissiflora' | bright yellow, full |
| R. 'Norma' | salmon pink |

Rhododendron 'Persil'

Rhododendron 'Klondike'

# Rhododendron

### AZALEA MOLLIS

The former scientific name has become the common name. The correct name is now *Rhododendron japonicum*. This *Rhododendron* is suitable for a solitary position or for filling a parterre. The bright colors are something you need to like! Before the buds open, it is hard to believe that before long there will not be a branch or stem to be seen: the shrub will be covered in flowers. These plants are usually supplied by color instead of named cultivar, for example with bright red, orange-red, or yellow flowers. The shrubs also have an attractive fall color. Their height is 1.5 to 2m (5–6ft).
**Hardiness: US Zone 6, Canadian Zone 5.**

| | |
|---|---|
| *R. japonicum* | red, orange, white, 2m (6ft) |

*Rhododendron japonicum*

# Rhus

### SUMAC

Rhus is particularly suitable for growing in a solitary position. *R. typhina*, whose lower branches always become bare, may very well serve as a tree in a small city garden. The highly pubescent branches and strong fall colors are its greatest decorative features. *R. glabra* has the best flower panicles. Plant in any soil in full sun. The suckers are a common source of annoyance.
**Hardiness: US Zone 4-3, Canadian Zone 3-2.**

| | |
|---|---|
| *R. aromatica* 'Grow–low'* | yellowish, Apr, 50cm (20in) |
| *R. glabra* | purplish red June, 2m (6ft) |
| *R. g.* 'Laciniata'! | wine red, delicate leaves, July–Aug, 2m (6ft) |
| *R. typhina* | greenish, July–Sept, 4m (13ft) |
| *R. t.* 'Dissecta' | green., delicate leaves, 4m (13ft) |

# Ribes

### CURRANT

The most popular cultivar is *R.* 'King Edward VII' with its large racemes of flowers. Others such as the very thorny and impenetrable *R. stenocarpum* are worthy of greater consideration. *R. alpinum*, with its red fruits, is suitable for underplanting; the cultivar 'Schmidt' retains its leaves longer and grows faster. *R. americanum* has thin pendulous branches and a beautiful fall color. Fast-growing *R. glandu-losum* is an addition to the ground-cover shrubs.
**Hardiness: US Zone 7-3, Canadian Zone 6-2.**

| | |
|---|---|
| *R. alpinum* | yellow, May–June, 1.5m (5ft) |
| *R. a.* 'Schmidt' | compact, dark green, 2m (6ft) |
| *R. glandulosum*** | pink, 50cm (20in) |
| *R. odoratum* | golden yellow, Apr, 2m (6ft) |
| *R. sanguineum* | pink, Apr, 2m (6ft) |
| *R. s.* 'Album'** | white, 2m (6ft) |
| *R. s.* 'King Edward VII' | red, 2.5m (8ft) |
| *R. s.* 'Pulborough Scarlet'* | dark red, white center, 2.5m (8ft) |

*Rhus typhina*

| R.s. 'Spring Snow' | white, 2m (6ft) |
| R. s. 'Splendens' | red, 2.5m (8ft) |
| R. stenocarpum** | 1m (3ft) |

*Ribes sanguineum* 'King Edward VII'

## Ribes

### BLACK CURRANT, RED CURRANT, WHITE CURRANT

Even if you do not like currants, it may be interesting to plant these fruit shrubs in your flower garden. At least they will attract a lot of birds! Remember that the gooseberry, *R. uva-crispa*, will not grow as tall as *R. nigrum* or *R. rubrum*, black, red or white currants. Birds eat hardly any white currants, which are therefore left for human consumption even if they are not netted.

**Hardiness: US Zone 6-3, Canadian Zone 5-2.**

| R. nigrum 'Baldwin' | black, late, 1.5m (5ft) |
| R.n. 'Black Reward'** | black, late, 1.5m (5ft) |
| R.n. 'Boskoop Giant' | black, mid-season, 1.5m (5ft) |
| R.n. 'Consort' | black, mid-season, 1.5m (5ft) |
| R.n. 'Swedish Black'** | black, early, 1.5m (5ft) |
| R. rubrum 'Jonkheer van Tets' | red, early, 1.2m (4ft) |
| R.r. 'Primus'** | white, late, 1.0m (3ft) |
| R.r. 'Red Lake' | red, late, 1.2m (4ft) |
| R.r. 'Rondum'** | red, late, 1.2m (4ft) |
| R.r. 'Rosetta'** | red, late, 1.2m (4ft) |
| R.r. 'Rotet'** | red, late, 1.2m (4ft) |

| R.r. 'White Pearl' | white, mid-season, 1.0m (3ft) |
| R. uva-crispa 'Achilles' | red, late, 75cm (30in) |
| R.u.'Early Sulphur'* | early, 75cm (30in) |
| R.u. 'Whitesmith'** | pale green, mid-season, 75cm (30in) |

*Ribes rubrum*

*R.u. 'Whinham's Industry' purplish red, medium early, 75cm (30in)*

## Robinia

### BLACK LOCUST

Robinias can be cultivated as trees or as shrubs. *R.* 'Pink Cascade', and *R. hispida* are thornless. Like *Gleditsia* 'Sunburst', *R. p.* 'Frisia' has strik-

*Robinia pseudoacacia* 'Frisia'

ing yellow leaves. 'Tortuosa' means twisted. Plant in full sun in well-drained soil that is not too rich. Do not put them in an inordinately windy position because of the risk of broken branches. **Hardiness: US Zone 6-5, Canadian Zone 5-4.**

| | |
|---|---|
| R. 'Pink Cascade' | pink. red, June, 2–5m (6–16ft) |
| R. hispida | pink, June–July, 3m (10ft) |
| R. pseudoacacia 'Frisia' | white, June, 5–8m (16–26ft) |
| R. p. 'Tortuosa' | twist. branches, 5–10m (16–33ft) |

## Rubus

### ORNAMENTAL BLACKBERRY, BRAMBLE

Some of these strong shrubs and low creeping plants (see also: Evergreen shrubs) are cultivated for their flowers, e.g., *R. odoratus*, *R. tridel* and *R. ulmifolius*; others are grown for their fruits, e.g. the common blackberry, raspberries and the Japanese wineberry (*R. phoeniculasius*). They are easy plants and tolerate full sun as well as shade. **Hardiness: US Zone 6-4, Canadian Zone 5-3.**

| | |
|---|---|
| R. 'Betty Ashburner'* | 30cm (12in) |
| R. odoratus | acid pink, June–Sept, 1.5m (5ft) |
| R. phoeniculasius** | bright red fruits, 3m (10ft) |
| R. spectabilis | purplish red, orange yellow fruits, Apr, 2.5m (8ft) |
| R. x tridel 'Benenden' | bright white, May, 2m (6ft) |
| R. ulmifolius 'Bellidiflorus'** | pink (d), July–Aug, 2.5m (8ft) |

*Rubus spectabilis*

## Rubus

### BLACKBERRY (THORNLESS), BRAMBLE

In a flower garden, thornless blackberries are preferable to those with thorns, as gardening near the shrubs will be a great deal pleasanter. Blackberries and raspberries make no special demands on the soil. Blackberries will grow in half-shade, but raspberries need full sun. Unlike currants, their old branches must be cut back after fruition; the new ones will bear next season's fruit. The fall raspberry is the exception: it bears fruit on one-year-old wood and may therefore be cut down to the base. This fall raspberry is not cultivated commercially and is therefore more difficult to obtain.

**Raspberry:**

| | |
|---|---|
| R. idaeus 'Amber' | yellow, fall |
| R.i. 'Autumn Bliss' | red, fall |
| R.i. 'Boyne' | red, summer |
| R.i. 'Brandywine' | purple, summer |
| R.i. 'Dormanred' | red, summer |
| R.i. 'Heritage' | red, fall |
| R.i. 'Latham' | red, summer |

**Blackberry:**

| | |
|---|---|
| R. laciniatus 'Hull Thornless' | early |
| R. l. 'Thornfree' | late |
| R. l. 'Thornless Evergreen' | mid-season |

## Salix

### WILLOW

A damp garden is not very suitable but, fortunately, there are many different kinds of willow. Willows like full sun. *S. elaeagnos* and *S. exigua* thrive in dry soil. The small well-known weeping willow (*S.* 'Pendula') is now called *S. capraea* 'Kilmarnock.' **Hardiness: US Zone 6-2, Canadian Zone 5-1.**

| | |
|---|---|
| S. bockii | gr., bedewed branches, 1.5m (5ft) |
| S. capraea 'Kilmarnock' | weeping form, 2m (6ft) |
| S. cinerea* | gr. pubescent branches, 3m (10ft) |

*Salix capraea 'Kilmarnock'*

| | |
|---|---|
| S. elaeagnos | red-brown branches, 1.5m (5ft) |
| S. exigua | gray. brown branches, 4m (13ft) |
| S. gracilistyla* | gray pub. branches, 50cm, 20in) |
| S. helvetica* | yel. catkins, gray leaves, 1m (3ft) |
| S. irrorata* | purple, white-bloomed shoots, 2–3m (6–10ft) |
| S. purpurea 'Nana' | yellow branches, 1m (3ft) |
| S. repens | yellow catkins, Apr, 2m (6ft) |
| S. r. var. nitida | yellow catkins, 1m (3ft) |

## Sambucus

**ELDER**

The American elder looks well in the countryside, but it is less suitable for gardens. There are, however, a great many magnificent cultivars, which unfortunately are available all too rarely. They all have large white domed flower heads in spring, followed in fall by heads of fruit, a treat for birds. Elders thrive in sun or shade in any soil (see also: Perennials).
**Hardiness: US Zone 5-4, Canadian Zone 4-3.**

| | |
|---|---|
| S. canadensis 'Aurea'* | large yellow leaves, 4m (13ft) |
| S. c. 'Maxima' | green, large leaves, 6m (20ft) |
| S. nigra | g. leav., bl. berr. 5–7m (16–23ft) |
| S. n. 'Aurea' | golden yellow leaves |
| S. n. 'Laciniata' | pinnate leaves, 5m (16ft) |
| S. n. 'Purpurea' | young leaves purple, 5m (16ft) |
| S. racemosa | red berries, Apr, 5m (16ft) |
| S. r. 'Plumosa Aurea' | pinnate yel. leaves, 3m (10ft) |
| S. r. 'Sutherland' | green.-yel. leaves, 3m (10ft) |

Sambucus nigra

## Sorbaria

The flower panicles of this shrub resemble those of meadowsweet and astilbes. Five species are cultivated, but they all look much the same. They develop underground runners and are therefore easy to divide. Plant them at the back of the shrub border: the flowers will show up from a distance. They will grow in any soil in sun or half-shade.
**Hardiness: US Zone 7-3, Canadian Zone 6-2.**

| | |
|---|---|
| S. aitchisonii | white, July–Aug, 4m (13ft) |
| S. sorbifolia | white, July–Aug, 4m (13ft) |

## Spartium

**SPANISH BROOM**

Spartium resembles, and is related to, *Cytisus*. The shrub has distinctly green branches which collectively look broom-shaped. Plant them in full sun in soil that is not too moist. They may be pruned after they have flowered.
**Hardiness: US Zone 9, Canadian Zone 8.**

| | |
|---|---|
| S. junceum | golden yellow, May–June, 40cm (16in) |

Spartium junceum

## Spiraea

This genus includes many species, all of which will grow in any soil in sun or half-shade. They will also grow in full shade, but flower less profusely. Late-flowering species may be cut down to the ground in winter as they flower on one-year-old wood.
**Hardiness: US Zone 7-2, Canadian Zone 6-2.**

| | |
|---|---|
| S. arcuata** | cream, Apr–May, 1.75m (5ft) |
| S. x arguta | white, May–June, 2.5m (8ft) |

| | |
|---|---|
| *S.* x *cinerea*** | white, May, 1.5m (5ft) |
| *S. prunifolia* | white, May, 1.75m (5ft) |
| *S.* x *vanhouttei* | white, May, 1.75m (5ft) |
| *S. bullata** | deep pink, June, 40cm (16in) |
| *S.* x *bumalda* | |
| 'Anthony Waterer' | red, June–Aug, 50cm (20in) |
| *S. b.* 'Darts Red' | deep carmine red |
| *S. b.* 'Froebelii' | pink, June–Aug, 1m (3ft) |
| *S. b.* 'Goldflame' | gol. yellow leaves, 80cm (32in) |
| *S. billardii* | pink, July, 2m (6ft) |
| *S. douglasii* | pink, July–Aug, 1.75m (5ft) |
| *S. japonica* 'Albiflora' | white, July–Aug, 50cm (20in) |
| *S. j.* 'Golden Princess'** | pink, June–July, 1m (3ft) |
| *S. h.* 'Little Princess' | pale pink, Aug, 50cm (20in) |
| *S. j.* 'Shirobana' | two-col., July–Aug, 70cm (28in) |
| *S. nipponica* | clear white, June, 2m (6ft) |
| *S. thunbergii* | white, Apr–May, 1m (3ft) |
| *S.* x *vanhouttei* | white, May–June, 2m (6ft) |

*Spiraea thunbergii*

# Staphylea

**BLADDERNUT**
This broadly upright, unspectacular-looking shrub for moisture-retentive, humus-rich soil produces pale green fruits, about 10cm (4in) long, which resemble nuts.
**Hardiness: US Zone 6, Canadian Zone 5.**

| | |
|---|---|
| *S. bipinnata* | |
| *S. colchica* | white, May, 3m (10ft) |

# Stephanandra

It seems incomprehensible that growers still cultivate nature's "failures". The cultivar 'Crispa' with its distorted leaves is an example of this phenomenon. This popular shrub looks mortally ill all through summer. It is up to you to decide whether to plant one! *S. tanakae* is larger, but has fewer flowers. They are all dense shrubs with cheerful green leaves, and need full sun.

*Stephanandra incisa*

*Staphylea bipinnata*

| | |
|---|---|
| *S. incisa*! | white, June, 1.5m (5ft) |
| *S. i.* 'Crispa'! | white, June, 50cm (20in) |
| *S. tanakae* | white, June, 2m (6ft) |

## *Symphoricarpos*

**SNOW BERRY**

This shrub is unjustly maligned: it is ideal for tree underplanting. It can be clipped at a level of 1 metre (3ft), which creates a large dense surface. In full sun, it will produce more white or pink berries, which remain on the shrub for a long time. Regular pruning of two- or three-year-old branches is needed to keep a free-standing shrub in shape. The branches are so thin that they can be cut off with ordinary pruning shears. The shrubs grow 1.5m (5ft) tall. The flowers are less important than the large berries. Snowberries will thrive in sun or shade, in sheltered urban gardens or in strong winds.

**Hardiness: US Zone 6-4, Canadian Zone 5-3.**

| | |
|---|---|
| *S. albus* | white berries |
| *S. a.* 'White Hedge'* | white berries |
| *S. chenaultii* | lilac berries |
| *S. c.* 'Hancock' | lilac berries |
| *S. doorenbosii* 'Erect'* | white berries |
| *S. d.* 'Magic Berry' | lilac berries |
| *S. d.* 'Mother of Pearl' | white berries |
| *S. orbiculatus* | white berries |
| *S. o.* 'Variegata' | variegated leaves |

*Symphoricarpos doorenbosii* 'Mother of Pearl'

## *Syringa*

**LILAC**

This spring-flowering shrub can grow up to 4m (13ft) tall. There are many botanical (natural) species in various sizes; these, however, are obtainable only from highly specialized growers. For the benefit of people with small gardens, several are listed here although they may be difficult to acquire. The others are the most popular cultivars of *S. vulgaris*, the common lilac. Most people simply ask for a blue or a white tree – there is much more choice! They will grow in any soil in full sun, and need very little pruning. Give them plenty of space. Lilacs are unsuitable for very small gardens!

**Hardiness: US Zone 5-3, Canadian Zone 4-2.**

*Syringa josikae*

**Botanical species:**

| | |
|---|---|
| *S. amurensis* | whitish lilac, June |
| *S. x chinensis* | lavender blue, May, 2m (6ft) |
| *S. josikaea* | mauve, May–June, 3m (10ft) |
| *S. laciniata* | lilac, May, 1m (3ft) |
| *S. meyeri* 'Palibin' | lilac, May–June, 2m (6ft) |
| *S. x persica* | lilac, May–June, 2m (6ft) |
| *S. pinnatifolia***! | white and lavend., May, 2.5m (8ft) |
| *S. reflexa* | purp. pink, May–June, 3m (10ft) |
| *S. x swegiflexa*** | pink, May, 3m (10ft) |
| *S. sweginzowii* | pink, May–June, 2m (6ft) |
| *S. villosa* | lilac pink, May, 2m (6ft) |
| *S. tomentella*** | mauv. pink, May–June, 4m (13ft) |

**Single cultivars of *S. vulgaris*!:**

| | |
|---|---|
| *S. v.* 'Andenken an Ludwig Späth' | mauve |
| *S. v.* 'Capitaine Baltet' | light pink |
| *S. v.* 'Decaisne' | dark blue |
| *S. v.* 'Ester Staley' | light blue |
| *S. v.* 'Flora'* | white |
| *S. v.* 'Leon Gambetta' | lilac |
| *S. v.* 'Lucie Baltet' | pink |
| *S. v.* 'Mme Florentine Stepman'* | white |
| *S. v.* 'Primrose' | cream |
| S.v. 'Sensation' | purple red |

**Double cultivars of *S. vulgaris*:**

| | |
|---|---|
| *S. v.* 'Charles Joly' | mauve |
| *S. v.* 'Michael Büchner' | blue |
| *S. v.* 'Mme Lemoine' | white |
| *S. v.* 'Belle de Nancy' | blue |
| *S. v.* 'Paul Thirion' | pinkish red |
| *S. v.* 'President Loubet' | wine red |

*Syringa vulgaris* 'Andenken an Ludwig Späth'

# Tamarix

### TAMARISK

*T. pentandra* is now called *T. ramosissima*. I have never seen a beautiful mature tamarisk, and yet in Europe they are very popular. The straggling branches have a soft haze of small pale mauve flowers. It is difficult to give sound advice on pruning this plant: cutting it down to the base every three years may well produce the best results, even though there will not be any flowers the following year. Plant in fairly dry soil in full sun.
**Hardiness: US Zone 5-4, Canadian Zone 4-3.**

| | |
|---|---|
| *T. parviflora* | deep pink, May, 3m (10ft) |
| *T. ramosissima* 'Pink Cascade' | pink, June–July, 3m (10ft) |
| *T. r.* 'Rubra' | reddish, June–July. 3m (10ft) |
| *T. tetandra* | pale pink, May–June, 3m (10ft) |

*Tamarix tetandra*

# Ulex

### GORSE

Gorse resembles broom, but it has sharp thorns and is also frost tender. You should therefore plant it in a sheltered position in full sun. Cover the roots for the winter: the shrub will then sprout again after it has been cut by frost. Pruning is not a pleasant chore: use branch loppers.

| | |
|---|---|
| *U. europaeus* | yellow, June–July, 2m (6ft) |

| | |
|---|---|
| *V. p.* 'Mariesii' | white, May–June, 4m (13ft) |
| *V. p.* 'Rosace'* | dark red and pink, 3m (10ft) |
| *V. p.* var. *tomentosum* | cream, May |
| *V. sargentii* 'Onondaga' | white, May–June, 2m (6ft) |

# Viburnum

A major disadvantage of these classic shrubs is that they are often eaten by viburnum beetle which often defoliates the plant. The first shrub on the list has clusters of beautiful shiny red berries. It is an essential feature for the grove for attracting birds. *V. p.* 'Mariesii' is also suitable for planting in parterres: its height will be 1.5m (8ft) if pruned annually. *V. opulus* 'Roseum' (syn. *V. opulus* 'Sterile') is the well-known old-fashioned snow-ball tree (see also: Evergreen shrubs).
**Hardiness: US Zone 8-3, Canadian Zone 7-2.**

| | |
|---|---|
| *V.* x *bodnantense* 'Dawn' | pink, Feb–Mar, 3m (10ft) |
| *V.* x *carlcephalum* | white, Apr–May, 2m (6ft) |
| *V. carlesii* | pink buds, white flowers, Apr–May, 2m (6ft) |
| *V. farreri* (=*fragrans*) | pink buds, white flowers, Feb–Mar, 3.5m (11fift) |
| *V. lantana* | cream, May–June, 4m (13ft) |
| *V. opulus* | white, flat umbels, June–July, 4m (13ft) |
| *V. o.* 'Compactum' | white, June–July, 1.5m (5ft) |
| *V. o.* 'Roseum' | w., spheric., June–July, 3m (10ft) |
| *V. plicatum* | cream, May–June, 3m (10ft) |

*Viburnum carlesii*

# Weigela

### WEIGELA
The drawback to this pleasant garden shrub is that it is in full leaf by the time the flowers appear, which makes them less eye-catching. *W. florida* is the first to flower in early May; the others follow later in the month or in early June. Weigelas are easy to care for: they thrive in any soil in sun or in semi-shade.
**Hardiness: US Zone 6, Canadian Zone 5.**

| | |
|---|---|
| *W. florida* | |
|   'Nana Purpurea'**! | 60cm (24in) |
| *W. f.* 'Nana Variegata'! | 60cm (24in) |
| *W. f.* 'Purpurea'!* | mauvish pink, 1m (3ft) |
| **Hybrids:** | |
| *W.* 'Bristol Ruby' | carmine red, 2m (6ft) |
| *W.* 'Candida' | white, 2m (6ft) |
| *W.* 'Centennial' | red, 2.5m (8ft) |
| *W.* 'Eva Rathke' | bright carmine red, 2m (6ft) |
| *W.* 'Newport Red' | bright red, 2m (6ft) |
| *W.* 'Rosabella'! | pink with paler edges, 2m (6ft) |
| *W.* 'Rosea' | pink, 2m (6ft) |

*Weigela* 'Newport Red'

# 3. Hedging plants

*Although hedging plants cannot be classified separately in botanical terms, a chapter is devoted to them in this book because of their special function. Designing a garden occasionally starts with choosing a suitable hedge. Alpine currant and cedar are often planted for this purpose, but that is really a pity because there is a far wider choice. Most of the plants listed here are also described in the chapters on trees and shrubs. It is difficult to make the right choice from the huge selection of suitable plants. Many shrubs can be trimmed to form hedges; only the principal kinds have been mentioned here. It is crucial to remember exactly which cultivar you bought originally: if a plant dies and is replaced by the wrong species or cultivar, the differ-ence in color will always be apparent (for instance, if* Berberis vulgaris *'Atropurpurea' is used to fill a gap in* B. thunbergii *'Atropurpurea'). The first figure given in the lists is the required number of plants per metre (3ft). The way in which these plants flower is described in other chapters; in the case of hedges it is important to know how fast they will grow and how often they should be pruned in the course of a year. The second figure therefore refers to the number of annual prunings. This is followed by the principal characteristics of the leaves. The des-cription of each genus states whether the shrub is evergreen or deciduous, and whether it is frost-tender. The height depends on the height required; the maximum height is indicated in meters (and feet in brackets).*

## Acer

### HEDGEMAPLE

The leaves of this deciduous fast-growing shrub are reminiscent of those of the hawthorn, and the two shrubs may be combined to form a hedge.
**Hardiness: US Zone 6, Canadian Zone 5.**

A. campestre                4, 2x, small leaves, 3m (10ft)

## Acer

### MAPLE

In summer, the deciduous maple forms a dense hedge which will need to be pruned twice. The hedge is suitable for windy places in open countryside.
**Hardiness: US Zone 5, Canadian Zone 4.**

A. platanoides              3, 3x, large leaves, 4m (13ft)
A. pseudoplatanus           3, 3x, large leaves, 4m (13ft)

*Acer pseudoplatanus*

## Alnus

### ALDER

The deciduous alder is suitable for damp conditions in open countryside, and can be grown as a windbreak. One drawback to this kind of hedge is the risk of attack by wooly aphid but this rarely does permanent damage to the hedge.
**Hardiness: US Zone 5, Canadian Zone 4.**

A. glutinosa      4, 3x, sticky leaves, 6m (20ft)

*Alnus glutinosa* alder tree

## Berberis

### BARBERRY

The hedge planted most frequently is *B. thunbergii* 'Atropurpurea'. Its maintenance is difficult: the spines are liable to cause ulcers to hands. Pruning, which needs to be done regularly, therefore becomes a disagreeable chore. An "open" hedge needs to be thinned every winter with branch loppers, and a clipped hedge must be trimmed twice every summer with hedge cutters. (See also: Evergreen shrubs.)
**Hardiness: US Zone 7-4, Canadian Zone 6-3.**

Evergreen:
B. julianae      3, 2x, green, 3.5m (11ft)

B. stenophylla      3, 2x, green, 2.5m (8ft)
**Deciduous:**
B. thunbergii      4, 2x, green, 1.5m (5ft)
B. t. 'Atropurpurea'      4, 2x, reddish brown, 1.5m (5ft)
B. t. 'Nana'      6, 1x, green, 40cm (16in)
B. vulgaris**      4, 2x, green, 2.5m (8ft)

*Berberis stenophylla*

## Buxus

### BOX

There is an almost infinite number of cultivars of the evergreen *Buxus sempervirens*. Only specialized nurseries supply specified named cultivars; those listed below are generally available. Some of them will grow up to 4m (13ft) tall. Box thrives in sun and half-shade. Trim box in June and August at a time when there is not much sun. This will reduce the risk of leaf burn.
**Hardiness: US Zone 6, Canadian Zone 5.**

B. sempervirens      6, 2x, green, yellow tips, 60cm (24in)
B. s. 'Suffruticosa'      7, 2x, round leaves, 30cm (12in)

*Buxus sempervirens*

# Carpinus

## EUROPEAN HORNBEAM

The leaves die but some of them remain on the hedge. The cultivar 'Fastigiata' drops all its leaves in fall. *Carpinus betulus* 'Fastigiata' is a separate story: the idea is for the upright principal bole to remain intact from the ground upwards; in other words: don't start clipping the tops of the shrubs until the required height has been reached! The side branches of the young hedge will need pruning. Most gardeners do not know how to treat this exclusive and expensive hedge (the plants are grafted). Because of its bareness in winter, it is more suitable for hedges within a garden than for dividing neighboring plots. *C. betulus* needs polling more frequently to obtain a denser hedge (see also: *Fagus*, Vines and wall plants, and Trees for large gardens).
**Hardiness: US Zone 6, Canadian Zone 5.**

| | |
|---|---|
| *C. betulus* | 4, 2x, narrow point., 10m (33ft) |
| *C. b.* 'Fastigiata' | 3.5, 2x, narrow pointed, 5m (16ft) |

*Carpinus betulus*

# Chamaecyparis

## "FALSE" CYPRESS

It is unwise to grow evergreen cypress hedges. The shrubs cannot tolerate "wet feet" and inevitably become bare at the base. Their grayish-blue appearance is out of keeping with other colors. They are difficult to prune, particularly compared with *Thuja*.
**Hardiness: US Zone 7, Canadian Zone 6.**

| | |
|---|---|
| *C. lawsoniana* 'Allumii' | 2.5, 2x, blueish green, 4m (13ft) |
| *C. l.* 'Columnaris' | 2.5, 2x, blueish gray, 4m (13ft) |

*Chamaecyparis lawsoniana* 'Allumii'

# Cornus

## DOGWOOD

This dense deciduous plant grows very slowly for the first few years. It is, however, possible to prune it to form hedges and even arbors. The entire hedge will be covered in yellow flowers in March–April.
**Hardiness: US Zone 5, Canadian Zone 4.**

| | |
|---|---|
| *C. mas* | 2, 3x, small leaves, yellow flowers, 4m (13ft) |
| *C. m.* 'Variegata'** | 2, 2x, variegat. leaves, 4m (13ft) |

*Cornus mas* 'Variegata'

## Crataegus

**HAWTHORN**

Hawthorns are deciduous and have long formed the most popular kind of hedge. It should not be planted in areas suffering from fireblight. Because of this disease, it makes sense to grow a mixed hedge: planting hedge maples and hawthorns alternately reduces the risk of total loss if the disease strikes. The leaves of the two shrubs are very similar. The trimmed hawthorn will flower less. The hawthorn thrives in sun and half-shade.

**Hardiness: US Zone 6-5, Canadian Zone 5-4.**

| | |
|---|---|
| *C. monogyna* | 4, 2–3x, white, fruits dull red, 4m (13ft) |
| *C. laevigata* | 4, 2–3x, white, 4m (13ft) |
| *C. l.* 'Paul's Scarlet' | 4, 2x, red (d), 4m (13ft) |

## Elaeagnus

This dense, tangled, and spiny evergreen hedge tolerates wind and is grafted on to a rootstock. Check regularly whether the rootstock is sprouting; it might take over later on. The suckers are easy to spot as they are deciduous. The hedge grows slowly in sun and half-shade.

**Hardiness: US Zone 8, Canadian Zone 7.**

*Crataegus laevigata* 'Paul's Scarlet'

*Elaeagnus* x *ebbingei*

| | |
|---|---|
| *E.* x *ebbingei* | 2, 1x, green, 2m (6ft) |
| *E. pungens* 'Maculata'* | 2, 1x, variegated leaves, 1.5m (5ft) |

## Escallonia

It is a pity that this dense, tangled evergreen shrub with small glossy leaves is rarely grown as a hedge. The escallonia needs full sun.

**Hardiness: US Zone 9, Canadian Zone 8.**

| | |
|---|---|
| *E.* 'Donard Seedling'** | 2, 1x, pink, 1m (3ft) |

## Fagus

### EUROPEAN BEECH

Hornbeam and beech hedges are sometimes

*Escallonia*, free-growing

confused, which creates an ugly effect if the wrong plant is chosen to fill a gap. The hornbeam has pointed leaves which turn grayish brown in winter, whereas the rounder leaves of the beech turn chestnut brown. If a beech hedge has grown too big and needs drastic pruning, you should cover it temporarily with, for instance, old sheets to prevent direct sunlight falling onto the branches. The covering may be removed as soon as new leaves have formed. The green *F. sylvatica* has reddish shoots.

*Fagus sylvatica*

**Hardiness: US Zone 7, Canadian Zone 6.**

| | |
|---|---|
| *F. sylvatica* | 4, 2x, green, 6m (20ft) |
| *F. s.* 'Purpurea' | 4, 2x, reddish brown, 5m (16ft) |

## Fuchsia

Fuchsias are suitable for sheltered positions only, and need extra protection during severe winters. Even so, as a clipped hedge the plant suffers less from frost than it does as a free-standing shrub, when it is not unusual for it to be cut right down to the base by frost. If this happens, simply cut off the dead wood and it will sprout again in spring. Fuchsias can also be used to form an open hedge; in that case cut them down to the soil every spring. (For cultivars see: Deciduous shrubs).
**Hardiness: US Zone 8, Canadian Zone 7.**

| | |
|---|---|
| general | 2, deciduous |
| *F. magellanica* | 2.5, 2x, red, July–Sept, 2m (6ft) |
| *F. m.* 'Riccartonii' | 2.5, 2x, July–Sept, 2m (6ft) |

## Hedera

### ENGLISH IVY

It is possible to create a splendid dense divider with a framework of wire netting or steel reinforcement sheets. The wild species (*H. helix*) is small-leafed and slow-growing; the other is faster. Ivy may be damaged by frost during a severe winter and should therefore not be planted where it might catch the wind.
**Hardiness: US Zone 6-5, Canadian Zone 5-4.**

*Fuchsia magellanica* 'Riccartonii'

| *H. helix* | 3, 1x, green, small–leafed, 4m (13ft) |
| *H. h.* 'Baltica' | 2, green, small–leafed, 4m (13ft) |

## *Hydrangea*

In mild areas the deciduous hydrangea can form a free-growing flowering hedge. The choice is between shrubs with round flower heads and lace-caps. *H. paniculata* is unsuitable because of its fragile branches. Pruning should consist of no more than slightly thinning the hedge. (For

*Hedera helix* 'Hybernica'

cultivars see: Deciduous shrubs.)
**Hardiness: US Zone 8, Canadian Zone 7.**

| *H. macrophylla* | 2, spherical flower heads |
| *H. serrata* | 2, flat flowers |

## *Hypericum*

### ST. JOHN'S WORT

These deciduous plants can be grown as an open flowering hedge and should be cut back to just above the base after the winter. You will then be

*Hydrangea macrophylla*

without a divider for a while. For best results, this hedge should have a sunny position.
**Hardiness: US Zone 7-6, Canadian Zone 6-5.**

| *H. androsaemum* | 3, yellow, black berries, 1m (3ft) |
| *H. a.* 'Autumn Blaze' | brown berries, 1m (3ft) |
| *H. a.* 'Excellent Flair' | reddish-brown berries, 1m (3ft) |
| *H. a.* 'Orange Flair' | reddish-brown berries, 1m (3ft) |
| *H.* 'Hidcote' | 3, yellow, 70cm (28in) |
| *H. moserianum* | yellow, 50cm (20in) |

## *Ilex*

### HOLLY

Evergreen holly can be grown as a free-growing shrub or as a hedge. Shrubs without too many spines to their leaves are advisable for the latter purpose because of maintenance problems; weeding underneath a hedge is unpleasant if

*Hypericum moserianum*

there is a lot of prickly foliage. The following cultivars have only a few spines.
**Hardiness: US Zone 8, Canadian Zone 7.**

**The following needs to be clipped:**
*I. aquifolium* 'Pyramidalis'**2.5, 1x, lots of berries, 3m(10ft)
**Free–growing or clipped:**
| *I. crenata* | 3, 1x, 1m (3ft) |
| *I. c.* 'Convexa' | 4, 1x, 1m (3ft) |
| *I. c.* 'Golden Gem'** | 5, 1x, 50cm (20in) |

## *Lavandula*

### LAVENDER

Lavender is lovely when combined with roses or

along a border of annuals. It is less suitable as a dividing hedge between neighboring plots because of annual pruning. (For cultivars see: Perennials).

*Ilex aquifolium* 'Pyramidalis'

**Hardiness: US Zone 6, Canadian Zone 5.**

| | | |
|---|---|---|
| *L. angustifolia* | 3, 1x, 60cm (24in) | |

## Ligustrum

**PRIVET**

There are many species of evergreen privet; only a few of them are ever planted as hedges. A privet hedge is fast-growing and unpretentious.

*Lavandula*

The snag is that it will need frequent trimming. A severe winter may kill the hedge, which should then be sawn off close to the ground. It will regain its former height within a year. Privet thrives in any soil and in all conditions.
**Hardiness: US Zone 6, Canadian Zone 5.**

| | | |
|---|---|---|
| *L. ovalifolium* | 4, 3x, green, 3m(10ft) | |
| *L. vulgare* 'Cheynne" | 4, 3x, green, 3m (10ft) | |
| *L. vulgare* 'Lodense' | 5, 3x, green, 50cm (20in) | |

## Lonicera

**HONEYSUCKLE**

Evergreen honeysuckle can be grown to form not only low clipped hedges, but also clipped

*Ligustrum ovalifolium*

surfaces. The latter can be clipped flat, but also into other shapes such as irregular undulations to suit one's own taste. Such shapes will look as attractive in a wild garden as in a formal one. (For cultivars see: Evergreen shrubs).
**Hardiness: US Zone 9-8, Canadian Zone 8-7.**

| | | |
|---|---|---|
| *L. nitida* | 3, 2x, green, 1m (3ft) | |
| *L. pileata* | 3, 2x, green, 1.5m (5ft) | |

*Lonicera pileata*

## Mahonia

Of all the evergreen mahonia shrubs, *M. aquifolium* is the one that is least beautiful and sold most frequently; the leaves of the others suffer less in appearance after a frost. They are not used very often, and are most suitable for a free-growing hedge. The leaves have sharp spines. The plant is also of interest for flower arrangements.
**Hardiness: US Zone 7-5, Canadian Zone 6-4.**

| | |
|---|---|
| *M. aquifolium* | 2.5, yellow flowers, 1m (3ft) |
| *M. wagneri* 'Pinnacle'!** | 2.5, yellow, prickly, 1m (3ft) |
| *M. w.* 'Vicaryi'** | 3, yellow, smaller, 80cm (32in) |

## Malus

### APPLE

Both apple and pear trees can be grown as cordons to form a deciduous hedge. The type known as "espalier trees" is not new since fruit trees shaped in this way were quite common in the nineteenth century. *Malus* is only suitable

*Mahonia aquifolium*

for growing on one's own land, not as a hedge between neighboring plots: the trees might be damaged by children picking the fruit. The small trees are grafted on to a "slow" rootstock, which means that they must not be grown in long grass and should be planted near the surface. They need permanent staking.
**Hardiness: US Zone 6-5, Canadian Zone 5-4.**

| | |
|---|---|
| *Malus* various cultivars | 3–4, 2x, green, 2.5m (8ft) |
| *Pyrus* various cultivars | 3–4, 1x, green, 2.5m (8ft) |

## Nepeta

### CATMINT

Catmint is more suitable as an edging plant than as a shrub. *N.* 'Six Hills' Giant' grows quite tall and can serve as a "hedge" round a kitchen garden or a rose bed. You should cut back the plants in early spring. Plant them in full sun. But beware: they do attract cats!
**Hardiness: US Zone 6, Canadian Zone 5.**

*Malus*

| | |
|---|---|
| *N.* 'Six Hills' Giant' | 5, pale blue, 50cm (20in) |

## Photinia

This more or less evergreen hedge with red shoots is suitable for a sheltered position. Like the *Enkanthius* (in the foreground of the photograph), it makes an expensive and exclusive hedge.
**Hardiness: US Zone 9, Canadian Zone 8.**

| | |
|---|---|
| *P. x fraseri* | 3, 2x, shiny leaves, 2m (6ft) |

## Picea

### SERBIAN SPRUCE

These evergreen spruces form a dense green hedge dividing two plots. *P. omorika* is tall and narrow; other species are less suitable as they spread too much. Allow for the fact that pruning is impossible. It is also inevitable that the spruces will become bare lower down as they grow older and will then need replacing by younger trees.

*Photinia*

The Serbian spruce needs acid soil and should not be planted too near the coast.
**Hardiness: US Zone 4, Canadian Zone 3.**

| | |
|---|---|
| *P. omorika* | grayish green, 10m (33ft) |

## Populus

### POPLAR

The deciduous poplar is more successful as a hedge than as a tree. Don't grow one, however, unless you are prepared to prune the trees back to the main bole annually (in winter) with branch loppers. The trees have an annual growth rate of over 1m (3ft): neglect would be disastrous! The older the trees, the more beautiful the knots become where the branches have been cut every year. You can gain quick results with this hedge. The poplar is therefore suitable for people planning to move house again soon!
**Hardiness: US Zone 4, Canadian Zone 3.**

| | |
|---|---|
| *P. nigra* 'Italica' | 3, 1x, green 3–6m (10–20ft) |

## Potentilla

This deciduous flowering hedge looks attractive in a bright and cheerful garden. Remember that the cultivars with yellow flowers can be very dominating; you are more likely to create a harmonious effect with those bearing white or red flowers. (For cultivars see: Decidous shrubs).
**Hardiness: US Zone 4-2, Canadian Zone 3-1.**

| | |
|---|---|
| *P. fruticosa* 'Abbotswood' | 4, 1x, white |
| *P. f.* 'Red Ace' | 4, 1x, red |
| *P. f.* 'Tangerine' | 4, 1x, apricot |

## Prunus

### CHERRY LAUREL, PURPLE LEAF SAND CHERRY

This extensive genus includes both evergreen

*Potentilla fruticosa* 'Tangerine'

*Populus nigra* 'Italica'

and deciduous species suitable for clipped or free–growing hedges. The evergreen varieties are best kept in shape with secateurs to prevent all the outer leaves being cut in half. In the case of small leaves that is less noticeable. *P. cistena* is a cross between *P. pumila* and *P. cerasifera*. *P. l.* 'Zabeliana' spreads considerably and is therefore less suitable for gardens.

**Hardiness: US Zone 8, Canadian Zone 7.**

**Evergreen:**

| | |
|---|---|
| *P. laurocerasus* 'Caucasica' | 2.5, 2x, dark green, 2.5m (8ft) |
| *P. l.* 'Otto Luyken' | 3, white flowers, 5cm (20in) |

**Deciduous:**

| | |
|---|---|
| *P. cistena* | 3, 2x, purple leaves, 2m (6ft) |

# Pyrus

**PEAR**

See *Malus.*

# Rhododendron

The rhododendron is evergreen, winter-hardy and reasonably fast-growing; it is therefore suit-

*Rhododendron* 'Pink Pearl'

*Prunus laurocerasus* 'Zabeliana' spreads considerably and is therefore not so uitable for small gardens

able for tall, dense, and broad hedges. They cannot be pruned satisfactorily. If they grow too tall, it is possible to saw them them down to just above the soil, after which they will once again produce dense, bushy shoots. They require acid, humus-rich soil and do not tolerate drying winds. Such a hedge will always be expensive.

**Hardiness: US Zone 7-5, Canadian Zone 6-4.**

| | |
|---|---|
| R. 'Catawbiense Album' | 2, white, 4m (13ft) |
| R. 'Catawbiense Boursault' | 2, lilac, 4m (13ft) |
| R. 'C. Grandiflorum' | 2, lilac, 4m (13ft) |
| R. 'Cunningham's White' | 2, pinkish white, 4m(13ft) |

| R. 'Nova Zembla' | 2, dark red, 4m (13ft) |
| R. 'Pink Pearl' | 2, pink, 4m (13ft) |
| R. 'Roseum Elegans' | 2, bright purplish pink, 4m (13ft) |

| R. pimpinellifolia | 2, 2x, rough hedge, pink, 1–1.5m (3–5ft) |
| R. rubiginosa | 2, 2x, rough hedge, pink, 1–1.5m (3–5ft) |
| R. rugosa | 3, flowering hedge, all colors, 1m (3ft)) |

## Ribes

### CURRANT

The common decorative shrub, which is also easy to propagate by cuttings, is quite suitable for hedging purposes. It will, however, flower a little less exuberantly.

**Hardiness: US Zone 8, Canadian Zone 7.**

*Rosa pimpinellifolia*

*Ribes sanguineum*

| R. sanguineum | 4, 3x, pink or red, 2m (6ft) |

## Rosa

### ROSE

A disadvantage of these small but prickly deciduous hedges along a public highway is that paper and rubbish get caught up in them. Allow for this in certain positions. You should thin them every winter or cut them down to the base every two years.

**Hardiness: US Zone 7-4, Canadian Zone 6-3.**

| R. nitida! | 3, flowering hedge, pink, 60–80cm (24–32in) |

## Salix

### WILLOW

The willow is deciduous, grows fast and is inexpensive, but requires a lot of pruning. For those who do not mind, any of the species is suitable. The willow even does well in very wet soil.

*Salix species*

Hardiness: **US Zone 4, Canadian Zone 3.**

*S. species*                    4, 3-4x, greenish gray, 3m (10ft)

## Sambucus

**ELDER**

This deciduous hedge's rapid growth during the first few years subsequently means a lot of pruning. The elder will not flower when grown as a hedge. The delicate leaves of the scarlet-berried elder (*S. racemosa*) are more beautiful.
Hardiness: **US Zone 5-4, Canadian Zone 4-3.**

| | |
|---|---|
| *S. canadensis* | |
| 'Plumosa Aurea' | 3, 3x, delicate leaves, 4m (13ft) |
| *S. nigra* | 3, 3x, coarse leaves, 4m (13ft) |
| *S. racemosa* | 3, 3x, delicate leaves, 4m (13ft) |

## Spiraea

*S. bumalda* and *S. japonica* are most suitable for a free-growing hedge; *S. arguta* is best clipped. Thin out the deciduous free-growing hedges by a third every winter; the hedge will thus be entirely renewed within three years. The low-growing *S. japonica* needs hardly any maintenance at all.
Hardiness: **US Zone 6-4, Canadian Zone 5-3.**

| | |
|---|---|
| *S. arguta* | 2.5, 2x, white, 1.75m (5ft) |
| *S. bumalda*, | |
| 'Anthony Waterer' | 4, pinkish red, 1m (3ft) |
| *S. b.* 'Froebelii' | 3, pinkish red, 1.5m (5ft) |
| *S. japonica* | 4, pink, 50cm (20in) |

*Sambucus canadensis* 'Plumosa Aurea'

## Symphoricarpos

**SNOWBERRY**

Few berries will remain on this deciduous hedge after it has been pruned. In the last century snowberries were often used for clipped hedges in particular. It thrives in any kind of soil in sun or shade.
Hardiness: **US Zone 6-4, Canadian Zone 5-3.**

*Spiraea arguta*

| | |
|---|---|
| S. albus | 3, 3x, white berries, 1.5m (5ft) |
| S. a. 'White Hedge'* | 3, 3x, white berries, 1.5m (5ft) |
| S. x chenaultii | 3, 3x, purple red berries, 1.8m (5ft 9in) |
| S. orbiculatus | 3, 3x, purple red berries, 1.8m (5ft 9in) |

*Symphoricarpos albus* 'White Hedge'

# Taxus

### YEW

Of all these evergreen plants, *T. media* 'Hicksii' is unfortunately the one most likely to be on sale. Its branches are fairly upright, so that the shrub may collapse under a heavy load of snow. It cannot be equated with *T. baccata*, as it will remain lower and is therefore unsuitable for dividing plots of land. The plant is grafted: all the young plants are therefore identical and will form a hedge which is uniform in color and growth. A hedge consisting of *T. baccata*, on the other hand, will look varied and marbled since the plants are grown from seed. This means that they are all slightly different: some are a little denser, whereas others are somewhat darker in color. These variations are invisible in a young hedge and do not appear until it has been clipped to a face. The branches of this more robust plant are also more horizontal and therefore do not suffer as a result of a heavy fall of snow. Unlike other conifers, they do not need acid soil. The ground must, however, be rich in humus and well drained, and some shade is permissible. The distance between plants may be slightly greater if a larger size is purchased.
**Hardiness: US Zone 6, Canadian Zone 5.**

| | |
|---|---|
| T. baccata! | 2,5, 2-3x, dark green, 5m (16ft) |
| T. b. 'Washingtonii' | 2, 2x, yellowish green, 2m (6ft) |
| T. media 'Hicksii' | 3, 2x, dark green, 2m (6ft) |

# Thuja

### WHITE CEDAR, WESTERN RED CEDAR

Thujas are evergreen, except that *T. occidentalis* turns bronze-colored in winter, which makes its appearance less attractive. Thujas used for hedging purposes must be cultivated with a single stem to prevent their collapsing under a load of snow later on. Multi-stemmed hedge plants should be cut wedge shaped to hold the snow load. This species is bronze-colored in winter and presents a gloomy appearance during that season. The cultivars listed below are much better. You can shorten the lateral branches which grow as tall as the stem. The top of the hedge should not be trimmed until it has reached the required height. *T. plicata* remains a shiny dark green in winter. It is less frost-hardy, especially if both frosty and windy.
**Hardiness: US Zone 6-4, Canadian Zone 5-3.**

| | |
|---|---|
| T. occidentalis 'Brabant' | 2.5, 2x, green 4m (13ft) |
| T. o. 'Spiralis' | 3, 2x, foliage in twisted sprays, 4m (13ft) |
| T. plicata! | 2.5, 2x, shiny green, 5m (16ft) |
| T. p. 'Atrovirens'! | 2.5, 2x, shiny green, 5m (16ft) |
| T. p. 'Zebrina' | 2.5, 2x, striated, 4m (13ft) |

# Tilia

### LIME

This old-fashioned deciduous hedge with its beautiful "lime-green" leaves was at one time often grown around the bleaching fields of old Dutch farmhouses. The wild shoots surrounding limes can also be cut into splendid shapes: round, spherical or cube-shaped. Lime trees often sprout halfway up the bole; these branches can also be shaped. Various species are suitable for gardens.
**Hardiness: US Zone 5, Canadian Zone 4.**

| | |
|---|---|
| T. europaea | 4, 3x, pale green, 3m (10ft) |

*Tilia europaea*

# Ulmus

## ELM

*U. minor* syn. *U. campestre, U. carpinifolia* was at one time often used as a hedging plant. Now that the risk of Dutch elm disease (see: Trees for large gardens) has greatly increased, this plant can no longer be recommended for hedges. If a single tree is planted, the risk may sometimes be acceptable, but in the case of a hedge all the plants may be lost within a year.

**Hardiness: US Zone 6, Canadian Zone 5.**

*U. carpinifolia*

*Ulmus carpinifolia*

# 4. Conifers

Most garden centers provide relatively far more space for conifers than is devoted to them in this book. The reason they do so is that compared with deciduous and even many evergreen plants, conifers look well in any season. If they do not belong to a needle-shedding species, their appearance is more or less the same in summer as in winter. Actually the great disadvantage of conifers is that they show no signs of the changing seasons that are so thrilling to watch: the first bulbs emerging from the earth; new leaves appearing on trees and shrubs; plants coming into flower; fall colors; falling leaves; the structure of branches, and so on. All this is lacking in the case of conifers. A garden with nothing but

conifers is therefore not to be recommended, but you can certainly grow them here and there as special features: their rich variety of shapes is virtually unlimited. Conifers require acid soil. Any exceptions to this rule are specifically mentioned. Pay special attention to heights: the "dwarf" conifer may turn out to grow quite tall after all! Conifers usually need sun; the exceptions – the species which tolerate shade – are specified.
Conifers suitable for hedging purposes are to be found in the chapter on Hedging plants.
Heights are indicated but not the speed of growth. This may vary considerably between species and even between cultivars. Work on the principle that the slower the growth, the smaller the tree will remain. That

is the reason why genuine dwarf conifers are far more expensive than those that grow taller.
The details given after the species list the color of the scale-leaves or needles, the type of growth, and the height in meters and feet, or in centimeters and inches if it is less than one meter (3ft).

## Abies

### SILVER FIR

This genus, which produces tall trees, makes few demands on the soil. The trees sustain considerable damage if subjected to long periods of dry winds. The differences between the genera *Abies* and *Picea* (Spruce) include the following: *Abies* has blunt needles with an indentation at their tips; *Picea* has sharp pointed needles. Another difference is the fact that if you pull a needle off an *Abies* twig, a small piece of bark will remain attached to it. This does not occur if you do the same with *Picea*, which has pointed buds

*Abies procera* 'Glauca'

without resin, whereas *Abies* has blunt buds, often resinous. The silver firs include the following species: common (*A. alba*); balsam (*A. balsamea*); giant (*A. grandis*); Spanish (*A. pinsapo*) and noble (*A. procera*).
**Hardiness: US Zone 7-2, Canadian Zone 6-2.**

| | |
|---|---|
| *A. alba* | two white stripes beneath, broad crown, 20m (65ft) |
| *A. a.* 'Pendula' | green, narrow weeping form, 15m (50ft) |
| *A. a.* 'Pyramidalis' | green, narrow columnar form, 10m (33ft) |
| *A. balsamea* | dark green, narrowly pyramidal, 15m (50ft) |
| *A. b.* 'Nana' | dark gr., broad sphere, 1m (3ft) |
| *A. concolor* | gray/green, pyramidal, 30m (100ft) |
| *A. grandis* | dark green, pyramidal, 20m (65ft) |
| *A. homolepsis!** | dark green, cylind., 25m (80ft) |
| *A. koreana* | dark green, blue cones, 15m (50ft) |
| *A. lasiocarpa* 'Compacta' | blue. gray, pyramidal, 1m (3ft) |
| *A. nordmanniana* | dark green, regular, 20m (65ft) |
| *A. pinsapo* | green, pyramidal, 20m (65ft) |
| *A. procera* | gray/green, conical, 25m (80ft) |
| *A. p.* 'Glauca' | gray/blue, conical, 20m (65ft) |

## *Araucaria*

**CHILE PINE, MONKEY PUZZLE**
This tree is very frost-tender when it is young, in spite of the fact that severe frosts also occur in its native habitat (southern Chile). Although this is not a genuinely spreading tree, it is only suitable for a large garden; the shiny dark green plates are too dominant for a small one. The branches form regular whorls around the bole.
**Hardiness: US Zone 8, Canadian Zone 7.**

| | |
|---|---|
| *A. araucana* | dark green, large tree, 15m (50ft) |

## *Calocedrus*

**INCENSE CEDAR**
The genus *Librocedrus* has been divided into three genera; the old name is retained for *L. bidwillii*, a frost-tender New Zealand tree. The *Calocedrus* will grow to about 45m (150ft). The straight columns are useful for stressing vertical lines in a garden design.
**Hardiness: US Zone 6, Canadian Zone 5.**

| | |
|---|---|
| *C. decurrens* | green, narrow column, 20m (65ft) |
| *C. d.* 'Aureovariegata' | yellow scales, columnar, 15m (50ft) |

*Calocedrus decurrens*

*Araucaria araucana*

# Cedrus

## CEDAR

The needles may be cut by frost in a severe winter. Although the tree will then look dead in spring, the buds will sprout as usual. The species Cedar of Lebanon (*C. libani*) is the most frost-tender. This tree grows pyramidally when it is young; later on its crown will flatten. The Atlas cedar (*C. atlantica* 'Glauca') is often planted in too small a garden, and will then need felling prematurely.
**Hardiness: US Zone 8-7, Canadian Zone 7-6.**

| | |
|---|---|
| *C. atlantica**  | blueish green, broad, 30m (100ft) |
| *C. a.* 'Aurea'** | yellowish green, broad, 15m (50ft) |
| *C. a.* 'Fastigiata'** | grayish blue, columnar, 15m (50ft) |
| *C. a.* 'Glauca' | blueish gray, broad, 15m (50ft) |
| *C. a.* 'Glauca Pendula' | blueish gray, broad, 5m (16ft) |
| *C. deodora* | light green, very broad, 20m (65ft) |
| *C. d.* 'Golden Horizon'* | greenish yellow, broad, 5m(16ft) |
| *C. d.* 'Pendula'** | green, weeping, broad, 3m (10ft) |
| *C. d.* 'Pygmy'** | gray, spherical, 50cm (20in) |
| *C. d. libani* | light and dark green, pyramidal, 20m (65ft) |
| *C. l.* 'Sargentii' | dwarf, blueish green, 1.5m (5ft) |

*Cedrus atlantica* 'Glauca'

# Cephalotaxus

## COWTAIL PINE

This conifer from Japan does not need acid soil but likes a sheltered position; it thrives in the shade of other trees. *Cephalotaxus* is an excellent conifer for medium-sized gardens but is rarely on sale.
**Hardiness: US Zone 9-8, Canadian Zone 8-7.**

| | |
|---|---|
| *C. fortunei* | dark green, irregular, 10m (33ft) |
| *C. harringtonia*** | shiny dark green, broad, 3m (10ft) |
| *C. h.* 'Fastigiata'* | dark green, columnar, 4m (13ft) |

# Chamaecyparis

## FALSE CYPRESS

This genus includes the greatest variety of shapes: not because of developments in nature, but as a result of hybridization by humans. Every imaginable color and shape is represented. The name false cypress is misleading and is used only to distinguish the tree from the common cypress, a conifer for subtropical climates. To prevent root rot caused by *Phytophtora cinnamomi*, *C. lawsoniana* in particular should not be planted in very wet soil. The scales first become lighter in color, then turn dry and brown as the plants die down. This may also occur when they are older.
**Hardiness: US Zone 7, Canadian Zone 6.**

| | |
|---|---|
| *C. lawsoniana** | green or blueish green, pyramidal, 30m (100ft) |
| *C. l.* 'Albovariegata' | white variegations, conical, 10m (33ft) |
| *C. l.* 'Alumii' | blueish green, pyramidal, 15m (50ft) |
| *C. l.* 'Alumigold'** | sulfur yellow, narrow, 10m (33ft) |
| *C. l.* 'Columnaris'** | blueish gray, columnar, 10m (33ft) |
| *C. l.* 'Ellwoodii'** | blueish green, conical, 5m (16ft) |

*Cephalotaxus harringtonia*

*Chamaecyparis lawsoniana* 'Ellwoodii'

*Chamaecyparis lawsoniana* 'Triomf van Boskoop'

| | |
|---|---|
| *C. l.* 'Erecta Virides'** | fresh green, pyramidal, 7m (23ft) |
| *C. l.* 'Filiformis Compacta' | green, dense, round, 50cm (20in) |
| *C. l.* 'Forsteckensis'** | blueish green, round, 1m (3ft) |
| *C. l.* 'Globe'** | gray, spherical, 1m (3ft) |
| *C. l.* 'Golden Spire' | yel., narr. columnar, 8m (26ft) |
| *C. l.* 'Golden Wonder' | yellowish green, pyramidal, 10m (33ft) |
| *C. l.* 'Green Globe'* | green, spherical, 1m (3ft) |
| *C. l.* 'Intertexta' | blue/green pyramidal, 10m (33ft) |
| *C. l.* 'Lane' | golden yellow, slender, 8m (26ft) |
| *C. l.* 'Lutea' | yellowish green, slender, slow, 7m (23ft) |
| *C. l.* 'Lutea Nana' | yellow, broad cone, 50cm (20in) |
| *C. l.* 'Minima Glauca' | blueish green, spherical, 1m (3ft) |
| *C. l.* 'Pygmaea'** | green, flat cone, 50cm (20in) |
| *C. l.* 'Silver Queen' | yellowish green, tips silvery white, 10m (33ft) |
| *C. l.* 'Spek' | grayish blue, conical, 7m (23ft) |
| *C. l.* 'Stewartii' | golden yel., pyramidal, 7m (23ft) |
| *C. l.* 'Triomf van Boskoop' | silvery blue, conical, 20m (65ft) |
| *C. l.* 'Wisselii' | blueish green, conical, slender, 10m (33ft) |
| *C. l.* 'Youngii'* | green, narrow cone, 10m (33ft) |
| *C. nootkatensis*! | fresh bright green, slender pyramidal, 30m (100ft) |
| *C. n.* 'Pendula' | green, weeping, 10m (33ft) |
| *C. obtusa** | deep green, conical, 15m (50ft) |
| *C. o.* 'Caespitosa'** | green, super dwarf, 30cm (12in) |
| *C. o.* 'Contorta'** | green, dwarf, 1m (3ft) |
| *C. o.* 'Filicoides' | shiny dark green, 1.5m (5ft) |
| *C. o.* 'Flabelliformis'** | green, spherical, slow, 1m (3ft) |

| | |
|---|---|
| *C. o.* 'Juniperioides'* | green, super dwarf, 20cm (8in) |
| *C. o.* 'Minima' | green, super dwarf, 30cm (12in) |
| *C. o.* 'Nana' | light gr. dwarf, irreg., 1m (3ft) |
| *C. o.* 'Nana Gracilis' | light green, irregular conical shape, 3m (10ft) |
| *C. o.* 'Pygmaea' | brown. gr., spherical, 1.5m (5ft) |
| *C. o.* 'Tetragona Aurea' | v. bright yellow, irregular, 2m (6ft) |
| *C. pisifera** | green, conical, 15m (50ft) |
| *C. p.* 'Boulevard' | grayish blue, broadly pyramidal, 1m (3ft) |
| *C. p.* 'Filiformis' | grayish green, pendulous, 1m (3ft) |
| *C. p.* 'Filifera Aurea' | golden yellow, pendulous, spherical, 2m (6ft) |
| *C. p.* 'Filifera Nana' | dark green, dwarf, 1m (3ft) |
| *C. p.* 'Gold Spangle' | yellow, pyramidal, 5m (16ft) |
| *C. p.* 'Nana' | green, spherical, slow, 50cm (20in) |
| *C. p.* 'Plumosa' | green, pyramidal, 7m (23ft) |
| *C. p.* 'Plumosa Aurea' | golden yel., pyramidal, 8m (26ft) |
| *C. p.* 'Plumosa Aurea Compacta' | golden yellow, small, 1m (3ft) |
| *C. p.* 'Squarrosa' | grayish blue, dense, broad, 7m (23ft) |
| *C. p.* 'Sungold' | yellow, broad, 7m (23ft) |

## *Cryptomeria*

### JAPANESE RED CEDAR

The cryptomeria, a tree imported from Japan, prefers a position sheltered from the east wind in sufficiently moisture-retentive soil. Several cul-

*Cryptomeria japonica*

tivars have been developed especially for their fasciation, an error of nature that we admire and propagate. This applies to the cultivars 'Bandai' and 'Jindai', from which the suffix '-sugi' is now omitted.
**Hardiness: US Zone 7, Canadian Zone 6.**

| | |
|---|---|
| C. japonica | bright gr., pyramidal, 25m (80ft) |
| C. j. 'Bandai' | mossy 'lumps', 1m (3ft) |
| C. j. 'Compacta' | green in summer, blueish in winter, 10m (33ft) |
| C. j. 'Cristata' | with fasciation, 5m (16ft) |
| C. j. 'Globosa Nana' | blueish green, compact spherical, 1m (3ft) |
| C. j. 'Jindai' | light gr., densely conical, 2m (6ft) |
| C. j. 'Spiralis' | light green, twisted branches, 10m (33ft) |
| C. j. 'Vilmoriana' | light green, rounded conical shape, 75cm (30in) |

## Cupressus

### TRUE CYPRESS
These trees can survive a few mild winters in very sheltered gardens, but are more suitable for large pots (with acid soil!) which can stand in the garage during the winter.
**Hardiness: US Zone 9, Canadian Zone 8.**

| | |
|---|---|
| C. sempervirens | blueish gray, columnar, 4m (13ft) |

*Cupressus sempervirens*

## x *Cupressocyparis*

### HYBRID CYPRESS
Hybrid cypresses and dawn redwoods are the fastest-growing conifers. That is as far as the similarity goes, as the metasequoia is bare in winter. The hybrid cypress is a cross between two genera (*Cupressus macrocarpa* x *Chamaecyparus nootkatensis*). The trees are very frost-tender when young, which makes it risky to grow them for hedging purposes.
**Hardiness: US Zone 8, Canadian Zone 7.**

| | |
|---|---|
| C. leylandii | light green, conical, 20m (65ft) |
| C. l. 'Castlewellan Gold' | yellow, conical, 10m (33ft) |
| C. l. 'Leighton Green'** | light green, conical, 10m (33ft) |
| C. l. 'Silver Dust' | spots with white variegations, conical, 10m (33ft) |

*Cupressocyparis leylandii*

## Juniperus

Most junipers are extremely hardy and have become the most popular shrub for foundation planting as they provide winter interest, but in my opinion they have been overplanted. Some so-called dwarf junipers do not remain dwarf for long. *J. squamata* 'Meyeri' has an attractive blue appearance when young, but the dwarf turns into

a small giant, whose brown needles will show up before long: you will have been conned!
**Hardiness: US Zone 5-3, Canadian Zone 4-2.**

| | |
|---|---|
| *J. chinensis*** | grayish green, pyramidal or broadly upright, 15m (50ft) |
| *J. c.* 'Keteleeri' | gray/green, conical, 10m (33ft) |
| *J. c.* 'Mountbatten' | grayish green, narrow, 3m (10ft) |
| *J. c.* 'Stricta'** | gray/blue, pyramidal, 5m (16ft) |
| *J. communis* | grayish green, various shapes, 4m (13ft) |
| *J. c.* 'Compressa'*! | green, dense column, 2m (6ft) |
| *J. c.* 'Depressa Aurea'* | yellow, broad, 50cm (20in) |
| *J. c.* 'Effusa'** | green, broad, 50cm (20in) |
| *J. c.* 'Hibernica'** | blue/green, columnar, 3m (10ft) |
| *J. c.* 'Hornibrookii'**! | green, very broad, 50cm (20in) |
| *J. c.* 'Nana' | golden yel., trailing, 50cm (20in) |
| *J. c.* 'Repanda'! | green, broad, 30cm (12in) |
| *J. c.* 'Suecica'! | gr., narrow column, 4m (13ft) |
| *J. horizontalis* 'Andorra Compact' | gray, broad, 50cm (20in) |
| *J. h.* 'Glauca' | see: 'Wiltonii' |
| *J. h.* 'Hughes' | blueish gr., broad, 50cm (20in) |
| *J. h.* 'Plumosa' | gray/green compact, 60cm (24in) |
| *J. h.* 'Wiltonii' | bl., broadly trailing, 30cm (12in) |
| *J. h.* 'Prostrata' | blue/green, trailing, 40cm (16in) |
| *J. media* 'Blaauw' | grayish blue, bushy, 1m (3ft) |
| *J.* x *media* 'Hetzii' | gray, broad, 5m (16ft) |
| *J. m.* 'Old Gold' | greenish yel., compact, 1m (3ft) |
| *J. m.* 'Pfitzeriana' | green, loose, 2m (6ft) |
| *J. m.* 'Pfitzeriana Aurea' | greenish yellow, 1.5m (5ft) |
| *J. m.* 'Pfitzeriana Glauca' | blueish green, loose, 2m (6ft) |
| *J. m.* 'Plumosa Aurea' | yellowish green, dense, 2m (6ft) |

*Juniperus horizontalis* 'Hughes'

*Junipera* x *media* 'Pfitzeriana Aurea'

| | |
|---|---|
| *J. m.* 'Sargentii' | bl./gr., very broad, 80cm (32in) |
| *J. procumbens* 'Nana'*** | green, very flat, 30cm (12in) |
| *J. sabina* | green, irregular, 2m (6ft) |
| *J. s.* 'Tamariscifolia' | blueish green, coarse, 1m (3ft) |
| *J. squamata* 'Blue Star' | gray/bl., spherical, 50cm (20in) |
| *J. s.* 'Blue Carpet' | blue./gray, broad, 50cm (20in) |
| *J. s.* 'Meyeri' | bad! |
| *J. s.* 'Pygmaea'** | green, compact, 50cm (20in) |
| *J. virginiana*! | blue./gr., pyramidal, 20m (65ft) |
| *J. v.* 'Canaertii' | gr., broadly columnar, 4m (13ft) |
| *J. v.* 'Glauca' | blue./gray, columnar, 5m (16ft) |
| *J. v.* 'Globosa'** | green, spherical, 1m (3ft) |
| *J. v.* 'Gray Owl' | gray/blue, shrubby, 2.5m (8ft) |
| *J. v.* 'Skyrocket' | grayish blue, very narrow, 4–7m (13–23ft) |

## Larix

### LARCH

The larch has fresh green shoots in spring and turns a beautiful color later on. *L. kaempferi* (Japanese larch) is still sold under its former name *L. leptolepis*. Excrescences resembling broomsticks are sometimes cultivated: an example of this is *L. kaempferi* 'Georgengarten' with a compact shape and branches haphazardly protruding from it.
**Hardiness: US Zone 4-3, Canadian Zone 3-2.**

| | |
|---|---|
| *L. decidua* | light green, narrow, 25m (80ft) |
| *L. d.* 'Corley'** | green, dwarf, 1m (3ft) |
| *L. d.* 'Pendula' | green, slender weeping shape, 15m (50ft) |
| *L. kaempferi* | light green, broad, 30m (100ft) |
| *L. k.* 'Blue Rabbit'** | blue. gray, dwarf, 50cm (20in) |
| *L. k.* 'Blue Ball'** | blueish gray, flat, 30cm (12in) |
| *L. k.* 'Georgengarten'** | light green, dwarf, 50cm (20in) |
| *L. k.* 'Pendula'** | green, broad, 4m (13ft) |
| *L. k.* 'Prostrata'** | green, broad, 50cm (20in) |

## Libocedrus

See: *Calocedrus.*

## Metasequoia

### DAWN REDWOOD, WATER FIR

Along with the *Cupressocyparis*, this is probably the fastest-growing conifer. It is a handsome tree with a very regular shape, and looks beautiful by a large pond or a lake. Its discovery in Central China in 1945 was the last time a large tree was found. Although the tree has only been imported into America for half a century, botanical gardens already have some giant specimens. It will grow in any soil and, like the larch, it is deciduous.
**Hardiness: US Zone 7, Canadian Zone 6.**

| *M. glyptostroboides* | light green, conical, 25m (80ft) |
|---|---|

## *Microbiota*

This conifer first became cultivated for a variety

*Metasequoia glyptostroboides*

*Larix decidua*

of purposes only a few years ago. Its low dense growth suppresses weeds. The tree's bright to light green summer color turns grayish brown in winter.

**Hardiness: US Zone 4, Canadian Zone 3.**

| *M. decussata* | green, broad, 1m (3ft) |
|---|---|

## *Picea*

**SPRUCE**

*P. abies* is grown mostly as a Christmas tree in many countries. The narrower *P. omorika* is also used for this purpose, although its branches are somewhat weaker. Green or blue *P. pungens* is more costly (the bluer it is, the more expensive it becomes): its sturdy branches are able to support large decorations. Of all the spruces, this is also the one that is most tolerant of wind, even sea breezes. There is a great demand for dwarf spruces, as watching the pale green buds come out in spring is an annual delight. The cultivars of *P. abies* are also among the very best dwarf conifers. From a distance, *P. breweriana* is very different from the others: the extremities of the horizontal branches become thin, pliant and pendulous for up to 2m (6ft). The large cones are first green, then purple, and finally brown (for the differences from *Abies*, see: *Abies*). The common names for the various spruces are: Norway

spruce (*P. abies*); Black spruce (*P. mariana*); Serbian spruce (*P. omorika*); Oriental spruce (*P. orientalis*); Colorado spruce or Blue spruce (*P. pungens*); and Sitka spruce (*P. sitchensis*).
**Hardiness: US Zone 5-2, Canadian Zone 4-1.**

| | |
|---|---|
| *P. abies* | Norway spruce, 15m (50ft) |
| *P. a.* 'Aurea' | yellow, pyramidal, 10m (33ft) |
| *P. a.* 'Capressina'** | dense, columnar, 10m (33ft) |
| *P. a.* 'Caerulea'** | steel blue |
| *P. a.* 'Clanbrassiliana' | spherical, very dense, 1m (3ft) |
| *P. a.* 'Columnaris'** | columnar shape |
| *P. a.* 'Compacta' | light gr., spherical, 50cm (20in) |
| *P. a.* 'Cupressina' | gr., slender column, 10m (33ft) |
| *P. a.* 'Diffusa'** | green, dense sphere, 10m (33ft) |
| *P. a.* 'Gregoryana'** | green, cushion–shaped, slow, 60cm (24in) |
| *P. a.* 'Hystrix'** | green, superdwarf |
| *P. a.* 'Inversa'! | green, weeping form, dense, narrow, 10m (33ft) |
| *P. a.* 'Nidiformis'! | dwarf, even growth, 1m (3ft) |
| *P. a.* 'Procumbens'*! | green, broad, dense, 1m (3ft) |
| *P. a.* 'Ohlendorfii' | green, conical, 2.5m (8ft) |
| *P. a.* 'Pygmaea' | green, regular, 1m (3ft) |
| *P. a.* 'Pyramidalis' | columnar |
| *P. a.* 'Remontii'* | green, dense cone, 2m (6ft) |

*Picea abies* 'Nidiformis'

*Picea breweriana*

| | |
|---|---|
| *P. a.* 'Repens' | green, very broad, 50cm (20in) |
| *P. breweriana* | gr., tall and broad, 30m (100ft) |
| *P. engelmanii* 'Glauca'* | gray/blue, pyramidal, 20m (65ft) |
| *P. glauca* | green, conical, 20m (65ft) |
| *P. g.* 'Conica' | light green, conical, dense, 1.5m (6ft) |
| *P. g.* 'Echiniformis' | green, dwarf, spherical, 30cm (12in) |
| *P. mariana* | blue/green, conical, 15m (50ft) |
| *P. m.* 'Argenteovariegata'* | nearly white, pyram., 3m (10ft) |
| *P. m.* 'Nana' | blueish green, flat, round, 30cm (12in) |
| *P. obovata*** | grayish green, narrowly pyramidal, 10m (33ft) |
| *P. omorika* | grayish green, narrowly pyramidal, 15m (50ft) |
| *P. o.* 'Nana' | blue/green, irregular, 1m (3ft) |
| *P. orientalis* | dark green, conical, 20m (65ft) |
| *P. o.* 'Aurea' | gol./yel. tips, conical, 15m (50ft) |
| *P. pungens* | grayish green, broadly pyramidal, 20m (65ft) |
| *P. p.* 'Glauca Globosa' | blue, compact, 1m (3ft) |
| *P. p.* 'Erich Frahm'** | blueish gray, 4m (13ft) |
| *P. p.* 'Hoopsii' | blueish gray, 5m (16ft) |
| *P. p.* 'Koster' | blue, pyramidal, 15m (50ft) |
| *P. p.* 'Oldenburg'** | blueish gray, broadly pyramidal, 15m (50ft) |
| *P. sitchensis* | green, two blue stripes beneath, broadly pyramidal, 5m (16ft) |

# Pinus

**PINE**

The commonest pine trees we see in northern woods are *P. strobus* and Red pine (*P. resinosa)* and the frequently planted *P. sylvestris*. The amount of choice is almost unlimited. The various species are sometimes difficult to distinguish from one another; apart from the color, the main difference is the number of needles combined in a bundle: 2, 3, or 5. Common names include: Arolla pine or Swiss stone pine (*P. cembra*); Bhutan pine (*P. Griffithii*); Mountain pine (*P. mugo*); Austrian pine (*P. n.* var. *austriaca*); white pine (*P. strobus*); and Scots pine (*P. sylvestris*).
**Hardiness: US Zone 5-3, Canadian Zone 4-2.**

| | |
|---|---|
| *P. cembra*** | blueish gr., slender, 20m (65ft) |
| *P. c.* 'Stricta' | blueish green, conical, 1m (3ft) |
| *P. densiflora* 'Globosa' | green, spherical, 1m (3ft) |
| *P. griffithii*** | blueish green, broadly pyramidal, 20m (65ft) |
| *P. mugo* | dark green, shrubby, 5m (16ft) |
| *P. m.* 'Gnom' | gr., broadly pyramidal, 2m (6ft) |
| *P. m.* var. *mughus* | dark green, compact, 2m (6ft) |
| *P. m.* var. *pumilio* | dwarf, broad, 1.5m (5ft) |
| *P. nigra* var. *austriaca*! | dark green, broadly ovoid, 10m (33ft) |

*Pinus cembra*

| | |
|---|---|
| *P. parviflora*! | blue/gr., irregular, 15m (50ft) |
| *P. p.* 'Glauca' | blueish gray, very irregular, 8m (26ft) |
| *P. peuce* | grayish green, narrowly pyramidal, 15m (50ft) |
| *P. p.* 'Aurea'** | yellow, pyramidal 12m (40ft) |
| *P. pinaster* | shiny green, conical, 20m (65ft) |
| *P. pumila* 'Dwarf Blue' | blue, spherical, 3m (10ft) |
| *P. strobus* | gray/gr., pyramidal, 15m (50ft) |
| *P. s.* 'Alba'* | grayish green, narrowly pyramidal, 8m (26ft) |
| *P. s.* 'Minima'* | light gr., spherical, 50cm (20in) |
| *P. s.* 'Radiata' | blueish gray, dwarf, 1.5m (5ft) |

*Pinus parviflora*

| | |
|---|---|
| *P. sylvestris* | green, irregular, 15m (50ft) |
| *P. s.* 'Aurea' | yellow (winter), irregular, 8m (26ft) |
| *P. s.* 'Globosa'* | green, round, 1m (3ft) |
| *P. s.* 'Pumila'* | blueish green, round, 2m (6ft) |
| *P. wallichiana* | see: *P. griffithii* |

## *Podocarpus*

**YELLOW WOOD**

This conifer is exceptional in that it tolerates limy soil. It provides low dense cover. There are many species of the genus *Podocarpus*, nearly all of which come from the warmer regions of the southern hemisphere. The species listed below tolerate shade and are sufficiently winter-hardy.
**Hardiness: US Zone 9, Canadian Zone 8.**

| | |
|---|---|
| *P. alpinus*\* | green, irregular, 2m (6ft) |
| *P. nivalis*\* | bright green, broad, 1m (3ft) |

## *Pseudolarix*

**GOLDEN LARCH**

This rare deciduous tree has a magnificent fall color and is only suitable for very large gardens. Its former name was *P. kaempferi*.
**Hardiness: US Zone 6, Canadian Zone 5.**

| | |
|---|---|
| *P. amabilis*\* | green, broadly pyramidal,15m (50ft) |

*Pseudolarix amabilis*

## *Pseudotsuga*

### DOUGLAS FIR

In Canada, where this tree is native, it will grow up to 60m (200ft) tall. Because of its rapid growth it is used a great deal for forestry purposes in Europe. The tree needs a sheltered position when young.
**Hardiness: US Zone 5, Canadian Zone 4.**

| | |
|---|---|
| *P. glauca* 'Pendula'* | blueish gr., weeping, 15m (50ft) |
| *P. menziesii* | green, broadly pyramidal, 30m (100ft) |

## *Sciadopitys*

### JAPANESE UMBRELLA PINE

This tree is immediately recognizable by its long, pine-like needles which, however, are fleshy and therefore rule out any possible confusion with pines. Umbrella pines need acid soil, not too dry, and tolerate shade.
**Hardiness: US Zone 4, Canadian Zone 3.**

| | |
|---|---|
| *S. verticillata* | shiny green, narrowly pyramidal, 20m (65ft) |

*Sciadopitys verticillata*

*Pseudotsuga menziesii*

## Sequoia

### REDWOOD

This is the world's tallest tree and grows up to 120m (400ft) tall in its natural environment in the coastal region of California. Although there are some tall specimens in Europe, the tree is not sufficiently winter-hardy throughout the continent.
**Hardiness: US Zone 8, Canadian Zone 7.**

| | |
|---|---|
| S. sempervirens* | green, narrow, 20m (65ft) |
| S. s. 'Prostrata'** | grayish green, flat, 50cm (20in) |

*Sequioa sempervirens*

## Sequoiadendron

### SIERRA REDWOOD

These trees grow to over 100m (330ft) tall in their natural environment, although they remain shorter than the sequoia. Young trees are frost-tender. Old trees are in danger of being struck by lightning, which is why damaged specimens are often to be seen in the grounds of country houses. The soft bark is remarkable.
**Hardiness: US Zone 8, Canadian Zone 7.**

| | |
|---|---|
| S. giganteum | dark grayish green, pyramidal, 30m (100ft) |
| S. g. 'Glaucum'* | silvery gray, narrow column, 8m (26ft) |

## Taxodium

### SWAMP CYPRESS, BALD CYPRESS

This slender deciduous tree grows well in very moist soil. Large knobs ("knees") are produced around the tree; these help the aeration of roots. The swamp cypress often grows near large ponds or lakes in country parks and has a beautiful fall color.
**Hardiness: US Zone 6, Canadian Zone 5.**

| | |
|---|---|
| T. distichem* | green, broadly pyramidal, 30m (100ft) |

*Taxodium distichem*

## Taxus

### YEW

This is one of the few conifers to do well in limy soil which, however, does need adequate humus. Yews do tolerate shade. The fleshy red berries are highly toxic. This relatively slow-growing tree can become very old. In the section on *Chamaecyparis*, a description is given of the root rot which may also affect young yews. The disease is transmitted slowly from one plant to another; the slight discoloration of the needles is indicative. (See also: Hedging plants.)

| | |
|---|---|
| *T. baccata* | green, broad and tall, 20m (65ft) |
| *T. b.* 'Adpressa' | dark green, broad shrubby form, 2.5m (8ft) |
| *T. b.* 'Aurea' | yellow, broad shrubby form, 10m (33ft) |
| *T. b.* 'Dovastoniana' | dark green, weeping, 10m (33ft) |
| *T. b.* 'Fastigiata' | dark green, columnar, 4m (13ft) |
| *T. b.* 'Fastigiata Aurea' | yellow, columnar, 4m (13ft) |
| *T. b.* 'Fastigiata Aureomarginata' | yel.-edged, columnar, 4m (13ft) |
| *T. b.* 'Lutea' | yellow berries, green needles, broad, 4m (13ft) |
| *T. b.* 'Repandens' | blueish green, horizontal growth, 50cm (20in) |
| *T. b.* 'Semperaurea' | yellow, broad, 2m (6ft) |
| *T. b.* 'Standishii' | yellow, columnar, later broad, 2m (6ft) |
| *T. b.* 'Summergold' | yellow, broad, 1m (3ft) |
| *T. b.* 'Washingtonii' | yellowish, broad, 2m (6ft) |
| *T. cuspidate* 'Capitata' | green, pyramidal, 12m (40ft) |
| *T.c.* 'Nana' | green, very broad, 1m (3ft) |
| T.c. 'Nana Aurescens' | yellow, low, 30cm (12in) |
| *T. cuspidata* 'Nana' | green, very broad!, 1m (3ft) |
| *T. c.* 'Rustique'** | bronze-col. (winter), broad |
| *T.c.* 'Thayerae' | green, wide spreading, 2.4m (8ft) |
| *T. media* 'Hicksii' | dark gr., broad. col., 2m (6ft) |
| *T.m.* 'Kelsey' | dark green, compact, 3m (10ft) |
| *T. m.* 'Nidiformis' | green, broad shrub, 1m (3ft) |

# Thuja

The thuja can tolerate wind and prefers soil that is not too dry, though it need not be acid. There are eastern (*T. occidentalis* – white cedar) and less common Chinese (*T. orientalis* – Chinese Arbovitae) species, as well as the giant *Thuja plicata* (western red cedar). *T. occidentalis* is green in summer, but often somewhat bronze-colored in winter; the plant also has a rather untidy growth. *T. plicata*, however, stays bright green and shiny in winter and also looks tidier (see also: Hedging plants).

**Hardiness: US Zone 8-4, Canadian Zone 7-3.**

| | |
|---|---|
| *T. occidentalis* 'Alba'** | white tips, pyram. 2.5m (8ft) |
| *T. o.* 'Brabant' | olive green, pyram. 4m (13ft) |
| *T. o.* 'Globosa'! | green. yel., spherical, 1.5m (5ft) |
| *T. o.* 'Frieslandia'** | light gr. pyramidal, 10m (33ft) |
| *T. o.* 'Little Champion'! | green, spherical, 1m (3ft) |
| *T. o.* 'Lutea'** | gol/yel., pyramidal, 10m (33ft) |
| *T. o.* 'Pyramidalis Compacta' | fresh green, narrow, 10m (33ft) |
| *T. o.* 'Recurva Nana' | green, compactly pyramidal, 2m (6ft) |
| *T. o.* 'Rheingold'* | golden yellow, full bush, 1.5m (5ft) |
| *T. o.* 'Rosenthalii'* | dark green, columnar, 5m (16ft) |
| *T. o.* 'Smaragd' | fresh green, pyramidal, 4m (13ft) |
| *T. o.* 'Spiralis'! | light green, slender conical form, 15m (50ft) |
| *T. o.* 'Sunkist' | yellow, upright, 10m (33ft) |

*Taxus baccata* 'Fastigiata Aurea'

*Thuja occidentalis* 'Rheingold'

| T. o. 'Umbraculifera'* | green, flat sphere, 1m (3ft) |
| T. orientalis* | green, broad column, 10m (33ft) |
| T. o. 'Pyramidalis Aurea'* | yellow, columnar, 10m (33ft) |
| T. plicata* | shiny green, conical, 25m (80ft) |
| T. p. 'Atrovirens'* | dark green, narrowly pyramidal, 20m (65ft) |
| T. p. 'Pumila'* | green, irregular, 4m (13ft) |
| T. p. 'Zebrina' | green/yel., conical, 15m (50ft) |

## Thujopsis

### HIBA ARBOVITAE

This strong conifer tolerates half-shade. It is too large for even medium-sized gardens: as the conifer ages, the lower branches spread across the ground, after which they grow vertically again to become tall broad shrubs. The shiny scales feel leathery to the touch and are white beneath.
**Hardiness: US Zone 7, Canadian Zone 6.**

| T. dolabrata | shiny green, shrub, 30m (100ft) |
| T. d. 'Nana' | green, flat sphere, 50cm (20in) |

## Torreya*

### NUTMEG TREE

This tree, which has large striking ovoid seeds, is suitable for a sheltered position in a large garden. It tolerates limy soil and shade.
**Hardiness: US Zone 10, Canadian Zone 9.**

| T. nucifera** | shiny dark green, shrub form, 10m (33ft) |

*Tsuga canadensis*

*Thujopsis dolabrata*

## Tsuga

### HEMLOCK

Do not plant these fast-growing, shade-tolerant trees in windy positions: the needles will be brown by spring if you do. The hemlock is native in North America.
**Hardiness: US Zone 8-5, Canadian Zone 7-4.**

| T. canadensis | dark green, pyramidal, pendulous, 25m (80ft) |
| T. c. 'Gracilis' | yellow. gr., flat sphere, 1m (3ft) |
| T. c. 'Minima' | green, dwarf, 50cm (20in) |
| T. c. 'Pendula'* | dark green, dwarf, weeping form, 2m (6ft) |
| T. heterophylla | fresh green, narrowly pyramidal, 20m (65ft) |

# 5. Roses

The roses in this chapter have been grouped partly along botanical and historical lines, but partly also according to their suitability for specific purposes. Cultivars of old roses, summer-flowering but wonderfully fragrant, are available again from some specialized nurseries, a good reason for devoting a reasonable amount of space to them. Hybrid Tea and Polyantha roses are always grafted, as are some of the old cultivars and species roses. Some roses are obtainable on their own rootstocks. The advantage of the first method is that, apart from the occasional sucker, no long rhizomes are formed. In a large rose bed, rhizomes are sometimes desirable for producing dense growth and thus suppressing weeds; in that case roses on their own roots are more satisfactory. Roses should only be planted in sunny, airy places; the wind should be able to blow through them. This also helps prevent some diseases and infestations. It also means that enclosed urban gardens are unsuitable for roses. Only a few cultivars, often old and once-flowering, are suitable for shady positions. The genuine rose collector should refer to specialized publications, but the average gardener should be able to manage with the following lists, even though they do not pretend to be comprehensive. Availability is difficult to assess. Roses are currently in vogue; more and more garden centers have a large assortment, but you will need to contact a specialized rose grower for exclusive species and cultivars. Most of them will despatch roses to you. The dates of the old roses are indicated to enable you to lay out a garden along historical lines. Roses which will grow in shady positions are mentioned separately. Old roses are usually double; species roses are always single. The height of roses is indicated in centimeters, with the number of inches in brackets or, if one meter or over, in meters, with the number of feet in brackets. The abbreviation (d) stands for double blooms; (sd) for semi-double.

## Alba roses

Alba roses are summer-flowering. An 1840 garden book lists 42 different albas; by 1860 there were over 60. Now there are only about a dozen left. The Jacobite rose (*R. alba* 'Maxima') is a well-known example and was cultivated for centuries at monasteries and ancient farmhouses. A near-white fragrant double flower emerges from a pale pink bud. The leaves are sea-green, as are those of most other albas. Its fragrance is unsurpassed.
**Hardiness: US Zone 6, Canadian Zone 5.**

| | |
|---|---|
| R. 'Bel Amour' | very old, intense pink, 2m (6ft) |
| R. 'Celestial' | 18th cent., fresh pink, 1.5m (5ft) |
| R. 'Félicité Parmentier' | 1828, pale pink, 1.5m (5ft) |
| R. 'Great Maiden's Blush' | 15th century, soft pink, 2m (6ft) |

*Rosa* 'Felicité Parmentier'

| | |
|---|---|
| R. 'Koenigin von Danemarck' | 1826, pink, 1.5m (5ft) |
| R. alba 'Maxima' | 15th century, white, soft pink buds, 2.5m (8ft) |
| R. 'Mme Legras de St. Germain' | 19th century, creamy white, 2m (6ft) |
| R. 'Mme Plantier' | 1835, white, pinkish-red buds, 2m (6ft) |

## Austin roses

Austin roses are perpetual flowering, except for R. 'Scintellatione' and 'Warwick Castle'. For some decades, the English grower David Austin has been engaged in crossing old and new cultivars with a view to preserving their ancient shapes and fragrance while combining them with resistance to disease and long flowering seasons. The open natural-looking shape has been retained as much as possible. It is a pity that the color of so many of these roses presents a neither-fish-nor-flesh appearance, a mixture of pink and yellow, for instance. The following examples are just a few from the extensive range. **Hardiness: US Zone 6, Canadian Zone 5.**

| | |
|---|---|
| R. 'Charles Austin' | apricot (d), 1m (3ft) |
| R. 'Chaucer' | silvery pink (sd), 1m (3ft) |
| R. 'Constance Spry' | deep pink (d), 3m (10ft) |
| R. 'Gertrude Jekyll' | deep pink, green centers, 1.8m (5ft) |
| R. 'Graham Stewart Thomas' | yellow (d), 1m (3ft) |
| R. 'Heritage' | pale pink (d), 1.2m (4ft) |
| R. 'Mary Webb' | lemon yellow (d), large, 1.2m (4ft) |
| R. 'Othello' | deep red (d), 1m (3ft) |
| R. 'Scintillation'* | pale pink, 1.3m (4ft 4in) |
| R. 'The Prioress' | white (sd), 1m (3ft) |
| R. 'The Squire' | velv. deep red (d), 70cm (28in) |
| R. 'The Wife of Bath' | pale pink (d), 1m (3ft) |
| R. 'The Yeoman' | pink (d), 1m (3ft) |

*Rosa* 'Chaucer'

| | |
|---|---|
| R. 'Warwick Castle' | soft pink, 70cm (28in) |
| R. 'William Shakespeare' | dark red (d), 90cm (36in) |

## Baby roses

See: Miniature roses.

## Ground cover roses

New developments are taking place in this perpetual flowering group, partly because park services need to economize, and partly because the use of tubs and containers on patios is one of the major current trends. These roses are suitable for flower beds, banks, and verges, and are tolerant of inexpert maintenance. Let them grow or cut them back to their base – either is possible! All these roses are also available on their own rootstock. A dozen or so cultivars are added annually; others are dropped. Pruning can do little harm, and the dense growth will suppress weeds. The latest cultivars are available from specialist rose growers, and from superior garden centers a year later. "Pavement" roses in every color are a novelty and have a more upright growth (see also: Rugosas). The following dimensions refer to the length of the branches. **Hardiness: US Zone 6, Canadian Zone 5.**

**Low trailing cultivars:**

| | |
|---|---|
| R. 'Alba Meidiland' | white (d), 70cm (28in) |
| R. 'Candy rose' | deep pink (sd), 70cm (28in) |
| R. 'Fil d'Ariane' | white (sd), 80cm (32in) |
| R. 'Friendship' | |
| R. 'Green Snake' | white (hips), 1.5m (5ft) |
| R. 'Immense' | white, slightly pink, 60cm (24in) |
| R. 'Lavender Dream' | lavender pink |
| R. 'Lavender Friendship' | |
| R. 'Max Graf' | luminous pink, 1.5m (5ft) |

*Rosa* 'Alba Meidiland'

| R. 'Partridge' | see: 'Weisse Immensee' |
| R. x 'Paulii' | white, large, 1m (3ft) |
| R. 'Pink Friendship' | |
| R. 'Pink Wave' | soft pink (sd), 60cm (24in) |
| R. 'Repens Meidiland' | white, 30cm (12in) |
| R. 'Silver River' | white, shaded pink, 70cm (28in) |
| R. 'Swany' | white (d), 60cm (24in) |
| R. 'Tapis Volant' | whitish pink, 1.25m (4ft 2in) |
| R. 'Weisse Immensee' | white, 60cm (24in) |
| R. wichuraiana | white, 5m (16ft) |
| R. w. 'Variegata' | variegated leaves, 1m (3ft) |

**Cultivars with more upright growth:**

| R. 'Bingo Meidiland' | |
| R. 'Bonica' | pink (d), 60cm (24in) |
| R. 'Candy Rose' | pink, 80cm (32in) |
| R. 'Ferdy' | salmon pink (d), 60cm (24in) |
| R. 'Fiona' | dark red (hd), 90cm (36in) |
| R. 'Heidetraum' | pinkish red (sd), 70cm (28in) |
| R. 'La Sevillana' | bright red, 70cm (28in) |
| R. 'Mozart' | carmine, white center, 1.2m (4ft) |
| R. 'Nozomi' | pale pink, 90cm (36in) |
| R. 'Pink Bells' | pink (d), 70cm (28in) |
| R. 'Smarty' | pale pink, 90cm (36in) |
| R. 'The Fairy' | soft pink, 45cm (18in) |
| R. 'White Spray' | white, spreading, 1.5m (5ft) |

## Species roses

Depending on how botanists classified these roses, there are between 100 and 200 different species. Only in the northern hemisphere are they found growing wild. They are very suitable for shrub borders. They flower briefly in summer, but their wonderful fragrance and red, orange or black hips in fall make up for this drawback. The branches, and the shape, color or quantity of the thorns are often beautiful in themselves. These roses thrive in sun or semi-shade.

**Hardiness: US Zone 7-4, Canadian Zone 6-3.**

| R. banksiae | see: Container plants |
| R. canina | dog rose, pink and white, red hips, 3m (10ft) |
| R. californica 'Plena'! | pink (d), 3m (10ft) |
| R. gallica 'Complicata' | pink, red hips, 1.5m (5ft) |
| R. glauca! | pinkish red, red hips, 2.5m (8ft) |
| R. hugonis | light yellow, early, 2.5m (5ft) |
| R. moyesii | dark red, bottle-shaped hips, 3m (10ft) |
| R. m. 'Geranium' | scarlet, orange hips, 1.5m (5ft) |
| R. multiflora | see: Climbing roses |
| R. nitida | bright pink, many small red |

*Rosa californica* 'Plena'

*Rosa* 'Bonica'

117

|                      | thorns, 50cm (20in)                          |
| -------------------- | -------------------------------------------- |
| *R. pendulina*       | mallow pink, 2m (6ft)                        |
| *R. pimpinellifolia* | burnet/Scotch rose, white, some-times pink, black hips, 1m (3ft) |
| *R. roxburgii*\*\*!  | pink, bush not rose-like, 2m (6ft)           |
| *R. rubiginosa*      | eglantine (sweet briar), pink, red hips, 2m (6ft) |
| *R. rubrifolia*      | see: *R. glauca*                             |
| *R. rugosa*          | see: Rugosas                                 |
| *R. spinosissima*    | see: *R. pimpinellifolia*                    |
| *R. virginiana*      | pink, round hips, 1.5m (5ft)                 |
| *R. woodsii* var. *fendleri*! | lacquer pink, 1.5m (5ft)            |

## Botanical roses, native

There are many native roses to be found in the meadows and woodlands of North America. These are a very neglected group of native shrubs and should be more widely planted. Some are not readily available even from nurseries specialising in native plants. *Rosa arvensis* is a wild rose found in Europe. These roses will not grow as tall as the height indicated below if they are thinned annually.
**Hardiness: US Zone 7-3, Canadian Zone 6-2.**

|                 |                        |
| --------------- | ---------------------- |
| *R. arvensis*\*\* | forest rose, 6m (20ft) |
| *R. blanda*     | meadow rose, 2m (5ft)  |
| *R. carolina*   | pasture rose, 2m (5ft) |
| *R. palustris*  | swamp rose, 1m (3ft)   |
| *R. setigera*   | prairie rose, 5m (15ft) |
| *R. virginiana* | virginia rose, 2m (5ft) |

## Bourbon roses

Bourbon roses are summer-flowering; a few of them are perpetual-flowering. The accidental crossing of a China rose and a Damascus rose on the island of Bourbon in 1817 led to the creation of a special rose which became the ancestor of an

*Rosa arvensis*

entire group of roses. A mere twenty of the more than 400 cultivars are still cultivated. Earthing up is essential. This group is fairly resistant to disease. *R.* 'Souvenir de la Malmaison' is frost-tender.
**Hardiness: US Zone 6, Canadian Zone 5.**

|                          |                                        |
| ------------------------ | -------------------------------------- |
| *R.* 'Boule de Neige'    | 1867, white, red edges, 1m (3ft)       |
| *R.* 'La Reine Victoria' | 1872, lilac pink, 1.2m (4ft)           |
| *R.* 'Louise Odier'      | 1851, lilac pink, 1.5m (5ft)           |
| *R.* 'Mme Pierre Oger'   | 1878, light silvery pink, 1.2m (4ft)   |
| *R.* 'Souvenir de la Malmaison'! | 1843, white, pink shadings, 80cm (32in) |
| *R.* 'Variegata di Bologna' | see: bi-color roses                 |
| *R.* 'Zéphirine Drouhin' | 1868, carmine pink, 2.5m (8ft)         |

## Centifolia roses

In the seventeenth century there were several hundred cultivars of this summer-flowering rose with its 100 flower petals. Only a few dozen are

*Rosa* 'Mme Pierre Oger'

left. *R.* 'De Meaux', which has pompon-shaped flowers, is particularly strong as a standard rose and hardly needs any protection. The centifolias are also called "Cabbage roses" or "Provence roses", names which refer to their shape or provenance.
**Hardiness: US Zone 6, Canadian Zone 5.**

|                             |                                        |
| --------------------------- | -------------------------------------- |
| *R.* 'Blanchefleur'         | white, slight flush (d), 1.2m (4ft)    |
| *R.* x *centifolia* 'Bullata' | 16th century, pink, 1.5m (5ft)       |
| *R.* 'De Meaux'!            | before 1789, bright pink, small, 70cm (28in) |
| *R.* 'Fantin Latour'        | c. 1900, soft pink, 1.5m (5ft)         |
| *R.* 'Petite de Hollande'   | 1800, bright pink, small, 1.2m (4ft)   |
| *R.* 'Reine des Centfeuilles' | 1824, bright pink, 1.5m (5ft)        |
| *R.* 'Tour de Malakoff'     | 1856, dark purple, 2.5m (8ft)          |

*Rosa* 'Fantin Latour'

# China roses

The oldest perpetual-flowering roses and ancestors of the hybrid teas, several are frost-tender and require earthing up every year. 'Old Blush', 'Mutabilis', and 'Viridiflora' are tolerant of shade. 'Viridiflora' is a botanical curiosity, and not to everyone's taste.
**Hardiness: US Zone 7, Canadian Zone 6.**

| | |
|---|---|
| R. 'Hermosa' | 1840, bright pink, 90cm (36in) |
| R. 'Mutabilis' | 1932, yellow/orange/red, 90cm (36in) |
| R. 'Old Blush' | 1789, silvery pink, 1.5m (5ft) |
| R. 'Slaters Crimson China' | 1792, carmine red, 90cm (36in) |
| R. 'Sophie's Perpetual' | pale pink, 2.5m (8ft) |
| R. 'Viridiflora' | 1833, green, 90cm (36in) |

# Damask roses

With just a few exceptions, these are summer-flowering double roses. *R.* 'Kazanlik' or 'Trigentipetala' is a Bulgarian cultured rose used for the production of rose oil. Its fragrant petals are particularly suitable for making potpourri.
**Hardiness: US Zone 7, Canadian Zone 6.**

| | |
|---|---|
| R. 'Bel Amour' | 1950, salmon pink, 1.5m (5ft) |
| R. 'Celsiana' | before 1750, bright pink, 1.5m (5ft) |
| R. 'Comte de Chambord' | warm pink, repeat-flowering, 1.2m (4ft) |
| R. 'Ispahan' | 1832, deep pink, grayish-green leaves, 1.5m (5ft) |
| R. 'Kazanlik' | very old, bright pink, 1.5m (5ft) |
| R. 'Leda' | before 1827, pinkish white, carmine edges, 1.4m (4ft 8in) |
| R. 'Marie Louise' | 1813, luminous pink, 1.2m (4ft) |
| R. 'Mme Hardy' | 1832, cream, pendulous, 1.8m (5ft) |
| R. 'Petite Lisette' | 1817, silvery-pinkish cream, 1.2m (4ft) |
| R. 'Trigintipetala' | ancient, old rose (d), 2m (6ft) |

# English roses

See: Austin roses.

# Single-flowered bush roses!

Although these perpetual-flowering roses have distinct characteristics of their own, they have never been classified as a distinct group. *R.* 'Sancta'** was known to the ancient Romans; the others date from the early part of the nineteenth century.
**Hardiness: US Zone 6, Canadian Zone 5.**

| | |
|---|---|
| R. 'Dainty Bess' | pink, 1m (3ft) |
| R. 'Ellen Willmott'* | pink buds, white flowers, 1.2m (4ft) |
| R. 'Goethe'** | fuchsia pink, 1.8m (ft) |

*Rosa* 'Old Blush'

*Rosa* 'Kazanlik'

| R. 'Golden Wings'* | pale yellow, 1m (3ft) |
| R. 'Mrs. Oakley Fisher' | copper orange to yellow, 70cm (28in) |
| R. 'Sally Holmes' | very pale pink, 1.3m (4ft 4in) |
| R. sancta** | white, 80cm (32in) |
| R. 'White Wings' | white, 1m (3ft) |

Rosa 'Dainty Bess'

## Floribunda and Polyantha roses

See: Polyantha roses.

## Gallica roses

At her château de Malmaison, the Empress Josephine had 150 different Gallicas, several of which are still cultivated. Along with the albas, the summer-flowering Gallicas are among the strongest old roses and tolerate light shade. The following species and cultivars are also suitable for hedging purposes; in that case they should be pruned immediately after flowering early in July. R. gallica 'Versicolor' (Rosa mundi) should not be confused with Rosa damascena 'Versicolor' (York and Lancaster roses).
**Hardiness: US Zone 5, Canadian Zone 4.**

| R. 'Belle de Crécy' | 1850, pink, 1.2m (4ft) |
| R. 'Charles de Mills' | old, bright pinkish violet, 1.2m (4ft) |
| R. 'Complicata' | very old, bright pink, 3m (10ft) |
| R. 'Duchesse de Montebello' | 1829, soft pink, 1.2m (4ft) |
| R. 'Maître d'Ecole' | 1840, pink w. violet, 90cm (36in) |
| R. g. 'Versicolor' | very old, pink with stripes, 90cm (36in) |

## Hybrid perpetuals

See: Remontant roses.

## Striped roses

Striped roses are summer-flowering old roses from the Bourbon (B), Gallica (G), Damask (D), and Centifolia (C) groups. Botanically, therefore, they do not form a single group, but lovers of two-color roses can enjoy themselves choosing from the following list. These are all bushes which need pruning (therefore thinning) just like other shrubs, and which grow to between 1.5 and 2m (5 and 6ft) tall. R. gallica 'Versicolor' sometimes mutates back to an ordinary large–flowered single pink rose, R. g. 'Officinalis', which, in fact, is also very beautiful.
**Hardiness: US Zone 6, Canadian Zone 5.**

| R. 'Château de Namur' (G) | soft pink, white stripes |
| R. 'Ferdinand Pichard' | carmine red, white stripes |
| R. 'Frankfurt'* (C) | red, scarlet stripes |
| R. 'Honorine de Brabant' (B) | pale pink, lilac spots |
| R. 'Mécène' | white, lilac pink stripes |
| R. 'Ouillet Parfait' (G) | white, red stripes |
| R. 'Pompon Panaché' (G) | cream, pink stripes |
| R. 'Sophie de Marsilly' (C) | pinkish-white stripes |

Rosa gallica 'Versicolor' and Rosa gallica 'Officinalis'

Rosa 'Charles de Mills'

| | |
|---|---|
| R. 'Tricolore de Flandre' (G) | light red, lilac stripes |
| R. 'Variegata de Bologna'! (B) | white, purple stripes |
| R. 'Versicolor' (G) | pinkish red, soft pink stripes |
| R. 'Village Maid' (C) | creamy white, lilac pink stripes |
| R. 'York and Lancaster' (D) | pale pink light stripes or white with pink stripes |

## Native roses

See: Species roses.

## Climbing roses

Except for the old cultivars, climbing roses are perpetual flowering. Don't plant climbing roses against a south-facing wall, as they are more sensitive to mildew in such a position. Walls facing south-east or south-west are satisfactory. Fix trellis or wires before planting: roses that have been carefully planted can grow fast. The small-flowered Noisette roses were popular climbers in the nineteenth century, but a greater variety of colors is now available. They are not easy to cultivate and are slightly frost-tender. Noisette-roses are not perpetual-flowering: they bloom during the last week in June and the first week in July. The named cultivars tolerate shade. **Hardiness: US Zone 7, Canadian Zone 6.**

**Small-flowered, Noisette roses:**

| | |
|---|---|
| R. 'Aimée Vibert' | white (d), almost thornless, 3.5m (11ft) |
| R. 'Blush Noisette' | purplish pink (sd), 2m (6ft) |
| R. 'Deschamps' | cherry red, few thorns, 4.5m (14ft) |
| R. 'Mme Alfred Carrière' | white/soft pink, perpetual, 6m (20ft) |

*Rosa* 'Blush Noisette'

**Species roses** (see also Ramblers and Scramblers)

| | |
|---|---|
| R. *moschata* | white, 6m (20ft) |
| R. *multibracteata* | purplish pink, 2m (6ft) |
| R. *multiflora* | white, brownish-red hips, fast growing, 5m (16ft) |

**Large-flowered Polyantha and Floribunda roses:**

| | |
|---|---|
| R. 'Bantry Bay' | d. pink, open flower, 3.5m (11ft) |
| R. 'Cl. Allgold' | bright yellow (sd), 4.5m (14ft) |
| R. 'Cl. Iceberg'! | white (d), 5.5m (18ft) |
| R. 'Cl. Queen Elizabeth' | bright silvery pink, 6m (20ft) |
| R. 'Crimson Shower' | deep red, 3m (10ft) |
| R. 'Heidelberg' | fiery red, 2m (6ft) |
| R. 'Mermaid' | sulfur yellow, 3.5m (11ft) |
| R. 'Phyllis Bide' | light apricot, 2m (6ft) |

**Hybrid Teas:**

| | |
|---|---|
| R. 'Aloha' | pink, full, 3m (10ft) |
| R. 'Cl. Superstar' | coral-vermillion, 3.5m (11fit |
| R. 'Cl. Suttersgold' | d. yel., or. a. p. haze, 3.5m (11ft) |
| R. 'Meg' | pink, yellow haze, almost single, 2.5m (8ft) |
| R. 'Mme Grégoire' Staechelin | dusty pink, early, 4.5m (13fift) |

*Rosa* 'Golden Showers'

**Other popular perpetual-flowering climbing roses:**

| | |
|---|---|
| R. 'Apollo' | yellow (d), 3m (10ft) |
| R. 'Compassion' | salmon pink and apricot, 3m (10ft) |
| R. 'Golden Showers' | golden yellow (sd), 2.5m (8ft) |
| R. 'New Dawn' | soft pink, 4m (13ft) |
| R. 'Paul's Scarlet Climber' | carmine red, 6m (20ft) |
| R. 'Pink Cloud' | salmon pink, large, 6m (20ft) |
| R. 'Pink Ocean' | pink, large, 4m (13ft) |
| R. 'Sympathie' | velvety red, 4m (13ft) |
| R. 'Zéphirine Drouhin' | carmine pink, 4m (13ft) |

**Old cultivars, summer–flowering:**

| | |
|---|---|
| R. 'Blush Noisette' | 1817, deep pink, 2m (6ft) |
| R. 'Cl. Pompon de Paris' | red, small (d), 4m (13ft) |
| R. 'Dorothy Perkins' | pink, small (d), 4m (13ft) |
| R. 'Excelsa' | crimson, 3.5m (11ft) |
| R. 'Félicité et Perpétue' | white, small, 5m (16ft) |
| R. 'Gloire de Dijon' | 1853, yel. and pink, 3.5m (11ft) |
| R. 'Mermaid' | 1918, golden yellow, 8m (26ft) |
| R. 'Mme Alfred Carrière' | 1879, creamy white, 6m (20ft) |
| R. 'Zéphirine Drouhin' | 1868, candy pink, 4m (13ft) |

## Lambertiana roses

See: Musk roses.

## Liaan roses

See: Rambler and Scrambler roses.

## Miniature roses

These are the smallest perpetual-flowering roses, and have a bushy growth. They are pruned like hybrid teas and floribundas. Use them in the same way as patio roses which, however, are considerably easier to maintain.

**Hardiness: US Zone 7-5, Canadian Zone 6-4.**

| | |
|---|---|
| R. 'Always a Lady' | mauve, fragrant, 60cm (24in) |
| R. 'Baby Gold Star'* | yellow, apricot, 30cm (12in) |
| R. 'Baby Carnival'* | lemon yellow/red pink, |
| (syn R. 'Baby Masquerade')* | 30-40cm (12-16 in) |
| R. 'Cinderella' | white and pink, 30cm (12in) |
| R. 'Green Ice' | white tinged green, 60cm (24in) |
| R. 'Little Ekimo'* | white, shade tolerant, 40cm (16in) |
| R. 'My Sunshine' | rich yellow, 30cm (12in) |
| R. 'Phoenix' | carmine and orange, 30cm (12in) |
| R. 'Pink Delight'** | pale pink (d), 30cm (12in) |
| R. 'Pink Heather'** | lilac pink, 20-30cm (8-12in) |

*Rosa* 'Dorothy Perkins' (right) and *Rosa* 'Paul's Scarlet Climber' (left)

| | |
|---|---|
| R. 'Red Cascade' | rich red, climber, 1.75m (5ft) |
| R. 'Starina' | red and orange, 35cm (14in) |
| R. 'Sweet Chariot' | mauve, fragrant, 30-40cm (12-16in) |
| R. 'Tom Thumb' | crimson and white, 10cm (4in) |
| R. 'Tinker Bell'** | mid pink, 30cm (12in) |
| R. 'Yellow Doll' | creamy yellow, 30cm (12in) |
| R. 'Vigilance'** | white climber, 1.75m (5ft) |
| R. 'White Charm' | white, fragrant, 30cm (12in) |

## Moss roses

Summer-flowering moss roses are to be found among Gallicas, Centifolias and Damask roses. The flower buds are covered in a moss-like growth. At a distance it looks as if the buds are covered in greenfly. *R.* 'Cristata' is also sold as 'Chapeau de Napoléon'.
**Hardiness: US Zone 6, Canadian Zone 5.**

| | |
|---|---|
| R. 'Blanche Moreau' | 1880, white, 1.2m (4ft) |
| R. 'Cristata' | 1826, deep pink, 1.5m (5ft) |
| R. 'Eugénie Guinoisseau' | 1864, deep pinkish violet, 1.8m (5ft) |
| R. 'Général Kléber' | 1856, soft deep pink (d), 1.5m (5ft) |
| R. 'Mousseline' | 1855, creamy pink, repeat flowering, 1.2m (4ft) |
| R. 'Nuits de Young' | 1845, velvety deep mauve (d), 1.2m (4ft) |
| R. 'René d'Anjou' | 1853, warm pink, repeat flowering, 1.5m (5ft) |
| R. centifolia 'Muscosa' | white, pinkish haze, 1.2m (4ft) |
| R. 'William Lobb' | 1855, violet red (sd), 3m (10ft) |

*Rosa* 'William Lobb'

## Musk roses

Musk roses are summer-flowering, usually followed by a repeat florescence in fall. Many of these hybrids were developed between 1904 and 1924 by the Reverend Pemberton, a clergyman who turned his back on the church when growing roses became his major passion. Several of his roses were launched by his former gardener J.A. Bentall, who introduced the famous roses 'The Fairy' (1932) and 'Ballerina' (1937) himself.
**Hardiness: US Zone 6, Canadian Zone 5.**

| | |
|---|---|
| R. 'Ballerina' | pale pink, 80cm (32in) |
| R. 'Bishop Darlington' | palest pink (hd) |
| R. 'Buff Beauty' | apricot (sd), 2.5m (8ft) |
| R. 'Cornelia' | pale pink (d) |
| R. 'Danae' | yellowy cream, small, 1m (3ft) |
| R. 'Felicia' | pink and salmon (d), 1.2m (4ft) |
| R. 'Francesca' | apricot a. cream (sd), 1.2m (4ft) |
| R. 'Kathleen' | pale pink, almost single |
| R. 'Moonlight' | cream, 1.5m (5ft) |
| R. 'Mozart' | bright red, white eye, 1m (3ft) |
| R. 'Penelope' | salm. pink a. w. (sd), 1.5m (5ft) |
| R. 'Prosperity' | cream (d), 2m (6ft) |
| R. 'Robin Hood' | pink (sd), 1m (3ft) |

*Rosa* 'Felicia'

## Park roses

These large round bushes, sometimes perpetual-flowering, are suitable for planting on their own, but also in the front row of a shrubbery. Prune them like shrubs: thin them but never cut them back.
**Hardiness: US Zone 7-6, Canadian Zone 6-5.**

| | |
|---|---|
| R. foetida 'Persian Yellow' | bright yellow (d), 2m (6ft) |
| R. 'Frülingsduft' | large, yellow (d), 2m (6ft) |
| R. 'Frülingsgold' | pale yellow (sd), 1.5m (5ft) |
| R. 'Frülingsmorgen' | carmine pink, 2m (6ft) |
| R. 'Frülingsschnee' | snow white (d), 1.5m (5ft) |
| R. macrantha 'Raubritter' | bright pink (sd), 90cm (36in) |
| R. 'Maigold' | br. golden yel., large (d), 2m (6ft) |
| R. moyesii 'Geranium' | scarlet, hips orange, 1.5m (5ft) |
| R. 'New Face' | brown. pink clusters, 1.5m (5ft) |
| R. 'Nevada'! | white, large, hips yel., 2m (6ft) |
| R. omeiensis 'Pteracantha' | cream, br. red thorns, 2m (6ft) |
| R. virginiana 'Harvest Song' | red, 1.25m (4ft 2in) |

*Rosa* 'Nevada'

*Rosa* 'Sweet Dream'

## *Patio roses*

Roses are usually divided into groups which enable one to work out their growth pattern. Perpetual-flowering patio roses are an exception to the rule: the name has more to do with where they are grown and what is considered to be their purpose. This group of modern roses has a leaf density corresponding to that of miniature roses, and a height similar to that of polyanthas, but the flowers are smaller. The plants do not spread to the extent of trailing roses. The group consists solely of modern scented cultivars. All the cultivars listed here were introduced after 1980.
**Hardiness: US Zone 7, Canadian Zone 6.**

| | |
|---|---|
| R. 'Anna Ford' | orange red, 45cm (18in) |
| R. 'Apricot Sunblaze' | orange red, 40cm (16in) |
| R. 'Arctic Sunrise' | whitish pink, 45cm (18in) |
| R. 'Cider Cup' | apricot, 45cm (18in) |
| R. 'Clarissa' | orange yellow, 60cm (24in) |
| R. 'Dainty Dinah' | salmon pink, 45cm (18in) |
| R. 'Hotline' | bright red, 30cm (12in) |
| R. 'Little Prince' | orange red, yellow centers, 45cm (18in) |
| R. 'Meillandina' | red, 40cm (16in) |
| R. 'Perestroica' | bright yellow, 40cm (16in) |
| R. 'Striped Meillandina' | red a. white stripes, 30cm (12in) |
| R. 'Sweet Dream' | apricot, 40cm (18in) |

## Polyantha and Floribunda roses

Some of these perpetual-flowering, but not very fragrant roses are grown on their own rootstock. They need earthing up in fall. *R.* 'Nancy Steen' is named after a great rose lover, who searched for old roses in the gardens of early settlers' homes and churchyards in New Zealand and published a book about them. It provided a further boost to the cultivation of old roses.
**Hardiness: US Zone 7, Canadian Zone 6.**

**Red and orange:**

| | |
|---|---|
| *R.* 'Allotria' | orange red (d), 60cm (24in) |
| *R.* 'Amsterdam' | br. red, dark leaves, 60cm (24in) |
| *R.* 'City of Belfast' | bright red, 60cm (24in) |
| *R.* 'Europeana'! | deep red, dark leav. 60cm (24in) |
| *R.* 'Fanal' | light red (sd), 50cm (20in) |
| *R.* 'Highlight' | scarlet vermilion, 60cm (24in) |
| *R.* 'Käthe Duvigneau' | luminous dark red (sd), 70cm (28in) |
| *R.* 'Korona' | bright orange red (d), 70cm (28in) |
| *R.* 'La Grande Parade' | bright red, 90cm (36in) |
| *R.* 'La Sevillana' | red (sd), 70cm (28in) |
| *R.* 'Magneet' | orange red (sd), 90cm (36in) |
| *R.* 'Montana' | luminous red (d), 60cm (24in) |
| *R.* 'Nina Weibul' | dark blood red (sd), 75cm (30in) |
| *R.* 'Orangeade' | bright vermilion orange, 90cm (36in) |
| *R.* 'Paprika'! | brick red (sd), 60cm (24in) |
| *R.* 'Skagerrak' | dark red (d), 70cm (28in) |
| *R.* 'Tornado' | scarlet (sd), 60cm (24in) |

*Rosa* 'City of Belfast'

**Pink:**

| | |
|---|---|
| *R.* 'Anneke Doorenbos' | deep pink (d), 90cm (36in) |
| *R.* 'Betty Prior' | carmine pink, 90cm (36in) |
| *R.* 'Bonica' | pale pink |
| *R.* 'Compassion' | salmon pink (d), 30cm (12in) |
| *R.* 'Fashion' | salmon-coral pink, 60cm (24in) |
| *R.* 'Märchenland' | salmon pink (sd), 90cm (36in) |
| *R.* 'Nancy Steen'** | soft pink, bronze-colored leaves, 75cm (30in) |
| *R.* 'Pernille Poulsen' | pink (d), 60cm (24in) |
| *R.* 'Pink Maiden' | salmon pink (sd), 70cm (28in) |
| *R.* 'Queen Elizabeth' | pure pink (d), 1.2m (4ft) |

**Yellow:**

| | |
|---|---|
| *R.* 'All Gold' | golden yellow (sd), 60cm (24in) |
| *R.* 'Apricot Queen' | apricot |
| *R.* 'Apricot Nectar' | apricot, 60cm (24in) |
| *R.* 'Chinatown' | yel., pink haze (d), 1.2m (4ft) |
| *R.* 'Friesia' | pure yellow (d), 60cm (24in) |
| *R.* 'Sunsilk' | creamy yellow, 70cm (28in) |

*Rosa* 'Friesia'

**White:**

| | |
|---|---|
| *R.* 'Iceberg'! | see: 'Schneewittchen' |
| *R.* 'Gruss an Aachen' | cream, peach haze, 45cm (18in) |
| *R.* 'Schneewitchen' (Iceberg) | pure white, (d), 90cm (36in) |
| *R.* 'White Queen' ('Elizabeth') | white (d), 1.2m (4ft) |

*Rosa* 'Schneewittchen' ('Iceberg')

## Portland roses

This group of roses was often grown in the nineteenth century following the introduction of hybrids resulting from the crossing of China and Damask roses by the Dukes of Portland. The result was a longer flowering season. The roses are summer-flowering; there is no question of their being genuinely remontant.

**Hardiness: US Zone 6, Canadian Zone 5.**

| | |
|---|---|
| R. 'Arthur de Sansal' | 1855, dark carmine violet, 90cm (36in) |
| R. 'Comte de Chambord' | 1863, warm pink, 90cm (36in) |
| R. 'Jacques Cartier' | 1868, deep pink, 90cm (36in) |
| R. 'Pergolèse' | 1860, carmine viol., 90cm (36in) |
| R. 'Rose du Roi' | 1815, pink. purple, 90cm (36in) |
| R. 'Rose de Resht'! | reintr., fuchsia red, 90cm (36in) |

*Rosa* 'Rose du Roi'

## Rambler roses

Because of their vigorous growth, these vigorous summer-flowering climbers roses are suitable for training over sheds or through trees. Adapt their height to the height of the tree (for the fastest-growing roses, see: Scrambler roses).

**Hardiness: US Zone 7, Canadian Zone 6.**

| | |
|---|---|
| R. 'Albéric Barbier' | cream (sd), 4.5m (14ft) |
| R. 'Blue Magenta' | deep violet (d), 4m (13ft) |
| R. 'Dr. W. van Fleet' | soft pink (sd), 4.5m (14ft) |
| R. 'Excelsa' | pinkish red (d), 4.5m (14ft) |
| R. 'Félicité et Perpétue' | pale pink (d), 4.5m (14ft) |

| | |
|---|---|
| R. 'François Juranville' | salmon pink, 6.5m (21ft) |
| R. 'Ghislaine de Féligonde' | light orange yellow (d), 2.5m (8ft) |
| R. 'Kew Rambler' | lilac pink, 6m (20ft) |
| R. *multiflora* | white, 5m (16ft) |
| R. 'New Dawn' | very pale pink (sd), 4m (13ft) |
| R. 'Phyllis Bide' | p. pink, yel., white (sd), 3m (10ft) |
| R. 'The Garland' | white (sd) (hips), 4.5m (14ft) |
| R. 'Veilchenblau' | lavend. purple (sd), 4.5m (14ft) |

*Rosa* 'Albéric Barbier'

## Remontant roses, Hybrid perpetuals

These roses flower in summer, followed by a second period of florescence. In the nineteenth century, remontant or repeat flowering roses were expensive and therefore only affordable by the well-to-do. Ordinary people had to make do with summer-flowering roses. Remontant roses became popular in about 1820, and were recognized as a separate group. Their popularity lasted until the First World War, probably until the arrival of the perpetual-flowering hybrid teas.

**Hardiness: US Zone 6, Canadian Zone 5.**

| | |
|---|---|
| R. 'Baron Girod de l'Ain' | red, white edges, 1.2m (4ft) |
| R. 'Baronne Prévost' | deep pink, thorny, 1.5m (5ft) |
| R. 'Eclair' | dark red, difficult, 1.2m (4ft) |
| R. 'Ferdinand Pichard' | carm. red, pink–strip. 1.5m (5ft) |

| | |
|---|---|
| R. 'Frau Karl Druschki' | buds red, flowers w., 1.75m (5ft) |
| R. 'John Hopper' | bright pink. mauve, 1.2m (4ft) |
| R. 'La Reine' | silvery pink, (frost–tender), 90cm (36in) |
| R. 'Mrs. John Laing' | silvery pink, 1.2m (4ft) |
| R. 'Paul Neyron' | warm pink, strong, 90cm (36in) |
| R. 'Reine des Violettes' | velvety mauve, almost thornless, 1.5m (5ft) |
| R. 'Roger Lambelin' | carm. red, w. edges, 1.2m (4ft) |

*Rosa* 'Paul Neyron'

## *Rugosa roses*

The strong summer-flowering, and often perpetual-flowering Rugosas are easily recognizable by their deeply veined leaves which distinguish them from all other roses. The disease-resistant and low-maintenance Pavement roses are new. The "Dwarf, Jozi, Pierette, Pink, Purple, Scarlet, Snow and White Pavement" roses are grown on their own rootstocks; they are tolerant of a polluted environment and of the salt used on icy roads. Rugosa roses are suitable for hedging purposes and the hips can be made into a preserve. If you order *R. rugosa* for hedging, you will nearly always receive a mixture. It is therefore advisable to order specific cultivars.
**Hardiness: US Zone 5, Canadian Zone 4.**

| | |
|---|---|
| R. *rugosa* | red, pink or white, hips red |
| R. r. 'Alba' | white, hips orange red, 1m (3ft) |
| R. r. 'Blanc Double de Coubert' | white (sd), 1.5m (5ft) |
| R.r 'David Thompson' | mid red, 1.2m (4ft) |
| R. r. 'Frau Dagmar Hastrup' | pure pink, 1.2m (4ft) |
| R. r. 'F.J. Grootendorst' | pinkish red, fragrant, 1m (3ft) |
| R. r. 'Hansa' | purpl. red, perpetual, 1m (3ft) |
| R.r 'Henry Hudson' | white, fragrant, 70cm (28in) |
| R.r 'Martin Frobisher' | light pink, 2m (6ft) |
| R. r. 'Max Graf' | pink, trailing, 40cm (16in) |

| | |
|---|---|
| R. r. 'Mrs. Anthony Waterer' | crimson (sd), 1.5m (5ft) |
| R. r. 'Pink Grootendorst' | pink, small, 1.5m (5ft) |
| R. r. 'Pink Hedge' | pink, bronze leaves, 1m (3ft) |
| R. r. 'Red Hedge' | red, red hips, low |
| R. r. 'Schneezwerg' | pure white, compact |
| R.r 'Thérèse Bugnet' | mid pink, 2m (6ft) |

*Rosa rugosa* 'Blanc Double de Coubert'

## *Rugosa hybrids*

Unlike the common Rugosas, these roses are more susceptible to disease. They do not really form a distinct group but, because of their tenderness, they are listed separately here. Earthing up is advisable. They are remontant or perpetual-flowering and grow much taller than the Rugosas listed above.
**Hardiness: US Zone 5, Canadian Zone 4.**

| | |
|---|---|
| R. 'Agnes' | bright yellow (d), 2.5m (8ft) |
| R. 'Conrad F. Meyer' | pink (d), tender, 3m (10ft) |
| R. 'Roseraie de l'Hay' | purple (d), 2.5m (8ft) |
| R. 'Sarah Van Fleet' | br. pink, yel. center, 3m (10ft) |

*Rosa* 'Roseraie de l'Hay'

## Shade-tolerant roses

Most roses, and in particular China and tea roses, hybrid teas, Austin roses, remontant hybrids, miniature and patio roses require full sun. Modern ground-cover roses, scramblers, ramblers, botanical, alba, and rugosa roses, and rugosa hybrids are tolerant of shade. Only a few cultivars from the other groups tolerate shade. To avoid discoloration, it is better not to plant deep purple roses where they will catch the fiercest midday sun.

## Scramblers

These are the most vigorous of all climbing roses, usually bearing small single flowers, sometimes followed by hips. They are the rose "festoons" for adorning uninteresting trees and covering garden sheds. They grow faster and larger than ramblers, are summer- flowering and will thrive in shade.
**Hardiness: US Zone 8-7, Canadian Zone 7-6.**

| | |
|---|---|
| R. arvensis | white, 6m (12ft) |
| R. banksiae | see: Container plants |
| R. 'Bobby James' | white, almost single, 9m (30ft) |
| R. brunonii | white, 10m (33ft) |
| R. filipes 'Kiftsgate' | jasmine-white, 9m (30ft) |
| R. gentiliana | cr., single to semi-double, 6m (20ft) |
| R. helenae | cream, 8m (25ft) |

*Rosa helenae*

*Rosa rugosa* 'Hansa'

| | |
|---|---|
| R. 'Himalayan Musk Rambler' | pale pinkish red, 10m (33ft) |
| R. longicuspis | white, 10m (33ft) |
| R. 'Rambling Rector' | cream (sd), 6m (20ft) |
| R. 'Seagull' | white (sd), 8m (26ft) |
| R. 'Wedding Day' | white, 9m (30ft) |

## Standard roses, standard weeping roses

It makes no sense to list all standard roses: every grower has a number of cultivars grafted on to stems. All hybrid teas and polyantha roses are basically suitable for growing as standards. Some growers will graft your favorite rose on to a stem

for you. A popular selection of weeping standards is available almost anywhere. They are much hardier than other roses and need very little protection against winter frosts.
**Hardiness: US Zone 8, Canadian Zone 7.**

| | |
|---|---|
| R. 'Ballerina' | pale pink, 1.5m (5ft) |
| R. 'Dorothy Perkins' | bright pink, small (d), 1.5m (5ft) |
| R. 'Excelsa' | pinkish red (d), 1.5m (5ft) |
| R. 'New Dawn' | soft pink, large (d), 1.5m (5ft) |
| R. 'Swany' | white, small (d), 1.5m (5ft) |
| R. 'White Dorothy' | bright white, small (d), 1.5m (5ft) |

## Thornless roses

In America, hybridization is currently taking place to produce thornless roses: the latest trend. The oldest one known is 'Zéphirine Drouhin', a low-growing climber introduced in 1868 which can also be planted as a bush. The others are hybrid teas from the rose growers Unwins.
**Hardiness: US Zone 7, Canadian Zone 6.**

| | |
|---|---|
| R. 'Smooth Angel'* | cream, 90cm (36in) |
| R. 'Smooth Lady'* | pink, 90cm (36in) |
| R. 'Smooth Prince'* | cherry red, 90cm (36in) |
| R. 'Smooth Velvet'* | dark red, 90cm (36in) |
| R. 'Sophie's Perpetual' | bordeaux red, 70cm (28in) |
| R. 'Zéphirine Drouhin' | candy pink, 3m ((10ft) |

*Rosa* 'Ballerina'

## Tea roses

Don't confuse this group with the hybrid teas which were introduced later. Tea roses were popular during the second half of the nineteenth century. Most of these perpetual-flowering roses are very frost-tender; the hardiest cultivars are listed below.
**Hardiness: US Zone 8, Canadian Zone 7.**

| | |
|---|---|
| R. 'Adam' | pink and apricot, 2m (6ft) |
| R. 'Gloire de Dijon' | pink and orange apricot, 4.5m (14ft) |
| R. 'Triomphe de Luxembourg' | salmon pink, 90cm (36in) |

*Rosa* 'Adam'

## Hybrid teas and large-flowered bush roses

These perpetual-flowering roses need earthing up every year. Anyone not prepared to undertake this task would do better to select plants from the groups for which it is not required. These roses, with their disappointing fragrance, are available almost anywhere.
**Hardiness: US Zone 6, Canadian Zone 5.**

**Red and orange:**

| | |
|---|---|
| R. 'Ace of Hearts' | deep red, 90cm (36in) |
| R. 'American Home' | dark red, 90cm (36in) |
| R. 'Double Delight' | red blend, fragrant, 90cm (36in) |
| R. 'Fragrant Cloud' | coral red, fragrant, 1.2m (4ft) |
| R. 'Granada' | red blend, 80cm (32in) |
| R. 'Mr. Lincoln' | dark red, fragrant, 1.2m (4ft) |
| R. 'Swathmore' | red blend, 80cm (32in) |

**Pink:**

| | |
|---|---|
| R. 'Bride' | light pink, 80cm (32in) |
| R. 'Curly Pink' | rich pink, 80cm (32in) |
| R. 'Dainty Bess' | see: Single-flowered bush roses |
| R. 'Electron' | warm pink, fragrant, 90cm (36in) |
| R. 'Elizabeth Taylor' | dark pink, 90cm (36in) |
| R. 'First Prize' | mid pink, fragrant, 1.2m (4ft) |
| R. "Miss All American Beauty" | rich pink, dark leaves, fragrant, 1.2m (4ft) |

| | |
|---|---|
| R. 'Savoy Hotel' | pink blend, 90cm (36in) |
| R. 'Tiffany' | pink blend, fragrant, 1.2m (4ft) |

**Yellow:**

| | |
|---|---|
| R. 'Gina Lollobrigida' | rich yellow, 90cm (36in) |
| R. 'Graceland' | medium yellow, 90cm (36in) |
| R. 'Jean Kenneally' | apricot yellow, fragrant, 35cm (14in) |
| R. 'Kings Ransome' | glowing yellow, 90cm (36in) |
| R. 'New Day' | medium yellow, 1.2m (4ft) |
| R. 'Party Girl' | apricot yellow, fragrant, 45cm (18in) |
| R. 'Rise and Shine' | mid yellow, 40cm (16in) |
| R. 'Oregold' | rich yellow, 80cm (32in) |
| R. 'Sutters Gold' | deep yellow, pink haze, 90cm (36in) |

**White:**

| | |
|---|---|
| R. 'Creamy white' | gr. white a yellow, 90cm (36in) |
| R. 'Kaiserin Auguste Viktoria' | creamy white, fragrant, 2m (6ft) |
| R. 'Pole Star' | clear white, 90cm (36in) |
| R. 'Pascali' | creamy white, 90cm (36in) |
| R. 'Honor' | clear white, 1.5m (5ft) |

## Weeping roses

See: Standard roses.

*Rosa* 'Fragrant Cloud'

# 6. Vines and wall plants

Anyone glancing at an English book on gardens will always find an exten-sive section on climbing plants. There are two reasons for this: first, the British like vines and, second, the climate is more favorable than it is in much of Europe and parts of North America, which gives those gardeners a far greater choice. This section is limited to the species, varieties and cultivars that are sufficiently frost-hardy to survive in less temperate areas. If they are not fully hardy, there is a note to that effect. After a succession of mild winters, nurseries tend to offer a wider selection of plants. Be careful! A severe winter will make you regret any impulsive purchases. Vines require a lot of maintenance: fixing wires or trellis, and then pruning later on. If you don't begrudge the effort spent on all that, your home may acquire the romantic atmosphere of an English country house. The heights provided are the maximum heights in meters, with the approximate number of feet in brackets. The "height" will also indicate how a plant can, for instance, be trained horizontally along the eaves.

## Actinidia

**KIWI PLANT, CHINESE GOOSEBERRY**
The small kiwi fruits of the *A. arguta* are edible, as are the larger fruits of the *A. chinensis*, of which a number of cultivars are grown. Although the plants are extensively cultivated in New Zealand, they originally came from China. A male plant is always needed for *A. chinensis* to bear fruits. *A. kolomikta* is cultivated mainly because of its tri-colored leaves. Give it a warm sunny position to let the fruits ripen. The plant produces large white flowers in May–June; the fruits ripen in October.
**Hardiness: US Zone 8-6, Canadian Zone 7-5.**

| | |
|---|---|
| *A. arguta* | white, June, 6m (20ft) |
| A.a 'Issai' | white, June, 6m (20ft) |
| *A. chinensis* | cream, June, 9m (30ft) |
| *A. c.* 'Bruno'* | female |
| *A. c.* 'Hayward' | female |
| *A. kolomikta* | yellowish, June, 5m (16ft) |

*Actinidia chinensis*

## Akebia

This semi-evergreen climber is good for growing into trees. Good soil preparation is essential: sometimes the plant refuses to grow. Provide wires for it to cling to.
**Hardiness: US Zone 6, Canadian Zone 5.**

| | |
|---|---|
| *A. quinata* | lilac, blue, May–June, 12m (40ft) |
| *A. trifoliata* | lilac, June–July, 9m (30ft) |

*Akebia quinata*

## Ampelopsis

At one time, the *Parthenocissus* was also classified as belonging to this genus. The ampelopsis is a smaller, hardy climber which can also be grown in pots or patios and in a cool greenhouse. The deeply lobed leaves with white specks and spots are very attractive.
**Hardiness: US Zone 7, Canadian Zone 6.**

*A. brevipedunculata*
   'Elegans'           variegated leaves, 1m (3ft)

*Ampelopsis brevipedunculata* var. *maximowiczii*

## Aristolochia

**DUTCHMAN'S PIPE**
This plant can climb up a north-facing wall, or preferably up a trellis on the front porch. The name refers to its brownish, pipe-shaped flowers, somewhat resembling old-fashioned German tobacco pipes. Unfortunately, the flowers hide behind the foliage and cannot be seen unless the leaves are held aside.
**Hardiness: US Zone 6, Canadian Zone 5.**

*A. macrophylla*      brownish, 10m (33ft)

## Campsis

**TRUMPET CREEPER**
The plant is self-clinging, but it is best to tie it in a few places to prevent it being blown off the wall when it is older. It is the best climber for a south-facing wall. The plant comes into leaf very late, and after planting it you should not worry too quickly as to whether it is dead.
**Hardiness: US Zone 6, Canadian Zone 5.**

| | |
|---|---|
| *C. grandiflora* | orange red, July–Sept, 10m (33ft) |
| *C. radicans* | orange, July–Sept 10m (33ft) |
| *C. r.* 'Flamenco' | red, Aug–Sept, 8m (26ft) |
| *C. r.* 'Flava' | yellow, Aug–Sept,8m (26ft) |
| *C. tagliabuana*'Mme Galen' | or. red Aug–Sept, 10m (33ft) |

## Carpinus

**HORNBEAM**
What is the European hornbeam doing in a

*Campsis tagliabuana* 'Mme Galen'

*Aristolochia manschurica*

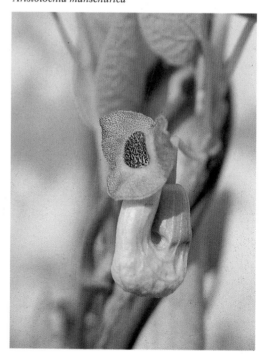

chapter on vines and wall plants? At one time, rooms were often provided with sun blinds, but many of them have disappeared because of high maintenance costs. By way of a substitute, you might plant a *C. betulus* 'Fastigiata' on either side of a window. Planted as a tree (3m/10ft tall), the end result will be rapidly achieved: cut the branches back to 10cm (4in) from the trunk and they will soon produce dense shoots. You will subsequently be able to keep the tree in shape with hedge cutters.
Hardiness: US Zone 6, Canadian Zone 5.

| | |
|---|---|
| *C. betulus* 'Fastigiata' | light green, 3m (10ft) |

## Celastrus

**BITTERSWEET**
This climber may also be grown as a shrub; it is suitable for a pergola or wire fence. Unfortunately, the common bittersweet is not usually supplied by name, which makes it impossible to tell whether you have bought a male or a female plant. With the exception of the 'Hermaphroditus' cultivar, both sexes are needed in order to produce berries. These berries (red balls inside orange and yellow seed vessels) can be dried and preserved.
Hardiness: US Zone 5, Canadian Zone 4.

| | |
|---|---|
| *C. orbiculata* 'Diana' | (female), or. berries, 8m (26ft) |
| *C. scandens* | orange berries, 10m (33ft) |
| *C.s.* 'Indian Brave' | (male), orange berries, 10m (33ft) |
| *C.s.* 'Indian Maid' | (female), orange berries, 10m (33ft) |

*Celastrus scandens*

## Clematis

**OLD MAN'S BEARD**
Except for *C. viticella*, the botanical species and their hybrids are less susceptible to the dreaded clematis wilt. Unfortunately, most of them are still hard to obtain: you should therefore look for a specialized grower. Never grow clematis on a south-facing wall; walls facing south-east or south-west are possible, but even then you should protect the base of the plant from direct sunshine. Many people do that by placing a flat stone against it, but a low-growing evergreen shrub would surely be more attractive. A separate book could be devoted to the large-flowered hybrids. The following list is limited to the most popular cultivars.
Hardiness: US Zone 7-2, Canadian Zone 6-1.

**Botanical species and their hybrids:**

| | |
|---|---|
| *C. alpina*** | 3m (10ft) |
| *C. a.* 'Columbine' | pale blue |
| *C. a.* 'Frances Rives' | blue |
| *C. a.* 'Frankie' | blue |
| *C. a.* 'Magnus Johnson' | bright blue |
| *C. a.* 'Pamela Jackman' | dark blue |
| *C. a.* 'Rosy Pagoda' | bright pink |
| *C. a.* 'Ruby' | dark purplish pink |
| *C. a.* 'Willy' | pale pink |
| *C. a.* 'Frances Rives' | blue |
| *C. a.* 'White Columbine' | white |
| *C. macropetala*** | 3m (10ft) |
| *C. m.* 'Blue Bird' | lilac, blue (d) |
| *C. m.* 'Floralia'* | pale blue |
| *C. m.* 'Jan Lindmark' | blueish violet (d) |
| *C. m.* 'Lagoon' | deep blue (d) |
| *C. m.* 'Maidwell Hall' | lavender blue (d) |
| *C. m.* 'Rosy O'Grady' | deep pink (d) |
| *C. m.* 'White Lady' | white |
| *C. m.* 'White Swan' | white |
| *C. montana* | May–June, 6–12m (20–40ft) |

*Clematis montana*

| | |
|---|---|
| C. m. 'Alexander' | cream |
| C. m. 'Elizabeth' | bright pink |
| C. m. 'Freda' | deep pink |
| C. m. 'Grandiflora' | bright white |
| C. m. 'Marjorie'* | creamy pink |
| C. m. 'Mayleen' | deep pink |
| C. m. 'Picton's Variety' | deep satin pink |
| C. m. var. rubens | pale pink |
| C. m. 'Superba' | white |
| C. m. 'Tetraroze' | lilac, pink |
| C. m. 'Vera'* | deep pink |
| C. orientalis* | yellow, July–Sept, 6m (20ft) |
| C. o. 'Bill Mackenzie' | yellow, July–Sept |

*Clematis viticella* 'Abundance'

| | |
|---|---|
| C. o. 'Bravo'* | yellow, July–Aug |
| C. o. 'Corry' | yellow, July–Sept |
| C. o. 'Golden Harvest'* | yellow, July–Sept |
| C. o. 'Orange Peel' | yellow, July–Sept |
| C. tangutica | yellow, July–Sept, 4m (13ft) |
| C. t. 'Aureolin' | yellow, July–Aug |
| C. vitalba | white, Aug–Oct, 15m (50ft) |
| C. viticella** | June–Aug, 3m (10ft) |
| C. v. 'Abundance' | bright violet |
| C. v. 'Alba Luxurians' | white, July–Sept |
| C. v. 'Blue Bell'* | violet blue |
| C. v. 'Etoile Violette' | violet |
| C. v. 'Kermesina' | deep wine red, Apr–May |
| C. v. 'Little Nell' | white, purple edges |
| C. v. 'Minuet' | cream, pinkish-purple margins |
| C. v. 'Royal Velours' | deep purplish red, June–Sept |
| C. v. 'Rubra' | wine red, May–June |
| C. v. 'Venosa Violacea' | violet, white-veined, May–Aug |

**Some large-flowered hybrids: 3m (10ft)**

| | |
|---|---|
| C. 'Barbara Jackman' | dark purple, July–Sept |
| C. 'Bees Jubilee' | pale pink, July–Sept |
| C. 'Ernest Markham'! | lilac, red, June–Aug |
| C. 'Gipsy Queen' | purple, June–Aug |
| C. 'Hagley Hybrid' | pink, June–Sept |
| C. 'Huldine' | white, July–Aug |
| C. 'Jackmannii' | mauve, May–Aug |
| C. 'Jackmannii Alba' | white, June–Aug |
| C. 'Jackmannii Superba' | mauve, June–Sept |
| C. 'Lady Betty Balfour' | mauvish blue, Aug–Sept |
| C. 'Lasurstern' | lilac, blue, July–Aug |
| C. 'Mme Le Coultre' | large-flowered, white, June–Aug |
| C. 'Mrs. Cholmondeley' | light blue, June–Aug |
| C. 'Miss Bateman' | white, June–Aug |
| C. 'Nelly Moser' | pink-striped, May–Aug |
| C. 'Perle d'Azur' | light blue, July–Sept |
| C. 'Pink Fantasy' | pale pink, July–Sept |
| C. 'Rouge Cardinal'! | wine red, June–Aug |
| C. 'The President' | purplish blue, May–Aug |
| C. 'Ville de Lyon' | "mass"-colored red, May–Aug |
| C. 'Vyvyan Pennell' | mauvish lilac, July–Sept |

*Clematis* 'Ernest Markham'

*Cotoneaster horizontalis*

## Cotoneaster

The deciduous species mentioned below can be grown as ground cover, but also as a low climber for walls. Its branches grow in a characteristic herringbone pattern. The small white flowers are followed in fall by red berries, a great treat for birds. If you grow it against a wall, cut back the protruding branches regularly. Like the pyracantha, the plant is highly susceptible to fireblight and therefore banned from importation into some countries.
**Hardiness: US Zone 6, Canadian Zone 5.**

| | |
|---|---|
| *C. horizontalis* | white, 2m (6ft) |

## Euonymus

The climbing species are all evergreen. *E. japonica* is very frost-tender, and should only be grown on patios or in sheltered courtyards. The following species will only grow adhesive roots if they are trained up a wall. There are many small-leafed cultivars of *E. fortunei*. After the winter they always look rather grubby. Except for *E. japonica*, the following species can also be grown as ground cover.
**Hardiness: US Zone 7-6, Canadian Zone 6-5.**

| | |
|---|---|
| *E. fortunei* var. *radicans* | dull green, 4m (13ft) |
| *E. f.* 'Variegatus'! | variegated leaves, 4m (13ft) |
| *E. f.* 'Vegetus'! | shiny green, 6m (20ft) |
| *E. japonica* | shiny green, 3m (10ft) |
| *E. j.* 'Variegata' | variegated leaves, 3m (10ft) |

## Fallopia

See: *Polygonum*.

*Euonymus fortunei* 'Variegatus'

## Forsythia

The long slender branches of this particular forsythia are convenient for training. The plant flowers a little less exuberantly than the bush forsythia. It is suitable for an east- or a west- facing wall.
**Hardiness: US Zone 7, Canadian Zone 6.**

| | |
|---|---|
| *F. suspensa* | light yellow, March–April, 3m (10ft) |
| *F.s. Sieboldii* | Mar-Apr, 3m (10ft) |
| *F. s.* 'Nymans'** | Mar–Apr, 3m (10ft) |

## Hedera

### IVY

Is there anyone who does not recognize ivy? Even so,

*Forsythia suspensa*

I should like to eliminate a source of misunderstanding: many people conveniently refer to any climber as "ivy." In addition, ivy is often regarded as a villain: the plant is supposed to affect walls and roofs, and even grow through them; it is believed to attract vermin such as mice (and even rats!) as well as insects, birds' nests. Now for the true story: ivy certainly affects pointing if it consists of soft, often limy, mortar. Usually this applies to walls built before 1940. Growing underneath roof shingles occurs only in the event of poor pruning. To prevent ivy growing too thick, it should be trimmed regularly with hedge cutters. What remains is a fine evergreen wall covering which provides excellent insulation. People used to know a good thing when they saw it! It is less well known that there are several species of ivy, and many cultivars of the "common" ivy (*H. helix*). Some of them are frost-tender. The fastest growers are: *H. helix* 'Woerner' and *H. hibernica*. A list of more or less frost-hardy species and cultivars with their leaf characteristics follows (see also: Evergreen shrubs).
**Hardiness: US Zone 6-5, Canadian Zone 5-4.**

| | |
|---|---|
| *H. colchica* | |
| 'Dentata Variegata'** | creamy white margins |

| | |
|---|---|
| *H. helix* | small leaves, dark green |
| *H. h.* 'Baltica' | small leaves |
| *H. h.* 'Caenwoodiana' | pointed |
| *H. h.* 'Deltoidea' | round leaves |
| *H. h.* 'Eva'* | creamy white, yellow margins |
| *H. h.* 'Glacier' | grayish green |
| *H. h.* 'Goldheart' | yellow centers |
| *H. h.* 'Green Ripple'* | deep green, ground cover |
| *H. h.* 'Green Survival'** | ground cover |
| *H. h.* 'Gruno'*! | ground cover |
| *H. h.* 'Irish Lace' | dark green |
| *H. h.* 'Ivalace' | ground cover |
| *H. h.* 'Königer's Auslese' ('Sagittifolia') | round |
| *H. h.* 'Minetta' | ground cover, bushy |
| *H. h.* 'Miniature Needle-point' | dwarf |
| *H. h.* 'Parsley Crested'* | crested at margins |
| *H. h.* 'Pin Oak'** | deeply lobed |
| *H. h.* 'Spletchley' | green, dwarf |
| *H. h.* 'Sulphurea' | yellow variegations |
| *H. h.* 'Très Coupé'* | deeply lobed |
| *H. h.* 'Woerner'* | green, marbled leaves |
| *H. hibernica* | dark green, large |

## Humulus

### HOP
The hop mentioned below may also be regarded

*Hedera helix*

as a perennial plant: it dies down to the soil every year and emerges again in spring. The rising shoots are edible. The female plants are more beautiful than the male ones, and produce those magnificent hops in August. It is a pity that it is impossible to distinguish between male and female plants at the time of purchase: buy three plants, wait and see, and then throw away the male plants. In a private garden they are not needed for pollination. If possible, grow them up free-standing posts to prevent other plants being overgrown by them. Underground runners, which can grow up to several meters (yards) long, need to be removed regularly.
**Hardiness: US Zone 5, Canadian Zone 4.**

| | |
|---|---|
| *H. lupulus* | greenish, Aug–Sept, 10m (33ft) |
| *H. l.* 'Aureus' | yellow leaves, 10m (33ft) |

## Hydrangea

### CLIMBING HYDRANGEA
Although the plant is self-clinging, it should be fixed at a few points: an older plant could be blown right off the wall. The flower stems may project from the wall for up to 50cm (20in), and should be cut back in the fall or early spring. The pale green sprouting leaves and large white flower heads are very beautiful. They should,

*Humulus lupulus* (female)

however, have a sheltered position on a north or east facing wall.
**Hardiness: US Zone 6, Canadian Zone 5.**

*H. petiolaris*!          white, June–Aug, 5m (16ft)

# Jasminum

**JASMIN**
The following jasmines are frost-hardy plants; *J. nudiflorum* (winter jasmine) needs to be tied to the wall. *J. beesianum* has small but intensely pink flowers, and will wind itself round wires. Provide this plant with some protection against the wind.

*Hydrangea petiolaris*

(For other species see: Container plants and some cool-greenhouse plants).
**Hardiness: US Zone 9, Canadian Zone 8.**

*J. nudiflorum*          yellow, Dec–Feb, 3m (10ft)

# Kadsura

The self-twining evergreen Kadsura should be removed from nurseries as the damage this vine has caused to the native flora in parts of the southern states is far too great as it is.

*K. japonica*          cream, June–July, 4m (13ft)

# Lathyrus

See: Perennials and Annuals and biennials.

*Kadsura japonica*

# Lonicera

**HONEYSUCKLE**
This rewarding climber is planted primarily because of its lengthy flowering season and fragrant flowers. It is a twining climber: give it something to wind itself round, preferably near a patio so that you can thoroughly enjoy its evening fragrance. Combine an early- and a late-flowering cultivar. *L. acuminata* is also suitable for ground cover. The shape of the flowers does not differ much, except for the cultivars of *L.* x *brownii*, which have tubular flowers. The plants will grow in any soil in sun or, preferably, semi-shade. Heights do not vary much: between 3m (10ft) and 4m (13ft); *L. japonica* grows up to 6m (20 ft) tall.
**Hardiness: US Zone 8-3, Canadian Zone 7-2.**

*Jasminum nudiflorum*

**Deciduous:**

| | |
|---|---|
| *L.* x *brownii* | |
|    'Dropmore Scarlet' | orange, June–Aug |
| *L. caprifolium** | light yellow, May–June |
| *L.* x *heckrottii* | orange pink, June–Aug |
| *L. h.* 'Goldflame' | orange pink, May–July |
| *L. periclymenum* | yellow and pink, May–Aug |
| *L. p.* 'Belgica Select' | yellow and pink, May–July |
| *L. p.* 'Cream Cloud'**! | whitish, May–Sept |
| *L. p.* 'Serotina'* | purplish red, May–July |
| *L. tellmaniana** | orange yellow, June–Aug |

**Evergreen/semi–evergreen:**

| | |
|---|---|
| *L. acuminata*** | rapid grower |
| *L. henryi* | brownish red, June–Aug |
| *L. japonica* | |
|    'Aureoreticulata' | variegated, yellow, June–Aug |
| *L. j.* 'Halleana'! | cream, May–Aug |
| *L. j.* 'Hall's Prolific'* | pale cream, June–Aug |
| *L. j.* var. *repens** | pale cream, May |
| *L. sempervirens* | orange red, June–July |
| *L. s.* 'Superba'** | red, June–July |

# Magnolia

This species of tree may well be grown as a climber in a cool climate to supplement the restricted range of available evergreen plants. Grow it against a south-facing wall to protect it from cold winds. The flowers are large, as are the leathery leaves.
**Hardiness: US Zone 8, Canadian Zone 7.**

| | |
|---|---|
| *M. grandiflora* | white, May–July, 3m (10ft) |

# Morus

**MULBERRY**

First fix a strong trellis for this climber, which is suitable for a south- or south-east-facing wall. The flowers are not striking, but the fruits are all the more so. The plant has large, light green, irregularly lobed leaves. *M. a.* 'Pendula' needs tying up firmly when it is young; the branches will subsequently become pendulous.
**Hardiness: US Zone 7-5, Canadian Zone 6-4.**

| | |
|---|---|
| *M. alba* 'Pendula' | fruits white or red, 4m (13ft) |
| *M. nigra* | fruits dark red to black, 4m (13ft) |

# Parthenocissus

This is the best self-clinging climber. The plant's decorative features include its young budding

*Lonicera* x *heckrottii*

138

leaves, fall color and berries. It is suitable for south-, east-, or west-facing walls. *P. quinquefolia*, the Virginia creeper, is also suitable for ground cover.

**Hardiness: US Zone 8-5, Canadian Zone 7-4.**

| | |
|---|---|
| *P. henryana**\* | blue berries, 10m (33ft) |
| *P. quinquefolia* | blue berries, 15m (50ft) |
| *P. tricuspidata* | |
| 'Green Spring'\* | large-leafed, 10m (33ft) |
| *P. t.* 'Veitchii' | young leaves purplish, 10m (33ft) |

## *Passiflora*

### PASSION FLOWER

A young passion flower plant can survive a few mild winters in a sheltered position. As the plant grows older, it becomes more tolerant of frost. If the first winter is severe, try again. Give the plant a sheltered position facing south. (For other species, see: Container plants and some cool-greenhouse plants).

**Hardiness: US Zone 9-8.**

| | |
|---|---|
| *P. caerulea* | lilac and white, July–Oct, 10m (33ft) |

*Parthenocissus tricuspidata* 'Veitchii'

## Polygonum

### RUSSIAN VINE

The Russian vine is reputed to be the fastest grower, but *Clematis vitalba* ('Traveller's Joy') surpasses it and has a more beautiful structure. It

*Passiflora caerulea*

is also more tolerant of wet soil. The Russian vine is less robust and will be damaged by frost in such a position. The two species listed below are often confused: they differ in color only. The botanical name also confuses: *Bilderdykia* and *Fallopia* are outdated. It is to be hoped that the name will not change again!
**Hardiness: US Zone 7, Canadian Zone 6.**

| | |
|---|---|
| *P. aubertii* | white and green, July–Oct, 12m (40ft) |
| *P. baldschanicum* | pinkish, July–Oct, 12m (40ft) |

## Prunus

### MORELLO CHERRY

Along with the *Aristolochia* and *Hydrangea*, this is the best plant for a north-facing wall. There is

*Polygonum aubertii*

always a solution for every corner of the garden! Fix wires to the wall before planting the cherry. The plant will only reach the indicated height if it is properly trained (and pruned). Birds are not too fond of this sour cherry.
**Hardiness: US Zone 5, Canadian Zone 4.**

| | |
|---|---|
| *P.* 'Meteor' | white, May, 3m (10ft) |
| *P.* 'Morelo' | white, May, 3m (10ft) |

## Prunus

### PEACH

Like the morello cherry, this is a good plant for

*Prunus* 'Morelo'

training along a wall, but in this instance one facing south or east. In early May you will be surprised by a sea of pink flowers, glossy oblong leaves and, later on of course, fruit. Because of the warmth of the wall, the fruits have more chance of ripening in such a position in a cool climate than if the peach were grown as a free-standing tree. Regularly water the young plants, just like all climbers on an east-facing wall, even if it is raining!
**Hardiness: US Zone 7, Canadian Zone 6.**

*Prunus persica* 'Amsden'

| | |
|---|---|
| *P. persica 'Amsden'**\** | early |
| *P. p.* 'Elberta' | late |
| *P.p.* 'Halehaven' | mid season |
| *P.p.* 'Redhaven' | early |

## *Pyracantha*

### FIRETHORN

The appeal of this evergreen climber is due to its clusters of white flowers and subsequent berries which the birds like so much. Firethorns usually look rather neglected, when in fact they can be trained very successfully. The process must be started when the plant is young and the branches are still flexible. Fix the wires before planting. The plants grow up to 5m (16ft) tall. The clusters of white flowers appear at the end of May.
**Hardiness: US Zone 7, Canadian Zone 6.**

| | |
|---|---|
| *P. coccinea* 'Red Mound' | red |

**Hybrids:**

| | |
|---|---|
| *P.* 'Mohave' | red |
| *P.* 'Orange Charmer' | orange |
| *P.* 'Orange Glow' | orange red |
| *P.* 'Teton' | dwarf |
| *P.* 'Yellow Berried' | yellow |

*Pyracantha* 'Orange Glow'

## *Rubus*

### WINEBERRY

Brambles require a sunny position. The two-year-old branches need to be cut down to the base every year in early spring. During the summer, the sprouting branches should be tied back every week: they are needed for producing the edible bright red fruits the following year. The leaves, the flowers and the densely spiny, reddish branches are all decorative. *R. henryi* is evergreen and bears black fruits. Plant in full sun against a wall or fence. (For blackberries see: Evergreen shrubs).
**Hardiness: US Zone 6, Canadian Zone 5.**

| | |
|---|---|
| *R. phoeniculasius* | white, May–June, 3m (10ft) |

## *Solanum*

### POTATO VINE

The solanum will only do well in sheltered courtyards and cold greenhouses. Protect the base: if the plant is killed off down to the base by frost, it will at least sprout again in spring. For the same reason, it should not be planted in very wet soil, except for the *S. dulcamara* which is very hardy.

*Rubus phoeniculasius*

| | |
|---|---|
| S. crispum | blue, June–Sept, 4m (13ft) |
| S. c. 'Glasnevin'** | blue, July–Sept, 4m (13ft) |
| S. dulcamara | purple, July–Aug, 3m (10ft) |
| S. d. 'Variegata'** | variegated leaves, July–Aug, 3m (10ft) |
| S. jasminoides | mauve, July–Sept, 4m (13ft) |
| S. j. 'Album'** | white, July–Sept, 4m (13ft) |

# Vitis

**VINE**

Some vines are grown for the color of their leaves in summer or fall, others for their

*Solanum crispum 'Glasnevin'*

bunches of grapes. The height of the edible vines (*V. vinifera, V. labruscana*) depends on how it is trained. Training should be started when the plant is very young. Remember that pruning the woody parts must not be done any later than February. The sap that is already rising would otherwise seep through the wound and would be hard to staunch.
**Hardiness: US Zone 6, Canadian Zone 5.**

| | |
|---|---|
| V. amurensis* | fall colors, 8m (26ft) |
| V. coignetiae! | fall colors, 8m (26ft) |
| V. labruscana 'Concord' | blue fruits |
| V. 'Concord Seedless' | blue fruits |
| V. 'Niagara' | white fruits |
| V. vinifera | |
|    'Boskoop Glorie'** | blue fruits |
| V.v. 'Chardonnay' | white fruits |
| V.v. 'Foch' | blue fruits |
| V.v 'Purpurea' | bright red and purple leaves, 8m (26ft) |

# Wisteria

One misunderstanding needs to be cleared up first of all: people often talk about "flowering" and "non-flowering" varieties of wisteria. *W. floribunda* does not flower for about ten years; *W. sinensis* will flower after three years. *W. floribunda*, which is not very fragrant, has longer racemes. The flowers appear at the same time as the leaves. *W. sinensis* is full of shorter racemes before the leaves appear and is fragrant. Because of those differences, they tend to be used in different ways. *W. floribunda* is better for growing over a pergola, where the longer racemes of flowers can hang down freely. *W. sinensis* is suitable for growing against a wall. The difference between the two is apparent at an early age: *W. floribunda* twists clockwise, whereas *W. sinensis* twists anti-clockwise.
**Hardiness: US Zone 7, Canadian Zone 6.**

| | |
|---|---|
| W. floribunda | blue, May–June, 10m (33ft) |
| W. f. 'Longissima Alba'*! | white, May, 10m (33ft) |
| W. f. 'Macrobotrys'! | blue, May, 10m (33ft) |
| W. f. 'Rosea' | mauve, May, 10m (33ft) |
| W. f. 'Violacea Plena'* | lilac, May, 10m (33ft) |
| W. sinensis | blue, May, 12ft, (40ft) |
| W. s. 'Alba' | white, May–June, 12m (40ft) |
| W. s. 'Prolific'* | lilac, Apr–May, 12m (40ft) |

*Wisteria sinensis*

*Vitis coignetiae*

# 7. Perennials

This chapter includes all the common perennials as well as special ones that are readily available or relatively easy to find. Those marked with asterisks are harder to track down, and may involve a time-consuming but pleasurable search for specialist growers/nurseries. Things are changing in the world of perennials: cultivars that were exclusive until quite recently are now popular, whereas others are disappearing. The size of the standard assortment, however, has rapidly increased. The question of where and how to grow the various plants takes pride of place in this chapter: that is the kind of information you need when you are gardening. If a plant is often combined with another one, that is also mentioned. Plants can, of course, be combined in innumerable ways – many more than could ever be incorporated in a single book. You will find a description of the genus as well as details about the color of the flowers, their flowering season and the height of the various species. The height will vary according to the kind of soil and the amount of feeding. In the case of foliage plants, for instance Aceana, the color of the leaves is mentioned as well.

You will find a few symbols and abbreviations:

! = the author is keen on this plant
\* = the plant is difficult to obtain
\*\* = the plant is available only from a few specialized nurseries
(d) = double flowers
(sd) = semi-double flowers

## Acaena

This plant is suitable for ground cover and can be walked on (lightly). The leaves are its main decorative feature. The creamy-white flowers (June-August) are insignificant, but the subsequent burrs form a handsome brownish carpet. Plant in relatively dry soil in full sun to show up the color. The colors in the following list refer to the leaves.
**Hardiness: US Zone 7-6, Canadian Zone 6-5.**

| | |
|---|---|
| A. anserinifolia | gr., large, June–Aug, 15cm (6in) |
| A. buchananii | light blueish green, June–Aug, 10cm (4in) |
| A. magellanica | deep blueish green, June–Aug, 20cm (8cm) |
| A. microphylla | bronzelike green, June–Aug, 10cm (4in) |
| A. m. 'Blue Haze' | gray. blue, June–Aug, 15cm (6in) |
| A. novae-zelandiae | gr., large, June–Aug, 20cm (8in) |

Acaena anserinifolia

## Acanthus

**BEAR'S BREECHES**

Acanthus leaves were often used as decorative features in Greek and Roman architecture; originally in the capitals of Corinthian columns. The acanthus requires a warm position. Tall

spikes of flowers rise above the thorny decorative leaves which resemble those of hogweed.
**Hardiness: US Zone 7, Canadian Zone 6.**

| | |
|---|---|
| A. mollis | pink and white, July–Sept, 1m (3ft) |
| A. hungaricus | pinkish lilac, June–Sept, 1m (3ft) |
| A. spinosus* | mauve, July–Sept, 1m (3ft) |

*Acanthus mollis*

# Achillea

### YARROW

This plant, a handsome plant for a border, is excellent for cutting and also attracts butterflies. It needs dry, sandy soil on reasonably dry

subsoil. The species can be found growing wild in verges. The hybrid cultivars with their stiff regular flower heads can be dried. The plant needs to be divided regularly.
**Hardiness: US Zone 4-3, Canadian Zone 3.**

| | |
|---|---|
| A. filipendulina 'Cloth of Gold' | yellow, July–Sept, 1m (3ft) |
| A. f. 'Parker' | yellow, July–Aug, 1m (3ft) |
| A. millefolium | white, June–Aug, 50cm (20in) |
| A.m. 'Borealis' | pink, July-Aug, 40cm (16in) |
| A. m. 'Cerise Queen' | pinkish red, 50cm (20in) |
| A. m. 'Heidi' | purple, 70cm (28in) |
| A. m. 'Hoffnung' | pale yellow, 60cm (24in) |
| A. m. 'Lilac Beauty' | lilac, 70cm (28in) |
| A.m. 'Paprika' | red, 60cm (24in) |
| A. m. 'Summer Wine' | dark wine red, 70cm (28in) |
| A. m. 'White Beauty' | white, 50cm (20in) |
| A. ptarmica 'Perry's White | white, June–Aug, 70cm (28in) |
| A. p. 'The Pearl' | white (d), June–Aug, 70cm (28in) |
| A. taygetea | pale yellow, June–Aug, 40cm (16in) |
| A. umbellata | white, gray leaves, June–Aug, 20cm (8in) |

**hybrid cultivars:**

| | |
|---|---|
| A. 'Coronation Gold' | soft yel., June–Sept, 80cm (32in) |
| A. 'Credo' | sulfur yel., June–Sept, 1m (3ft) |
| A. 'Martina' | sulfur yellow, June–Sept, 70cm (28in) |
| A. 'Moonshine' | yellow, June–Aug, 60cm (24in) |
| A. 'Schwellenburg' | lem. yel., July–Aug, 30cm (12in) |

*Achillea filipendulina* 'Parker'

*Achillea millefolium* 'Cerise Queen'

## Aconitum

**MONKSHOOD**

The flowers are so shaped that only drones can reach the nectar: a good example of co-operation between a plant and an animal species. Although the plant's growth structure resembles that of the delphinium, it prefers a shady position. The leaves are a handsome shade of dark green, in contrast with those of the delphinium, which are light green. Monkshood is suitable for borders and for cutting; it requires moisture-retentive soil.

**Hardiness: US Zone 5-4, Canadian Zone 4-3.**

| | |
|---|---|
| A. x cammarum 'Bicolor' | blue and white, July–Aug, 1.4m (4ft 6in) |
| A. c. 'Bressingham Spire' | viol. blue, July–Aug, 90cm (36in) |
| A. carmichaelii | blue. violet, Sept–Oct, 1m (3ft) |
| A. henryi 'Spark' | blue. violet, July–Aug, 1.2m (4ft) |
| A. lamarckii* | sulf. yel., June–Aug, 1.2m (4ft) |
| A. lycoctonum: | see A. lamarkii |
| A. napellus | dark blue, June–July, 1.2m (4ft) |
| A. n. 'Album' | white, June–Aug, 1m (3ft) |
| A. n. 'Carneum'* | pink, June–July, 1.4m (4ft 6in) |
| A. n. 'Rubellum' | pale pink, June–Aug, 1m (3ft) |
| A. septentrionale 'Ivorine'* | ivory, May–June, 70cm (28in) |

Aconitum x cammarum 'Bicolor'

## Adonis

The great attraction of this old-fashioned plant is its early florescence and delicate foliage. The plant is suitable for any kind of soil, and likes sun or half-shade. The species amurensis needs rather more protection (see also: Annuals and biennials).

**Hardiness: US Zone 5-4, Canadian Zone 4-3.**

| | |
|---|---|
| A. amurensis | yellow, Mar–May, 30cm (12in) |
| A. a. 'Pleniflora' | yellow (d), Mar–May, 25cm (10in) |
| A. vernalis | golden yellow, Mar–May, 20cm (8in) |

## Ajuga

The ajuga is one of the best plants for ground cover on rich, well-drained soil. Feed it well: after two years the plant tends to be much smaller and to flower less exuberantly. The flowers appear in April–May. Plant in sun or semi-shade. Excellent under planting for spring bulbs. Easily propagated by dividing into individual rosettes or dividing up clumps. Plant just a few at first to find out whether your chosen position is suitable.

**Hardiness: US Zone 3, Canadian Zone 3.**

| | |
|---|---|
| A. reptans 'Alba' | white, green leaves, May–June, 15cm (6in) |
| A. r. 'Atropurpurea' | blue, dark leaves, 15cm (6in) |
| A. r. 'Burgundy Glow' | blue, tricol. leaves, 15cm (6in) |
| A. r. 'Delightful' | blue, whitish pink leaves, 15cm (6in) |
| A. r. 'Jungle Beauty' | blue, 30cm (12in) |
| A. r. 'Multicolor' | blue, varieg. leaves, 20cm (8in) |
| A. r. 'Purple Torch' | purplish pink, green leaves, 15cm (6in) |
| A. r. 'Rosea' | pink. red, red leaves, 20cm (8in) |
| A. r. 'Rubra' | mauv. bl., dark leaves, 15cm (6in) |

Ajuga reptans 'Burgundy Glow'

## Alchemilla

**LADY'S MANTLE**

**LADY'S MANTLE**

This trouble-free edging plant is also suitable for filling parterres, in among roses, and so on. *A. vulgaris* is a botanical species with much smaller flowers. This plant can also grow well in moist grass that is not cut more than twice a year. It needs sun or half-shade.

**Hardiness: US Zone 3, Canadian Zone 3.**

| | |
|---|---|
| *A. alpina* | greenish yellow, May–Sept, 20cm (8in) |
| *A. erythropoda* | pale yel., May–Sept, 30cm (12in) |
| *A. mollis* | yel. gr., June–Aug, 40cm (16in) |
| *A. m.* 'Robustica' | yellow, June–Aug, 50cm (20in) |

*Alchemilla erythropoda*

## Alstroemeria

Alstroemerias are not entirely frost-hardy; keep them covered during the winter. The plant needs full sun and well-drained soil to reduce the risk of damage by frost. The flowers are good for cutting and keep well. In central Chile these plants grow by the wayside like dandelions. They tend to proliferate.

**Hardiness: US Zone 7, Canadian Zone 6.**

| | |
|---|---|
| *A. aurantiaca* | orange, July–Aug, 80cm (32in) |
| *A. a.* 'Orange King' | orange, 90cm (36in) |
| *A. ligtu\** | various pastel shades, July–Aug, 70cm (28in) |

## Althaea

Althaeas resemble hollyhocks but are smaller and are generally less spectacular. The species *ficifolia* and *rosea* are now classified under the genus *Alcea* (see: Annuals and biennials). The plant needs full sun.

**Hardiness: US Zone 4, Canadian Zone 3.**

| | |
|---|---|
| *A. officinalis* | pale pink, May–Sept, 1.7m (5ft 4in) |

## Alyssum

This low-growing ground cover for full sun on dry soil is suitable for edging and for growing over low walls. It is also pretty in between

*Alyssum saxatile*

*Alstroemeria aurantiaca*

paving stones on a patio. It is a pity that the plant looks less attractive after it has flowered.
**Hardiness: US Zone 4, Canadian Zone 3.**

| | |
|---|---|
| *A. montanum* | bright yel, May–June, 20cm (8in) |
| *A. murale* | dark yel., June–Aug, 30cm (12in) |
| *A. saxatile* | golden yel, May–June, 30cm (12in) |
| *A. s.* 'Golddust' | gold. yel., Apr–June, 20cm, (8in) |
| *A. s.* 'Plenum' | yel. (d), May–July, 30cm (12in) |
| *A. s.* 'Sulphureum' | pale yel., Apr–June, 40cm (16in) |

## *Anaphalis*

### PEARL EVERLASTING

The small white papery flowers appear between gray leaves. The anaphalis needs full sun and soil that is not too moist. It is recommended for a gray-and-white border.
**Hardiness: US Zone 3, Canadian Zone 3.**

| | |
|---|---|
| *A. margaritacea* | white, June–Sept, 40cm (16in) |
| *A. m.* 'Neuschnee' | snowy white, July–Sept, 50cm (20in) |

## *Anchusa*

The Italian anchusa is a very hairy, coarse-leafed plant with borage-like flowers. They survive the

*Anaphalis margaritacea*

winter better in well-drained soil. Plant in full sun. Propagate by division.
**Hardiness: US Zone 6, Canadian Zone 5.**

| | |
|---|---|
| *A. azurea* 'Dropmore' | sky blue, June–Sept, 1.25m (4ft 2in) |
| *A. a.* 'Little John' | blue, June–Sept, 40cm (16in) |
| *A. a.* 'Loddon Royalist' | gentian blue, June–Sept, 1m (3ft) |

*Anchusa azurea* 'Loddon Royalist'

147

# Androsace

This low-growing rock plant needs a sunny spot and well-drained soil.
**Hardiness: US Zone 6-5, Canadian Zone 5-4.**

| | |
|---|---|
| A. carnea ssp. *brigantiaca* | white, May–July, 10cm (4in) |
| A. sarmentosa | bri. pink, May–June, 10cm (4in) |
| A. sempervivoides | lilac pink, June–July, 5cm (2in) |

*Androsace sarmentosa*

# Anemone

Anemones with tubers and rhizomes are spring-flowering plants; those listed here flower in fall. Although they come from the whole of southern and eastern Asia, they are called Japanese anemones. Several species have been crossed to create hybrids which are eminently suitable for growing in borders. Propagate by seed.
**Hardiness: US Zone 6-2, Canadian Zone 5-1.**

| | |
|---|---|
| A. hupehensis | pink, Aug–Oct, 60cm (24in) |
| A. h. 'Prinz Heinrich' | purpl. red, Aug–Oct, 80cm (32in) |
| A. h. 'September Charm' | d. pink, Aug–Oct, 90cm (36in) |
| A. h. 'Splendens' | deep purplish red, Sept–Oct, 80cm (32in) |
| A. x hybr. 'Elegans' | pink, Aug–Oct, 80cm (32in) |
| A. 'Honorine Jobert' | white, long-flowering, 1.2m (4ft) |
| A. 'Königin Charlotte' | purplish pink, Sept–Oct, 1m (3ft) |
| A. 'Margarette' | pink (d), Aug–Oct, 80cm (32in) |
| A. 'Pamina' | d. red (d), Sept–Oct, 80cm (32in) |
| A. 'Robustissima' | bright pink, July–Sept, 1m (3ft) |
| A. 'Whirlwind' | white, Sept–Oct, 90cm (36in) |
| A. x lesseri | carmine red, May–June, 25cm (10in) |
| A. multifida | creamy white, June–July, 25cm (10in) |

| | |
|---|---|
| A. rioularis* | white, blue outside, June–July, 80cm (32in) |
| A. sylvestris | white, May–July, 25cm (10in) |
| A. s. 'Macrantha'* | white, May–July, 30cm (12in) |
| A. tomentosa 'Robustissima' | bri. pink, Aug–Oct, 80cm (32in) |

# Anethum

This plant is known as dill, a culinary herb, but its delicate foliage also looks pretty in a border. It has umbelliferous flowers, and resembles fennel which grows in similar places.
**Hardiness: US Zone 6, Canadian Zone 5.**

| | |
|---|---|
| A. graveolens | yel. gr., June–July, 60cm (24in) |

*Anethum graveolens*

*Anemone 'Honorine Jobert'*

## Antennaria

### CAT'S EARS

Antennaria is a very low-growing ground-cover plant for the driest possible soil in full sun. It can be walked on (lightly) when not in flower. The grayish leaves are wooly and look well in rockeries or growing over walls.
**Hardiness: US Zone 3, Canadian Zone 3.**

| | |
|---|---|
| A. dioica | p. white, May–June, 10cm (4in) |
| A. d. var. borealis | white, May–June, 10cm (4in) |
| A. d. 'Rubra' | candy p., May–June, 10cm (4in) |

Antennaria dioica 'Rubra'

## Anthemis

### CHAMOMILE, DOG FENNEL

The common anthemis with its small daisy-like flowers is a long-flowering plant for dry and sunny positions. It needs well-drained soil and full sun.
**Hardiness: US Zone 4, Canadian Zone 3.**

| | |
|---|---|
| A. carpatica | white, May–July, 15cm (6in) |
| A. cretica var. cupaniana | white, 50cm (20in) |
| A. x hybr. 'E.C. Buxton' | lem. yel., June–Sept, 80cm (32in) |
| A. hybr. 'Kelwayi' | yellow, June–Sept, 80cm (32in) |
| A. h. 'Wargrave' | pale yel., June–Sept, 80cm (32in) |

Anthemis cretica var. cupaniana

## Aquilegia

### COLUMBINE

Like peonies and asters, this is an old-fashioned perennial. Aquilegias are also sold as seeds, but then they are mixed. You can collect seed yourself from the best plant and sow it, even though the plant will not always keep its color. It needs sun or half-shade. The height may vary. When combining them with other plants, remember that aquilegias always flower between May and July.
**Hardiness: US Zone 5-3, Canadian Zone 4-3.**

| | |
|---|---|
| A. alpina | d. blue, May–June, 70cm (28in) |
| A. caerulea | blue and yellow, 50cm (20in) |
| A. chrysantha 'Yellow Queen' | golden yellow, 60cm (24in) |
| A. clematifolia | lilac and white, no spurs, Apr–May, 45cm (18in) |
| A. flabellata 'Alba' | white, May–June, 20cm (8in) |
| A. viridiflora | greenish yellow, May–June, 25cm (10in) |
| A. vulgaris | purplish blue, 50cm (20in) |
| A. v. 'Nivea' | white, 50cm (20in) |
| A. v. 'Plena' | mixed (d), 75cm (30in) |
| **Hybrid cultivars:** | |
| A. 'Biedermeier' | mixed, June–July, 40cm (16in) |
| A. 'Crimson Star' | carm. red and white, 60cm (2ft) |
| A. 'Ministar' | blue and white, 15cm (6in) |
| A. 'Nora Barlow' | red and white (d), 80cm (32in) |
| A. 'Rosea' | pink, 60cm (2ft) |
| A. 'Silver Queen' | white, 50cm (20in) |

Aquilegia 'Nora Barlow'

# Arabis

This undemanding, fully evergreen plant is suitable for edging and growing over low walls in full sun. It is undemanding. *A. procurrens* has white flowers, but there is also a variegated cultivar.
**Hardiness: US Zone 7-4, Canadian Zone 6-3.**

| | |
|---|---|
| *A.* x *arendsii* 'La Fraicheur' | pink, April–May, 15cm (6in) |
| *A. a.* 'Rosabella' | purplish pink, large, Apr–May, 15cm (6in) |
| *A. blepharophylla*\* | pink, Mar–Apr, 10cm (4in) |
| *A. caucasica* 'Bakkely' | white, Apr–May, 20cm (8in) |
| *A. c.* 'Pinkie' | dark pink, Apr–May, 10cm (4in) |
| *A. c.* 'Plena' | white, full, Apr–May, 15cm (6in) |
| *A. c.* 'Rosea' | pink, Apr–May, 20cm (8in) |
| *A. c.* 'Schneehaube' | white, Apr–May, 20cm (8in) |
| *A. c.* 'Snow Cap' | white, Apr–May, 20cm (8in) |
| *A. c.* 'Variegata' | white, white margins to leaves, Apr–May, 20cm (8in) |
| *A. ferdinandi-coburgii* | white, Apr–June, 15cm (6in) |

*Arabis arendsii* 'Rosabella'

# Armeria

**SEA PINK, THRIFT**

Thrift tolerates salty sea breezes and even salty soil. This rock plant needs full sun and is also suitable for edging purposes. The leaves are grass-like although the plant does not belong to any of the grass families. Regular renewal is required to avoid the deteriorating appearance of the plant's center.
**Hardiness: US Zone 8-4, Canadian Zone 7-3.**

| | |
|---|---|
| *A. girardii* | pale pink, May–July, 10cm (4in) |
| *A. maritima* | pink, May–July, 15cm (6in) |
| *A. m.* 'Alba' | white, May–July, 20cm (8in) |
| *A. m.* 'Düsseldorfer Stolz' | carmine red, May–July, 15cm (6in) |
| *A. m.* 'Splendens' | pinkish red, 15cm (6in) |

| | |
|---|---|
| *A. pseudoarmeria* | lilac pink, May–July, 25cm (10in) |
| *A. p.* 'Bees Ruby' | clear purplish red, May–July, 40cm (16in) |

# Artemisia

**WORMWOOD**

Wormwood is familiar as a culinary herb but the species described here are decorative as well as aromatic foliage plants, essential for a gray and white garden. The flowers are insignificant. Like most gray-leafed and gray wooly plants, they need full sun. *A. abrotanum* (lad's love, old man, southernwood), *A. absinthium* (wormwood), *A. dracunculus* (tarragon) and *A. vulgaris* are all herbs. Drought is not a problem and the plants will

*Artemisia smidtiana* 'Nana'

*Armeria maritima*

grow in any kind of soil. Except for *A. lactiflora*, all the following have gray leaves.

**Hardiness: US Zone 5-3, Canadian Zone 4-2.**

| | |
|---|---|
| *A. abrotanum* | gray leaves, 90cm (36in) |
| *A. arborescens* 'Powis' | July–Sept, 60cm (24in) |
| *A. lactiflora* | creamy white, Aug–Sept,1.75m (5ft) |
| *A. ludoviciana* 'Silver Queen' | silvery, 60cm (24in) |
| *A. l.* 'Valerie Finnis' | coarse leaves, 40cm (16in) |
| *A. smidtiana* 'Nana' | silvery white, 20cm (8in) |
| *A. stelleriana* | white felt-like, yellow flowers, 40cm (16in) |

## Aruncus

This ideal plant for growing by itself in a shady position is also suitable for borders and woodland areas. The strong plants have loose plumes of flowers resembling those of astilbes. Plant in moist positions to prevent the leaves dying off too early in the season.

**Hardiness: US Zone 6-4, Canadian Zone 5-3.**

| | |
|---|---|
| *A. aetusifolius* | cr. white, May–July, 30cm (12in) |
| *A. dioicus* | cr. white, June–July, 1.5m (5ft) |
| *A. d.* 'Kneiffii' | delicate leaves, June–Aug, 50cm (20in) |
| *A.d.*'Zweiweltenkind' | white, red leaves, July–Aug, 1.5m (5ft) |

*Aruncus aetusifolius*

## Asarum

### WILD GINGER

Wild ginger is suitable for deepest shade and moist soil – is there anyone who can still claim that there is so little choice for a shady garden? The flowers are produced underneath the leaves and are almost invisible. *A. nadense* has dull leaves; the smaller leaves of *A. europaeum* are shiny dark green. Both are evergreen.

**Hardiness: US Zone 5-4, Canadian Zone 6-5.**

| | |
|---|---|
| *A. canadense* | purple, Mar–Apr, 15cm (6in) |
| *A. europaeum*! | purple, Mar–Apr, 10cm (4in) |

*Asarum europaeum*

## Asclepias

### BUTTERFLY WEED

This plant needs a warm sunny position in dry soil. Growth is slow in spring, and it is not easily transplanted. Seed pods are showy and can be used in dry flower arrangements The plants spread slowly using underground rhizomes.

**Hardiness: US Zone 4-3, Canadian Zone 3-2.**

| | |
|---|---|
| *A. syriaca* | purpl. pink, July–Sept, 2m (6ft) |
| *A. tuberosa* | orange, July–Sept, 50cm (20in) |

*Asclepias tuberosa*

# Asphodeline

**YELLOW ASPHODEL**

This grass-like Mediterranean plant needs a dry sunny position. With its green fruits at the end of the dead flower spikes, it looks old-fashioned and exotic. Propagate by division; the seeds will produce flowering plants after three years.
**Hardiness: US Zone 8-6, Canadian Zone 7-5.**

| | |
|---|---|
| *A. liburnica*\* | yellow, May–June, 90cm (36in) |
| *A. lutea*! | yellow, May–June, 80cm (32in) |

# Aster

**MICHAELMAS DAISY**

There is a huge diversity: tall plants that need supports, and others low and bushy. So be careful what you order! There are even some summer-flowering cultivars. They all need sun. The leaves of some low-growing species are affected by mildew in fall, which makes them less attractive. The species *cordifolius*, *ericoides* and *lateriflorus* have small flowers resembling gypsophila. By way of exception, *A. linosyrus* has golden yellow flowers with insignificant petals. Although not all cultivars are likely to be immediately available everywhere, they can be ordered from specialist nurseries.
**Hardiness: US Zone 4-3, Canadian Zone 3-2.**

| | |
|---|---|
| *A.* x *alpellus* 'Triumph' | blue with orange centers, June–July, 20cm (8in) |
| *A. alpinus* | bl. purple, May–June, 20cm (8in) |
| *A. a.* 'Albus' | white, May–June, 20cm (8in) |
| *A. a.* 'Dunkele Schöne' | violet, May–June, 30cm (12in) |
| *A. a.* 'Goliath' | light blue, Apr–June, 20cm (8in) |
| *A. a.* 'Happy End' | pink, May–June, 30cm (12in) |
| *A. amellus* 'Blue King' | viol. blue, Aug–Sept, 60cm (24in) |
| *A. a.* 'Breslau' | viol.pur., Sept–Oct, 40cm (16in) |
| *A. a.* 'Joseph Lakin' | light blueish mauve, Aug–Oct, 50cm (20in) |
| *A. a.* 'King George' | viol. blue, Aug–Oct, 60cm (24in) |
| *A. a.* 'Lac de Genève' | soft blue, Aug–Oct, 60cm (24in) |
| *A. a.* 'Peach Blossom' | viol. pink, Aug–Oct, 60cm (24in) |
| *A. a.* 'Rudolf Goethe' | lav. blue, Aug–Sept, 60cm (24in) |
| *A. a.* 'Veilchenkönigin' | deep viol. Aug–Sept, 50cm (20in) |
| *A. cordifolius* 'Ideal' | light violet blue, June–Aug, 90cm (36in) |
| *A. c.* 'Little Carlow' | blue, Sept–Oct, 80cm (32in) |
| *A. c.* 'Lovely'! | pink, Aug–Sept, 70cm (28in) |
| *A. divariticus* | white, Sept–Oct, 60cm (24in) |
| **A. dumosus hybrids:** | |
| *A. d.* 'Alice Haslam' | pink. red, Sept–Oct, 30cm (12in) |
| *A. d.* 'Audrey' | dark pink, Aug–Oct, 50cm (20in) |
| *A. d.* 'Blue Baby' | pure blue (sd), Aug–Oct, 25cm (10in) |
| *A. d.* 'Herbstgrüss von Bresserhof' | lilac, Sept–Oct, 35cm (14in) |
| *A. d.* 'Jenny' | red (d), Aug–Oct, 30cm (12in) |
| *A. d.* 'Lady in Blue' | blue (sd), Sept–Oct, 25cm (10in) |
| *A. d.* 'Oktoberschnee-kupfel' | white, Sept–Oct, 40cm (16in) |
| *A. d.* 'Peter Harrison' | pink, Aug–Oct, 30cm (12in) |
| *A. d.* 'Peter Pan' | br. pink, Aug–Oct, 25cm (10in) |
| *A. d.* 'Prof A. Kippenberg' | lav. blue, Sept–Oct, 40cm (16in) |
| *A. d.* 'Rosenwichtel' | br. pink, Aug–Oct, 20cm (8in) |
| *A. d.* 'Schneekissen' | white, Sept–Oct, 25cm (10in) |
| *A. d.* 'Snowsprite' | white (sd), Sept–Oct, 50cm (20in) |
| *A. ericoides* 'Blue Star' | lav. blue, Sept–Oct, 80cm (32in) |
| *A. e.* 'Brimstone' | w./yel., Sept–Oct, 60cm (24in) |
| *A. e.* 'Cinderella' | pale lilac, Sept–Oct, 80cm, (32in) |
| *A. e.* 'Esther' | pink, Sept–Oct, 60cm (24in) |
| *A. e.* 'Herbstmyrte' | violet, Aug–Oct, 90cm (36in) |
| *A. e.* 'Schneetanne' | white, Aug–Oct, 1.8m (5ft 8in) |
| *A. laevis* | lilac, Sept–Oct, 1.5m (5ft) |
| *A. lateriflorus* 'Coombe Fishacre'! | lil. pink, Sept–Oct, 80cm (32in) |
| *A. l.* 'Horizontalis'! | pink. lilac, Aug–Oct, 80cm (32in) |
| *A. novae-angliae* 'Barr's Blue' | purpl. blue, Aug–Oct, 1.5m (5ft) |
| *A. n.* 'Barr's Pink' | bright pink, Aug–Oct, 1.5m (5ft) |
| *A. n.* 'Harrison's Pink' | salmon pink,Aug–Oct, 1.25m (4ft 2in) |
| *A. n.* 'Roter Stern' | crimson, Aug–Oct, 1.5m (5ft) |
| *A. novi belgii* 'White Lady's' | white, Aug–Oct, 1m (3ft) |
| *A. n.* 'Winston Churchill' | crimson, Aug–Oct, 90cm (36in) |
| *A. n.* 'Burgundy Glow' | wine red, Aug–Sept, 70cm (28in) |
| *A. sedifolius* 'Nanus' | lil. blue, Aug–Sept, 50cm (20in) |
| *A. tongolensis* 'Berggarten' | May–June, 60cm (24in) |

*Aster* x *alpellus* 'Triumph'

| | |
|---|---|
| *A. t.* 'Napsbury' | dark lilac, yellow center, May–July, 40cm (16in) |
| *A. t.* 'Wartburgstern' | lilac, yellow center, May–June, 60cm (24in) |

*Aster sedifolius* 'Nanus'

## Astilbe

Astilbes are divided into several groups with one thing in common: their beautiful vigorous plumes. If planted in a moist position, the leaves will not curl up and turn brown. It is therefore best to grow them in the shade. A garden without astilbes is almost inconceivable! Note the height to which the plants will grow before planting them. **Hardiness: US Zone 6-5, Canadian Zone 5-4.**

*Astilbe* 'Sprite'

| | |
|---|---|
| *A. chinensis* 'Finale' | br. pink, Aug–Sept, 50cm (20in) |
| *A. c.* 'Intermezzo' | sal. pink, July–Sept, 50cm (20in) |
| *A. c.* 'Pumila' | lil. pink, July–Sept, 30cm (12in) |
| *A. c.* 'Serenade' | pink.red, July–Sept, 45cm (18in) |
| *A. c.* 'Superba' | purpl. pink, July–Sept, 1.2m (4ft) |
| *A. c.* 'Veronica Klose' | dark purplish pink, Aug–Sept, 40cm (16in) |
| ***Arendsii* hybrids:** | |
| *A.* 'Amethyst' | mauve lilac, July–Aug, 80cm (32in) |
| *A.* 'Bressingham Beauty' | pink, July–Aug, 90cm (36in) |
| *A.* 'Bridal Veil' | white, June-July, 80cm (32in) |
| *A.* 'Bumalda' | white and pink, June–July, 40cm (16in) |
| *A.* 'Cattleya' | deep pink, July–Aug, 1m (3ft) |
| *A.* 'Erika' | pink, July–Aug, 80cm (32in) |
| *A.* 'Etna' | dark red, July–Aug, 60cm (24in) |
| *A.* 'Fanal' | pom. red, July–Aug,60cm (24in) |
| *A.* 'Feuer' | coral, Aug–Sept, 60cm (24in) |
| *A.* 'Gloria | deep pink, July–Aug, 80cm (32in) |
| *A.* 'Glut' | fluor. red, Aug–Sept, 80cm (32in) |
| *A.* 'Irrlicht' | light pinkish white, July–Aug, 60cm (24in) |
| *A.* 'Snowdrift' | white, July–Aug, 70cm (28in) |
| *A.* 'Weisse Gloria' | white, July–Aug, 90cm (36in) |
| ***Crispa* hybrids:** | |
| *A.* 'Liliput' | sal. pink, July–Aug, 20cm (8in) |
| *A.* 'Perkeo'! | dark pink, July–Aug, 20cm (8in) |
| ***Japonica* hybrids:** | |
| *A.* 'Deutschland' | br. white, June–July, 50cm (20in) |
| *A.* 'Europa' | br. pink, June–July, 50cm (20in) |
| *A.* 'Koblenz' | carm. red, July–Aug, 50cm (20in) |
| *A.* 'Peach Blossom' | light salmon pink, July–Aug, 50cm (20in) |
| *A.* 'Red Sentinel' | dark red, July–Aug, 50cm (20in) |
| *A.* 'Rheinland' | carm. pink, June–July, 60cm (24in) |
| *A.* 'Vesuvius' | carm. red, July–Aug, 60cm (24in) |
| ***Simplicifolia* hybrids:** | |
| *A.* 'Aphrodite' | pink, June–Aug, 50cm (20in) |
| *A.* 'Bronze Elegans' | pink, July–Aug, 30cm (12in) |
| *A.* 'Buchanan' | cr. white, July–Aug, 30cm (12in) |
| *A.* 'Dunkellachs' | salmon pink, brown foliage, July–Aug, 30cm (12in) |
| *A.* 'Praecox Alba' | white, July–Aug, 50cm (20in) |
| *A.* 'Sprite' | soft pink, Aug–Sept, 40cm (16in) |
| ***Thunbergii* hybrids:** | |
| *A.* 'Moerheimii' | cream, July–Aug, 80cm (32in) |
| *A.* 'Prof Van der Wielen' | white, July–Aug, 125m, (4ft 2in) |

## Astilboides

This plant is frequently sold under its former name *Rodgersia*. If planted in semi-shade in moist soil, the leaves will not die prematurely. The plant will be less affected by late night frosts

if it is grown under trees or close up against the house. The arching plumes provide another focal point. Even the small green fruits on the faded plumes are highly decorative.
**Hardiness: US Zone 6, Canadian Zone 5.**

*A. tabularis*! cream, June–July, 1m (3ft)

*Astilboides tabularis*

*Aubrieta* 'Red Carpet'

## *Astrantia!*

**MASTERWORT**

Astrantias are popular for flower arrangements and borders: they are sturdy plants, flower for a long period, and are suitable for sunny or shady positions – the choice is yours. It is best to plant them in moist soil.
**Hardiness: US Zone 5, Canadian Zone 4.**

| | |
|---|---|
| *A. carniolica* 'Rubra'* | wine red, July–Aug, 50cm (20in) |
| *A. major* | greenish white and pink, July–Aug, 70cm (28in) |
| *A. m.* 'Alba' | white, June–Aug, 60cm (24in) |
| *A. m.* 'Lars'* | dark red, June–Oct, 80cm (32in) |
| *A. m.* 'Margery Fish'* | white and green |
| *A. m.* 'Rosea' | pink and green, 50cm (20in) |
| *A. m.* 'Rosensinfolie'* | reddish, 75cm (30in) |
| *A. m.* 'Rubra' | purplish red, 70cm (28in) |
| *A. m.* 'Shaggy'* | white and green, June–Sept, 80cm (32in) |
| *A. maxima* | silvery pink, June–July, 50cm (20in) |

## *Aubrieta*

This mat-forming plant resembles arabis and is suitable for edging, ground cover, in between paving stones, and especially for clambering over walls. Aubrietias need a sunny position that

*Astrantia major* 'Rubra'

is not too dry. Propagation is easiest by division in fall, but sowing in April is also possible; the plants will flower the following year. Aubrietias start flowering shortly after the last frost; all of them flower in April and May. Their maximum height is 10cm (4in).
**Hardiness: US Zone 5, Canadian Zone 4.**

**Hybrid cultivars:**

| | |
|---|---|
| A. 'Argenteovariegata' | light mauve, variegated leaves |
| A. 'Blue King' | soft violet |
| A. 'Cascade Blue' | blue |
| A. 'Cascade Purple' | purplish blue |
| A. 'Cascade Red' | carmine red |
| A. 'Double Stockflowered Pink' | pale pink (d), large |
| A. 'Dr. Mules' | blue violet |
| A. 'Gloriosa' | pink |
| A. 'Golden Emperor' | violet, leaves with golden variegations |
| A. 'Hendersonii' | light blue |
| A. 'Leightlinii' | carmine pink |
| A. 'Red Carpet' | deep red |
| A. 'Novalis' | clear blue |
| A. 'Royal Red' | deep red |
| A. 'Vera Prichard' | pink |
| A. 'Whitewell Gem' | violet purple, large |

## *Aurinia*

See: *Alyssum*.

## *Azorella*

This ground-covering plant has small green leaves and needs well-drained soil and sun or semi-shade.
**Hardiness: US Zone 7, Canadian Zone 6.**

| | |
|---|---|
| *A. trifurcata* | yel. green, June–July, 10cm (4in) |

*Azorella trifurcata*

## *Bergenia*

This evergreen plant has large leaves and is suitable for edging, in borders, or in parterres. The leaves of some cultivars turn reddish in winter. Plant in sun or half-shade and divide regularly.
**Hardiness: US Zone 4-3, Canadian Zone 3.**

| | |
|---|---|
| *B. cordifolia* | lilac pink, Mar–May, 40cm (16in) |
| *B. c.* 'Purpurea' | purp. red, Mar–May, 40cm (16in) |
| *B. purpurascens* | dark lilac red, Apr–May, 40cm (16in) |

**Hybrid cultivars**:

| | |
|---|---|
| *B.* 'Abendglut' | dark red, Mar–May, 25cm (10in) |
| *B.* 'Baby Doll' | pale to bright pink, Apr–May, 25cm (10in) |
| *B.* 'Bressingham Salmon' | salmon pink, Apr–May, 30cm (12in) |

*Bergenia* 'Silberlicht'

| | |
|---|---|
| *B.* 'Bressingham White' | white and pale pink, Apr–May, 40cm (16in) |
| *B.* 'Glockenturm' | pink. red, Mar–May, 60cm (24in) |
| *B.* 'Morgenröte' | dark purplish red, Mar–May, 40cm (16 in) |
| *B.* 'Öschberg' | pinkish red, 50cm (20in) |
| *B.* 'Perfect' | bright lilac red, Apr–May, 60cm (24in) |
| *B.* 'Silberlicht' | white, pink later, Apr–May, 40cm (16in) |
| *B.* 'Sunningdale' | carmine lilac, Apr–May, 45cm (18in) |
| *B.* 'Wintermärchen' | red, Apr–May, 40cm (16in) |

# Bletilla

This undemanding hardy orchid needs an eye-catching position by a patio, in open ground, full sun and well-drained soil.
**Hardiness: US Zone 7, Canadian Zone 6.**

| | |
|---|---|
| *B. striata* | lilac pink, June–July, 40cm (16in) |
| *B. s.* 'Alba' | white, May–June, 30cm (12in) |

*Bletilla striata* 'Alba'

# Borago

**BORAGE**

This undemanding plant for any condition is perennial but also self-seeds. The flowers are edible and look decorative in salads (see also: Annuals and Biennials).
**Hardiness: US Zone 7, Canadian Zone 6.**

| | |
|---|---|
| *B. pygmeae***! | pale bl., June–Sept, 40cm (16in) |

# Brunnera

**SIBERIAN BUGLOSS**

This shade-loving plant for borders or wooded corners of the garden has highly decorative, large, round, dark green leaves and small blue flowers. It is suitable for rather moist soil.
**Hardiness: US Zone 4, Canadian Zone 3.**

| | |
|---|---|
| *B. macrophylla* | sky blue, Apr–May, 60cm (24in) |
| *B. m.* 'Variegata' | blue, variegated leaves, 50cm (20in) |

*Brunnera macrophylla*

# Buphtalmum

**YELLOW OX-EYE**

This bright yellow, daisy-like flower provides a cheerful splash of color in midsummer. Ox-eyes need a sunny position and are especially good for cutting. The plant has no other special requirements. For *B. speciosum* see *Telekia*, whose flowers really do resemble ox-eyes.
**Hardiness: US Zone 4, Canadian Zone 3.**

| | |
|---|---|
| *B. salicifolium* | yellow, June–Sept, 50cm (20in) |

# Caltha

**MARSH MARIGOLD, KINGCUP**

See: Water plants.

# Campanula

**BELLFLOWER**

There are tall campanulas for flower borders (they need staking) and low ones which are more suitable for rockeries. They flourish in any kind of soil and need full sun. *C. rapunculoides* is invasive and should be avoided. *C. punctata* is good for shady locations. Campanulas of any kind are among the most rewarding of all garden plants.

**Hardiness: US Zone 7-4, Canadian Zone 6-3.**

| | |
|---|---|
| *C. carpatica* | blue, June–Aug, 30cm (12in) |
| *C. c.* 'Alba' | white, June–Aug, 30cm (12in) |
| *C. c.* 'Blue Clips' | sky blue, June–Aug, 20cm (8in) |
| *C. c.* 'Karl Foerster' | blue, June–Aug, 20cm (8in) |
| *C. c.* 'Kobaltglocke' | d. blue, June–Aug, 20cm (8in) |
| *C.c.* 'White Clips' | white, June–Aug, 20cm (8in) |
| *C.c* 'White Star' | white, June–Aug, 20cm (18in) |
| *C. c.* 'White Star' | June–Aug, 25cm (10in) |
| *C. garganica* | lilac, Apr–May, 10cm (4in) |
| *C. glomerata* 'Alba' | white, May–June, 70cm (28in) |

| | |
|---|---|
| *C. g.* 'Joan Elliott' | d. blue, May–July, 60cm (24in) |
| *C. g.* 'Schneekrone' | br. white, May–June, 50cm (20in) |
| *C. g.* 'Superba'! | d. violet, June–July, 40cm (16in) |
| *C. lactiflora* | viol. bl., June–July, 90cm (36in) |
| *C. l.* 'Loddon Anne' | lil. pink, June–Aug, 90cm (36in) |
| *C. l.* 'Prichard's Variety' | viol. blue, June–Aug, 60cm (24in) |
| *C. latifolia* var. *macrantha* | mauv. blue, June–Aug, 1m (3ft) |
| *C. l.* 'Alba' | white, June–Aug, 1m (3ft) |
| *C. persicifolia* | br. blue, June–July, 80cm (32in) |
| *C. p.* 'Alba' | white, June–July, 80cm (32in) |
| *C. p.* 'Coerulea' | pure blue, June–July, 80cm (32in) |
| *C. portenschlageana*! | mauvish blue, June–Sept 20cm(8in) |

*Campanula garganica*

*Buphtalmum salicifolium*

| C. p. 'Resholt' | d. blue, June–Sept, 10cm (4in) |
| C. poscharskyana! | viol. blue, June–July, 25cm (10in) |
| C. p. 'E.H. Frost' | porcelain white, blue center, June–July, 15cm (6in) |
| C. punctata | pink, July-Aug, 60cm (24in) |
| C. x pulloides 'G.F.Wilson' | bl. mauve, July–Aug, 15cm (6in) |
| C. pyramidalis | blue, dark center, July–Sept, 1.2m (4ft) |
| C. p. 'Alba' | white, July–Sept, 1.2m (4ft) |
| C. rapunculoides | br. violet, June–Aug, 80cm (32in) |

Campanula portenschlageana

## Cardamine

**BITTER CRESS**

The common bitter cress is suitable for planting in damp grass that is cut late in the season. No further care is required. *C. trifolia* can be used for

Cardamine pratensis

evergreen ground cover and can be walked on. Plant in a shady and moderately damp position.
**Hardiness: US Zone 5-3, Canadian Zone 4-3.**

| C. pratensis | l. mauve, May–June, 30cm (12in) |
| C. p. 'Plena' | light mauve (d) |
| C. trifolia*! | white, May–June, 10cm (4in) |

## Centaurea

**KNAPWEED**

Perennial centaureas are far larger than the wild annual cornflowers. If you cut back *C. montana* immediately after they have bloomed, they will flower for a second time. Centaureas look very well in old-fashioned gardens. Support them before they are blown over. *C. macrocephala* looks more like an artichoke than a cornflower.
**Hardiness: US Zone 5, Canadian Zone 5.**

| C. dealbata | purplish pink, June–Aug, 60cm (24in) |
| C. macrocephala | yellow, July–Aug, 1.25m (50in) |
| C. montana | cornflower blue, May–Sept, 70cm (28in) |
| C. m. 'Alba' | white, May–Sept, 70cm (28in) |
| C. m. 'Grandiflora' | viol. blue, June–Aug, 50cm (20in) |
| C. m. 'Purham Variety'* | lilac mauve, May–Sept, 70cm (28in) |

Centaurea montana

# Centranthus

### RED VALERIAN

The pinkish red color of the flowers and sea-green leaves do not blend in well with most other plants. It might be better to choose the white variety – if you can find it! The plant will tolerate extremely dry conditions and even grow on top of brick walls constructed with lime-rich mortar.
**Hardiness: US Zone 6, Canadian Zone 5.**

| | |
|---|---|
| C. ruber | fuchsia pink, June–Aug, 80cm (32in) |
| C. r. 'Albus' | white, June–Aug, 70cm (28in) |
| C. r. 'Coccineus' | pink. red, June–Aug, 70cm (28in) |

*Centranthus ruber* 'Albus'

# Cerastium

### SNOW IN SUMMER

Cerastiums are the most suitable edging plants for a dry position in full sun. Let them clamber over a low wall if possible. *C. biebersteinii* has grayish-green leaves; *C. tomentosum* has gray leaves; and *C. t.* var. *columnae* has silvery white leaves.
**Hardiness: US Zone 4, Canadian Zone 3.**

| | |
|---|---|
| C. biebersteinii | white, May–June, 20cm (8in) |
| C. tomentosum | white, May–June, 15cm (6in) |
| C. t. var. columnae | white, May–June, 10cm (4in) |

# Ceratostigma

In spring, this plant looks as though fall has already arrived, a point that is not in its favor. Plant in sun or half-shade, preferably in dry sandy soil.

**Hardiness: US Zone 7, Canadian Zone 6.**

| | |
|---|---|
| C. plumbaginoides | gentian blue, Aug–Sept, 30cm (12in) |
| C. willmottianum | gentian blue, Aug–Oct, 90cm (36in) |

*Ceratostigma plumbaginoides*

# Chelone

### TURTLE-HEAD

This undemanding plant is suitable for cutting and will grow in any soil in sun or semi-shade without needing to be staked. Turtle-heads will

*Cerastium tomentosum*

provide late-season color in flower borders.
**Hardiness: US Zone 5, Canadian Zone 5.**

| | |
|---|---|
| C. obliqua | pink, July–Oct, 70cm (28in) |
| C. o. 'Alba' | white, July–Sept, 60cm (24in) |

*Chelone obliqua*

## Chiastophyllum

This genus was formerly called *Cotyledon*. The arching sprays of small yellow flowers are unlike those of any other plant. The succulent leaves grow in rosettes. The plant requires full sun and moderately dry soil.
**Hardiness: US Zone 5, Canadian Zone 5.**

| | |
|---|---|
| C. oppositifolium | yellow, June–July, 20cm (8in) |

*Chiastophyllum oppositifolium*

## Chrysanthemum

**PERENNIAL CHRYSANTHEMUM, MARGUERITE**

This extensive genus includes tall and low-growing botanical species as well as various groups of hybrids: the former *Pyrethrums* (painted daisies) now come under *Coccineum* hybrids. Marguerites are classified as *Maximum* hybrids, with the exception of *C. leucanthemum*. Pay special attention to the various heights! You will find the fall chrysanthemums under *Rubellum* hybrids. They are all undemanding garden plants suitable for a position in full sun.
**Hardiness: US Zone 5-2, Canadian Zone 4-2.**

| | |
|---|---|
| C. arcticum 'Roseum' | soft pink, Sept–Oct, 40cm (16in) |
| C. leucanthemum | |
|   'Maikönigin' | white, Apr–May, 70cm (28in) |
| C. serotinum | w., yel center, Sept–Oct, 2m (6ft) |
| ***Maximum* hybrids - marguerite:** | |
| C. 'Alaska' | w., yel. center, June–July, 1m (3ft) |
| C. 'Silver Princess' | white, yellow center, June–July |
| C. 'Snow Dwarf Lady' | white, yellow center, May–July, 20cm (8in) |
| C. 'Wirral Supreme' | w.(d), July–Aug, 90cm (36in) |
| ***Coccineum* hybrids (formerly: *Pyrethrum*):** | |
| C. 'James Kelway' | scarlet, May–June |
| C. 'Robinson's Red' | bri. red, May–June, 70cm (28in) |
| C. 'Robinson's Rose' | pink, May–June, 80cm (32in) |
| ***Rubellum* hybrids:** | |
| C. 'Clara Curtis' | pure pink, Sept–Oct, 80cm (32in) |
| C. 'Mary Stoker' | soft yellow, Sept–Oct, 1m (3ft) |

*Chrysanthemum* 'Wirral Supreme'

## Cimicifuga

**BUGBANE**

Grow this plant in the shade at the back of a border or in a wild garden. The tall bright spikes of flowers resemble candles. The flowers bend over when it rains. Plant bugbane in humus-rich woodland soil. The long flower stems will need some support.

**Hardiness: US Zone 5-4, Canadian Zone 4-3.**

| | |
|---|---|
| C. acerina | white, Aug–Sept, 80cm (32in) |
| C. dahurica | cr. white, Aug–Sept, 1.5m (5ft) |
| C. racemosa | white, Sept–Oct, 2m (6ft) |
| C. r. 'Atropurpurea'* | red leaves, Aug–Oct, 1.5m (5ft) |
| C. simplex 'White Pearl' | white, Oct–Nov, 1.25m (4ft 2in) |

*Cimicifuga dahurica*

## Clematis

The name clematis usually brings to mind vines, but there are also several less familiar species which do not have climbing tendencies and die down to the soil every year. In order to resist the notorious clematis wilt, plant clematis a little deeper than usually.

**Hardiness: US Zone 5-4, Canadian Zone 4-3.**

| | |
|---|---|
| C. x bonnstedtii 'Crepuscule' | light blue, July–Oct, 1m (3ft) |
| C. x durandii | indigo blue, July–Oct, 2.5m (8ft) |
| C. douglasii var. scottiae* | viol.blue, May–June, 50cm (20in) |
| C. integrifolia | viol. bl., June–Sept, 60cm (24in) |
| C. jouiana 'Mrs Robert Brydon' | creamy blue, July–Aug, 2.5m (8ft) |
| C. j. 'Praecox' | creamy lilac, Aug–Sept, 1.5m (5ft) |
| C. recta | white, Aug–Sept, 2m (6ft) |
| C. recta 'Purpurea'! | white, July–Aug, 2m (6ft) |

## Codonopsis

Although this perennial is not very well known, some thirty species are cultivated. The bell-shaped flowers do not have eye-catching colors, but add an extra dimension to nature's rich variety of forms. Plant close to a path or patio as the delicate little plants are not very striking from a distance.

**Hardiness: US Zone 5, Canadian Zone 4.**

| | |
|---|---|
| C. clematidea* | light bl., July–Aug, 40cm (16in) |

## Convallaria

**LILY-OF-THE-VALLEY**

This fragrant plant is related to Solomon's seal. The low-growing plants can cover large areas in semi-shade. Propagation is simply by division in summer.

**Hardiness: US Zone 4, Canadian Zone 3.**

| | |
|---|---|
| C. majalis | white, May, 20cm (8in) |
| C. m. 'Rosea' | pale pink, May, 20cm (8in) |

*Convallaria majalis*

*Clematis integrifolia*

## Coreopsis

These native summer-flowering perennials should be given a position in full sun. They are undemanding and good for cutting.

**Hardiness: US Zone 5-4, Canadian Zone 4-3.**

C. grandiflora 'Badengold' yellow, July–Aug, 1m (3ft)
C. g. 'Sonnenkind'      gold. yel., June–Aug, 30cm (12in)
C. g. 'Sunray'          d. yellow, June–Sept, 75cm (30in)
C. lanceolata 'Baby Gold' yellow, July–Sept, 50cm (20in)
C. l. 'Sterntaler'      yel., brownish ring, 40cm (16in)
C. rosea 'American
  Dream'!               d. pink, June–Sept, 30cm (12in)
C. verticillata!        yellow, July–Sept, 50cm (20in)
C. v. 'Grandiflora'     d. yellow, July–Oct, 60cm (24in)
C. v. 'Moonbeam'!       lem. yel., July–Oct, 40cm (16in)
C. v. 'Zagreb'          yellow, July–Oct, 25cm (10in)

Coreopsis rosea 'American Dream'

## Cornus

Dogwood requires humus-rich soil; the rhizomes will only push their way through a thick layer of leaf mould or peat, which always needs to be slightly moist. The flowers are followed by bright red fruits.

**Hardiness: US Zone 2-3, Canadian Zone 2-1.**

C. canadensis           creamy white, May–June,
                        15cm (6in)

## Corydalis

The Corydalis rewards you with a long flowering season and lovely delicate light green foliage. Plant in half-shade in moisture-retentive soil. C. lutea can self seed extensively; keep it within bounds! The plant is undemanding (see also: Bulbs and tuberous plants).

**Hardiness: US Zone 5, Canadian Zone 4.**

C. cheilantifolia       yellow, May–June, 20cm (8in)
C. lutea                yellow, June–Oct, 40cm (16in)
C. ochroleuca*          creamy white, July–Aug,
                        30cm (12in)

Corydalis lutea

Cornus canadensis

# Cotula

It is possible to walk – lightly – on this mossy-looking plant. Its flowers are insignificant: small creamy yellow buttons in July–August. Plant in moisture-retentive soil in full sun or semi-shade. **Hardiness: US Zone 8, Canadian Zone 7.**

| | |
|---|---|
| C. hispida | gray foliage, June–Aug, 5cm (2in) |
| C. potentillina | gray. green, July–Aug, 5cm (2in) |
| C. squalida | green, June–Aug, 10cm (4in) |

Cotula hispida

# Crambe

**SEA KALE**

Grown by itself at the edge of a large lawn, sea kale resembles a giant version of gypsophila. Plant in well-drained humus-rich soil; the plant may be damaged by frost in an excessively moist spot. Sea kale needs a sunny position. The bleached leaf stems of the much shorter *C. maritima* may be eaten as a vegetable. **Hardiness: US Zone 6, Canadian Zone 5.**

| | |
|---|---|
| C. cordifolia! | white, large leaves, June–July, 3m (10ft) |
| C. maritima | white, gray leaves. May–June, 70cm (28in) |

# Cymbalaria

**KENILWORTH IVY, IVY-LEAFED TOADFLAX**

This plant can cover large areas clambering over walls in the rockery, but also grows in stony soil and in walls in the shade. Although cymbalarias looks so fragile, they are tolerant of considerable drought. It is best to plant them in limy soil. The small flowers look more striking in full sun; the leaves will develop better in semi-shade. **Hardiness: US Zone 8-5, Canadian Zone 7-4.**

| | |
|---|---|
| C. aquitriloba* | violet and yellow, May–Aug, 5cm (2in) |
| C. hepaticifolia* | white-veined leaves, May–Sept, 5cm (2in) |
| C. muralis | lilac, May–Nov, 10cm (4in) |

# Darmera

**UMBRELLA PLANT**

This plant is still sold under the name *Peltiphyllum*. It bears pink flowers on bare stems which emerge straight from the soil. The large round leaves appear later and turn a magnificent shade of red in fall. The

Crambe cordifolia

Cymbalaria muralis

leaves may suffer serious damage from unexpected frost as they emerge, but this does not matter in the long run: new leaves will be formed nevertheless.
**Hardiness: US Zone 6, Canadian Zone 5.**

| | |
|---|---|
| *D. peltata* | pink, Apr–May, 75cm (30in) |

*Darmera peltata*

# Delphinium

Delphiniums require full sun and need staking. They look well  combined with large-flowered perennials, but also with roses and lilies. The flowers are good for cutting. If cut back immediately after flowering (June–July), they may produce somewhat shorter blooms later in the season. The following list is merely a brief selection from the vast assortment. Take special note of the various heights.
**Hardiness: US Zone 4, Canadian Zone 3.**

**Small-flowered hybrids, branching plants:**

| | |
|---|---|
| *D. grandiflorum* | |
| 'Blue Dwarf' | blue, June–Sept, 20cm (8in) |
| *D. g.* 'Butterfly' | navy blue, June–July, 25cm (10in) |

**Belladonna hybrids:**

| | |
|---|---|
| *D. bellamosum* | dark blue, 1.2m (4ft) |
| *D.* 'Blue Bees' | blue, June–Aug, 80cm (32in) |
| *D.* 'Clivedon Beauty' | dark blue, 90cm (36in) |
| *D.* 'Moerheimii' | white, 1.25m (4ft 2in) |
| *D.* 'Piccolo' | bright blue, June–Aug, 1m (3ft) |
| *D. nudicaule* | or. red, June–July, 40cm (16in) |
| *D.* x *ruysii* 'Pink Sensation' | pink, June–July, 80cm (32in) |

**Large-flowered hybrids, flower spikes:**

| | |
|---|---|
| *D.* 'Astolat' | pink, black eyes, 1.5m (5ft) |
| *D.* 'Azurriese' | azure, white eyes, 1.7m (5ft 4in) |

| | |
|---|---|
| *D.* 'Black Knight' | dark violet blue, 1.5m (5ft) |
| *D.* 'Blue Bird' | gentian blue with white eyes, 1.5m (5ft) |
| *D.* 'Blue Jay' | blue with white eyes, 1.5m (5ft) |
| *D.* 'Blue Whale' | blue with brown eyes, 2m (6ft) |
| *D.* 'Capri' | bright blue with white eyes, 80cm (32in) |
| *D.* 'Galahad' | snow-white with large spikes, 1.5m (5ft) |
| *D.* 'Guinevere' | mauve, 1.5m (5ft) |
| *D.* 'King Arthur' | violet with white eyes |
| *D.* 'Lady Guinevere' | mauve lilac with light blue, 1.5m (5ft) |
| *D.* 'Percival' | white, black eyes, 1.75m (5ft) |
| *D.* 'Polar Night' | blueish violet, 1.25m (4ft 2in) |
| *D.* 'Summer Skies' | blue, white centers, 1.5m (5ft) |
| *D.* 'Sungleam' | pale yellow, 1.5m (5ft) |
| *D.* 'Waldenburg' | deep dark blue with black eyes, 1.5m (5ft) |
| *D.* 'Zauberflöte' | blue with pink and white eyes, 1.8m (5ft 8in) |

# Dianthus

### CARNATION PINK

Carnations and pinks are a matter of personal taste: some people love them and others hate them. It is important to know that the flowers of *D. plumarius* are always flattened when it rains.

*Delphinium* 'Polar Night'

The plants are suitable for borders and for edging purposes. *D. deltoides* (Maiden pink) is one of the best rock plants. Occasional renewal is required. All carnations and pinks need full sun.
**Hardiness: US Zone 4, Canadian Zone 3.**

*Dicentra spectabilis* 'Alba'

| | |
|---|---|
| *D. allwoodii* 'Romeo' | reddish brown, white margins, May–Aug, 40cm (16in) |
| *D. deltoides* 'Albiflorus' | white, pink rings, June–Sept, 15cm (6in) |
| *D.d.* 'Brilliant' | crimson, 15cm (6in) |
| *D. d.* 'Flashing Light' | br. red, June–Aug, 20cm (8in) |
| *D. plumarius* 'Albus Plenus' | white (d), May–July, 30cm (12in) |
| *D.p.* 'Cheyenne' | bright pink (d), June-Sept, 30cm (12in) |
| *D.p.* 'Cyclops' | deep red, June-July, 30cm (12in) |
| *D. p.* 'Helen' | pink, May–July, 20cm (8in) |
| *D. p.* 'Heidi' | carmine red (d), May–July, 40cm (16in) |
| *D.p.* 'John Ball' | white, red eye (d), 30cm (12in) |
| *D. p.* 'Munot' | d. red, June–Sept, 40cm (16in) |
| *D. p.* 'Rose de Mai' | sal. red (d), June–Aug, 30cm (12in) |
| *D.p.* 'Mrs Sinkins' | white (d), June-July, 30cm (12in) |

## *Dicentra*

### BLEEDING HEARTS

There are tall as well as low-growing species.

*Dianthus allwoodii* 'Romeo'

The *eximina* cultivars have gray bedewed leaves, which makes them the very best kind of plants for a gray-and-white border. This old-fashioned garden plant, which belongs to the *Papaveraceae* family, prefers semi-shade.
**Hardiness: US Zone 5-3, Canadian Zone 4-2.**

| | |
|---|---|
| *D. eximina* 'Alba' | white, May–Sept, 30cm (12in) |
| *D. e.* 'Boothman's Variety' | soft pink, May–Sept, 30cm (12in) |
| *D. formosa* 'Bountiful' | carmine pink, May–Sept, 40cm (16in) |
| *D. f.* 'Luxuriant' | purplish pink, May–Sept, 40cm (16in) |
| *D. spectabilis* | pinkish red, May–June, 60cm (24in) |
| *D. s.* 'Alba' | white, May–June, 50cm (20in) |

## Dictamnus

### GAS PLANT

If you hold a lighted match to this plant on a still summer evening, a large flame will shoot up above the spikes of flowers and cause a herbal fragrance to be released. This does not harm the flowers. Plant in full sun in rather dry soil. Note the names: 'Albiflorus' is white, but not *D. albus*.
**Hardiness: US Zone 4, Canadian Zone 3.**

*Dictamnus albus*

| | |
|---|---|
| *D. albus*! | purpl. pink, June–July, 70cm (28in) |
| *D. a.* 'Albiflorus' | white, June–July, 60cm (24in) |

## Digitalis

### FOXGLOVE

The species listed below may be classified as perennial; see also under Annuals and biennials. Foxgloves grow naturally in cleared woodland and on the fringes of woods. The plant therefore requires sun or semi-shade. Plant in moisture-retentive humus-rich soil.
**Hardiness: US Zone 7-4, Canadian Zone 6-3.**

| | |
|---|---|
| *D. ferruginea* | brownish yellow, June–Aug, 1.25m (4ft 2in) |
| *D. grandiflora* | yellow, June–July, 80cm (32in) |
| *D. lutea* | pale yel., June–July, 80cm (32in) |
| *D. mertonensis* | sal. pink, May–June, 80cm (32in) |

## Dodecatheon

### SHOOTING STARS

The soil must be rich in humus, nutrients, and be moist. The plant is closely related to primulas and cyclamens, and is most like the latter. The

*Digitalis mertonensis*

flower stems emerge from a rosette of leaves. The height depends largely on the kind of soil, and the plants seem to prefer humus-rich clay.
**Hardiness: US Zone 5-4, Canadian Zone 4-3.**

| | |
|---|---|
| D. jeffryi* | lilac, Apr–May, 20cm (8in) |
| D. meadia | pink, May–June, 40cm (16in) |
| D. m. 'Album' | white, May–June, 40cm (16in) |
| D. pulchellum | pinkish purple, May–June, 30cm (12in) |
| D. p. 'Red Wings' | reddish, May–June, 30cm (12in) |

*Dodecatheon pulchellum* 'Red Wings'

## Doronicum

**LEOPARD'S BANE**

These rewarding plants bear yellow flowers in spring. Camouflage the leaves of *D. orientale*, which soon become ugly, by placing a taller plant in front of them. They will grow in any soil in sun or semi-shade.
**Hardiness: US Zone 6-5, Canadian Zone 5-4.**

| | |
|---|---|
| D. orientale | gold yel., Apr–May, 50cm (20in) |
| D. o. 'Finesse' | yellow, May–June, 50cm (20in) |
| D. o. 'Magnificum'* | yellow, Apr–June, 50cm (20in) |
| D. pardalianches | yellow, June–July, 80cm (32in) |
| D. plantagineum | yellow, June–July, 90cm (36in) |
| D. p. 'Excelsum' | br. yel., May–June, 1.25m (4ft 2in) |

## Draba

**YELLOW WHITLOW GRASS**

This low cushion-forming and delicate-looking plant is suitable for ground cover and thrives beside low walls and other dry spots in full sun. *D. aizoides* is

now called *D. lasiocarpa*, an evergreen plant.
**Hardiness: US Zone 5-1, Canadian Zone 4-1.**

| | |
|---|---|
| D. lasiocarpa | sul. yellow, Apr–May, 5cm (2in) |
| D. sibirica | yellow, Apr–Aug, 10cm (4in) |

*Draba lasiocarpa*

## Dryas

**MOUNTAIN AVENS**

This evergreen ground cover for full sun is suitable for rockeries or an alpine patio garden in containers. Dryas requires limy soil.
**Hardiness: US Zone 1, Canadian Zone 1.**

| | |
|---|---|
| D. octopetala | white, June–Sept, 10cm (4in) |
| D. x suendermanii | cream, June–Sept, 15cm (6in) |

*Dryas octopetala*

*Doronicum pardalianches*

## Duchesnea

### INDIAN STRAWBERRY

This luxuriant ground cover for any kind of soil bears small tasteless red strawberries. Only its flowers differs from those of the wild strawberry, which are white.
**Hardiness: US Zone 4, Canadian Zone 3.**

| | |
|---|---|
| *D. indica* | yellow, June–Sept, 20cm (8in) |

*Duchesnea indica*

## Echinacea

### CONEFLOWER

The genus *Echinacea* has been separated from that of *Rudbeckia*. Echinaceas are vigorous native perennials which do not need support. The flowers have strong stems and are suitable for cutting.

*Echinacea purpurea*

**Hardiness: US Zone 4, Canadian Zone 3.**

| | |
|---|---|
| *E. purpurea*! | purplish pink, July–Sept, 80cm (32in) |
| *E. p.* 'Leuchtstern' | purplish red, July–Sept, 80cm (32in) |
| *E. p.* 'Bright Star' | white, dark center, July–Sept, 80cm, (32in) |

## Echinops

### GLOBE THISTLE

This tall perennial with bluish gray leaves attracts many butterflies; the flowers are suitable for drying. It requires full sun to half-shade and does well in any kind of soil.
**Hardiness: US Zone 5-4, Canadian Zone 4-3.**

| | |
|---|---|
| *E. banaticus* | violet blue, July–Aug, 1m (3ft) |
| *E. b.* 'Blue Globe' | dark blue, July–Sept, 1m (3ft) |
| *E. b.* 'Taplow Blue' | blue, July–Sept, 1m (3ft) |
| *E. ritro* | blue, July–Sept, 1m (3ft) |

## Epimedium

This evergreen perennial requires a sheltered spot in acid soil. If its position is excessively windy, the leaves will dry up and turn brown in winter. The plant should therefore be grown in a half-shady to shady position.
**Hardiness: US Zone 5, Canadian Zone 4.**

| | |
|---|---|
| *E. grandiflorum* | white, May–June, 30cm (12in) |
| *E. x rubrum* | red/yel., May–June, 25cm (10in) |
| *E. x versicolor* 'Sulphureum' | yellow, May–June, 25cm (10in) |
| *E. youngianum* 'Niveum' | white, May–June, 25cm (10in) |
| *E. y.* 'Roseum' | pink, May–June, 25cm (10in) |

Right: *Echinops banaticus* 'Taplow Blue'
*Epimedium youngianum* 'Roseum'

## Eremurus

FOXTAIL LILY, KING'S SPEAR

See: Bulbs and tuberous plants.

## Erigeron

FLEABANE

Erigerons require full sun; suitable for cutting, their flowers resemble asters. There are many cultivars. They are undemanding and will thrive in any kind of soil.
**Hardiness: US Zone 3, Canadian Zone 2.**

| | |
|---|---|
| *E. speciosus* | lilac blue, May–Aug, 50cm (20in) |
| **Hybrid cultivars:** | |
| *E.* 'Dignity' | pink, June–Aug, 40cm (16in) |
| *E.* 'Darkest of All' | d. violet, June–Sept, 50cm (20in) |
| *E.* 'Foersters Darling' | pinkish red (sd), June–Aug, 60cm (24in) |
| *E.* 'Pink Jewel' | pink, May–Aug, 50cm (20in) |
| *E.* 'Pink Triumph' | pink (d), June–Aug, 60cm (24in) |
| *E.* 'Red Sea' | d.red, June–Aug, 60cm (24in) |
| *E.* 'Black Sea' | viol. blue, June–Aug, 60cm (24in) |
| *E.* 'Summer Snow' | white, June–Aug, 60cm (24in) |

*Erigeron* 'Pink Triumph'

## Erodium

This perennial is sometimes invasive; it resembles the geranium. The difference is in the flower stem, which reminds one of the curved neck of a heron, whereas the geranium has a straight stem like a stork's neck. Don't bother too much about finding a suitable position – the plant will thrive almost anywhere in the garden.
**Hardiness: US Zone 9-5, Canadian Zone 8-4.**

| | |
|---|---|
| *E. manescavii* | purpl. pink, June–Sept, 40cm (16cm) |
| *E. reichardii* 'Album' | white, May–Aug, 5cm (2in) |
| *E.* x *variabele* 'Bishop's Form' | purplish pink, June–Sept, 5cm (2in) |
| *E. v.* 'Flore Pleno' | pink (d), June–Sept, 5cm (2in) |
| *E. v.* 'Roseum' | purpl. pink, June–Sept, 5cm (2in) |

*Erodium* x *variabele* 'Bishop's Form'

## Eryngium

SEA HOLLY

Sea holly requires dry sandy soil and bright sunshine, which also shows up the color of the leaves to better advantage. It is suitable for borders and rock gardens. The flowers are suitable for cutting and drying.
**Hardiness: US Zone 7-4, Canadian Zone 6-3.**

| | |
|---|---|
| *E. agavifolium* | gr. white, July–Sept, 1.5m (5ft) |
| *E. alpinum* 'Blue Star' | d. blue, June–Aug, 80cm (32cm) |
| *E. bourgatii* | steel blue, July–Sept, 50cm (20in) |
| *E. giganteum* | cream, July–Aug, 70cm (28in) |
| *E.* x *oliverianum* | blue, July–Aug, 75cm (30in) |
| *E. planum* | light blue, July–Aug, 1m (3ft) |
| *E. p.* 'Blue Dwarf' | d. blue, July–Aug, 60cm (24in) |

*Eryngium planum* 'Blue Dwarf'

## *Eupatorium*

This tall perennial blooms in fall and should form part of every border for that reason. It also attracts many butterflies. The plant is undemanding and will thrive in full sun or half-shade. The common name for *E. purpureum* is Joe Pyeweed.
**Hardiness: US Zone 5-4, Canadian Zone 4-3.**

| | |
|---|---|
| *E. cannabinum* | pink, July–Sept, 1.25m (4ft 2in) |
| *E. c.* 'Plenum' | pink (d), Aug–Sept, 1.5m (5ft) |
| *E. maculatum* | |
| 'Atropurpureum' | deep pink, Aug–Sept, 2m (6ft) |
| *E. m.* 'Album'*! | white, Aug–Sept, 2.2m (6ft 8in) |
| *E. purpureum* | purplish pink, Aug–Sept, 2m (6ft) |
| *E. rugosum*! | white, July–Aug, 1m (3ft) |

*Eupatorium purpureum*

## *Euphorbia*

**SPURGE**

Euphorbias look well in a green and yellow border, and need well-drained soil in full sun. *E. cyparissias* in particular may be repeated throughout a border. The others are suitable for borders as well as for solitary positions. Plant them in full sun or semi-shade; they are undemanding as far as soil is concerned. It is said that this plant keeps away moles. Some people are allergic to the plant's milky sap.
**Hardiness: US Zone 6-4, Canadian Zone 5-3.**

| | |
|---|---|
| *E. amygdaloides* | yellow, leaves green, Apr–May, 40cm (16in) |
| *E. a.* 'Purpurea' | red leaves, Apr–May, 40cm (16in) |
| *E. cyparissas* | yellowish green, Apr–July |
| *E. griffithii* | red, May–July, 60cm (24in) |
| *E. myrsinites* | yellow, Apr–May, 25cm (10in) |
| *E. polychroma* | yel. green, May–June, 40cm (16in) |

*Euphorbia myrsinites*

## *Filipendula*

**MEADOWSWEET**

With the exception of *F. vulgaris*, meadowsweet is a plant for sun to half-shade in moist soil. Its full, graceful plumes are its principal beauty. The plants look well in borders and beside the water.
**Hardiness: US Zone 5-4, Canadian Zone 4-3.**

| | |
|---|---|
| *F. palmata* | pale pink, June–Aug, 90cm (36in) |
| *F. p.* 'Nana' | deep pink, July–Aug, 20cm (8in) |
| *F. purpurea* | pink. red, June–Sept, 70cm (28in) |

F. rubra 'Venusta Magnifica'pink, June–Aug, 2.5m (8ft)
F. vulgaris                  white, June–Aug, 60cm (24in)
F. v. 'Plena'                white (d), June–Aug, 40cm (16in)

*Filipendula rubra* 'Venusta Magnifica'

## Foeniculum

### FENNEL

Fennel looks wonderful in between tall hybrid tea
roses. The bright colors of the roses are mellowed to
some extent by its delicate foliage. But beware: fennel
may self-seed alarmingly! Cut back several stems
before the longest day to extend its flowering season.
**Hardiness: US Zone 5, Canadian Zone 4.**

F. vulgare              yel. green, June–Sept, 1.5m (5ft)
F. v. 'Bronze Giant'    yellowish green, June–Sept,
                        1.7m (5ft 4in)
F. v. 'Purpureum'       yellowish green, June–Sept,
                        1.5m (5ft)

## Fuchsia

See: Deciduous shrubs.

## Gaillardia

### BLANKET FLOWER

This plant's daisy-like flowers are good for cutting
and look best in full sun. It is not the prettiest of

border plants, and is therefore more suitable for a
special section for cut flowers, where it will flower
over a long period. Gaillardias thrive in any kind of
soil provided it is well drained.
**Hardiness: US Zone 4, Canadian Zone 3.**

**Hybrid cultivars:**
G. 'Aurea Pura'      yellow, June–Sept, 60cm (24in)
G. 'Bremen'          yellow, red ring, June–Sept,
                     70cm (28in)
G. 'Burgundy'        br. red, June–Sept, 50cm (20in)
G. 'Dazzler'         golden yellow, brownish red
                     center, July–Sept, 40cm (16in)
G. 'Goblin'          yel/red, June–Sept, 35cm (14in)

*Gaillardia* 'Kobold'

*Foeniculum vulgare*

| G. 'Golden Goblin' | yellow, June–Sept, 40cm (16in) |
| G. 'Monarch Strain' | yel., red margins, June–Sept, 60cm (24in) |

## Galium

### BEDSTRAW

Galiums are suitable for borders and edging purposes, and really belong in a herb garden. (A small sprig adds a distinctive flavor to white table wine). Propagate the plant by dividing the fast-growing clumps; this can be done in the second year, so there is no need to buy large quantities. Some wild galiums are available from specialist nurseries. One of them is *G. verum*, which is suitable for ground cover and will thrive in any kind of soil. It will tolerate sun at any time of day.

*Galium odoratum*

**Hardiness: US Zone 5, Canadian Zone 5.**

| G. odoratum | white, May–June, 30cm (12in) |

## Gaura

This gracefully arching, grass-like plant with its red-spotted leaves needs to be sheltered from the wind. The plants may be grown individually between paving stones or cobbles provided their position is in full sun or half-shade.

**Hardiness: US Zone 5, Canadian Zone 4.**

| G. lindheimeri | pinkish white, July–Sept, 1m (3ft) |
| G. l. 'Whirling Butterflies' | white, July–Oct, 1m (3ft) |

## Gentiana

### GENTIAN

Gentians require special care and cool, moist, well-drained soil is essential. It may be five years before *G. lutea* flowers. These expensive plants are only worth planting if the soil is genuinely suitable for them.

*Gentiana septemfida*

*Gaura lindheimeri*

| | |
|---|---|
| G. acaulis | d. blue, Apr–May, 15cm (6in) |
| G. asclepidea | br. blue, Aug–Oct, 50cm (20in) |
| G. cruciata | br. blue, July–Aug, 25cm (10in) |
| G. dahurica | d. blue, June–Sept, 20cm (8in) |
| G. lutea** | yellow, July–Sept, 1.5m, (5ft) |
| G. septemfida | blue, green centers, July–Sept, 20cm (8in) |
| G. sino–ornata | light blue, greenish stripes, Sept–Oct, 15cm (6in) |
| G. tibetica | cream, July–Aug, 40cm (16in) |
| G. triflora | blue, Aug–Oct, 1.2m (4ft) |

## Geranium

### CRANESBILL

Plant geraniums in moisture-retentive soil in semi-shade: they tend to droop in full sun. *G. phaeum* requires deep shade; *G. nodosum* needs shade. This species provides garden designers with unlimited opportunities: the blue, mauve, pink, and white flowers can go in any border except those with red, yellow, or orange flowers. The differences in the size of flowers and in the foliage are so great that several species will fit into a border. Within the scope of this book it is impossible to mention every species or the ever-increasing number of cultivars. *G. robertianum* self-seeds extensively and is therefore suitable for a wild garden or in old garden walls.
**Hardiness: US Zone 6-4, Canadian Zone 5-3.**

| | |
|---|---|
| G. cantabrigiense 'Biokovo' | white and pink, May–June,15cm (6in) |
| G. cinereum 'Ballerina'! | lil. pink, June–Sept, 15cm (6in) |
| G. c. 'Splendens' | pink. red, June–July, 10cm (4in) |
| G. clarkii 'Kashmir White' | pink, white veins, June–July, 30cm (12in) |
| G. dalmaticum 'Roseum' | pink, June–July, 15cm (6in) |
| G. endressii | soft pink, June–Aug, 30cm (12in) |
| G. e. 'Wargrave Pink' | sal. pink, June–Aug, 30cm (12in) |
| G. eriostemum | lilac blue, June–Aug, 40cm (16in) |
| G. macorrhizum 'Bevan's Variety' | pinkish red, June–July, 30cm (12in) |
| G. m. 'Ingwerson's Variety' | viol. p., June–July, 30cm (12in) |
| G. m. 'Spessart'! | white, red calyx, June–July, 30cm (12in) |
| G. magnificum | violet, June–Aug, 50cm (20in) |
| G. nodosum | lil. pink, June–July, 30cm (12in) |
| G. phaeum | deep brownish purple, May–July, 50cm (20in) |
| G. p. 'Album' | white, May–July, 50cm (20in) |
| G. p. 'Lily Lovell'*! | lilac, May–July, 50cm (20in) |
| G. platypetalum | br. blue, June–Aug, 40cm (16in) |
| G. pratense | soft blue, June–Aug, 70cm (28in) |
| G. p. 'Galactic' | white, June–Aug, 50cm (20in) |
| G. p. 'Grandiflorum' | |
| G. p. 'Johnson's Blue' | br. blue, June–July, 50cm (20in) |
| G. renardii | white, leaves gray, June–July, 25cm (10in) |

| | |
|---|---|
| G. robertianum | mauve, May–Oct, 20cm (8in) |
| G. sanguineum | red, June–Aug, 20cm (8in) |
| G. s. 'Album' | white, June–Sept, 20cm (8in) |
| G. s. 'Max Frei' | pur. red, June–Aug, 20cm (8in) |
| G. s. 'Nanum' | pur. red, June–Sept, 15cm (6in) |
| G. sylvaticum | viol. red, June–July, 50cm (20in) |

*Geranium cinereum* 'Splendens'

| | |
|---|---|
| G. s. 'Album' | white, buds pink, June–July, 50cm (20in) |
| G. s. 'Mayflower' | viol. blue, June–Aug,50cm (20in) |

## Geum

### AVENS

This plant for sun or semi-shade has remarkable seed heads after flowering. Most geums bloom twice. The plants tend to spread and are therefore suitable for ground cover. The nodding water avens (*G. rivale*) also grows in deepest shade. The common avens (*G. urbanum*) has insignificant yellow flowers; it is suitable for both woodland and botanical gardens.
**Hardiness: US Zone 5-4, Canadian Zone 4-3.**

| | |
|---|---|
| G. coccineum 'Borisii' | orange red, May–Aug, 40cm (16in) |
| R. rivale | orange, May–July, 50cm (20in) |
| G. r. 'Album' | white, 50cm (20in) |
| G. r. 'Leonard' | coppery red, 40cm (16in) |

| G. r. 'Lionel Cox'* | light apricot, 30cm (12in) |
| G. urbanum | yellow, May–July, 60cm (24in) |
| **Hybrid cultivars:** | |
| G. 'Georgenberg' | or. yellow, May–July, 25cm (10in) |
| G. 'Mrs. Bradshaw' | carmine red, 60cm (24in) |
| G. 'Lady Stratheden' | yel. (sd), May–Aug, 70cm (28in) |
| G. 'Red Wings' | scarlet (sd), June–Aug, 60cm (24in) |

*Glechoma hederacea*

## Glaucium

### HORNED POPPY

This member of the poppy family comes from coastal regions and has very long seed heads. Plant in sandy soil in full sun.
**Hardiness: US Zone 7, Canadian Zone 6.**

| G. flavum | yellow, July–Sept, 40cm (16in) |

*Glaucium flavum*

## Glechoma

### GROUND IVY

Ground ivy provides ideal deciduous ground cover for a wild garden or shady waterside. It thrives in moisture-retentive soil in deepest shade. Variegated ground ivy is suitable for containers and will completely overhang the edges. Flowers are produced over a long period, but mainly in April.
**Hardiness: US Zone 4, Canadian Zone 3.**

| G. hederacea | violet blue, Mar–Sept, 20cm (8in) |
| G. h. 'Variegata' | variegated leaves |

*Geum rivale 'Lionel Cox'*

## Gunnera

The foliage plant G. *magellanica* is not quite winter-hardy. It may be grown as ground cover in a cool greenhouse. The large gunnera must be kept dry in winter and insulated against frost: fix wire netting around the plant; fill the space with leaves; and cover the plant to protect it from rain. Remove the leaves in good time in spring and cover the sprouting leaves with, for instance, blankets if there is any chance of late night frosts. Let it have plenty of space: it can grow huge. It looks magnificent beside a very large pond, where its reflection will double the effect. The plant needs moisture-retentive soil in full sun.

175

| G. magellanica! | gr. leaves, July–Aug, 15cm (6in) |
| G. manicata** | large leaves, June–July, 2.5m (8ft) |
| G. tinctoria | green/brown, June–July, 3m (10ft) |

Gunnera manicata

# Gypsophila

Note the various heights: plant the taller cultivars in the border and let the low-growing ones clamber over low walls or in a rockery. Gypsophilas are good plants for mixing with others: the delicate flowers soften hard colors and help to blur unsuccessful color combinations. Plant in moderately dry soil and full sun.
**Hardiness: US Zone 4, Canadian Zone 3.**

| G. paniculata 'Bristol Fairy' | white, July–Aug, 1.5m (5ft) |
| G. p. 'Flamingo' | 1.5m (5ft) |
| G. p. 'Pacifica' | many flowers, July–Aug, 1m (3ft) |
| G. repens | white pink, July–Sept, 20cm (8in) |
| G. hybr. 'Rosy Veil' | pale pink, 30cm (12in) |

Gypsophila paniculata 'Bristol Fairy'

# Helenium

**SNEEZEWEED**

It is not easy to tell all the summer-flowering yellow blooms apart; this one is recognizable by its convex center. Like all the others, it requires full sun and a position that is not excessively moist.
**Hardiness: US Zone 7-4, Canadian Zone 6-3.**

| H. autumnale | |
|   'Pumilum Magnificum' | yellow, Aug–Sept, 90cm (36in) |
| H. bigelovii 'The Bishop' | yel./br., June–Aug, 60cm (24in) |
| H. hoopesii | deep gol. yel, May–June, 50cm (20in) |
| **Hybrid cultivars:** | |
| H. 'Butterpat' | yellow, July–Oct, 1.2m (4ft) |
| H. 'Moerheim Beauty' | brown red, July–Sept, 90cm (36in) |
| H. 'Wyndley' | yellow, July–Sept, 75cm (30in) |

Helenium bigelovii 'The Bishop'

# Helianthemum

**ROCKROSE**

Helianthemums require a dry sunny spot in a rock garden. To avoid the risk of damage by frost, it is advisable to protect the plants with bracken. The cultivars 'Snow Queen' and the two 'Wisleys' have gray leaves. The plants look like miniature shrubs and grow to a maximum height of 20cm (8in). They flower from June to August.
**Hardiness: US Zone 5, Canadian Zone 5.**

| **With double flowers:** | |
| H. 'Cerise Queen' | carmine pink |
| H. 'Orange Double' | orange |
| H. 'Sulphureum Plenum' | yellow |

**With single flowers:**

| | |
|---|---|
| H. 'Ben Hope' | pink and orange |
| H. 'Fire Dragon' | brick red |
| H. 'Golden Queen' | yellow |
| H. 'Henfield Brilliant' | orange red |
| H. 'Laurenson's Pink' | pale pink |
| H. 'Snow Queen' | white |
| H. 'Sudbury Gem' | pink-red |
| H. 'Supreme' | purple-red |
| H. 'Wisley Pink' | pink |
| H. 'Wisley Primrose' | pale yellow |

*Helianthemum, mixed*

## Helianthus

### SUNFLOWER

Like the annual plants, perennial sunflowers require full sun. The late, yellow flowers will seem brighter if the sun can shine on them. They are convenient for cutting, but should be staked in good time. *H. salicifolius* (the willow-leafed sunflower) is cultivated for its narrow, light green foliage.
**Hardiness: US Zone 6-4, Canadian Zone 5-3.**

| | |
|---|---|
| *H. atrorubens* | golden yellow, Aug–Oct, 1.75m (5ft) |
| *H. maximilianii* | yellow, Aug–Sept, 3m (10ft) |
| *H. salicifolius!* | yellow, Sept–Oct, 2m (6ft) |

## Heliopsis

All plants of the sunflower type resemble one another and are not always easy to tell apart. Heliopses are tall early-flowering perennials. They need staking and, like heleniums, helianthuses, and rudbeckias, prefer full sun. Heliopses will do well in any soil.
**Hardiness: US Zone 4, Canadian Zone 3.**

| | |
|---|---|
| *H. helianthoides* var. scabra | bright yellow, June–Sept, 1m (3ft) |
| *H. h.* 'Golden Plume' | golden yellow (d), July–Sept, 1.3m (4ft 4in) |
| *H. h.* 'Gold Green heart' | yel. (d), June–Sept, 1.2m (4ft) |
| *H. h.* 'Concave Mirror' | orange yellow, large, July–Sept, 1.3m (4ft 4in) |

*Heliopsis helianthoides* 'Golden Plume'

*Helianthus salicifolius*

# Helleborus

The helleborus is popular because of its unusual flowering season and evergreen foliage. If you would like to have a Christmas rose (*H. niger*) in flower by Christmas, you should dig up the plant in late fall and force it in a hothouse. Move it to a cooler place if the flower buds develop too soon – it is all quite tricky! In a severe winter the plant will flower later. The flowers will droop if it is frosty but they straighten out again when it thaws. Christmas roses require half-shade and moisture-retentive soil.

**Hardiness: US Zone 7-5, Canadian Zone 6-4.**

| | |
|---|---|
| *H. argutifolius* | light green, Feb–Apr, 40cm (16in) |
| *H. atrorubens* | mauve, Feb–Apr, 30cm (12in) |
| *H. foetidus* | green, Feb–Apr, 50cm (20in) |
| *H. niger* | white, Jan–Apr, 30cm (12in) |
| *H. orientalis* | red, March–May, 50cm (20in) |
| *H. viridis** | green, Feb–Apr, 50cm (20in) |

*Helleborus atrorubens*

# Hemerocallis

This edible plant looks attractive as the light green foliage appears in early spring. Day lilies require sun or half-shade in any kind of soil. A careful selection of cultivars will enable you to have constant flowers from May to September.

**Hardiness: US Zone 4, Canadian Zone 3.**

**Hybrid cultivars:**

| | |
|---|---|
| *H.* 'American Revolution' | dark purplish brown, July–Sept, 80cm (32in) |
| *H.* 'Aten' | or. yellow, July–Sept, 90cm (36in) |
| *H.* 'Atlas' | yellow, June–July, 1.1m (3ft 6in) |
| *H.* 'Bonanza' | yel. /br., June–Aug, 70cm (28in) |
| *H.* 'Corky' | yellow, June–Aug, 60cm (24in) |
| *H.* 'Frans Hals' | br. yel., June–Sept, 90cm (36in) |
| *H.* 'Gold Imperial' | yellow, June–Aug, 70cm (28in) |
| *H.* 'Hyperion' | pure yel., June–Aug, 70cm (28in) |
| *H.* 'Matador' | or., yel. center, July–Aug, 1.2m (4ft) |
| *H.* 'Northbrook Star'* | yellow, June–July, 70cm (28in) |
| *H.* 'Pink Charm' | pink, June–Aug, 70cm (28in) |
| *H.* 'Prairie Moonlight' | soft yellow, June–Aug, 90cm (36in) |
| *H.* 'Sammy Russell' | red, June–Aug, 70cm 28in) |
| *H.* 'Stella de Oro' | yellow, May–Sept, 30cm (12in) |
| *H.* 'Valiant' | orange, July–Sept, 90cm (36in) |

*Hemerocallis*, hybride

# Hepatica

This delicate evergreen plant requires heavy clay soil. Its flowers closely resemble those of the *Anemone*, in which genus it was formerly included.

**Hardiness: US Zone 5, Canadian Zone 4.**

| | |
|---|---|
| *H. acutiloba* | blue, white, Mar-Apr, 15cm (6in) |
| *H. americana* | blue, white, Mar-Apr, 15cm (6in) |
| *H. nobilis* | blue, Mar–Apr, 10cm (4in) |

*Hepatica nobilis*

*Heuchera micrantha* 'Palace Purple'

## Heracleum

**HOGWEED**
See: Annuals and biennials.

## Hesperis

**DAME'S VIOLET, SWEET ROCKET**
See: Annuals and biennials.

## Heuchera

**ALUM ROOT**
The species listed below do not greatly resemble one another. *H. brizoides* is the most familiar one. The tall feathery sprays of flowers tend to be flattened by rain. Heights may vary considerably depending on the type of soil, which needs to be moisture-retentive. Heucheras require sun or semi-shade. The cultivar 'Palace Purple' has handsome dark red leaves.
**Hardiness: US Zone 5, Canadian Zone 5.**

| | |
|---|---|
| *H. brizoides* 'Rain of Fire' | deep red, June–Aug, 70cm (28in) |
| *H. b.* 'Snowstorm' | white, June–Aug, 50cm (20in) |
| *H. b.* 'Walker's Variety' | pink, June–Aug, 50cm (20in) |
| *H. micrantha* 'Palace Purple'! | white, June–Aug, 50cm (20in) |
| *H. sanguinea* | red, May–July, 50cm (20in) |

## Hosta

**FUNKIA, PLANTAIN LILY**
This foliage plant can be grown for various purposes: for a position by itself, for edging, for borders, and for filling an entire flower bed. Plant only the largest cultivars in solitary positions. Semi-shade in fairly moist soil is best. It takes many cultivars several years to mature. The foliage becomes increasingly beautiful over the years; the gray-leafed kind in particular is often still greenish when the plant is young. The indicated height refers to the flower stems. The foliage colors show up best in the sun.
**Hardiness: US Zone 4, Canadian Zone 3.**

**Blueish-gray foliage:**

| | |
|---|---|
| *H.* hybr. 'Big Daddy' | lilac, June–July, 90cm (36in) |
| *H. h.* 'Blue Cadet' | lav. blue, July–Aug, 35cm (14in) |
| *H. h.* 'Krossa Regal'! | mauve, July, Aug, 90cm (36in) |
| *H. fortunei* 'Hyacinthina' | July–Aug, 60cm (24in) |

*Hosta fortunei* 'Hyacinthina'

179

| | |
|---|---|
| H. sieboldiana | mauve, June–July, 80cm (32in) |
| H. s. 'Elegans' | white, June–July, 60cm (24in) |
| H. s. 'Hadspun Blue' | July–Aug, 40cm (16in) |
| H. x tardiana 'Blue Moon' | July–Aug, 20cm (8in) |
| H. t. 'Blue Wedgwood' | June–July, 25in (10in) |
| H. t. 'Halcyon' | June–July, 40cm (16in) |

**Green foliage:**

| | |
|---|---|
| H. albomarginata 'Alba' | white, July–Aug, 50cm (20in) |
| H. fortunei 'Hyacinthina' | July–Aug, 70cm (28in) |
| H. f. 'Obscura' | purple, July–Aug, 70cm (28in) |
| H. f. 'Rugosa' | light purple, dark green, July–Aug, 70cm (28in) |
| H. hybr. 'Honey Bells' | lilac, Aug–Sept, 90cm (36in) |
| H. ventricosa | d. purple, July–Aug, 80cm (32in) |

**White-edged foliage:**

| | |
|---|---|
| H. crispula* | deep purple, white sinuate, July–Aug, 80cm (32in) |
| H. decorata | d. mauve, June–July, 70cm (28in) |
| H. undulata purple, 'Albomarginata' | l. purple, June–July, 60cm (24in) |

**White-striped foliage:**

| | |
|---|---|
| H. fortunei 'Francee' | lav. blue, July–Aug, 60cm (24in) |
| H. undulata 'Albomarginata'! | June–Sept, 90cm (36in) |
| H. u. 'Mediovariegata' | l. purple, July–Aug, 70cm (28in) |

**Yellow-edged foliage:**

| | |
|---|---|
| H. fortunei 'Aureomarginata' | violet, July–Aug, 70cm (28in) |
| H. hybr. 'Golden Tiara' | mauve, June–Aug, 60cm (24in) |
| H. h. 'Wide Brem' | l. mauve, June–July, 40cm (16in) |
| H. sieboldiana 'Frances Williams' | pale lilac, June–July, 60cm (24in) |

**Yellow foliage:**

| | |
|---|---|
| H. fortunei 'Aurea' | l. purple, July–Aug, 50cm (20in) |
| H. fortunei 'Albopicta' | green margins, lilac, 60cm (24in) |
| H. hybr. 'August Moon' | l. mauve, July–Aug, 80cm (32in) |
| H. h. 'Zounds' | violet, July–Aug, 50cm (20in) |

Hosta 'Golden Tiara'

# Houttuynia

This low-growing perennial can rapidly cover a large area under light-filtering trees. It does well in humus-rich soil and is suitable for moist positions beside streams or ponds. Propagate by division. **Hardiness: US Zone 5, Canadian Zone 4.**

| | |
|---|---|
| H. cordata | white, June–Aug, 30cm (12in) |
| H. c. 'Chameleon' | leaves with red variegations, June–Aug, 30cm (12in) |
| H. c. 'Plena' | (d), June–Aug, 30cm (12in) |

Houttuynia cordata 'Chameleon'

# Hypericum

### ST. JOHN'S WORT

H. calycinum is evergreen and suitable for semi-shade; H. perforatum prefers full sun and dry soil (see also: Evergreen and deciduous shrubs). **Hardiness: US Zone 6-5, Canadian Zone 5-4.**

| | |
|---|---|
| H. calycinum | yellow, July–Sept, 30cm (12in) |
| H. polyphyllum | yellow, June–Aug, 25cm (10in) |

Hypericum polyphyllum

## Iberis

**CANDYTUFT**

This ground-cover plant requires sun and is suitable for edging purposes or for a border of low-growing plants. *I.s.* 'Little Gem' looks attractive in a rock garden, but may also be used to fill an entire bed. Prune regularly to prevent it becoming too woody.
**Hardiness: US Zone 4, Canadian Zone 3.**

| | |
|---|---|
| *I. sempervirens* | white, May–June, 20cm (8in) |
| *I. s.* 'Snowflake' | white, May–June, 20cm (8in) |
| *I. s.* 'Little Gem' | white, Apr–June, 10cm (4in) |

*Iberis sempervirens*

## Incarvillea

**HARDY GLOXINIA**
See: Bulbs and tuberous plants.

## Inula

Inulas belong to the "sunflower" type of plants. The low-growing species are good for rock gardens; the taller ones look well in a border. They may also be planted in solitary positions. They are all tolerant of drought.
**Hardiness: US Zone 6-5, Canadian Zone 5-4.**

| | |
|---|---|
| *I. ensifolia* | yellow, July–Aug, 30cm (12in) |
| *I. orientalis* | or. yel., June–July, 50cm (20in) |
| *I. Royleana* | yellow, July-Aug, 60cm (24in) |

## Iris

The assortment of irises is so vast that only a limited selection is mentioned here. The following list will show you how wide a choice there is, and that many different plants may be combined. In Germany, many older cultivars have been preserved in specialized iris gardens known as iridaria. The soil should be wet for *I. lutea*; very moist for *I. kaempferi*; moist for *I. siberica*; and dry for *I. barbata*, *I. pumila*, and the larger *I. germanica* hybrids. The species and cultivars listed below are, on the whole, readily available. It is best to order from specialized growers.
**Hardiness: US Zone 4, Canadian Zone 3.**

| | |
|---|---|
| *I. kaempferi* | June–July, 80cm (32in) |
| *I. k.* 'Blue King' | dark blue |
| *I. k.* 'Carnival Prince' | soft blue, violet veins |
| *I. k.* 'Darling' | soft lilac pink |
| *I. k.* 'Gipsy' | violet blue, darker veins |
| *I. k.* 'Iso-No-Nami' | soft purple, white veins |
| *I. k.* 'Jodlesong' | purplish red, yellow honey guide |
| *I. k.* 'Loyalty' | violet blue, yellow honey guide (d) |
| *I. k.* 'Sensation' | purplish red, yellow honey guide (d) |
| *I. k.* 'Variegata' | blue, variegated leaves |
| *I. sibirica* | June–July, 70cm (28in) |
| *I. s.* 'Blue Cape' | pure blue |
| *I. s.* 'Blue King' | pure violet blue |

*Inula orientalis*

| I. s. 'Ego' | blue, sinuate margins |
| I. s. 'Emperor' | dark blue |
| I. s. 'Mountain Lake' | soft blue |
| I. s. 'Perry's Blue' | sky blue, large |
| I. s. 'Sparkling Rose' | bright pink |
| I. s. 'White Sails' | white |

**Germanica hybrids** (flowering season June):

| I. g. 'Alcazar' | lavender blue and purplish violet, 80cm (32in) |
| I. g. 'Ambassadeur' | bronze violet and deep violet, 1m (3ft) |
| I. g. 'Californian Gold' | dark yellow, 80cm (32in) |
| I. g. 'Constant Wattez' | pink, 1m (3ft) |
| I. g. 'Empress of India' | light blue, 1m (3ft) |
| I. g. 'Gentius' | pure violet, 50cm (20in) |
| I. g. 'Helge' | light lemon yellow, 50cm (20in) |
| I. g. 'Louvois' | brown, 1m (3ft) |
| I. g. 'Lugano' | white, 1m (3ft) |
| I. g. 'Moonbeam' | lemon yellow, 80cm (32in) |
| I. g. 'Mrs Horace Darwin' | white with lilac veins, 80cm (32in) |
| I. g. 'Nightfall' | purplish blue, 80cm (32in) |
| I. g. 'Red Orchid' | deep wine red, 50cm (20in) |
| I. g. 'Senlac' | dark wine red, 80cm (32in) |
| I. g. 'White Knight' | snow white, 60cm (24in) |

**Pumila hybrids** (flowering season April–May):

| I. p. 'Atroviolacea' | deep violet blue, 15cm (6in) |

*Iris kaempferi* 'Sensation'

| I. p. 'Aurea' | yellow, 20cm (8in) |
| I. p. 'Blue Denim' | light blue, 20cm (8in) |
| I. p. 'Brassie' | golden yellow, 20cm (8in) |
| I. p. 'Bright White' | silvery white, 20cm (8in) |
| I. p. 'Cyanea' | dark blue, 20cm (8in) |
| I. p. 'Die Braut' | white and creamy yellow |
| I. p. 'Pastel Charme' | purple, 15cm (6in) |

## *Kirengeshoma*

This tall plant requires shade and prefers humus-rich, moisture-retentive soil. It needs staking. The flowers of *K. koreana* are upright; *K. palmata* has pendent bell-shaped flowers.
**Hardiness: US Zone 5, Canadian Zone 5.**

| K. koreana | soft yellow, Aug–Sept, 1m (3ft) |
| K. palmata | soft yellow, Sept–Oct, 1m (3ft) |

## *Kniphofia*

**RED-HOT POKER, TORCH LILY**

Kniphofias are old-fashioned plants for solitary positions. Plant in full sun.
**Hardiness: US Zone 6, Canadian Zone 5.**

*Iris pumila* 'Aurea'

| K. uvularia | yellow/red, Aug–Sept, 1m (3ft) |

**Hybrid cultivars:**

| K. 'Alcazar' | garnet red, July–Sept, 1m (3ft) |
| K. 'Earliest of All' | red/yellow, June–July, 1m (3ft) |
| K. 'Little Maid' | yellow, July–Sept, 60cm (24in) |
| K. 'Royal Standard' | yellow/red, Aug–Oct, 1m (3ft) |

# Lamiastrum

## YELLOW ARCHANGEL

This fast-growing ground cover for a shady position was formerly classified as belonging to the genus *Lamium*. If it is not cut back, the plant may grow up to 60cm (24in) tall as it ages.
**Hardiness: US Zone 4, Canadian Zone 3.**

| L. galeobdolon | yellow, May–June, 40cm (16in) |
| L. g. 'Florentinum' | yellow, leaves variegated, 35cm (14in) |
| L. g. 'Hermann's Pride' | silver-flecked leaves, 40cm (16in) |

# Lamium

## DEADNETTLE

The common deadnettle is less rampant than *L.*

*Lamiastrum galeobdolon* 'Hermann's Pride'

*galeobdolon*, but requires a similar shady position. Deadnettles will grow in any kind of soil.
**Hardiness: US Zone 6-4, Canadian Zone 5-3.**

| L. maculatum 'Album' | white, Apr–July, 30cm (12in) |
| L. m. 'Beacon Silver' | silvery leaves, 15cm (6in) |
| L. m. 'Roseum' | pink, Apr–July, 30cm (12in) |
| L. m. 'White Nancy' | silvery leaves, 15cm (6in) |
| L. orvala*! | mauve, May–July, 80cm (32in) |

# Lathyrus

## SWEET PEA

*Lamium maculatum* 'White Nancy'

The sweet pea is one of the few "climbing" perennials. *L. vernus* provides ground cover for sun or half-shade.
**Hardiness: US Zone 5-4, Canadian Zone 4-3.**

| L. latifolius 'Pink Pearl' | pink, July–Aug, 1.5m (5ft) |
| L. l. 'Red Pearl' | car. red, July–Aug, 1.5m (5ft) |
| L. l. 'White Pearl' | white, July–Aug, 1.5m (5ft) |
| L. vernus! | violet, Apr–May, 40cm (16in) |
| L. v. 'Alboroseus' | pink and white, Apr–May, 40cm (16in) |

*Lathyrus latifolius* 'Red Pearl'

## Lavandula

**LAVENDER**

Lavender is really a semi-shrub, but here it is classified as a perennial for practical reasons. Prune the plants every year in spring; it is also possible to do this immediately after they have flowered, but a bare plant in midsummer is not very attractive. Pruning keeps the plants compact and makes them flower more abundantly. Plant lavender in a sunny position, perhaps combined with roses, or in a border of gray-leafed plants. It also makes a good edging plant, although it is slightly frost-tender. *L. officinalis* is called *L. angustifolia* nowadays. The late-flowering *L. dentata* 'Royal Crown' is not sufficiently winter-hardy: bring it indoors for the winter.
**Hardiness: US Zone 5, Canadian Zone 5.**

| | |
|---|---|
| *L. angustifolia* | blue, July–Aug, 40cm (16in) |
| *L. a.* 'Hidcote' | mauvish blue, 40cm (16in) |
| *L. a.* 'Loddon Pink'* | blue, 50cm (20in) |
| *L. a.* 'Munstead' | lilac mauve, 45cm (18in) |
| *L. a.* 'Rosea' | lilac pink, 40cm (16in) |

*Lavandula angustifolia* 'Munstead'

## Lavatera

**TREE MALLOW**

Like some campanulas, lavateras are among the perennials with the longest flowering season. They also look well combined with other plants.

Grow them in a sunny spot. Older plants become frost tender: cover the base thoroughly or, even better, take cuttings of older plants in August and let them overwinter indoors. Cut back the plants in spring: they will soon sprout again.
**Hardiness: US Zone 7-5, Canadian Zone 7-4.**

| | |
|---|---|
| *L. cachemiriana* | pink, July–Sept, 1.8m (6ft) |
| *L.* (hybr.cult.) 'Bredon Spring' | pink, June–Oct, 1.5m (5ft) |
| *L. thuringiaca* 'Barnsley'! | white with pink centers, June–Oct, 1.5m (5ft) |
| *L. olbia* 'Rosea' | bright pink, July–Oct, 1.5m (5ft) |

**Hybrid cultivars:**

| | |
|---|---|
| *L.* 'Candy Floss' | pale pink, June–Sept, 1.5m (5ft) |
| *L.* 'Ice Cool' | white to pale pink, June–Sept, 1.5m (5ft) |

*Lavatera thuringiaca* 'Barnsley'

## Leontopodium

**EDELWEISS**

This small rock plant for a dry sunny position is protected in Switzerland, but the plants available from garden centers have all been cultivated.
**Hardiness: US Zone 5, Canadian Zone 4.**

| | |
|---|---|
| *L. alpinum* | white, leaves gray, June–Aug, 25cm (10in) |
| *L. a.* 'Mignon' | w. small June–July, 10cm (4in) |

*Leontopodium alpinum* 'Mignon'

## Leucanthemella

See: *Chrysanthemum serotina*.

## Lewisia

Lewisias are suitable plants for rock gardens; they require well-drained soil as they are frost-tender. Cover the plants in winter and make sure they are growing in full sun.
**Hardiness: US Zone 6, Canadian Zone 5.**

| | |
|---|---|
| *L. cotyledon* | pink, June–Aug, 20cm (8in) |
| *L.* hybr. 'Sunset Strain' | pink, June–Aug, 25cm (10in) |
| *L. h.* 'Pinkie' | pink, June–Aug, 20cm (8in) |

*Lewisia* hybrid 'Pinkie'

## Liatris

**GAY FEATHERS**
See: Bulbs and tuberous plants.

## Ligularia

Because of their red leaves, 'Othello' and 'Desdemona' are the most familiar cultivars. The others, however, are no less beautiful. All ligularias like a moist position in full sun or half-shade. Pond edges are particularly suitable, but a solitary position is also effective. *L. przewalskii* has spikes of flowers; all the others are daisy-like. The tallest species are more suitable for very large gardens.
**Hardiness: US Zone 5-4, Canadian Zone 4-3.**

| | |
|---|---|
| *L. dentata* | orange yellow, July–Sept, 1m (3ft) |
| *L. d.* 'Desdemona' | orange, 1m (3ft) |
| *L. d.* 'Othello' | orange, July–Sept, 80cm (32in) |
| *L. x hessei* | orange yellow, July–Sept, 1.2m (4ft) |
| *L. x palmatiloba* | orange, Aug–Sept, 1.2m (4ft) |
| *L. przewalskii* | yellow, June–July, 1m (3ft) |
| *L. tangutica* | yellow, July–Sept, 1.2m (4ft) |
| *L. veitchiana* | yellow, July–Aug, 1.5m (5ft) |
| *L. wilsoniana* | golden yellow, Aug–Sept, 1.5m (5ft) |

*Ligularia przewalskii*

# Limonium

### SEA LAVENDER

Like armerias and eryngiums, this is a typical plant for coastal regions. It tolerates sea breezes as well as salty soil. Plant in full sun. Sea lavender can be dried (see also: Annuals and biennials).

**Hardiness: US Zone 6-5, Canadian Zone 5-4.**

| | |
|---|---|
| *L. dumosum* | white, June–Sept, 40cm (16in) |
| *L. latifolium* | lavender blue, June–Aug, 40cm (16in) |

# Linaria

### TOADFLAX

Toadflax requires dry sandy soil in full sun. It also grows well on old walls, although it is quite unlike the ivy-leafed toadflax (*Cymbalaria*). The plant is usually short-lived, but self-seeds freely.

**Hardiness: US Zone 5-4, Canadian Zone 5-4.**

| | |
|---|---|
| *L. alpina* | blue with orange throat, July–Aug, 10cm (4in) |
| *L. purpurea* | purplish violet, July–Oct, 60cm (24in) |
| *L. p.* 'Canon J. Went' | pale pink, June–Aug, 1m (3ft) |

*Linaria purpurea* 'Canon J. Went'

# Linnaea

### TWIN FLOWER

This delicate rock plant for acid soil in sun or semi-shade develops runners which can extend up to 4m (13ft) in length. Pictures of the great botanist Linnaeus often show him wearing Lapp clothing and holding this tubular-shaped flower. He introduced the binary classification used in this book: the name of the genus, species, variety (preceded by the word "var"), and cultivar. Cultivars are developed by human beings; varieties occur in nature.

**Hardiness: US Zone 1, Canadian Zone 1.**

| | |
|---|---|
| *L. borealis*\* | pink or white, June–Aug 15cm (6in) |

*Linnaea borealis*

# Linum

### FLAX

Flax has slender airy stems with light-green foliage and brightly colored flowers. It is suitable for borders, or for rock or heather gardens. The plant prefers dryish soil and full sun.

**Hardiness: US Zone 5, Canadian Zone 5.**

| | |
|---|---|
| *L. flavum* | yellow, June–July, 30cm (12in) |
| *L. perenne* | l. blue, June–July, 45cm (18in) |
| *L. p.* 'Album' | June–July, 45cm (18cm) |
| *L. p.* 'Diamant' | white, June–Aug, 25cm (10in) |
| *L. p.* 'Blue Sapphire' | sky blue, June–Aug, 25cm (10in) |

# Liriope

### LILLYTURF

This is a perennial for acid and humus-rich soil, in sun or semi-shade. The plant will grow if it likes its position. Liriopes are frost-hardy. *L. spicata* produces large black fruits after it has flowered.

*Linum perenne*

*Liriope muscari* 'Variegata'

**Hardiness: US Zone 7, Canadian Zone 6.**

| | |
|---|---|
| *L. muscari* | violet spikes, Aug-Oct, 60cm (24in) |
| *L. m.* 'Variegata' | silver-striped leaves, Aug-Oct, 40cm (16in) |
| *L. spicata* | l. violet, July-Sept, 40cm (16in) |

## Lobelia

These lobelias are at first sight different from the annual species, but if you look at the flowers closely, you will see the resemblance. Lobelias require a moist position in full sun or half-shade.

**Hardiness: US Zone 9-3, Canadian Zone 8-2.**

| | |
|---|---|
| *L. cardinalis* | red, July–Oct, 90cm (36in) |
| *L. fulgens* 'Queen Victoria' | br. red, July–Sept, 80cm (32in) |
| *L.* x gerardii 'Vedrariensis' | mauve, July–Sept, 90cm (36in) |
| *L. siphilitica*! | br. blue, July–Sept, 70cm (28in) |
| *L. s.* 'Alba' | white, July–Sept, 60cm (24in) |

*Lobelia fulgens* 'Queen Victoria'

## Lupinus

**LUPIN**

This genus includes as many as 200 species. *L. arboreus* (tree lupin) is woody. Herbaceous lupins

*Lupinus* 'The Pages'

are perhaps the least demanding of all garden plants as far as position and cultivation are concerned. To propagate, take seeds from the finest plants only. Cut back plants not required for seeds immediately after they have flowered to ensure a second flush of blooms in August.
**Hardiness: US Zone 5, Canadian Zone 5.**

| | |
|---|---|
| L. 'Chandelier' | yellow, June–Aug, 80cm (32in) |
| L. 'Noble Maiden' | white, 1m (3ft) |
| L. 'The Châtelaine' | pink and white, 1m (3ft) |
| L. 'The Governor' | blueish white, 1m (3ft) |
| L. 'The Pages' | carmine red, 1m (3ft) |

# Lychnis

Lychnes are undemanding and rewarding summer-flowering plants which require full sun. *L. coronaria* needs drier soil; its cultivars have finer colors than the species. The leaves are gray and hairy. The common name of *L. chalcedonica* is Jerusalem cross or Maltese cross; that of *L. viscaria* is red German catchfly.
**Hardiness: US Zone 4, Canadian Zone 3.**

| | |
|---|---|
| L. alpina 'Rosea' | pink, May–June, 10cm (4in) |
| L. arkwrightii 'Vesuvius'! | or. red, June–July, 70cm (28in) |
| L. chalcedonica | or. red, June–July, 1.3m (4ft 4in) |
| L. c. 'Carneum' | sal. pink, June–July, 80cm (32in) |
| L. coronaria | candy pink, June–Aug, 70cm (28in) |
| L. c. 'Alba'! | white, June–Aug, 70cm (28in) |
| L. c. 'Oculata'! | white with pink centers, June–Aug, 70cm (28in) |
| L. viscaria 'Plena' | pinkish red (d), July, 40cm (16in) |
| L. v. 'Splendens'! | pink, June–July, 40cm (16in) |

*Lychnis arkwrightii* 'Vesuvius'

# Lysimachia

**L O O S E S T R I F E**

The various heights and growth patterns make this a very diverse genus. Creeping Jenny (*L. nummularia*) is a moisture-loving prostrate perennial suitable for ground cover and for growing beside a pond. Garden loosestrife (*L. punctata*) is an invasive old-fashioned cottage-garden plant that can even be grown by complete beginners. The others bear elegant flowers for cutting and may be grown in borders or as edging. All lysimachias require full sun.
**Hardiness: US Zone 7-4, Canadian Zone 6-3.**

| | |
|---|---|
| L. atropurpurea* | pur. red, June–Aug, 50cm (20in) |
| L. barystachys | white, July–Aug, 70cm (28in) |
| L. ciliata! | yellow, July–Sept, 60cm (24in) |
| L. clethroides | white, July–Aug, 80cm (32in) |
| L. ephemerum | white, July–Sept, 1.2m (4ft) |
| L. nummularia | yellow, July–Sept, 10cm (4in) |
| L. punctata | yellow, June–Sept, 90cm (36in) |
| L. vulgaris | yellow, June–Aug, 80cm (32in) |

*Lysimachia clethroides*

# Lythrum!

**P U R P L E   L O O S E S T R I F E**

In nature, purple loosestrife grows alongside the water and up to 10cm (4in) under water. When grown on land, it should therefore be given a moist position in full sun. Choose the shorter cultivars for growing beside ponds. This plant is extremely invasive and must not be grown close to natural wetlands.
**Hardiness: US Zone 4, Canadian Zone 3.**

| | |
|---|---|
| L. salicaria | viol. pink, June–Aug, 1.5m (5ft) |

| | |
|---|---|
| L. s. 'Gypsy Blood' | dark red, July–Sept, 1.2m (4ft) |
| L. s. 'Mordon's Pink' | bright pink, June–Aug, 1m (3ft) |
| L. s. 'Robert'! | mauvish red, June–Aug, 80cm (32in) |

*Lythrum salicaria*

## Macleaya

**PLUME POPPY**

This plant does not look at all like a poppy, but if you break off a leaf you will find that the sap is similar. In large gardens, macleayas may be planted at the back of a deep border. The feathery plumes look well combined with helianthus, echinops and eupatorium.

**Hardiness: US Zone 5-4, Canadian Zone 4-3.**

| | |
|---|---|
| M. cordata | buff-white, July–Sept, 2m (6ft) |
| M. microcarpa | |
| 'Kelway's Coral Plume' coral pink, July–Sept, 2m (6ft) | |

*Maclaya cordata*

## Maianthemum

**CANADIAN MAY FLOWER**

May flowers make good ground cover for shady woodland corners. They require humus-rich, moisture-retentive soil. Each stem will produce only two leaves.

**Hardiness: US Zone 1, Canadian Zone 1.**

| | |
|---|---|
| M. canadense | white, May, 20cm (8in) |

## Malva

**MALLOW**

The malva family has produced several good garden plants: lavateras (perennials); althaeas (biennials), and malopes (annuals). All species require full sun and soil that is not excessively wet.

**Hardiness: US Zone 6-5, Canadian Zone 5-4.**

| | |
|---|---|
| M. moschata | pink, June–Sept, 60cm (24in) |
| M. m. 'Alba' | white, June–Sept, 60cm (24in) |
| M. sylvestris | pink, June–Sept, 50cm (20in) |

*Malva moschata*

## Meconopsis

**BLUE POPPY**

Blue poppies sometimes look more like annuals, but are more difficult to grow successfully.

189

People are tempted again and again by its unusual shade of blue, and are prepared to accept any amount of disappointment. *Salvia patens* has the same color and requires similar care. Plant both of them in full sun in well-drained soil. *M. cambrica* is a small undemanding poppy available in bright shades of red, orange, and yellow.
**Hardiness: US Zone 5, Canadian Zone 4.**

| | |
|---|---|
| M. betonicifolia | azure, June–July, 50cm (20in) |
| M. cambrica | orange or yellow, May–Aug, 30cm (12in) |

## Mertensia*

**VIRGINIA BLUEBELL**

This plant resembles a forget-me-not and has intensely blue flowers. It does well in shade, and is sufficiently winter-hardy. Mertensias die down early in summer, which makes them appear to be dead, but they will sprout again the following spring.
**Hardiness: US Zone 5, Canadian Zone 4.**

| | |
|---|---|
| M. sibirica* | blue, Apr–May, 50cm (20in) |
| M. virginica | blue, Apr–May, 50cm (20in) |

*Mimulus* 'Orange Glow'

*Meconopsis betonicifolia*

# Mimulus

**MONKEY MUSK**

Mimulus requires semi-shade or sun and a moist environment. It flowers exuberantly over a long period, and needs to be covered lightly in winter. **Hardiness: US Zone 8, Canadian Zone 7.**

| | |
|---|---|
| M. luteus | yellow, May–Aug, 30cm (12in) |
| M. primuloides | yellow, small, May–Sept, 10cm (4in) |

**Hybrid cultivars**:

| | |
|---|---|
| M. 'Major Bees' | yellow, brownish red spots, May–Sept, 30cm (12in) |
| M. 'Orange Glow' | orange, May–Sept, 25cm (10in) |
| M. 'Scarlet Bees' | red, May–Sept, 20cm (8in) |

# Monarda

**BERGAMOT**

No garden should be without this old-fashioned cottage-garden plant. Its flowers are very suitable for cutting and will provide all kinds of color combinations. The plant will grow in full sun or semi-shade, and is undemanding as far as soil is concerned. Divide and transplant regularly. **Hardiness: US Zone 4, Canadian Zone 3.**

| | |
|---|---|
| M. 'Adam' | cherry red, July–Aug, 1m (3ft) |
| M. 'Alba' | white |
| M. 'Aquarius' | l. mauve, July–Aug, 1.3m (4ft 4in) |
| M. 'Balance' | br. pink, July–Aug, 1.2m (4ft) |
| M. 'Blue Stocking' | blueish mauve, July–Aug, 1m (3ft) |

Monarda 'Prairie Night'

| | |
|---|---|
| M. 'Cambridge Scarlet' | scarlet, July–Aug, 80cm (32in) |
| M. 'Croftway Pink' | pink, July–Aug, 80cm (32in) |
| M. 'Prairie Fire' | dark red, July–Aug, 80cm (32in) |
| M. 'Prairie Night' | mauve, July–Aug, 1.2m (4ft) |
| M. 'Scorpion' | bright violet, July–Sept, 1.4m (4ft) |
| M. 'Snow White' | white, July–Aug, 80cm (32in) |
| M. 'Sunset' | purplish red, July–Aug, 1m (3ft) |
| M. 'Violet Queen' | dark violet, July-Aug,80cm (32in) |

# Montbretia

See: *Crocosmia*, Bulbs and tuberous plants.

# Nepeta

**CATMINT, CATNIP**

Nurseries quite often confuse *N. faassenii* and *N. mussinii*, even though they are different species. The low-growing species are more appropriate for small gardens; the tall ones are best in large gardens. Catmint is also suitable for edging purposes. The taller, less familiar, *N. grandiflora* is a good plant for borders. Cat-haters beware: cats like to lie down in the middle of the plant. **Hardiness: US Zone 6, Canadian Zone 5.**

| | |
|---|---|
| N. faassenii | lav. blue, May–Sept, 40cm (16in) |
| N. f. 'Six Hill's Giant' | blue, June–Aug, 50cm (20in) |
| N. f. 'Snowflake' | white and blue, May–Sept, 30cm (12in) |
| N. govaniana | soft yellow, July–Sept,80cm (32in) |
| N. grandiflora | blue, June–Sept, 1m (3ft) |

Nepeta sibirica

| N. mussinii | light blue, June–July, 20cm (8in) |
| N. nervosa | blue, June–Aug, 1m (3ft) |
| N. racemosa | see: N. mussinii |
| N. sibirica | blue, July–Aug, 80cm (32in) |

| O. verna | blue, Apr–May, 15cm (6in) |
| O. v. 'Alba' | white, Apr–May, 15cm (6in) |

Omphalodes verna

## Oenothera

**EVENING PRIMROSE**

The flowers are large in proportion to the plant itself, and the flowering season is quite long. Evening primroses require full sun and dry, well-drained soil. The flowers close suddenly in the evening. There are several cultivars of *O. tetragona* which do not differ much from the species; only 'Summer Solstis', which has red buds, grows considerably taller.
**Hardiness: US Zone 5-4, Canadian Zone 4-3.**

| O. caespitosa* | white, June–Aug, 20cm (8in) |
| O. fruticosa | yellow, June–Aug, 70cm (28in) |
| O. missouriensis! | yellow, June–Aug, 30cm (12in) |
| O. speciosa* | soft pink, June–Aug,40cm (16in) |
| O. tetragona | yellow, June–Aug, 50cm (20in) |

Oenothera missouriensis

## Pachysandra

This evergreen plant is useful for ground cover and requires shade or partial shade. The leaves turn somewhat yellowish in full sun, which is unattractive. For some reason that is hard to pinpoint, the plant does not thrive everywhere. It is therefore best to try out just a few plants at first.
**Hardiness: US Zone 5, Canadian Zone 5.**

| P. terminalis | white, Apr–May, 20cm (8in) |
| P. t. 'Green Carpet' | white, Mar–May, 15cm (6in) |
| P. t. 'Variegata'* | white, Apr–May, 15cm (6in) |

Pachysandra terminalis 'Variegata'

## Omphalodes

This small plant has light green leaves and makes good ground cover in partial shade. It needs moisture-retentive soil to prevent it drying out.
**Hardiness: US Zone 5, Canadian Zone 5.**

| O. cappadocica | gentian blue, Apr–May, 20cm (8in) |

# Paeonia

## PEONY

The large double-flowered peonies in three colors are the most familiar. The full flowers are so heavy that they tend to droop and need support. The *lactifloras* remain more upright. The question that growers are asked most frequently is why the peonies will not flower. Plant – in semi-shade – on top of richly fertilized soil. Leave the plants undisturbed for years and add fertilizer annually. The plants flower in June–July. The following list is a small selection from the vast number of cultivars.
**Hardiness: US Zone 5, Canadian Zone 5.**

| | |
|---|---|
| *P. officinalis* 'Alba Plena' | white, full, 70cm (28in) |
| *P. o.* 'Rosea Plena' | pink, full, 70cm (28in) |
| *P. o.* 'Rubra Plena' | red, full, 70cm (28in) |

*Lactiflora* **hybrids** (single flowers):

| | |
|---|---|
| *P.* 'Bowl of Beauty' | light red, yellow center, 1m (3ft) |
| *P.* 'l'Eclatante' | crimson, dark, 1m (3ft) |

*Lactiflora* **hybrids** (double flowers):

| | |
|---|---|
| *P.* 'Duchesse de Nemours' | creamy white, yellow center, 70cm (28in) |
| *P.* 'Karl Rosenfeld' | purplish red, 80cm (32in) |
| *P.* 'Lady Alexandra Duff' | pink to white, 1m (3ft) |
| *P.* 'Sarah Bernhardt' | silvery pink, 1m (3ft) |
| *P.* 'Victoire de la Marne' | silvery red, 1m (3ft) |

*Paeonia* 'Duchesse de Nemours'

# Papaver

## POPPY

Several species occur in nature. The low-growing *P. nudicaule* is perennial and easy to grow from seed; there are several hybrids varying in height from 25cm (10in) to 60cm (24in). *P. orientale* is the taller oriental poppy. All poppies need sun and thrive in any kind of soil.
**Hardiness: US Zone 5, Canadian Zone 4.**

| | |
|---|---|
| *P. orientale* 'Harvest Moon' | orange, May–July, 1m (3ft) |
| *P. o.* 'Helen Elizabeth' | pink, June–July, 70cm (28in) |
| *P. o.* 'Karine' | pink, May–June, 60cm (24in) |
| *P. o.* 'Orange Glow' | orange, May–July, 70cm (28in) |
| *P. o.* 'Perry's White' | white, May–July, 70cm (28in) |
| *P. o.* 'Pinnacle' | pink, white center, May–July, 70cm (28in) |
| *P. o.* 'Rembrandt' | dark red, May–July, 80cm (32in) |

*Papaver orientale*

# Penstemon

Penstemons are among the best red border plants. They require full sun, flower abundantly, and are suitable for any kind of soil.
**Hardiness: US Zone 8-5, Canadian Zone 7-5.**

| | |
|---|---|
| *P. barbatus* 'Coccineus' | scarlet, July–Sept, 1m (3ft) |
| *P. b.* 'Praecox nanus' | carmine pink, June–Sept, 50cm (20in) |
| *P. hirsutus* 'Pygmaeus' | violet, June–Aug, 15cm (6in) |
| *P. pinifolius* | scarlet, July–Aug, 15cm (6in) |

**Hybrid cultivars:**

| | |
|---|---|
| *P.* 'Garnet' | deep red, July–Sept, 50cm (20in) |

| P. 'Blue Spring' | blue, June–Aug, |
| | 50cm (20in) |
| P. 'Firebird' | red, June–Aug, |
| | 70cm (28in) |

*Penstemon* 'Firebird'

## *Petasites*

**BUTTERBUR**

An old English gardening book describes this plant as a genuine weed not worth cultivating. I share this view for a different reason: the foliage is attacked by insects early in the summer and dies down in August. Butterbur is often grown beside large ponds and may be planted up to the water line. The (expensive) *Darmera peltata* is more suited to such positions and conditions.

*Petasites hybrides*

**Hardiness: US Zone 5-4, Canadian Zone 4-3.**

| P. hybridus | pink, Mar–Apr, 80cm (32in) |
| P. japonicus 'Giganteus' | cream, Mar–Apr, 1.2m (4ft) |

## *Phlomis*

The phlomis is a suitable plant for full sun or half-shade. The strong upright flowers grow on the stems in tiers and are good for cutting.
**Hardiness: US Zone 8-5, Canadian Zone 7-4.**

| P. italica* | lilac pink, June–July, |
| | 60cm (24in) |
| P. fruticosa | yellow, June–July, 70cm (28in) |
| P. russeliana | yellow, June–July, 90cm (36in) |
| P. samia* | purple, June–July, 90cm (36in) |
| P. tuberosa* | pur. pink, June–July, 1.5m (5ft) |

*Phlomis russeliana*

## *Phlox*

In the case of this genus, we need to distinguish between the ground-cover plant for low walls (*P. subulata*) and the much taller border plants (*P. maculata* and *P. paniculata*), the former being rather more graceful and delicate than the latter. Cut back one-third of the flower stems before the longest day: these stems will flower later and thus extend the flowering season. All the plants are suitable for a sunny border and even do well on heavy clay. Water sufficiently to prevent drooping. The following list is a small selection from the vast assortment.
**Hardiness: US Zone 5, Canadian Zone 4.**

| | |
|---|---|
| *P. maculata* 'Alpha' | br. pink, June–Aug, 80cm (32in) |
| *P. m.* 'Delta' | white with lilac eyes, July–Aug, 1.2m (4ft) |
| *P. m.* 'Omega' | w. with. lil. eyes, July–Aug, 1m (3ft) |
| *P. paniculata* 'Amethyst' | soft blue, July–Sept, 75cm (30in) |
| *P. p.* 'Blue Ice' | white, July–Aug, 80cm (32in) |
| *P. p.* 'Border Gem' | viol. blue, July–Sept, 80cm (32in) |
| *P. p.* 'Flamingo' | flam. pink, July–Sept, 1m (3ft) |
| *P. p.* 'Graf Zeppelin' | white with red eyes, 1m (3ft) |
| *P. p.* 'Iris' | d. mauve, June–Aug, 80cm (32in) |
| *P. p.* 'Orange Perfection' | deep orange, 50cm (20in) |
| *P. p.* 'Starfire' | luminous red, 90cm (36in) |
| *P. p.* 'Tenor' | red, 1m (3ft) |
| *P. p.* 'The King' | blue, 80cm (32in) |
| *P. p.* 'White Admiral' | white, July–Aug, 80cm (32in) |
| *P. subulata* 'Benita' | lav. blue, May–June, 15cm (6in) |
| *P. s.* 'G.F. Wilson' | lilac blue, Apr–May, 15cm (6in) |
| *P. s.* 'May Snow' | white, May–June, 15cm (6in) |
| *P. s.* 'Moerheimii' | pink and carmine red, May–June, 15cm (6in) |
| *P. s.* 'Purple Beauty' | lilac, May–June, 10cm (4in) |
| *P. s.* 'Scarlet Flame' | br. red, Apr–June, 15cm (6in) |
| *P. s.* 'Temiscaming' | br. red, May–June, 10cm (4in) |
| *P. s.* 'White Delight' | white, Apr–June, 10cm (4in) |

*Phlox maculata* 'Alpha'

# Physalis

### CHINESE LANTERN

This plant's appeal is due not so much to its flowers as to the calyces and fruits produced in fall and suitable for dried flower arrangements. The plant behaves like a weed in the garden: the rhizomes are unstoppable.
**Hardiness: US Zone 5, Canadian Zone 5.**

| | |
|---|---|
| *P. alkekengi* | or. red, Sept–Oct, 80cm (32in) |

*Physalis alkekengi*

# Physostegia

### OBEDIENT PLANT

This strong and rather tall border perennial does not need staking. It produces good flowers for cutting and likes all soils.
**Hardiness: US Zone 4, Canadian Zone 3.**

| | |
|---|---|
| *P. virginiana* 'Bouquet Rose' | viol. pink, July–Sept, 70cm (28in) |
| *P. v.* 'Summer Snow' | white, July–Sept, 70cm (28in) |
| *P. v.* 'Summer Spire' | d. pink, July–Sept, 70cm (28in) |
| *P. v.* 'Vivid' | pink, July–Sept, 60cm (24in) |

*Physostegia virginiana* 'Summersnow'

## Phytolacca

**POKEWEED**

This plant originated in North America, but it has become naturalized in large parts of Europe. Its full racemes of black berries in fall are its main beauty. Propagation is by seed or division.
**Hardiness: US Zone 4, Canadian Zone 3.**

| | |
|---|---|
| P. acinosa | white, July–Sept, 1.5m (5ft) |
| P. americana | white, July–Sept, 1.2m (4ft) |

Phytolacca americana

## Plantago

The following cultivars of this common weed are of interest for gardens. They will grow in the most unlikely places, but prefer limy soil in among stones or gravel. They will not even be put off by highly compressed soil. 'Rosularis' has pompon-shaped flowers; 'Rubrifolia' has red leaves.
**Hardiness: US Zone 5, Canadian Zone 4.**

| | |
|---|---|
| P. major 'Rosularis'* | yellowish green, June–Sept, 30cm (12in) |
| P. m. 'Rubrifolia'* | brownish red leaves, June–Aug, 40cm (16in) |

## Platycodon

**BALLOON FLOWER**

Balloon flowers look rather like campanulas, although they are flatter. The English name refers to the shape of the flower buds. It is an undemanding border plant for a position in full sun. P. grandiflorus is the wild species from China.
**Hardiness: US Zone 4, Canadian Zone 3.**

| | |
|---|---|
| P. grandiflorus 'Albus' | white, July–Sept, 40cm (16in) |
| P. g. 'Mariesii' | lilac blue, June–Aug, 40cm (16in) |
| P. g. 'Shell Pink' | pink, June–Aug, 40cm (16in) |
| P. g. 'Dwarf' | blue, June–Aug, 10cm (4in) |

Platycodon grandiflorus 'Mariesii'

## Polemonium

**JACOB'S LADDER**

Polemoniums do well in a sunny border and produce good flowers for cutting. The leaves also look attractive before the plant comes into flower. Light support may be required. The plant thrives in any kind of soil and is undemanding.
**Hardiness: US Zone 7-4, Canadian Zone 6-3.**

| | |
|---|---|
| P. caeruleum | blue, June–July, 70cm (28in) |
| P. c. 'Album' | June–Aug, 40cm (16in) |
| P. pauciflorum* | l. yellow, June–Aug, 50cm (20in) |
| P. reptans | blue, Apr–June, 40cm (16in) |
| P. r. 'Blue Pearl' | June–Aug, 40cm (16in) |

*Polemonium caeruleum*

*Polygonatum falcatum* 'Variegatum'

plants and vines). They are all vigorous plants for sun and semi-shade and can be grown for many purposes: for borders, ground cover, rockeries (low species), and parterres.
**Hardiness: US Zone 7-3, Canadian Zone 6-2.**

| | |
|---|---|
| *P. affine* | d. pink, Aug–Oct, 30cm (12in) |
| *P. a.* 'Superbum' | pink, abundant flowers, Aug–Oct, 30cm (12in) |
| *P. amplexicaule* | red, July–Oct, 80–90cm (32–36ft) |
| *P. a.* 'Roseum' | pink, July–Oct, 1.2m (4ft) |
| *P. a.* 'Speciosum' | red, July–Sept, 1–1.2m (3–4ft) |
| *P. vaccinifolium* | pink, July–Oct, 25cm (10in) |

*Polygonum vaccinifolium*

## Polygonatum

### SOLOMON'S SEAL

Apart from the whorled Solomon's seal *(P. verticillatum)*, the various species closely resemble one another. Only the height differs: choose the right one to go with the size of the border. They require full sun to semi-shade, moist humus-rich soil, and are suitable for natural planting or a woodland corner. The white flowers are suspended from curved stems, suggesting a sow with piglets.
**Hardiness: US Zone 6-2, Canadian Zone 5-2.**

| | |
|---|---|
| *P. commutatum** | white, 1.2m (4ft) |
| *P. falcatum* 'Variegatum' | white margins to leaves, 25cm (10in) |
| *P. multiflorum* | white, May–July, 60cm (24in) |
| *P. odoratum* | white, May–July, 40cm (16in) |
| *P. verticillatum** | white, 70cm (28in) |

## Polygonum

### KNOTWEED

This genus comprises a large number of species, including some naturalized ones like knotgrass and lady's thumb. The tall Japanese polygonums are called *Reynoutria* nowadays (see also: Water-

*Potentilla erecta*

## *Potentilla*

**CINQUEFOIL**

These small undemanding plants have a tendency to flatten a little. They tolerate dryish soil, but should be watered regularly.

**Hardiness: US Zone 5, Canadian Zone 4.**

| | |
|---|---|
| *P. alba* | white, May–June, 15cm (6in) |
| *P. atrosanguinea* | d. red, June–July, 30cm (12in) |
| *P. aurea* | yellow, May–June, 10cm (4in) |
| *P. nepalensis* 'Miss Willmott' | car. red, July–Sept, 40cm (16in) |
| *P. neumanniana* 'Nana' | yellow, Apr–May, 5cm (2in) |
| *P. recta* | yellow, June–Aug, 80cm (32in) |
| *P. rupestris* | white, July–Aug, 60cm (24in) |
| *P. tongei* | or. red, July–Aug, 20cm (8in) |

*Primula denticulata*

# Primula

**PRIMROSE**

The name makes most people think of spring-flowering plants, but there is a lot of variety. Make sure you note the height and flowering season when using the following list. They all require half-shade and a soil rich in humus. *P. bessiana*, *P. bullesiana*, *P. bulleyana*, *P. japonica* and *P. pulverulenta* are candelabra primulas with flowers borne in tiered whorls, on long stems, they prefer a moist soil. *P sieboldi*, a Japanese species is the most tolerant of sun, heat and drought. *P. vialii* is moderately winter-hardy and should be protected.
**Hardiness: US Zone 5, Canadian Zone 4.**

| | |
|---|---|
| *P. auricula* | mixed, May–June, 15cm (6in) |
| *P. beesiana*! | purplish red, June–July, 50cm (20in) |
| *P. bullesiana*! | mix. col., June–July, 60cm (24in) |
| *P. bulleyana* | orange, June–Aug, 40cm (16in) |
| *P. chionantha* | white, May–July, 40cm (16in) |
| *P. denticulata* | lilac, Apr–May, 15cm (6in) |
| *P. d.* 'Alba' | white, Apr–May, 15cm (6in) |
| *P. d.* 'Rubra' | red, Apr–May, 15cm (6in) |
| *P. florindae*! | yellow, July–Sept, 90cm (36in) |
| *P. japonica* 'Alba' | white, May–July, 50cm (20in) |
| *P. juliae* 'Aurea' | yellow, Mar–May, 20cm (8in) |
| *P. j.* 'Betty Green' | red, Mar–Apr, 10cm (4in) |
| *P. j.* 'Upper Silesia' | mauve, Mar–Apr, 15cm (6in) |
| *P. j.* 'Snow Cushion' | white, Mar–Apr, 20cm (8in) |
| *P. j.* 'Wanda' | viol. purple, Feb–Apr, 15cm (6in) |
| *P. pulverulenta* | purplish red, May–June, 50cm (20in) |
| *P. rosea* 'Grandiflora' | pink, Mar–Apr, 20cm (8in) |
| *P. sieboldii* | pink, June, 20cm (8in) |
| *P. vialii*! | red/violet, June–July, 30cm (12in) |

# Prunella

**SELF-HEAL**

This undemanding perennial flowers well and merits greater interest. It thrives in any kind of soil, in sun or half-shade.
**Hardiness: US Zone 5, Canadian Zone 4.**

| | |
|---|---|
| *P. grandiflora* | violet blue, June–Aug, 25cm (10in) |
| *P. g.* 'Alba' | pure white |
| *P. g.* 'Carminea' | |
| *P. g.* 'Loveliness' | lilac pink, June–Sept, 20cm (8in) |
| *P. vulgaris* | blueish mauve, June–Aug, 25cm (10in) |
| *P.* x *webbiana* 'Rosea' | pink, June–Aug, 25cm (10in) |

# Pseudofumaria

See: *Corydalis*.

# Pulmonaria

**LUNGWORT**

This good evergreen plant attracts bees and flowers early in the season. Like *Ajuga reptans*, it tends to be affected by mildew in a dry position. Spraying makes little sense: it is simply growing in the wrong place. Nearly all flowers fade from blue to pink; in the following list, only the color of the colorfast plants is mentioned.
**Hardiness: US Zone 5-4, Canadian Zone 4-3.**

| | |
|---|---|
| *P. angustifolia* 'Azurea'! | azure, Apr–May, 25cm (10in) |
| *P. longifolia*! | blue, Apr–June, 30cm (12in) |
| *P. officinalis* | Mar–May, 30cm (12in) |
| *P. o.* 'Sissinghurst White' | white, Mar–Apr, 40cm (16in) |
| *P. rubra* | red, Mar–Apr, 30cm (12in) |
| *P. saccharata* | sky blue, Mar–May, 25cm (10in) |

*Prunella* x *webbiana*

*Pulmonaria longifolia*

| P. s. 'Mrs. Moon' | lilac pink, Apr–May, 30cm (12in) |
| P. s. 'Pink Dawn' | pink, Apr–May, 25cm (10in) |

## Pulsatilla

### PASQUE FLOWER

Year after year it comes as a surprise to see how relatively large flowers emerge straight from the cold soil. The taller seed heads are also highly decorative as they glisten in the sun. This is a good reason for planting them in a sunny spot although they can tolerate light shade.
**Hardiness: US Zone 5, Canadian Zone 4.**

| P. vulgaris | blueish mauve, Mar–Apr, 40cm (16in) |
| P. v. 'Alba' | white, Mar–Apr, 30cm (12in) |
| P. v. 'Red Bells' | red, Mar–Apr, 30cm (12in) |
| P. v. 'Rubra' | dark brownish red, Mar–Apr, 25cm (10in) |

Pulsatilla vulgaris 'Rubra'

## Pyrethrum

Pyrethrine, still the best biological pesticide to use against aphids and caterpillars, is extracted from this plant. See also: *Chrysanthemum (coccineum* hybrids).

## Ranunculus

### BUTTERCUP

Wild buttercups are to be found in moist soil by the roadside. The creeping buttercup, *R. repens*, is a tiresome weed. The following species are suitable for the side of a pond or not too dry a border.
**Hardiness: US Zone 6-5, Canadian Zone 5-4.**

| R. aconitifolius | white, May–July, 50cm (20in) |
| R. acris 'Multiplex' | yellow (d), May–Aug, 60cm (24in) |
| R. ficaria | yellow, Mar–Apr, 15cm (6in) |
| R. f. 'Alba' | white, Mar–Apr, 10cm (4in) |

Ranunculus acris 'Multiplex'

## Reynoutria

### JAPANESE KNOTWEED

This plant was called *Polygonum cuspidatum* until recently. Because of its bamboo-like stems, there is quite a difference between this species and the other knotweeds. They naturalize easily and can become a very aggressive weed. Grow with great caution.

| R. japonica var. compacta | pink, July–Sept, 40cm (16in) |
| R. j. 'Rosea' | pink, July–Sept, 1.75m (5ft) |
| R. sachalinensis* | white, Aug–Oct, 4m (13ft) |

## Rheum

### ORNAMENTAL RHUBARB

The huge leaves of this plant are highly decorative. It is suitable for planting by itself on the lawn or beside a medium-size pond. A

*Reynoutria japonica* var. *compacta*

**Hardiness: US Zone 6-5, Canadian Zone 5-4.**

| | |
|---|---|
| *R. aesculifolia*! | white/pink, June–July, 1m (3ft) |
| *R. pinnata* | pale pink, May–Aug, 1m (3ft) |
| *R. sambusifolia*! | white, June–July, 70cm (28in) |

*Rodgersia sambusifolia*

moisture-retentive soil and semi-shade are best for preventing the leaves from drooping.
**Hardiness: US Zone 6-5, Canadian Zone 5-4.**

| | |
|---|---|
| *R. australe* | greenish white, June–July, 2m (6ft) |
| *R. palmatum*! | pink, 1.5m (5ft) |
| *R. p.* var. *tanguticum* | red, May–July, 1.5m (5ft) |

*Rheum palmatum* var. *tanguticum*

# Rodgersia

See also: *Astilboides*. This is a foliage plant for a shady position and preferably moist soil. The handsome flower plumes, followed by green seed heads, are a further bonus.

# Rudbeckia

## CONEFLOWER

The rudbeckia's striking yellow flowers are a welcome addition to the assortment of perennials. Find a sunny spot for them and note their height: some of them are unsuitable for small gardens. For *R. purpurea* see: *Echinacea*.
**Hardiness: US Zone 6-4, Canadian Zone 5-3.**

| | |
|---|---|
| *R. fulgida* 'Goldsturm' | yellow, black centers, Aug–Oct, 60cm (24in) |
| *R. f.* var. *speciosa* | orange yellow, brown centers, July–Sept, 60cm (24in) |
| *R. laciniata* | yellow, July–Sept, 70cm (28in) |
| *R. maxima* | yellow, July–Sept. 1.5m (5ft) |

*Rudbeckia fulgida* 'Goldsturm'

# Ruta

### RUE

Dogs apparently hate this herb, which requires well-drained sandy soil. The plant's blueish green leaves may be used in meat and fish recipes. Some people are allergic to the herb.
**Hardiness: US Zone 6, Canadian Zone 5.**

| | |
|---|---|
| *R. graveolens* | yellow, May–Sept, 50cm (20in) |
| *R. g.* 'Jackman's Blue' | yellow, May–Sept, 40cm (16in) |

*Ruta graveolens* 'Jackman's Blue'

# Sagina

Sagina sometimes grows like a weed, but it may also be planted as ground cover in places that are walked on from time to time.
**Hardiness: US Zone 4, Canadian Zone 3.**

| | |
|---|---|
| *S. subulata* | white, May–Aug, 5cm (2in) |
| *S. s.* 'Aurea' | white, golden yellow leaves, 5cm (2in) |

*Sagina subulata*

# Salvia

### SAGE

This border plant for full sun has a lengthy flowering season and provides long-lasting cut flowers – no garden should be without it! Cut back the plant soon after it has bloomed: you will be rewarded with a second flush of flowers. *S. nemorosa* was formerly called *S. superba*.
**Hardiness: US Zone 6, Canadian Zone 5.**

| | |
|---|---|
| *S. nemorosa* 'Blaukönigin' | pur. blue, June–Aug, 40cm (16in) |
| *S. n.* 'Lubeca' | deep purplish blue, June–Aug, 80cm (32in) |
| *S. n.* 'May Night' | d. blue, May–Aug, 60cm (24in) |
| *S. n.* 'East Friesland' | pl. blue, July–Sept, 40cm (16in) |
| *S. n.* 'Rose Queen' | pink, June–Aug, 70cm (28in) |
| *S. n.* 'Tänzerin' | purple, June–Aug, 70cm (28in) |
| *S. pratensis*! | blue, June–Aug, 40cm (16in) |
| *S. verticillata* | blue, July–Sept, 80cm (32in) |
| *S. v.* 'Purple Rain' | lilac, June–Aug, 80cm (32in) |

*Salvia nemorosa* 'Tänzerin'

*Sambucus ebulus*

# Sambucus

An elder among the perennials? Yes, because this plant dies down to the soil every year. Large white flowers stand out above the fresh green leaves – it really is worth recommending! The plant is suitable for any soil but is highly invasive.
**Hardiness: US Zone 5, Canadian Zone 5.**

S. ebulus!          white, July, 2.5m (5ft)

# Sanguisorba

### BURNET

Like the alchemilla, this plant is recognizable by the water droplets that remain on its leaves. *S. minor* is a kitchen herb; *S. obtusa*, formerly classified as belonging to the *Poterium* genus, is suitable for borders. The plant requires sun and humus-rich, well-drained soil.
**Hardiness: US Zone 5-4, Canadian Zone 4-3.**

S. obtusa!            lilac pink, July–Sept, 80cm (32in)
S. tenuifolia 'Alba'*    white, Aug–Sept, 1.75 (5ft)

*Sanguisorba obtusa*

# Santolina

These sub-shrubs become woody with age. Prevent this by pruning the plants in spring. Give them a sunny position in, for example, a rock or a heather garden, but, because of their frost-tenderness, it is preferable not to grow them as edging plants. It is advisable to cover the base in winter. *S. rosmarinifolia* has green leaves; those of the following species are gray.
**Hardiness: US Zone 7, Canadian Zone 6.**

S. chamaecyparissus    yellow, July–Aug, 40cm (16in)
S. serratifolia        yellow, July–Aug, 35cm (14in)

*Santolina serratifolia*

# Saponaria

### SOAPWORT

This fast-growing and rewarding plant is capable of ousting other plants in the rock garden. It requires full sun and prefers not too moist a position. The low-growing species listed below are good, fast-growing rock plants.
**Hardiness: US Zone 6-4, Canadian Zone 5-3.**

S. ocymoides        pink, May–July, 20cm (8in)
S. o. 'Alba'        white
S. officinalis      pink, June–Sept, 60cm (24in)
S. o. 'Rosea Plena'   warm pink (d), June–Sept, 70cm (28in)
S. x oliviana       pink, May–July, 5cm (2in)

*Saponaria ocymoides*

# Saxifraga

SAXIFRAGE

*S. umbrosa* is an old-fashioned edging plant for sun or half-shade. *S. cuneifolia*, smaller in every way, may serve the same purpose. The *arendsii* hybrids are cushion-forming; the plants need to be renewed regularly as the center of the plants dies after a few years. The following list is just a brief selection: there are more than 300 species and cultivars. They are nearly all rock plants for full sun. One exception is *S. cortusifolia*, which prefers semi-shade and acid soil. The plant flowers extremely late. As a writer of books on plants, I am restrained in my choice of words and rarely use terms such as magnificent, wonderful, outstanding and so on, except when referring to this plant, because it really is wonderful. London pride, *S. umbrosa*, has a new name: *S. x urbium*.

**Hardiness: US Zone 6-5, Canadian Zone 5-4.**

| | |
|---|---|
| *S. arendsii* | red, pink or white, Apr–June, 15cm (6in) |
| *S. a.* 'Gaiety' | pink |
| *S.a* 'Purple Rose' | *purple* |
| *S. a.* 'Snow Carpet' | white |
| *S. cortusifolia*! | white, Oct–Nov, 40cm (16in) |
| *S. c.* var. *fortunei*! | white, red leaves, Oct–Nov, 50cm (20in) |
| *S. c.* 'Rubrifolia'! | white, red leaves, Oct–Nov, 50cm (20in) |
| *S. cuneifolia* | pink, May–June, 15cm (6in) |
| *S. x urbium* | pink, May–June, 30cm (12in) |
| *S. x u.* 'Clarence Elliot' | pink, May–June, 30cm (12in) |
| *S. u.* 'Variegata' | pale pink, yellow-spotted leaves |

*Saxifraga* x *urbium* 'Clarence Elliott'

# Scabiosa

SCABIOUS

This plant bears excellent flowers for cutting. It has a long flowering season and is suitable for sunny borders. Scabious needs limy, well-drained soil.

**Hardiness: US Zone 4, Canadian Zone 3.**

| | |
|---|---|
| *S. caucasica* | lilac blue, June–Sept, 70cm (28in) |
| *S. c.* 'Alba' | white, June–Sept, 70cm (28in) |
| *S. c.* 'Clive Greaves' | l. blue, June–Sept, 70cm (28in) |
| *S. c.* 'Stäfa' | d. blue, June–Sept, 80cm (32in) |

*Scabiosa caucasica* 'Stäfa'

# Sedum

STONECROP

This succulent requires as much sun as possible, and dry to very dry soil. Good drainage is

*Sedum acre*

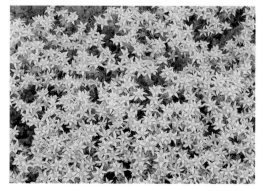

needed to prevent the plants rotting. Regular division will prevent *S. spectabile* and *S. spurium* disintegrating. The following list includes the commonest species.

**Hardiness: US Zone 6-4, Canadian Zone 5-3.**

| | |
|---|---|
| *S. acre* | yellow, June–July, 10cm (4in) |
| *S. album* | off-white, June–July, 15cm (6in) |
| *S. a.* 'Murale' | white, June–Aug, 15cm (6in) |
| *S. ewersii* | d. pink, July–Sept, 20cm (8in) |
| *S. glaucum* | w./pink, June–July, 15cm (6in) |
| *S. kamtschaticum* | g. yellow, June–Sept, 15cm (6in) |
| *S. lydium* | w./pink, June–July, 15cm (6in) |
| *S. reflexum* | yellow, June–Aug, 25cm (10in) |
| *S. spathulifolium* | yellow, June–July, 15cm (6in) |
| *S. spectabile* | pink, Aug–Oct, 30cm (12in) |
| *S. s.* 'Brilliant' | lilac pink, Aug–Oct, 30cm (12in) |
| *S. s. Spurium* 'Dragons Blood' | red, July–Sept, 10cm (4in) |
| *Sedum spurium* 'Fuldaglow' | red, July–Aug, 15cm (6in) |
| *S. s.* 'Robustum' | pink. red, July–Sept, 40cm (16in) |
| *S. stenopetalum* | yellow, June–Sept, 10cm (4in) |

*Sedum spectabile* 'Brilliant'

# Sempervivum

## HOUSELEEK

Sempervivum continues to grow in extremely dry conditions such as rough-surfaced roof tiles that are not set at too steep an angle. It is a good idea to plant houseleeks in shallow bowls in small alpine gardens. Gray, green, sea-green, or reddish fleshy leaves protect the plants against fierce sunlight. Some of them are covered in webs of hairs for the same reason. The pink flowers grow on 15cm (6in) stems. They flower in June–July. The following colors refer to the leaf rosettes.

**Hardiness: US Zone 5, Canadian Zone 4.**

| | |
|---|---|
| *S. arachnoideum* | gray, with web of hairs |
| *S. tectorum* 'Bicolor' | grayish blue |
| *S. t.* var. *glaucum* | grayish blue |
| *S. t.* 'Rubrum' | reddish |

**Hybrid cultivars:**

| | |
|---|---|
| *S.* 'Granat' | purplish red |
| *S.* 'Othello' | brownish red, large |
| *S.* 'Pseudo-ornatum' | reddish green |
| *S.* 'Ruby' | ruby red |
| *S.* 'Triste' | light purplish brown |

*Sempervivum arachnoideum*

# Sidalcea!

### PRAIRIE MALLOW

This is an ideal plant for borders: a long flowering season, strong stems, and still attractive after it has flowered. Provides cut flowers for carefree people! Combine it with phlox, purple loosestrife, and lavender.

**Hardiness: US Zone 5, Canadian Zone 4.**

*Sidalcea* 'Interlaken'

| | |
|---|---|
| S. candida | white, June–Aug, 80cm (32in) |
| S. oregana 'Brilliant' | car. red, July–Sept, 80cm (32in) |
| **Hybrid cultivars**: | |
| S. 'Elsie Heugh' | satin pink, June–Aug, 1m (3ft) |
| S. 'Rosanna' | pink, July–Aug, 1m (3ft) |
| S. 'Rose Beauty' | d. pink, June–July, 70cm (28in) |
| S. 'Rosy Gem' | carmine and lilac, 1m (3ft) |
| S. 'Sussex Beauty' | silvery pink, 1.2m (4ft) |

## Smilacina

### FALSE SPIKENARD

The flowers are not spread out like those of Solomon's seal; instead, they grow in astilbe-like sprays at the end of pendulous stems. The plant is suitable for deepest shade, but is not averse to sun. The flowers are good for cutting and look well combined with primulas.
**Hardiness: US Zone 4, Canadian Zone 3.**

| | |
|---|---|
| S. racemosa | white, June, 80cm (32in) |

Smilacina racemosa

## Solidago

### GOLDEN ROD

This little-grown, old-fashioned cottage garden plant is widely grown in Europe. Beware of some of the native species and the older, often tall-growing varieties, which can be very invasive. However, the more modern varieties are usually lower growing, making more compact clumps, and are suitable for borders. They grow well in any kind of soil and in full sun. Occasionally the lower leaves are affected by mildew. This plant is often accused of causing allergies in the fall, but is innocent, the culprit being ragweed.
**Hardiness: US Zone 5-4, Canadian Zone 4-3.**

| | |
|---|---|
| S. 'Cloth of Gold' | yellow, July–Sept, 40cm (16in) |
| S. 'Golden Dwarf' | yellow, Aug–Sept, 30cm (12in) |
| S. 'Goldkind' | pure yellow, Aug–Sept, 60cm (24in) |

| | |
|---|---|
| S. 'Laurin' | golden y., Aug–Sept, 40cm (16in) |
| S. 'Praecox' | yellow, July–Aug, 60cm (24in) |
| S. 'Crown of Rays' | bright yellow, Aug–Sept, 60cm (24in) |

Solidago 'Golden Dwarf'

## Solidaster

This plant's former name was Asterago, a cross between asters and golden rod. It is a good cold-greenhouse plant for cutting, but less suitable for gardens because of its weak stems. A warm windless spot or good support will remedy this. It thrives in any kind of soil.
**Hardiness: US Zone 5, Canadian Zone 4.**

| | |
|---|---|
| S. leteus | l. yellow, July–Sept, 60cm (24in) |
| S. i. 'Lemore' | yellow, Aug–Sept, 70cm (28in) |

Solidaster luteus 'Lemore'

## Stachys

**WOUNDWORT**

Stachys is pre-eminently an edging plant. As you take your daily walk down your garden path, you will not be able to resist bending down to feel whether the leaves are still just as soft as they were yesterday. Stachys avoids the need to plant an edging of box around rose borders. Like roses, the plants need sun, and soil that is not excessively moist. *S. grandiflora* is more of a woodland plant, with labiate flowers produced in (apparent) whorls around the stems, and green leaves.
**Hardiness: US Zone 5, Canadian Zone 4.**

| | |
|---|---|
| *S. grandiflora* 'Superba' | lil. pink, June–Aug, 50cm (20in) |
| *S. g.* 'Rosea' | pink, June–Aug, 60cm (24in) |
| *S. byzantina* 'Cotton Ball' | hooded flowers, July–Aug, 40cm (16in) |
| *S. b.* 'Lamb's Ears' | gray, July–Aug, 60cm (24in) |
| *S. b.* 'Silver Carpet' | no flowers!, 20cm (8in) |
| *S. spicata* 'Alba' | white, June–Aug, 25cm (10in) |
| *S. s.* 'Rosea' | pink, June–Aug, 25cm (10in) |

*Stachys byzantina* 'Lambs Lugs'

## Symphitum

**COMFREY**

This excellent evergreen ground-cover plant for deepest shade is invasive! It will thrive in any kind of soil. *S. caucasicum*, a border plant, is different from the others. Beware: this plant moves around!
**Hardiness: US Zone 5, Canadian Zone 4.**

| | |
|---|---|
| *S. caucasicum** | sky blue, June–Aug, 80cm (32in) |
| *S. grandiflorum* | cream, Mar–May, 40cm (16in) |
| *S. g.* 'Wisley Blue' | l. blue, May–July, 40cm (16in) |
| *S. officinale* | purple or white, May–Aug, 70cm (28in) |
| *S. x rubrum* | red, June–Aug, 30cm (12in) |

## Telekia

Telekias are strong plants with large bright green leaves. They are suitable for large gardens, in solitary positions, or as tall hedges. They are undemanding: plant in sun or semi-shade.
**Hardiness: US Zone 5, Canadian Zone 4.**

| | |
|---|---|
| *T. speciosa*! | bright orange yellow, July–Aug, 1.25cm (4ft 2in) |

*Telekia speciosa*

## Tellima

Tellimas are not spectacular, but no natural-looking woodland garden should be without them! They require deep shade and moisture-retentive soil. The plants resemble tolmieas, but are taller and deciduous.
**Hardiness: US Zone 5, Canadian Zone 4.**

*Symphitum grandiflorum*

| | |
|---|---|
| *T. grandiflora* | gr. yel., May–July, 50cm (20in) |
| *T. g.* 'Rubra' | gr. yel., May–July, 50cm (20in) |

*Tellima grandiflora* 'Rubra'

# Thalicthrum

**MEADOW RUE**

This genus resembles the familiar columbine. The plants need similar positions and meet the same requirements. They do, however, need more support, or they will fall over but in return will provide you with long stems for tall flower arrangements. The name *T. dipterocarpum* has been replaced by *T. delavayi*.
**Hardiness: US Zone 5, Canadian Zone 4.**

| | |
|---|---|
| *T. aquilegifolium* | bl. purple, May–July, 1.4m (4ft) |
| *T. delavayi* 'Album' | white, July–Sept, 1.5m (5ft) |
| *T. d.* 'Hewitt's Double' | light lilac mauve, 1.5m (5ft) |
| *T. rochebruneanum* | lilac, July–Sept, 1.75m (5fift) |

*Thalicthrum aquilegifolium*

# Thymus

**THYME**

The wooly thyme is still frequently sold under the name *T. brittannicus*, but its latest name is *T. praecox* var. *pseudolanuginosus*. The cushions of aromatic leaves look attractive scrambling over low walls and in rockeries. They are all mat-forming; the kitchen herb *T. vulgaris* is shaped like a small shrub. Plant in well-drained soil in full sun; a warm spot will be appreciated.
**Hardiness: US Zone 5-4, Canadian Zone 4-3.**

| | |
|---|---|
| *T. citriodorus*! | lilac pink, July–Aug, 10cm (4in) |
| *T. c.* 'Aureus' | lilac pink, yellow foliage |
| *T. c.* 'Silver Queen' | lilac pink, variegated foliage |
| *T. pseudolanuginosus*! | June–July, 10cm (4in) |
| *T. serpyllum* | lilac, June–July, 20cm (8in) |
| *T. s.* 'Albus' | white, June–July, 10cm (4in) |
| *T. s.* 'Coccineus' | pur. red, June–July, 10cm (4in) |
| *T. vulgaris* | pale lilac, May–July, 30cm (12in) |

*Thymus serpyllum* 'Coccineus'

# Tiarella

This low native evergreen ground-cover plant with lime-green leaves in spring and a reddish shade in fall forms a dense carpet preferring semi-shaded conditions. Plant under shrubs or in a woodland garden.
**Hardiness: US Zone 5-4, Canadian Zone 4-3.**

| | |
|---|---|
| *T. cordifolia* | cream, May–June, 30cm (12in) |
| *T. c.* 'Rosalie'* | pale pink, June–July, 30cm (12in) |
| *T. wheryi*! | cream, May–Sept, 30cm (12in) |

*Tiarella cordifolia*

beguiling that they are still among the "top twenty" border plants. They are old-fashioned, suitable for sunny or shady positions, for dry or moist soil – in other words: indestructible. Their flowering season is from June to September.
**Hardiness: US Zone 5, Canadian Zone 4.**

**T. andersoniana hybrids:**

| | |
|---|---|
| T. a. 'Blue Stone' | light blue, 70cm (28in) |
| T. a. 'Charlotte'** | bright pink, 50cm (20in) |
| T. a. 'Innocence' | pure white, 60cm (24in) |
| T. a. 'J.C. Weguelin' | blue, 70cm (28in) |
| T. a. 'Leonora' | blueish violet, 70cm (28in) |
| T. a. 'Osprey' | white and violet, 70cm (28in) |
| T. a. 'Purple Dome' | purple, 70cm (28in) |
| T. a. 'Rubra' | purplish red, 70cm (28in) |

## Tolmiea

**PICK-A-BACK PLANT**

Tolmieas have inconspicuous flowers, but they are good, dense, fast-growing ground-cover plants for dark corners. They look well combined with tall ferns. The plants like rather moist soil but are otherwise undemanding. Although they are frost-hardy, these evergreen plants were formerly often grown as indoor plants.
**Hardiness: US Zone 6, Canadian Zone 5.**

| | |
|---|---|
| T. menziesii | greenish yellow, May–June, 25cm (10in) |

## Tradescantia

**SPIDERWORT**

The plants look untidy, but the flowers are so

*Tradescantia andersoniana* 'Innocence'

## Tricyrtus

**TOAD LILY**

This plant is of interest because of its late flowering season. Its flowers are not striking, but its glossy green leaves help to make the plant look more decorative. It belongs to the lily family, but reminds one more of an orchid. Toad lilies require sun or semi-shade as well as acid soil: add garden peat.
**Hardiness: US Zone 7-5, Canadian Zone 6-4.**

| | |
|---|---|
| T. formosana | lilac, Aug–Oct, 40cm (16in) |
| T. hirta | br. lilac with white speckles, Sept–Nov, 80cm (32in) |
| T. latifolia* | white with purple veins, June–Aug, 70cm (28in) |
| T. pilosa** | yellow, June–July, 60cm (24in) |

*Tricyrtus hirta*

## Trifolium

### CLOVER

Anyone familiar with this plant will cease to regard clover as a weed. It needs a sunny spot (to make the red leaves show up better) in limy soil, preferably between stones.
**Hardiness: US Zone 5, Canadian Zone 4.**

*T. repens* 'Pentaphyllum'** May–June, 20cm (8in)

*Trifolium repens* 'Pentaphyllum'

## Trollius

### GLOBEFLOWER

This member of the buttercup family is a rewarding border plant which needs moist soil to achieve perfection. It is an undemanding plant for sun or partial shade.
**Hardiness: US Zone 5, Canadian Zone 5.**

*T. europaeus*          yellow, June–Aug, 80cm (32in)

*Trollius* 'Lemon Queen'

| | |
|---|---|
| *T. ledebourii** | orange, June–July, 60cam (2ft) |
| *T. pumilus* | yellow, June–July, 20cm (8in) |
| **Hybrid cultivars:** | |
| *T.* 'Earliest of All' | orange, y. May–July, 50cm (20in) |
| *T.* 'Etna' | d. orange, May–July, 60cm (24in) |
| *T.* 'Fire Globe' | orange, May–July, 70cm (28in) |
| *T.* 'Golden Queen' | yellow, Apr–June, 50cm (20in) |
| *T.* 'Lemon Queen' | yellow, Apr–June, 50cm (20in) |
| *T.* 'Orange Princess' | orange yel. May–July, 50cm (20in) |
| *T.* Prichard's Giant' | dark orange yellow, June, 90cm (36in) |

## Veratrum*

### FALSE HELLEBORE

The veratrum is a tall plant for a shady position. The full-grown leaf is pleated like an accordion, which gives the plant an oriental appearance. It introduces a special atmosphere, especially in older gardens. In spite of making a slow start, it requires a lot of space. The plant is poisonous.
**Hardiness: US Zone 6-5, Canadian Zone 5-4.**

| | |
|---|---|
| *V. album*** | white, June–July, 1.5m (5ft) |
| *V. californicum*** | white, July–Aug, 2.5m (8ft) |
| *V. nigrum*** | chestnut brown, June–July, 1.75m (5ft) |

*Veratrum album*

## Verbascum

### MULLEIN
See: Annuals and biennials.

## Verbena

Verbenas produce one or several stiffly upright heads of flowers. They make good, undemanding border plants and require full sun. They may not be fully hardy but, to compensate for this, they self-seed extensively. *V. officinalis* is a kitchen herb used all too rarely. For *V. bonariensis* see: Annuals and biennials.
**Hardiness: US Zone 4, Canadian Zone 3.**

| | |
|---|---|
| *V. hastata* 'Alba' | white, July–Aug, 1.25cm (4ft 2in) |
| *V. h.* 'Rosea'! | pink, June–Sept, 60cm (24in) |

## Veronica

The long-leafed and Virginian species have racemes of flowers; the others have spikes. They all require good, moisture-retentive soil in full sun. That is where the gentian-blue colors show up best.

*Veronica gentianoides* 'Pallida'

**Hardiness: US Zone 6-3, Canadian Zone 5-2.**

| | |
|---|---|
| *V. austriaca* 'Royal Blue' | dark blue, May–June, 40cm (16in) |
| *V. gentianoides* | blueish violet, May–June, 20cm (8in) |
| *V. g.* 'Pallida' | light blue, June–Aug, 30cm (12in) |
| *V. g.* 'Variegata' | variegated leaves, May–June, 20cm (8in) |
| *V. longifolia* | blue, July–Aug, 80cm (32in) |
| *V. virginica* | blue, July–Aug, 1.5m (5ft) |
| *V. v.* 'Alba' | white |
| *V. v.* 'Albo-Rosea' | whitish pink |
| *V. spicata* 'Blue Peter' | blue, June–July 40cm, (18in) |
| *V. s.* 'Red Fox' | dark pinkish red |
| *V. s.* 'Icicle' | white |

## Vinca

### PERIWINKLE
Along with the *Pachysandra*, vincas are among the most popular ground-cover plants. They are evergreen and suitable for sun or shade. Remember that the cultivars of *V. minor* grow less exuberantly than the species. Don't plant the variegated cultivars in too shady a spot. *V. major*, which has long runners, may be cut by a severe frost.
**Hardiness: US Zone 7-5, Canadian Zone 6-4.**

| | |
|---|---|
| *V. major** | blue, Apr–Sept, 40cm (16in) |
| *V. m.* 'Variegata' | blue, Apr–July, 30cm (12in) |
| *V. minor* | blue, Apr–July, 30cm (12in) |
| *V. m.* 'Gertrude Jekyll' | white, Apr–July, 10cm (4in) |
| *V. m.* 'Atropurpurea'* | wine red, Apr–June, 15cm (6in) |
| *V. m.* 'Plena' | light blue (d), Apr–June, 25cm (10in) |

*Vinca major* 'Variegata'

# Viola

Perennial violets may be divided into small-flowered spring violets, small-flowered (wild) summer violets, and large-flowered summer violets, the *Cornuta* hybrids (see also: Annuals and biennials). Wild violets are suitable for a sunny or half-shady position; the others prefer sun. *V. sororia* is very invasive. *V. labradorica*, called *V. riviniana* in England, has dark leaves.
**Hardiness: US Zone 7-3, Canadian Zone 6-2.**

| | |
|---|---|
| *V. canina* | blue, Apr–May, 10cm (4in) |
| *V. labradorica*! | blue. violet, Apr–June, 10cm (4in) |
| *V. odorata* | mauve, evergreen, Mar–May, 20cm (8in) |
| *V. o.* 'Alba'* | white, Mar–May, 20cm (8in) |
| *V. o.* 'Rubra'* | red, Mar–May, 20cm (8in) |
| *V. o.* 'Queen Charlotte'* | violet blue |
| *V. sororia*! | white with blue spots, Apr–May, 20cm (8in) |

**Cornuta hybrids:**

| | |
|---|---|
| *V.* 'Boughton Blue' | blue, May–Sept, 20cm (8in) |
| *V.* 'Foxbrook Cream' | creamy white |
| *V.* 'Gazelle' | warm yellow |
| *V.* 'Helen Mount' | soft blue |
| *V.* 'Milkmaid' | cream and slightly blue |
| *V.* 'Molly Sanderson' | purplish black |
| *V.* 'Netty Britton' | lilac blue |
| *V.* 'Penny Black' | almost black |
| *V.* 'Talitha' | blueish violet, with white center |
| *V.* 'Victoria Cowthorne' | lilac pink |
| *V.* 'White Superior' | white, large |

# Waldsteinia

This small, evergreen, strawberry-like plant provides undemanding ground cover (without

*Viola* 'White Superior'

fruits). It resembles *Duchesnea*, which produces small, inedible, strawberries. Propagate by division. Waldsteinias tolerate shade.
**Hardiness: US Zone 5-3, Canadian Zone 4-2.**

| | |
|---|---|
| *W. geoides*! | yellow, Apr–May, 25cm (10in) |
| *W. ternata* | yellow, Apr–May, 15cm (6in) |

*Waldsteinia ternata*

# Yucca

There is some confusion about the nomenclature relating to yuccas. Yet, there are differences. *Y. flaccida* has stiffly projecting leaves, whereas *Y. filamentosa* has less rigid, arching leaves. They require full sun on well-drained soil. They flower best in a warm spot. Like pampas grass (see: Grasses, bamboos, ferns) it is a good plant to grow by itself on a lawn.
**Hardiness: US Zone 6-5, Canadian Zone 5-4.**

| | |
|---|---|
| *Y. filamentosa* | white, July–Sept, 1.2m (4ft) |
| *Y. f.* 'Bright Edge' | variegated leaves, July–Aug, 1m (3ft) |
| *Y. flaccida* | white, July-Aug, 1.2m (4ft) |

*Yucca flaccida*

# 8. Bamboos, ferns, and grasses

The names of bamboos are subject to frequent change. In older books, you will find many bamboos listed under the names Arundinaria *and* Sinarundinaria; *now they are classified in far more genera. They should be used sparingly and with discrimination as they present a rather exotic appearance, which does not always blend in well with the local countryside. Winter sunshine is disastrous for bamboos as it causes damage to leaves. Grasses, including sedges, rushes, and ferns, are, in my opinion, grown far too rarely. This chapter will show how varied they are and you may well come to the conclusion that there is a good position for them in your garden. Grasses are not only handsome in summer, but also look well in winter, when the wintry sunshine caresses the often gleaming plumes and spikes of the dead tufts. In the case of bamboos, ferns, rushes, and sedges, the color of the leaves and the height of the plants (in meters or centimeters, followed by inches or feet) are their principal characteristics. The flowering season of grasses is mentioned, unless the leaf color is of greater significance. The second set of figures refers to the height including the spikes or plumes if they are considerably taller than the grass itself.*

## Adiantum

**MAIDENHAIR FERN**

Tropical species are now regarded as old-fashioned indoor plants, which do not thrive in modern centrally heated houses. The two ferns listed here are garden plants for a moist sunless corner of the garden.
**Hardiness: US Zone 3, Canadian Zone 2.**

| | |
|---|---|
| A. pedatum | light green, 30cm (12in) |
| A. p. 'Japonicum' | reddish, 60cm (24in) |

*Adiantum pedatum*

## Alopecurus

**GOLDEN FOXTAIL (GRASS)**

This species of grass is often found by the wayside. The flower spikes can be dried, although, when fresh, they also look attractive in wildflower arrangements. The popular golden foxtail is invasive; remove some of it every year.
**Hardiness: US Zone 5, Canadian Zone 4.**

A. pratensis 'Aureovariegatus' var. leaves, June–July, 70cm (28in)

*Alopecurus pratensis* 'Aureovariegatus'

## Arrhenatherum

This plant requires dry, slightly acid, sandy soil in full sun and looks well combined with *Eryngium*.
**Hardiness: US Zone 5, Canadian Zone 4.**

| | |
|---|---|
| *A. bulbosum* 'Variegatum' | white-striped, July–Aug, 30cm (12in), 50cm (20in) |

*Arrhenatherum bulbosum* 'Variegatum'

## Arundinaria

**BAMBOO**

This bamboo species resembles *Fargesia*, but has a more delicate appearance. The plant is evergreen and fast-growing; it requires sun or semi-shade.
**Hardiness: US Zone 8-7, Canadian Zone 7.**

| | |
|---|---|
| *A. jaunsarensis*** | dark stems, 2.5m (8ft) |

## Asplenium

**MAIDENHAIR SPLEENWORT**

This small but delicate plant requires moist humus-rich soil in a shady spot; it should be covered in winter. *A. ruta-muraria* is wall rue, which is suitable for the north side of old garden walls.
**Hardiness: US Zone 4-2, Canadian Zone 3-1.**

| | |
|---|---|
| *A. trichomanes* | green, 20cm (8in) |
| *A. ruta-muraria*** | blueish green, 30cm (12in) |

## Athyrium

**LADY FERN**

The lady fern grows wild in damp deciduous forests in Europe and can be propagated by division.

**Hardiness: US Zone 6, Canadian Zone 5.**

| | |
|---|---|
| *A. filix-femina* | green, large, 70cm (28in) |
| *A. f.* 'Cristatum' | fan-shaped top, 70cm (28in) |
| *A. f.* 'Fieldiae' | forked fronds, 60cm (24in) |
| *A. f.* 'Frizelliae' | narrow fronds, 40cm (16in) |
| *A. f.* 'Multifidum' | comb-shaped, 60cm (24in) |
| *A. f.* 'Plumosum'** | fine, 50cm (20in) |
| *A. nipponicum* 'Metallicum' | reddish purple fronds, 50cm (20in) |

## Avena

**BLUE OAT GRASS**
See: *Helictotrichon*.

*Athyrium felix-femina*

## Blechnum

**HARD FERN**

This dark green native-European fern is low-growing and evergreen. It is identifiable by its fronds: those that are more or less horizontal are sterile, whereas

*Asplenium trichomanes*

the fertile ones are upright. The latter are covered with brown spores. *B. penna-marina*, which grows naturally in some coastal regions, should be covered in winter when there are severe frosts.

**Hardiness: US Zone 8-5, Canadian Zone 7-4.**

| | |
|---|---|
| *B. spicant* | dark green, 30cm (12in) |
| *B. penna-marina* | dark green, 30cm (12in) |

*Blechnum spicant*

## Bouteloua

**BLUE GRAMA, MOSQUITO GRASS**

This native species of grass, which needs full sun, is easily identifiable: the flower spikes are at right angles to the stem and have pendent stamens.

**Hardiness: US Zone 4, Canadian Zone 3.**

| | |
|---|---|
| *B. gracilis* | brown flower spikes, July–Sept, 30cm (12in), 50cm (20in) |

## Briza

**QUAKING GRASS**

Quaking grass is native to Europe, and suitable for dry positions. It requires well-drained soil in full sun. *B. maxima* is an annual plant and the most suitable one for dried-flower arrangements. The smallest, *B. minor*, has the longest flowering season.

**Hardiness: US Zone 5, Canadian Zone 4.**

| | |
|---|---|
| *B. media* | heart-shaped spikelets, May–Aug, 40cm (16in), 60cm (24in) |
| *B. minor* | May–Sept, 30cm (12in), 45cm (18in) |

*Briza media*

*Bouteloua gracilis*

## Calamagrostis

These tall tufts have erect flower spikes and narrow leaves, slender and graceful. They remain in position in full sun until far into the winter. The less common *C. arundinacea* 'Overdam' is slightly shorter and has yellow-edged leaves.

**Hardiness: US Zone 5, Canadian Zone 4.**

| C. x *acutiflora* | erect, 1m (3ft), 1.5m (5ft) |
| C. a. 'Karl Foerster' | fine, Jul.–Aug, 1m (3ft), 1.5m (5ft) |

*Calamagrostis acutiflora* 'Karl Foerster'

## Carex

**SEDGE**

The taller species form clumps and the lower ones carpets. All require moist soil in shady positions. The species *morrowii* and *plantaginea* are evergreen. *C. muskenguensis* is the most handsome species for growing in a solitary position. These sedges are suitable for partial to full shade.
**Hardiness: US Zone 8-3, Canadian Zone 7-2.**

| C. *buchananii* | red. br., June–July, 50cm (20in) |
| C. *grayi* | star-shaped fruits, May–July, 60cm (24in) |
| C. *hachyoensis* 'Evergold' | leaves with yellow variegations, May–July, 20cm (8in) |

*Carex morrowii* 'Variegata'

| C. *morrowii* | green, Apr–May, 50cm (20in) |
| C. m. 'Variegata' | white-striped leaves, May–June, 60cm (24in) |
| C. *muskenguensis* | non-flowering, 80cm (32in) |
| C. *ornithopoda* 'Variegata' | w. vari., Apr–May, 20cm (8in) |
| C. *pendula!* | dark green, Apr–May, 60cm (24in), 1.2m (4ft) |

## Ceterach

**RUSTY–BACK FERN**

This small dainty fern will also grow in walls and crevices.
**Hardiness: US Zone 7, Canadian Zone 6.**

| C. *officinarum*** | dull green, 20cm (8in) |

*Ceterach officinarum*

## Chasmantium

This graceful, brightly colored grass is clump-forming and produces flat flower spikelets on pendent racemes. It requires full sun.
**Hardiness: US Zone 6, Canadian Zone 5.**

| C. *latifolium* | sea-green leaves, Aug–Sept, 80cm (32in), 1.2m (4ft) |

*Chasmantium latifolium*

# Cortaderia

This most popular plant for growing in solitary positions needs well-drained soil to prevent its being damaged by frost. It should be wrapped up for the winter: put wire netting around the plant and fill up the cavity with fallen leaves. It is difficult to cut back large clumps in spring: a small pruning saw is the most convenient tool for this. **Hardiness: US Zone 8, Canadian Zone 7.**

| | |
|---|---|
| *C. selloana* | white plume, Aug–Oct, 1.5m (5ft), 3m (10ft) |
| *C. s.* 'Pumila' | white, Aug–Nov, 80cm (32in), 1.2m (4ft) |
| *C. s.* 'Rosea' | pink, Aug–Nov, 1m (3ft), 1.75m (5ft) |

*Cortaderia selloana*

# Cyperus

See: Water and marsh plants.

# Cyrtomium

**FISHTAIL FERN, HOLLY FERN**

This evergreen fern may be grown in a sheltered position, but can also be placed under propagating tables in a cool greenhouse. A cold dark position in a house is also suitable. **Hardiness: US Zone 8, Canadian Zone 7.**

| | |
|---|---|
| *C. falcatum* | dark green, 60cm (24in) |
| *C. fortunei* | fresh green, 50cm (20in) |

*Cyrtomium falcatum*

# Dactylis

**COCK'S FOOT, ORCHARD GRASS**

Cock's foot is often seen growing like a weed on verges. The following species is decorative because of its white-edged leaves; the flower spikes look attractive in dried-flower arrangements. The plant can be grown in either dry or wet conditions. **Hardiness: US Zone 4, Canadian Zone 3.**

| | |
|---|---|
| *D. glomerata* 'Variegata' | variegated leaves, May–June, 45cm (18in), 75cm (30in) |

# Deschampsia

**TUFTED HAIR GRASS**

Deschampsia grows naturally on European

*Deschampsia cespitosa*

heathlands and therefore needs a sunny position and dry sandy soil, although it will survive in wet conditions. It is unspectacular as a garden plant, and it is only at sunset that the flower spikes have a beautiful color. This grass is easily identifiable by the attractive little twists in the flower stems. For lovers of native European plants, there are also the less familiar cultivars 'Bronze Veil', 'Gold Veil' and 'Gold Dust'.
**Hardiness: US Zone 5, Canadian Zone 4.**

| | |
|---|---|
| *D. cespitosa* | green leaves, June–July, 50cm (20in), 1m (3ft) |

## Dryopteris

**BUCKLER FERN, MALE FERN**

The semi-evergreen *D. austriaca* (*D. dilatata*) is a large woodland fern and requires a humus-rich damp soil. *D. filix-mas*, also semi-evergreen, is the familiar male fern often grown in old-fashioned gardens.
**Hardiness: US Zone 8-2, Canadian Zone 7-2.**

| | |
|---|---|
| *D. austriaca* | arching, 1m (3ft) |
| *D. erythrosora* | dark green, 70cm (28in) |
| *D. filix-mas* | semi-evergreen, 75cm (30in) |
| *D. f.* 'Cristata'** | branching at the top, 75cm (30in) |
| *D. f.* 'Linearis' | much divided and narrow, 75cm (30in) |
| *D. marginalis* | doubly pinnate, 60cm (24in) |
| *D. wallichiana* | leathery fronds, 1m (3ft) |

*Dryopteris austriaca*

## Elymus

**LYME GRASS**
See: *Leymus*.

## Fargesia

**BAMBOO**

This plant is often for sale under the name of *Sinarundinaria*. It is one of the bamboos most frequently used for fencing and, compared with others, it is also the cheapest. Only a small proportion of the leaves remains on the plant in winter. The leaves curl up in fierce sunlight, and it is therefore better to grow this plant in semi-shade.
**Hardiness: US Zone 7, Canadian Zone 6.**

| | |
|---|---|
| *F. muriliae* | small leaves, bright green, 3m (10ft) |
| *F. nitida* | blueish green leaves, 3m (10ft) |
| *F. n.* 'Nymphenburg'** | arching, 2.5m (8ft) |

*Fargesia nitida*

## Festuca

**FESCUE**

Blue fescue (*F. glauca* + cultivars) is the species planted most frequently in rock and heather gardens. The handsome round tufts are attractive to look at even when they are not in flower. Plant them in full sun to make the blueish-green color show up well.
**Hardiness: US Zone 5, Canadian Zone 4.**

| | |
|---|---|
| *F. gautieri** | br. green, May–July, 30cm (12in) |
| *F. glauca* | blue, May–June, 30cm (12in) |

| F. g. 'Blue Fox' | blueish green, May–June, 30cm (12in) |
| F. g. 'Elijah's Blue' | dark blueish green, May–June, 30cm (12in) |

*Festuca glauca*

## Glyceria

This rampant grass is suitable for moist and wet soil. It makes excellent ground cover for the sides of large ponds.
**Hardiness: US Zone 5, Canadian Zone 4.**

| G. *maxima* 'Variegata' | July–Aug, 60cm (24in), 1m (3ft) |

## Helictotrichon

**BLUE OAT GRASS**

Plant in dry well-drained sandy soil in full sun to make the blueish color of the leaves show up to its best advantage. The flower spikes are yellow and violet.
**Hardiness: US Zone 5, Canadian Zone 4.**

| H. *sempervirens* | blueish green, May–July, 50cm (20in), 1.2m (4ft) |

## Hibanobambusa

**BAMBOO**

This highly invasive medium-sized bamboo has delicate striped leaves and is tolerant of drought and frost. It is a good plant for growing in a solitary position in a medium-sized garden. It is best to plant the bamboo in a spot sheltered from the wind.
**Hardiness: US Zone 7, Canadian Zone 6.**

| H. *tranquillans* f. *kimmei*\*\* | yellow stripes, 1.5m (5ft) |
| H. *t.* f. *shiroshima*\*\* | yellowish white stripes, 1.75m (5ft) |

## Holcus

**CREEPING SOFT GRASS**

Until recently, this grass for either moist or dry soil was called *H. lanatus*. The wild species is native to Europe. The plant is more or less carpet-forming. Remove seeds before self-seeding occurs. Holcus will grow in any soil in sun or semi-shade.
**Hardiness: US Zone 6, Canadian Zone 5.**

| H. *mollis* 'Albovariegatus' | June–July, 20cm (8in), 30cm (12in) |

*Holcus mollis*

## Indocalamus

**BAMBOO**

This is a highly unusual genus of bamboos: the plants have very large leaves (up to 50cm/20in) and need shade. *S. tsuboianus* is altogether smaller than *S. tesselatus*. Both are good evergreen plants for small (urban) gardens.
**Hardiness: US Zone 8, Canadian Zone 7.**

| I. *tessalatus* | arching, 1.5m (5ft) |
| I. *tsuboianus* | green stems, 1m (3ft) |

## Juncus

**CORKSCREW RUSH**

See: Water and marsh plants.

## Koeleria

Koeleria is stronger than *Festuca glauca*, but cannot rival its beauty. The plant is carpet-forming. Like most grasses, this one likes dry, preferably limy soil and full sun.
**Hardiness: US Zone 4, Canadian Zone 3.**

| | |
|---|---|
| *K. glauca* | grayish green, May–Aug, 20cm (8in), 35cm (14in) |

*Koeleria glauca*

## Leymus

**LYME GRASS**

*Leymus*, formerly *Elymus*, can grow in windy sunny positions in the very driest sandy soil. It blends beautifully with dark-leafed shrubs or other grasses. The grass grows rapidly, preferably without fertilizer.
**Hardiness: US Zone 4, Canadian Zone 3.**

*Leymus arenarius*

| | |
|---|---|
| *L. arenarius* | blueish gray, May–July, 60cm (24in), 1.2m (4ft) |

## Luzula

**WOODRUSH**

Rushes and sedges usually require humus-rich, moisture-retentive soil in semi-shade or even shade. The following are no exception. *L. pilosa* (hairy woodrush) and *L. sylvatica* (greater woodrush) are both native European plants: all have delicate leaves.
**Hardiness: US Zone 6, Canadian Zone 5.**

| | |
|---|---|
| *L. nivea* | grayish green, June–Aug, 30cm (12in), 50cm (20in) |
| *L. pilosa* | white, Apr–June, 30cm (12in), 50cm (20in) |
| *L. sylvatica* | fresh green, Apr–June, 30cm (12in), 60cm (24in) |
| *L. s.* 'Marginata' | yellow leaves, Apr–June, 30cm (12in), 60cm (24in) |

*Luzula nivea*

## Matteuccia

**OSTRICH FERN**

These funnel- or vase-shaped ferns are a bright shade of light green, and are easy to grow in moist to wet soil. The leaf margins often turn brown in dry soil. The ferns are inclined to be invasive if their position suits them. Because of their long underground runners, they often re-emerge from the soil at some distance from their original position.
**Hardiness: US Zone 4, Canadian Zone 3.**

| | |
|---|---|
| *M. pensylvanica* | dark green, 1.5m (5ft) |
| *M. struthiopteris*! | light green, 1m (3ft) |

*Matteuccia struthiopteris*

*M. ciliata*     white flower spikes, May–July, 30cm (12in), 60cm (24in)

## Miscanthus

### AMUR SILVER GRASS

Miscanthus is sometimes on sale as bamboo, but bamboos do not die down in winter. The grass is also much easier to cultivate, so look out! *M. floridulus* (syn. *M. sinensis* var. *giganteus*) and *M. sacchariflorus* become very invasive. The flower plumes appear late in the year and are not much taller than the plant itself. The grass requires full sun.
**Hardiness: US Zone 6-5, Canadian Zone 5-4.**

| | |
|---|---|
| *M. floridulus* | arch. leaves, Sept–Oct, 3m (10ft) |
| *M. sacchariflorus* | large plumes, Sept–Nov, 2.5m (8ft) |
| *M. sinensis* 'Gracillimus' | nar. leaves, Sept–Oct, 40cm (16in) |
| *M. s.* 'Silver Feather' | wh. plumes, Sept–Oct, 1.5m (5ft) |
| *M. s.* 'Strictus' | yel.spots Aug–Sept, 1.75m (5ft) |
| *M. s.* 'Variegatus' | white-striped, Aug–Sept, 1.75m (5ft) |
| *M. s.* 'Zebrinus' | yellow horizontal stripes, Sept–Oct, 1.5m (5ft) |

*Miscanthus sacchariflorus*

## Melica

### MELIC

This fresh green ornamental grass from central and southern Europe sometimes becomes invasive further north. It has white to dusty-yellow flower spikes. The plant requires limy soil. The less familiar low-growing *M. uniflora* 'Variegata' has a white stripe and may be planted in a shady position. *M. ciliata* requires sun to half-shade.
**Hardiness: US Zone 6, Canadian Zone 5.**

*Melica ciliata*

## Molinia

### MOOR GRASS

This is a clump-forming grass for infertile high humus soils. The tufts have beautiful fall colors, especially in wintry sunshine. The grass requires sun to half-shade.
**Hardiness: US Zone 5, Canadian Zone 4.**

| | |
|---|---|
| *M. arundinaria* | green, July, 1m (3ft),1.5m (5ft) |
| *M. a.* 'Karl Foerster' | dark green, Aug–Sept, 1m (3ft), 1.5m (5ft) |

| M. caerulea | green, Aug–Oct, 60cm (24in), 1.2m (4ft) |
| M. c. 'Moor Witch'** | dark spikes, Aug–Oct, 40cm (16in), 80cm (32in) |
| M. c. 'Variegata' | white variegations, Aug–Oct, 30cm (12in), 60cm (24in) |

*Molinia caerulea* 'Moor Witch'

## Onoclea

**SENSITIVE FERN**

This is a native fern for a wet position as the fragile light green fronds are inclined to dry up. The wetter the soil, the sunnier the plant's position can be.
**Hardiness: US Zone 4, Canadian Zone 3.**

| O. sensibilis | fresh green, 50cm (20in) |

*Onoclea sensibilis*

## Osmunda

**ROYAL FERN**

The royal fern requires a moist position in sun or semi-shade to shade. The sterile fronds are light green; the fertile brown flower spikes are in the center at the ends of taller fronds.
**Hardiness: US Zone 3, Canadian Zone 2.**

| O. regalis | light green, 1m (3ft) |
| O. r. 'Purpurascens'* | red stems, 1m (3ft) |

*Osmunda regalis*

## Panicum

**PANIC GRASS**

This very erect, rather insignificant grass looks particularly attractive in late summer. The cultivar 'Strictum' turns golden yellow in fall. The plant is suitable for any soil, in sun or light shade.
**Hardiness: US Zone 5, Canadian Zone 4.**

| P. virgatum 'Rehbraun' | brownish red, July–Aug, 80cm (32in), 1.25m (4ft 2in) |
| P. v. 'Strictum'* | more erect, July–Aug, 90cm (36in), 1.5m (5ft) |

## Pennisetum

**CHINESE FOUNTAIN GRASS**

These tufts are suitable for growing in solitary positions. They look well when combined with trailing roses or other kinds of ground cover. The grass requires nutritious, well-drained, but moisture-retentive soil and full sun.
**Hardiness: US Zone 6, Canadian Zone 5.**

| | |
|---|---|
| *P. alopecuroides*! | brownish, Aug–Oct, 80cm (32in), 1m (3ft) |
| *P. a.* 'Hameln'! | more abundant florescence, July–Sept, 50cm (20in), 60cm (24in) |

*Pennisetum alopecuroides* 'Hameln'

## *Phalaris*

### GARDENER'S GARTERS

Phalaris is highly invasive and is suitable for any kind of soil. It is a plant for gardens where everything else fails. Don't confuse the grass with *P. canariensis*, the annual canary seed that looks so attractive in dried-flower arrangements. This perennial may be cut back in summer to produce a second flowering. It will tolerate either a dry or a wet position and will do well in either sun or shade.
**Hardiness: US Zone 4, Canadian Zone 3.**

| | |
|---|---|
| *P. arundinacea* 'Picta' | white-striped, July–Aug, 80cm (32in) |

## *Phyllitis*

### HART'S-TONGUE FERN

The fronds of this native fern, the only ones that are neither divided nor lobed, emerge from the soil like tongues, often frilled.

**Hardiness: US Zone 5, Canadian Zone 5.**

| | |
|---|---|
| *P. scolopendrium* | light green, 50cm (20in) |
| *P. s.* 'Angustifolia'* | long and narrow, 50cm (20in) |
| *P. s.* 'Cristata'* | comb-shaped, 40cm (16in) |
| *P. s.* 'Furcatum'* | comb-shaped, 40cm (16in) |

*Phyllitis scolopendrium*

## *Phyllostachys*

### BAMBOO

The color indications *aurea* and *nigra* of this fully evergreen bamboo for rather moist soil do not refer to its leaves: both species are green-leafed. Bamboo requires sun or semi-shade. *P. bissetii* has the best color in winter; *P. bambusoides* is moderately winter-hardy.
**Hardiness: US Zone 7-6, Canadian Zone 6-5.**

| | |
|---|---|
| *P. aurea* | yellowish green, small-leafed, 3.5m (11fift) |
| *P. aureosulcata* | fresh green, kinks, 4.5m (14ft) |

*Phalaris arundinacea* 'Picta'

| | |
|---|---|
| *P. bambusoides* | thicker stems, 5.5m (18ft) |
| *P. bissetii* | dark green, shrubby, 4m (13ft) |
| *P. flexuosa* | light green stems, 3m (10ft) |
| *P. nidularia* | dark green, bushy, 2.5m (8ft) |
| *P. nigra* | dark green, small, 4m (13ft) |
| *P. n.* 'Boryana'!* | stems spotted in the sun, 4.5m (14ft) |
| *P. n.* 'Henon' | green stems, 9m (30ft) |
| *P. viridi-glaucescens** | dark green stems, 9m (30ft) |

## *Pleiobastus*

**BAMBOO**

This is a dense low-growing bamboo; *P. humilis* var. *pumilus* is suitable for the most difficult of all positions: dry and shady. The others, too, may be grown in sun or shade.
**Hardiness: US Zone 6-5, Canadian Zone 6-5.**

| | |
|---|---|
| *P.* chino 'Elegantissimum' | white-striped leaves, 75cm (30in) |
| *P. c.* f. *angustifolius** | small leaves, 2m (6ft) |
| *P. pygmaeus* | erect, narrow leaves, 30cm (12in) |
| *P. simonii* 'Variegatus'* | |
| *P. viridi-striatus* 'Auricoma' | golden variegations, 80cm (32in) |

*Pleiobastus viridi-striatus* 'Auricoma'

## *Polypodium*

**COMMON POLYPODY**

*P. vulgaris* likes growing on old tree stumps and, unlike most ferns, is tolerant of a reasonable period of drought. It also grows on old roof tiles, provided the roof is in the shade.
**Hardiness: US Zone 4, Canadian Zone 3.**

| | |
|---|---|
| *P. vulgare* | bright green, 30cm (12in) |
| *P. v.* 'Virginianum' | evergreen fronds, 90cm (36in) |

## *Polystichum*

**GIANT HOLLY FERN, CHRISTMAS FERN**

These strong evergreen ferns are relatively undemanding, but don't plant them in a sunny position. *P. setiferum* (soft shield fern) is suitable for a solitary position.
**Hardiness: US Zone 5, Canadian Zone 4.**

| | |
|---|---|
| *P. acrostichoides* | dark green, 50cm (20in) |
| *P. aculeatum* | large fronds, 75cm (30in) |
| *P. braunii* | pale green, 80cm (30in) |
| *P. minutum* | d. green leathery, 75cm (30in) |
| *P. rigens* | dark green, mat, 40cm (16in) |
| *P. setiferum* | much divided, 40cm (16in) |
| *P. s.* 'Herrenhausen'! | broad, 70cm (28in) |
| *P. tsus-simense* | dark green, small, 30cm (12in) |

*Polystichum setiferum*

*Polypodium vulgare*

## Pseudosasa

**ARROW BAMBOO, METAKE**

This dark green bamboo has erect young shoots; after a year they arch over. The plant is useful as a divider, but also as a container plant for large tubs. It is winter-hardy, but the appearance of the foliage may be spoilt by frost, especially in a windy location. In a warm position, the plant may grow 1m (3ft) or so taller than the indicated height.
**Hardiness: US Zone 6, Canadian Zone 5.**

| | |
|---|---|
| *P. japonica* | green, large leaves, 2.5m (8ft) |

*Pseudosasa japonica*

## Pteridium

**BRACKEN FERN**

Always buy cultivated plants in pots, as this fern does not like being transplanted. After they have taken to a position, they are unstoppable. Underground runners will spread for many meters (yards) per annum and are almost impossible to eradicate. Pteridiums will grow in either sun or shade.
**Hardiness: US Zone 5, Canadian Zone 4.**

| | |
|---|---|
| *P. aquilinum**\** | single fronds, 1.5m (5ft) |

## Sasa

**BAMBOO**

The dead margins of the large older leaves are cream-colored, and the leaves therefore appear to be variegated. Like *Pleiobastus*, sasas are highly invasive and may thus suppress weeds. The taller *S. palmata*, also known as *S. cernua* var. *nebulosa*, is therefore suitable for large gardens only. Several large-leafed species have been classified as belonging to the genus *Indocalamus*. Sasas require sun or semi-shade in any kind of soil.
**Hardiness: US Zone 8-7, Canadian Zone 7-6.**

| | |
|---|---|
| *S. palmata* | palmate leaves, 2.5m (8ft) |
| *S. veitchii* | broad leaves, lighter margins, 75cm (30in) |

*Sasa veitchii*

## Sasaella

**BAMBOO**

The named cultivars of these two large-leafed species have variegated leaves. They are compact

*Pteridium aquilinum*

and keep their color quite well in winter. They resemble *Himanobambusa*.
**Hardiness: US Zone 8, Canadian Zone 7.**

*S. masamuneana*
   'Albostriata'       variegated leaves, 1.5m (5ft)

## *Sesleria*

**BLUE MOUNTAIN GRASS**

Seslerias prefer limy, rather moist soil, and sun or semi-shade. The large round tufts are suitable for heather or larger rock gardens.
**Hardiness: US Zone 5, Canadian Zone 4.**

*S. caerulea*       silvery gray, July–Aug, 20cm
               (8in), 30cm (12in)

## *Sinarundinaria*

**BAMBOO**

See: *Fargesia.*

## *Spartina*

Spartina requires moist to wet soil and is tolerant of salty soil. The plant develops underground runners, but is not invasive. The greenish flower spikes with mauve stamens are suitable for dried-flower arrangements.
**Hardiness: US Zone 5, Canadian Zone 4.**

*S. pectinata*'Aureomarginata'yell green, 1.2m (4ft), 1.5m (5ft)

*Spartina pectinata*

## *Stipa*

**FEATHER GRASS**

This delicate and elegant arching ornamental grass from southern Europe is suitable for dried-flower arrangements, and is also attractive for winter gardens. Plant in full sun in soil that is not excessively acid.
**Hardiness: US Zone 7-6, Canadian Zone 6-5.**

*S. capillata*       open plumes, July–Aug, 80cm
               (32in), 1.2m (4ft)
*S. pennata*       narrow plumes, June–July,
               50cm (20in), 75cm (30in)

## *Thelypteris*

**MARSH BUCKLER FERN**

Marsh buckler ferns often grow alongside water plants, but will also tolerate a drier position in sun or semi-shade. You will sometimes find this plant classified under *Dryopteris* or *Lastrea*.
**Hardiness: US Zone 4, Canadian Zone 3.**

*T. palustris*       fresh green, erect, 40cm (16in)

## *Woodsia*

This native fragile little fern for a special position, for instance in a rock garden, looks well combined with the more delicate flowering plants. Woodsias require semi-shade.
**Hardiness: US Zone 4, Canadian Zone 3.**

*W. obtusa*       delicate, bright green, 40 (16in)

*Stipa pennata*

# 9. Bulbs and tuberous plants

*An attempt has been made in this chapter to provide a complete list of the range of botanical bulbs, tubers, and rootstocks sold during the bulb season. Plants that are very frost-tender have either been omitted or special mention is made of this fact. The usual summer-flowering tubers such as dahlias and gladioli are, however, included. The botanical (natural) species of such plants are, of course, always available, but it is best to refer to up-to-date catalogs for current cultivars. There are specialized growers and garden centers as well as mail-order firms which will send you catalogs so that you can make your own choice at home. The following symbols have been used in this chapter:*

\* *= available only from specialized trade dealers*

\*\* *= difficult to obtain and relatively expensive.*

## Acidanthera *(syn.* Gladiolus*)*

### ABYSSINIAN GLADIOLUS

Plant this gladiolus in May and dig up the corms when the cormlets have formed in October–November. Choose a warm and sunny position. The plants are also suitable for large pots.
**Hardiness: US Zone 5, Canadian Zone 4.**

| | |
|---|---|
| A. bicolor | cream with purple spots, Aug, 80cm (32in) |
| A. tubergenii | white, dark center, 80cm (32in) |

## Agapanthus

### AFRICAN LILY

This old-fashioned container plant is still one of the best. Sometimes the plants refuse to flower: let them overwinter in a cool and frost-free place and put them in a pot that is well-drained but not too large. There need not be much light. You can move them to a warm and sunny spot out of doors from mid-May; give them plenty of water at that time. The plants can also remain in the ground provided they are well covered (see also: Perennials).
**Hardiness: US Zone 8, Canadian Zone 7.**

| | |
|---|---|
| A. africanus | blue, 1m (3ft) |
| A. a. 'Albidus' | white, Aug–Sept, 70cm (28in) |
| A. (hybrid cultivar) 'Blue Triumphator' | blue, Aug–Sept, 80cm (32in) |
| A. 'Liliput' | blueish purple, July–Aug, 45cm (18in) |
| A. orientalis | blue, smaller, 50cm (20in) |

*Agapanthus* 'Blue Triumphator'

*Acidanthera tubergenii*

# Allium

All alliums are among the last plants to flower in spring, and some of them are still flowering in summer. Plant them in full sun, and not too near the surface. The soil should be limy or neutral, and not too moist. The leaves are often not very beautiful, and it is therefore best to combine alliums with perennials so that the leaves are not too conspicuous. Some native European species are rather unattractive. Ramsons, *A. ursinum*, however, is an excellent ground–cover plant, although its leaves die down as early as July. *A. cepa* var. *viviparum* (tree onion or Egyptian onion) is a handsome onion for kitchen gardens. *A. schoenophrasum* is the familiar chive, which is also attractive in borders or for edging purposes, and is now also available in a lilac red shade. Chinese chives with flat leaves are more suitable for kitchen gardens. *A. ostrowskianum* is called *A. oreophyllum* nowadays.

**Hardiness: US Zone 5-4, Canadian Zone 3-2.**

| | |
|---|---|
| *A. afluatense* | lilac and pink, May, 75cm (30in) |
| *A.a.* 'Purple Sensation' | deep purple, May, 50cm (20in) |
| *A. albopilosum* | lilac, May, 50cm (20in) |
| *A. atropurpureum* | aubergine, May, 70cm (28in) |
| *A. caeruleum* (*A. azureum*) | sky blue, June, 50cm (20in) |

*Allium giganteum*

| | |
|---|---|
| *A. caesium* | |
| (*A. urseolatum*)** | violet blue, 40cm (16in) |
| *A. cernuum* | lilac, July, 30cm (12in) |
| *A. christophii* | silvery mauve, May, 30cm (12in) |
| *A. flavum* | golden yel., July–Aug, 30cm (12in) |
| *A. giganteum* | violet, July, 1.2m (4ft) |
| *A. karataviense* | green and white, May, 20cm (8in) |
| *A. moly* (*A. luteum*) | yellow, June–July, 20cm (8in) |
| *A. narcissiflorum** | mauve, June–July, 30cm (12in) |
| *A. nigrum!** | white, green center, June, 70cm (28in) |
| *A. oreophyllum* | mauve, June–July, 15cm (6in) |
| *A. roseum** | white, June, 30cm (12in) |
| *A. schoenophrasum* | mauve, May–July, 40cm (16in) |
| *A. s.* 'Forescate' | d. lilac red, May–July, 30cm (12in) |
| *A. siculum* | brown and green, June, 60cm-1m (2–3ft) |
| *A. sphaerocephalum* | purplish red, July, 40cm (16in) |
| *A. stipitatum** | deep pink, July, 1.6m (5ft 2in) |
| *A. unifolium* | soft pink, May–June, 40cm (16in) |
| *A. zebdanense** | white, Apr, 25cm (10in) |

# Anemone

A distinction is made between spring-flowering tubers and the larger ones which bloom later. These larger tubers, *A. coronaria*, flower in April to May if they are covered over in winter to protect them from frost. Others, for instance the wood anemone (*A. nemorosa*), a native European plant, have thin rhizomes. Do not let these dry out before planting them. The small rock-hard tubers need soaking for 24 hours before they are planted. *A. blanda* is usually sold in mixed colors; it is worth trying to buy single colors, as there is quite a difference in growth patterns and size of flowers; it is likely that white flowers will predominate. The white *A. blanda* will grow to about 20cm (8in), and the large-flowered cultivars a little taller; all the others will remain shorter. They flower in April.

**Hardiness: US Zone 8-5, Canadian Zone 7-4.**

**Spring-flowering with tubers:**

| | |
|---|---|
| *A. apennina** | bright blue, Mar–Apr, 10cm (4in) |
| *A. blanda* 'Blue Shades' | shades of blue, 10cm (4in) |
| *A. b.* 'Charmer' | deep pink, 10cm (4in) |
| *A. b.* 'Pink Star' | pinkish-mauve, 10cm (4in) |
| *A. b.* 'Radar' | purplish red, white center, 10cm (4in) |
| *A. b.* 'Rosea' | cyclamen purple, 10cm (4in) |
| *A. b.* 'White Splendour' | white, large flowers, 15cm (6in) |
| **A. coronaria De Caen-type, large-flowered single-flowered, Apr–May, 25cm (10in):** | |
| *A. c.* 'The Bride' | white |
| *A. c.* 'Hollandia' | red |
| *A. c.* 'Mr. Fokker' | violet and blue |
| *A. c.* 'Sylphide' | violet |

*Anemone coronaria*, De Caen Series, single-flowered

**double-flowered, Apr–May, 25cm (10in):**

| | |
|---|---|
| A. c. 'King of the Blues' | dark blue |
| A. c. 'Lord Derby' | violet and blue |
| A. c. 'Lord Lieutenant' | deep blue (sd) |
| A. c. 'Mount Everest' | white (sd) |
| A. c. 'Surprise' | red |
| A. c. 'Queen of the Violets' | purple |
| A. fulgens | scarlet (s), Apr–May, 25cm (10in) |

**Spring-flowering with rhizomes:**

| | |
|---|---|
| A. nemorosa | white, soft pink outside, 10cm (4in) |
| A. n. 'Alba Plena'* | white (d), 10cm (4in) |
| A. n. 'Robinsoniana'** | light blue, 10cm (4in) |
| A. ranunculoides* | dark yellow, 10cm (4in) |

*Anemone ranunculoides*

# Arisarum

## MOUSE PLANT

This ground-cover plant for light shade and humus-rich soil has small dark green leaves reminiscent of arum leaves. Small green berries appear in fall.
**Hardiness: US Zone 5, Canadian Zone 4.**

| | |
|---|---|
| A. proboscideum | chestnut brown, Mar–Apr, 20cm (8in) |

*Arisarum proboscideum*

# Arum

## CUCKOO PINT, LORDS AND LADIES

This is a winter-hardy plant with arrow-shaped leaves and, between them, a large dark red flower with a black spadix. Garden arums have fleshy rhizomes. The leaves appear in fall and die down in spring: a cycle which is the reverse of that of hostas; the two plants are therefore ideal to combine. The bright orange seed heads appear after July, those of *A. maculatum* a little earlier, and those of *A. italicum* a little later. The poisonous plants tolerate deep shade under deciduous trees. For *Arum dracunculus* see: *Dracunculus vulgaris*.
**Hardiness: US Zone 6, Canadian Zone 5.**

| | |
|---|---|
| A. italicum | gr. white, Apr–May, 40cm (16in) |

| A. i. 'Pictum'** | greenish white, leaves with light green veins, 40cm (16in) |
| A. maculatum | greenish white, spotted leaves, 40cm (16in) |

*Arum italicum*

## Begonia

### TUBEROUS BEGONIA

There are over a thousand species of begonia; just a few of them are frost-hardy. Most of them are cultivated as indoor plants. Bedding begonias are of course very well known. The begonias listed below have tubers. Treat them like dahlias, but don't plant them out too early: a late night frost may cause considerable damage. If the plants are already above ground when a frost is expected, they should be earthed up so that the leaves are covered again; alternatively, you can place inverted flower pots over the

*Begonia*, large-flowered, mixed

plants. Lift them again in good time, about mid-October, and let them overwinter in a cool place in dry peat dust. It would be inappropriate to provide details of the constantly changing assortment of cultivars, and only the various groups are listed here.

**Large-flowered hybrids:**
rose-like flowers
fringed flowers
marbled flowers
striped flowers
**Small-flowered hybrids:**

| B. 'Bertinii' | orange, hanging |

## Begonia

### WINTER-HARDY TUBEROUS BEGONIA

Only one begonia is winter-hardy, provided it is covered up well during periods of frost. Plant in a warm spot – but not in full sun – and in well-drained soil to prevent the tuber rotting in winter. Propagate by means of the bulbils in the leaf axils.
**Hardiness: US Zone 8, Canadian Zone 7.**

| B. grandis** | pale pink, July–Sept, 30cm (12in) |
| B. g. 'Alba'** | white, July–Sept, 30cm (12in) |

*Begonia grandis*

## Brodiaea

This good flower for cutting looks rather like an agapanthus. Plant in moist, well-drained soil and in full sun to semi-shade (see also: *Ipheion*).
**Hardiness: US Zone 7, Canadian Zone 6.**

| B. californica | blueish violet, June, 70cm (28in) |

*Brodiaea californica*

## Camassia

This native plant is suitable for perennial borders and may be used for naturalizing. It requires a moist to wet, nutritious position and full sun. The plant flowers in June–July.
**Hardiness: US Zone 5-3, Canadian Zone 5-2.**

| | |
|---|---|
| *C. cusickii* | sky blue, 60cm (24in) |
| *C. leichtlinii* | light blue, 60cm (24in) |
| *C.l.* 'Alba' | white, 80cm, (32in) |
| *C. l.* 'Plena' | white, 80cm, (32in) |
| *C. quamash* (*C. esculenta*) | light blue, 40cm (16in) |
| *C. quamash* | light blue, 40cm (16in) |

*Camassia quamash (C. esculenta)*

## Chionodoxa

**GLORY-OF-THE-SNOW**

Chionodoxas are among the earliest-flowering bulbs, and should therefore be planted close to the house, so that you can enjoy them through the window. They are suitable for naturalizing, for underplanting, and also for rock gardens. These undemanding plants grow up to 15cm (6in) tall.
**Hardiness: US Zone 5, Canadian Zone 4.**

| | |
|---|---|
| *C. luciliae* | lavender blue, white eyes |
| *C. l.* 'Alba' | bright white |
| *C. l.* 'Blue Giant' | blue |
| *C. l.* 'Pink Giant' | soft pinkish violet |
| *C. l.* 'Zwanenburg' | bright blue, white eyes |
| *C. sardensis* | bright gentian blue |

*Chionodoxa luciliae*

## Colchicum

This bulb flowers in September and will also produce flowers without soil, for instance on a window sill. The plant will not suffer if it is returned to the garden immediately after flowering. It is difficult to give an indication of its height: the rather weak-stemmed flowers grow up to 15–20cm (6–8in) tall, but the glossy dark green leaves, which do not appear until spring and die down again in June, grow up to 40–60cm (16–24in) tall. Colchicums are sometimes confused with fall crocuses. They are good plants for naturalizing between deciduous shrubs. The plants are poisonous.
**Hardiness: US Zone 7-5, Canadian Zone 6-4.**

| | |
|---|---|
| *C. agrippinum* | reddish purple, speckled, Sept–Oct |
| *C. autumnale* | light mauvish pink, early Sept |
| *C. a.* 'Album'* | white, Aug–Sept |
| *C. a.* 'Album Plenum'** | white (d), Aug–Sept |
| *C. a.* 'Roseum Plenum'** | violet, Oct |
| *C. byzantinum* | mauvish pink, Sept |
| *C. b.* 'Album'* | white, Sept |
| *C. cilicum* | light pinkish violet, late Sept |
| *C. luteum** | orange yellow, Jan–Mar |

| C. hybr. 'Waterlily' | pinkish mauve, Sept–Oct |
| C. speciosum | bright violet pink, Sept–Oct |
| C. s. 'Album'** | white, Sept–Oct |
| C. 'Waterlily' | lilac pink (d), Sept–Oct |

Colchicum byzantinum

## Corydalis

C. bulbosa and C. solida closely resemble each other. The former, however, is easier to propagate by seed, and the latter by division of the clumps of small attractive tubers. These species are eminently suitable for naturalizing under trees or shrubs: after a few years, they will form a carpet of flowers. They require humus-rich soil. All of them flower early (see also: Perennials).
**Hardiness: US Zone 5, Canadian Zone 4.**

| C. angustifolia** | white, Mar–Apr, 20cm (8in) |

Corydalis solida

| C. bulbosa! (C. cava) | pinkish mauve or white, Apr, 30cm (12in) |
| C. diphyla** | white and purple, Apr, 10cm (4in) |
| C. solida! | pale lilac, Mar–Apr, 25cm (10in) |

## Crinum

This bulb should be planted in a ground bed in a cool greenhouse, although it can overwinter out of doors provided it is well covered. Then plant out in a sheltered position with well-drained soil. Allow 40cm (16in) between bulbs and let the neck of the tall bulb extend above the ground.
**Hardiness: US Zone 7, Canadian Zone 6.**

| C. powelii | pink, Aug–Sept, 1m (3ft) |
| C. p. 'Album' | white, Aug–Sept, 1m (3ft) |

Crinum powelii

## Crocosmia

**MONTBRETIA**

These plants resemble freesias, but grow taller. Some species are frost-hardy, but even then covering them in winter is advisable. Plant new corms from the end of March. They can remain in the same position for a number of years. Propagate by planting out cormlets.
**Hardiness: US Zone 7-6, Canadian Zone 6-5.**

| C. masonorum | orange, Aug, 1m (3ft) |
| C. x crocosmiiflora | orange, 70–90cm (28–36in) |
| C. x c. 'Carmen Brilliant'* | carmine red (small-flowered) |
| C. x c. 'Lady Wilson'** | orange |
| C. x c. 'Lucifer'! | red, fairly winter-hardy |

# Crocus

There are fall- and spring-flowering species. Some self-seed extensively, for instance the fall-flowering *C. speciosus* and the spring-flowering *C. tommasinianus*. The Dutch, or spring, crocus, which looks like a "common" crocus, does so to a lesser extent. Buy crocuses in large quantities. You can plant them in single- or mixed-color groups. Try creating a gradual blending of colors, shading, for instance, from a deep color near a tree to a light one further away; scatter them according to color and exchange a few bulbs where the two colors meet. This will achieve a gradual transition without any severe lines. *C. sativus* may be planted in a herb garden: the stigmas yield saffron. Fall-flowering crocuses should be planted in July. As a rule, they are only available from specialized bulb dealers.

Hardiness: US Zone 8-3, Canadian Zone 7-2.

### Small-flowered species and cultivars:

| | |
|---|---|
| *Crocus chrysanthus* | |
| 'Blue Bird' | white, grayish blue outside |
| *C. c.* 'Blue Pearl' | silvery blue, soft blue outside |
| *C. c.* 'Blue Peter' | purplish blue with yellow throat |
| *C. c.* 'Buttercup' | golden yellow, brown inside |
| *C. c.* 'Cream Beauty' | creamy yellow, purple stripes |
| *C. c.* 'E.P. Bowles' | lemon yellow |
| *C. c.* 'Ladykiller' | purplish violet with white margin |
| *C. c.* 'Snowbunting' | white, purple-striped outside |
| *C. c.* 'Zwanenburg Bronze' | bronze, yellow inside |
| *C. tommasinianus* | light lavender blue |
| *C. t.* 'Albus'** | pure white |
| *C. t.* 'Pictus'** | lavender, purple-spotted |
| *C. t.* 'Barr's Purple' | violet pink |
| *C. t.* 'Ruby Giant' | ruby purple |
| *C. t.* 'Whitewell Purple'* | reddish violet |

*Crocosmia* x *crocosmiiflora*

| | |
|---|---|
| *C. vernus* | all colors |
| *C. versicolor* 'Picturatus' | white, purple stripes |

### Large-flowered cultivars:

| | |
|---|---|
| *C.* 'Blue Pearl' | blue |
| *C.* 'Jeanne d'Arc' | white |
| *C.* 'King of the Striped' | blue, striped |
| *C.* 'Pickwick' | silvery gray with lilac blue stripes |
| *C.* 'Purpureus Grandiflorus' | mauvish blue |
| *C.* 'Remembrance' | purplish blue |
| *C.* 'Yellow Mammoth' ('large yellow') | deep yellow |

### Fall-flowering species and cultivars:

| | |
|---|---|
| *C. goulimyi** | soft lilac, 15cm (6in) |
| *C. karduchorum*** | light lavender pink, 10cm (4in) |
| *C. pulchellus*** | light lilac and violet stripes, 10cm (4in) |
| *C. sativus** | lilac, 10cm (4in) |
| *C. speciosus** | dark violet blue, 15cm (6in) |

# Cyclamen

Cyclamens, well known as indoor plants, are still far too unfamiliar as garden plants, even though they are not difficult to cultivate.

*Crocus tommasinianus* 'Whitewell Purple'

Sowing, in fact, is easy enough: in the spot where they are to flower. The seed, however, must be fresh: plant it straight from its parent in a moisture-retentive spot in semi-shade. If a cyclamen has been in a permanent position for years, you will be rewarded with a carpet of flowers. When buying bulbs, make sure that they have come from a nursery and were not stolen from the wild in Turkey or Greece! Cyclamens make ideal rockery plants. *C. coum* flowers in spring, in a mild winter sometimes as early as January. *C. cilicum* is not altogether hardy.

**Hardiness: US Zone 10-5, Canadian Zone 9-5.**

| | |
|---|---|
| *C. cilicium* | pinkish red, Sept–Nov, 5cm (2in) |
| *C. coum* | pinkish mauve, Dec–Mar, 5cm (2in) |
| *C. hederifolium* (*C. neapolitanum*) | pink, Sept–Nov, 10cm (4in) |
| *C. h.* 'Album'* | white, Sept–Nov, 10cm (4in) |
| *C. persicum* | white with pink sheen, Dec–Mar, 5cm (2in) |

*Cyclamen persicum*

# *Dahlia*

Dahlias are usually sold ready packaged. When buying them don't just look at the pretty color picture, but inspect the contents as well: the size of tubers varies considerably. Plant dahlias at the same time as potatoes, from the first of May. If the plants are already coming up when there is a late night frost, invert a flower pot over them. They can be cut down and lifted again in November. Store them in a cool frost-free place. Don't let the tubers dry out; preferably put them in a box filled with dry sand or peat dust. Do not water the corms, as that might rot them. Removing the top pair of lateral buds will give you a large flower on a straight stem. Dahlias require good fertilization! The number of cultivars is huge; only the various groups are listed here.

Anemone-flowered dahlia 30–40cm (12–16in)

| | |
|---|---|
| Mignon dahlia | 40–70cm (16–28in) |
| Miniature dahlia | 30cm (12in) |
| Collerette dahlia | 30–40cm (12–16in) |
| Cactus and semi-cactus dahlia | 80cm–1.2m (32in–4ft) |
| Decorative dahlia | 80cm–1.2m (32in–4ft) |
| Pompon dahlia | 1–1.2m (3–4ft) |
| Water-lily dahlia | 70cm–1m (28in–3ft) |

The anemone-flowered dahlia 'D. Guinea'

Cactus dahlia 'Red Pygmy'

Pompon dahlia 'Golden Scepter'

## Dracunculus

Although the tubers are hardy, covering them in winter is recommended. Storing them frost-free is my personal preference. These arums are suitable for planting by themselves in a woodland corner or as container plants. They are still often sold under the name *Arum*, which they resemble, although they are much taller. The plants require semi-shade. The tubers are preferably planted in spring.
**Hardiness: US Zone 8, Canadian Zone 9.**

| | |
|---|---|
| D. vulgaris* | red/black, May–June, 80cm (32in) |

*Dracunculus vulgaris*

## Endymion

**BLUEBELL**

See: *Hyacinthoides*.

## Eranthis

**WINTER ACONITE**

Winter aconites are among the earliest-flowering plants; they are not much affected by frost or snow. In clay soil they can self-seed extensively. Seed should be sown again immediately. The hard "shapeless" tubers should be soaked before planting. Plant them quite deep: about 15cm (6in) down.
**Hardiness: US Zone 5, Canadian Zone 4.**

| | |
|---|---|
| E. cilicica | yellow, Mar, 10cm (4in) |
| E. hyemalis | yellow, Feb, 10cm (4in) |

## Eremurus

**FOXTAIL LILY, KING'S SPEAR**

Young plants are frost-tender. Cover them in winter and plant them in a sunny, sandy spot. The plants have long fleshy rootstocks that you will never forget. Preferably plant eremurus in among medium-sized perennials so that the rather unattractive leaves will be out of sight.
**Hardiness: US Zone 7-5, Canadian Zone 6-4.**

| | |
|---|---|
| E. 'Cleopatra' | orange and dark red, June, 1.4m (4ft 6in) |
| E. himalaicus | white, May–June, 90cm (36in) |
| E. olgae* | soft pink, July–Aug, 90cm (36cm) |
| E. robustus | soft pink, Aug, 2.5m (8ft) |

*Eremurus* 'Rexona'

*Eranthis hyemalis*

## Erythronium

This tuberous plant should be grown more frequently. Plant the tubers relatively deep and cover in winter. Do not let them dry out: plant immediately after delivery or store in moist peat dust. The bright green leaves are decoratively speckled or veined.

**Hardiness: US Zone 6-3 Canadian Zone 5-2.**

| | |
|---|---|
| *E. californicum* | |
| 'White Beauty' | white, Apr–May, 20cm (8in) |
| *E. dens-canis* | white, pink or mauve, Mar, 30cm (12in) |
| *E.* 'Pagoda' | sulfur yellow, Apr–May, 30cm (12in) |
| *E. tuolumnense* | gold, Apr–May, 30cm (12in) |

*Erythronium tuolumnense*

*Eucharis grandiflora*

## Eucharis

This luxurious plant is suitable for an artificially heated ground bed in a hothouse. Growth will be retarded if cultivated in pots. The flowers of this "flattened daffodil" are incorporated individually in bridal bouquets. The plant is only suitable for an experienced enthusiast.

| | |
|---|---|
| *E. grandiflora*** | white, spring/fall, 70cm (28in) |

## Eucomis

### PINEAPPLE FLOWER

The flower spikes with a tuft of leaves on top resemble pineapples. In spring, the large bulbs are often even on sale in street markets. Because of its brownish green color, however, this remarkably-shaped, undemanding container plant has not really caught on over the years. Propagate by seed; it will take three years to produce a flowering plant. Store in a cool place during the winter, but not below 8°C (48°F).

**Hardiness: US Zone 9, Canadian Zone 8.**

| | |
|---|---|
| *E. autumnalis* | bright white, Aug, 30cm (12in) |
| *E. bicolor* | light green with purple margins, Aug, 50cm (20in) |
| *E. b.* 'Alba' | off-white, Aug, 50cm (20in) |
| *E. comosus* | white, lilac centers, Aug, 50cm (20in) |

In the foreground: *Eucomis bicolor*

## Freesia

A few are suitable for gardens, but it is better to grow them in a greenhouse. Store them at 20°C (68°F), the last few months at 30°C (86°F). It is almost impossible to meet these requirements oneself, and it is therefore preferable to buy new corms annually. The prepared corms are supplied by growers in spring. They will only be successful in a dry, sunny, and warm position in a fine summer. Unfortunately, freesias are usually supplied only in mixtures of single or double flowers.

*Freesia*

## *Fritillaria*

### CROWN IMPERIAL, SNAKE'S HEAD

Nearly all fritillaries flower in April or May. Grow them in a moist position. The bulbs must not dry out: plant them immediately. *F. imperialis* is suitable for flower beds. The name crown imperial refers to its seed heads: although the flowers are pendent, the seed heads begin to stand upright and form a crown. Moles will remain at a distance of some meters (yards) from the bulbs, but the suggestion that the bulbs will dispel them is untrue. The characteristic but penetrating scent of the bulbs and flowers is perceptible at a considerable distance. Plant the bulbs at a depth of 20cm (8in) to enable you to plant annuals above them. Pansies can be planted in the same place in fall, which will give you a bed of flowering plants all the year round. The fritillary *F. meleagris* can be planted on a wet bank beside a stream, or in a very moist lawn that is not mown for the first time until late spring. Fasciation sometimes occurs naturally in crowns imperial; the cultivar 'Fasciata', with brownish red flowers, is grown especially for that purpose. The cultivars 'Argenteovariegata' and 'Aureovariegata' have silver and gold variegations respectively.

**Hardiness: US Zone 8-4, Canadian Zone 7-3.**

| | |
|---|---|
| *F. assyriaca\** | br., yel. margins, 40cm (16in) |
| *F. camtschatcensis\** | almost black, 25cm (10in) |
| *F. imperialis* | |
|    'Lutea Maxima' | yellow, 1m (3ft) |
| *F. i.* 'Rubra Maxima' | red, 1m (3ft) |
| *F. meleagris* | mixed colors, 20cm (8in) |
| *F. meleagris* 'Alba' | white, 20cm (8in) |
| *F. persica* | dark mauve, 1m (3ft) |
| *F. pontica\** | green, brown spots, 30cm (12in) |
| *F. verticillata\** | cream, green veins, 60cm (24in) |

*Fritillaria persica*

## *Gagea*

The following list consists of the field, spathaceous, meadow, and woodland gagea, in that order. All these species are native to Europe, but even so they are difficult to find in the bulb trade. Gageas are only suitable for clayey soil, and do well even in heavy clay. They can be grown in lawns. The clumps are tall and grass-like; the star-shaped flowers do not appear until the plant begins to die down.

**Hardiness: US Zone 7-6, Canadian Zone 6.**

| | |
|---|---|
| *G. lutea\*\** | yellow, Mar–May, 20cm (8in) |
| *G. pratensis\*\** | yellow, Mar–Apr, 10cm (4in) |

| G. spathacea** | yellow, Apr–May, 20cm (8in) |
|---|---|

*Gagea lutea*

## Galanthus

### SNOWDROP

To prevent the bulbs from drying out in summer when they are resting, they should be planted at a depth of 15cm (6in), preferably in partial shade. In some places snowdrops will self-seed on a massive scale: the first ones will begin to flower in the second year. Propagate simply by lifting the clumps carefully while they are in flower and dividing them. There are dozens of species; the commonest are listed below. *G. reginaeolgae* is a fall-flowering snowdrop for a dry and sunny spot.
**Hardiness: US Zone 7-4, Canadian Zone 6-3.**

| G. elwesii | white, Feb–Mar, 30cm (12in) |
|---|---|
| G. ikariae** | white, Mar, 35cm (14in) |

*Galanthus elwesii*

| G. nivalis | white, Mar, 20cm (8in) |
|---|---|
| G. n. 'Flore Pleno' | white, Feb–Mar, 20cm (8in) |

## Galtonia

### CAPE HYACINTH, SUMMER HYACINTH

White bell-shaped flowers are suspended from a long stem. They are not winter-hardy; they are, however, suitable as container plants. Let them overwinter in a cool dark place indoors. Plant in April and lift again in October.
**Hardiness: US Zone 7, Canadian Zone 6.**

| G. candidans | white, July–Aug, 1.5m (5ft) |
|---|---|
| G. viridiflora* | white and green, Aug–Sept, 70cm (28in) |

*Galtonia candidans*

## Geranium

### CRANESBILL

Plant the small fleshy rootstocks in well-drained, not excessively moist soil in semi-shade. This genus consists of hundreds of species, most of which are classified as perennials.
**Hardiness: US Zone 8, Canadian Zone 7.**

| G. malviflorum | dark lilac, June, 30cm (12in) |
|---|---|
| G. tuberosum | pink to light mauve, Apr–June, 25cm (10in) |

## x Gladanthera**

This is a cross between the gladiolus and the acidanthera, what is known as a bigeneric hybrid. The flowers bear some resemblance to

*Geranium tuberosum*

*Gladiolus* 'Green Bird'

those of the gladiolus; the fragrance is similar to that of the acidanthera. This botanical curiosity was produced in New Zealand in 1955.

# Gladiolus

The large-flowered gladiolus suitable for cutting is generally familiar; the corms need to be lifted every year. They require the same treatment as dahlias. The corms are usually supplied by color or mixed, rather than by specifically named cultivars. The following list consists of several plants with special colors. They need full sun and should be supported with canes. The smaller, less familiar, and more or less frost-hardy wild gladioli are suitable for growing as perennials. These gladioli are native plants from South Africa, the Mediterranean countries, and Central Europe. There are numerous cultivars, which are divided into a number of groups: dwarf, miniature, small-flowered, medium-sized, large-flowered, giant-flowered, and botanical species.
**Hardiness: US Zone 6, Canadian Zone 5.**

| | |
|---|---|
| G. carneus | white and soft pinkish mauve, Apr–May, 60cm (24in) |
| G. communis | pinkish violet and red, May–June, 50cm (20in) |
| G.c. byzantinus | purple-red, May, 60cm (24in) |
| G. imbricatus** | dark mauve, June–July, 75cm (30in) |

**Large-flowered cultivars:**

| | |
|---|---|
| G. 'Green Bird' | creamy green |
| G. 'Invitation' | orchid-pink to mauve |
| G. 'Memorial Day' | greenish purple |
| G. 'My Love' | cream, pink fringe |
| G. 'White Friendship' | pure white |

# Gloriosa

**GLORY LILY**

Gloriosas are only suitable for greenhouses. The plant can grow up to 3m (10ft) tall. Cut it down in fall and let it overwinter in a warm spot. It is not a difficult plant to grow, provided the temperature is always kept high enough. It is often sold just as an indoor plant in summer.

| | |
|---|---|
| G. rothschildiana | yel./red, July–Sept, 3m (10ft) |

*Gloriosa rothschildiana*

## Hermodactylus

**WIDOW IRIS**

These rapidly spreading plants resemble irises. Plant them in sunny, sandy, well-drained soil. They have tuberous rootstocks.

*H. tuberosus*\*!  dark-purplish brown, Apr–May, 30cm (12in)

*Hermodactylus tuberosus*

## Hyacinthoides

**BLUEBELL**

It is difficult to tell what is the top of the potato-like bulbs. Planting by guesswork, however,

*Hyacinthoides hispanica* 'Danube'

cannot do much harm. Bluebells are frequently still sold as *Scilla campanulata*. The truest bluebell is *H. non-scripta*, recognizable by the flowers which are all suspended from one side of the flower stem. Hybridization between species, however, occurs frequently. In northern areas where deciduous trees leaf rapidly after snow melt, rather than planting in shade under trees, plant in locations which are sunny for most of the day. In Southern states, plant in a moist, cool, semi-shaded position. They are often supplied in mixed colors; buying individual colors provides more opportunities for combining them as liked.

**Hardiness: US Zone 5-4, Canadian Zone 4.**

| | |
|---|---|
| *H. hispanica* 'Blue Queen' | lavender blue |
| *H. h.* 'Dainty Maid' | purplish pink |
| *H. h.* 'Danube' ('Donau') | dark blue |
| *H. h.* 'Rosabella' | soft pink |
| *H. h.* 'Rose Queen' | deep pink |
| *H. h.* 'White City' | pure white |
| *H. non-scripta* | blue, May, 20–40cm (8–16in) |

## Hyacinthus

**HYACINTH**

Hyacinths are suitable bulbs for flower beds and edging. Plant about fifty bulbs per sq m (9 sq ft) at a depth of 10cm (4in). Store the bulbs at room temperature before planting. Wear gloves when planting them: the bulbs cause irritation. At least two thousand different cultivars must have been developed at some time, most of which have been lost again. Propagation is possible by cutting a shallow star in the underside of the bulb with a sharp kitchen knife; bulblets will then appear at the sides and will be ready to flower in three years' time. The bulbs known as multiflora!-hyacinths produce flowers on several stems at once. These can remain in the soil. The bulbs marked + are suitable for flowering indoors after preliminary forcing.

**Hardiness: US Zone 5, Canadian Zone 4.**

| | |
|---|---|
| *H.* 'Anna Marie' | soft pink, early, + |
| *H.* 'Bismarck' | light blue, very early |
| *H.* 'Blue Jacket' | dark blue and purple stripes, + |
| *H.* 'Carnegie' | white, early, + |
| *H.* 'City of Haarlem' | light yellow, medium early |
| *H.* 'Delft Blue' | light blue, early, + |
| *H.* 'l'Innocence' | white, + |
| *H.* 'Jan Bos' | red, white center, + |
| *H.* 'Lady Derby' | pink, late |
| *H.* 'Lord Balfour' | violet, late |
| *H.* 'Maria Christina' | apricot |
| *H.* 'Mulberry Rose' | pink |

| | |
|---|---|
| H. 'Ostara' | blue and mauve, early, + |
| H. 'Pink Pearl' | pink, + |
| H. 'Prins Hendrik' | light yellow, early |

*Hyacinthus* 'Ostara'

## Hymenocallis

**PERUVIAN DAFFODIL**

It is best to plant Peruvian daffodils indoors in February, using pots which can go out of doors in summer. You can also plant them in a warm spot in open ground in May. Bring them indoors again in October.

| | |
|---|---|
| H. festalis | white, June-July, 60cm (24in) |
| H. longipetala* | white, June, 50cm (20in) |

*Hymenocallis festalis*

## Incarvillea

This plant requires a warm and sunny position; not too moist as it is frost-tender. Cover thoroughly in winter. It is also suitable as a container plant and is often sold as a perennial.

Keep the rootstock moist; the plant can be forced in a greenhouse.
**Hardiness: US Zone 6, Canadian Zone 5.**

| | |
|---|---|
| I. delavayi | pink, June, 60cm (24in) |

*Incarvillea delavayi*

## Ipheion

This is one of the least expensive small bulbs which, unfortunately, is rarely cultivated. The plant is low-growing and has leaves smelling of onions. The flowers are a radiant shade of blue. Ipheions are still often sold as *Brodiaeas*.
**Hardiness: US Zone 6, Canadian Zone 5.**

| | |
|---|---|
| I. uniflorum | violet blue, May–June, 25cm (10in) |
| I. u. 'Rolf Fiedler'** | deep blue, April, 15cm (6in) |
| I. u. 'Wisley Blue' | light blue, May, 20cm (8in) |

*Ipheion uniflorum*

# Iris

There are spring-flowering bulbs, summer-flowering bulbs, and perennial irises. *I. danfordiae* and *I. reticulata* are conspicuous among the spring-flowering species because of their extremely early flowering season. Their height is 20cm (8in). Every garden should have some! Plant the irises close together to make the low-growing bulbs show up well. The foliage remains erect and is therefore not distracting.
**Hardiness: US Zone 6-4, Canadian Zone 5-3.**

**Early-flowering:**

| | |
|---|---|
| *I. danfordiae* | bright yellow, Feb, 15cm (6in) |
| *I. histrioides** | deep blue, Feb, 15cm (6in) |
| *I. h.* 'George' | mauve, darker marks |
| *I. h.* 'Major'* | deep blue |
| *I. reticulata* 'Alba'* | white, Feb, 15cm (6in) |
| *I. r.* 'Cantab' | flax blue, orange marks |
| *I. r.* 'Clairette'* | sky blue, deep purple lips |
| *I. r.* 'Harmony' | cornflower blue, darker lips |
| *I. r.* 'Hercules' | velvety purple, orange marks |
| *I. r.* 'Joyce' | bright blue, orange marks |
| *I. r.* 'Royal Blue'* | deep purplish blue, yellow marks |
| *I. r.* 'Violet Beauty'* | violet, dark lips, orange marks |

**Early-summer-flowering:**

| | |
|---|---|
| *I. bucharica** | cream, yellow spots, May, 30cm (12in) |
| *I. hoogiana*** | lavender blue, May, 60cm (24in) |
| *I. h.* 'Alba'*** | white, May, 50cm (20in) |
| *I. magnifica*** | soft lilac, May, 60cm (24in) |

*Iris reticulata* 'Harmony'

# Ismene

See: *Hymenocallis*.

# Ixia

This is an ideal plant for well-drained, humus-rich soil. Plant late to prevent new growth being damaged by frost, and close together (ten to an area the size of a saucer). They need to be well-covered in winter. Lift immediately after flowering and keep them warm in summer to simulate the dry South African summer. These details may show that the bulb, if grown for cut flowers, will do best in a greenhouse. Unfortunately, it is usually supplied in a mixture of excessively bright shades of red, pink, yellow, orange, and cream, all with a brightly colored darker center. Propagate by planting out the corms and cormlets again.
**Hardiness: US Zone 8, Canadian Zone 7.**

| | |
|---|---|
| *I. hybride* 'Giant' | white, red center, June–Aug, 70cm (28in) |
| *I.* 'Mabel' | deep pink, July, 40cm (16in) |
| *I. h.* 'Rose Emperor' | soft pink, red center, July, 60cm (24in) |
| *I. paniculata* | pink, Aug–Sept, 40cm (16in) |
| *I. speciosa** | red, Aug, 50cm (20in) |
| *I. viridiflora*** | green, Aug, 50cm (20in) |

*Ixia* 'Mabel'

# Ixiolirion

This is another bulb for a warm spot. For method of planting and treatment, see: *Ixia*.
**Hardiness: US Zone 6, Canadian Zone 6.**

| *I. tataricum*\* | d. blue, May–June, 30cm (12in) |

*Ixiolirion montanum (palassii)*

## *Leucojum*

**SNOWFLAKE**

*L. vernum*, the spring snowflake, flowers earlier than snowdrops. It has shiny dark green leaves which appear during the winter months. Like the summer snowflake, *L. aestivum*, this bulb requires moist, humus-rich soil in a semi-shady position.
**Hardiness: US Zone 6, Canadian Zone 5.**

| *L. aestivum* | white and green, Apr–May, 25-35cm (10–14in) |
| *L. a.* 'Gravetye Giant' | white and green, May–June, 40cm (16in) |
| *L. vernum* | white, Feb–Mar, 20cm (8in) |

*Leujocum aestivum*

## *Liatris*

**GAY FEATHERS**

This summer-flowering native bulbous plant is usually listed as a perennial. It make a good cut flower, with flower heads which have the peculiarity of opening from the top downwards.
**Hardiness: US Zone 4, Canadian Zone 3.**

| *L. spicata* | pur. pink, July–Aug, 70cm (28in |
| *L. s.* 'Floristan White' | white, July–Aug, 90cm (36in) |
| *L. s.* 'Kobold'! | violet lilac, strong, June–Sept, 50cm (20in) |

*Liatris spicata*

## *Lilium*

**LILY**

Plant lilies in well-drained soil and cover them in winter to protect them from frost. The species listed below are reasonably winter-hardy, but consult an up-to-date catalog to find suitable hybrids. Do not let the fleshy bulbs dry out: first store them in moist peat dust or plant them immediately. March is the time to plant them. Some bulbs only develop roots on the underside of the bulb (*L. candidum*); do not plant them at too great a depth. The bulbs that also develop roots on the flower stems (by far the most) may be planted at a normal depth (15cm/6in).Lilies are very prone to virus diseases which seriously weaken the plant, and the recently introduced pest lily beetle is becoming a major problem which must be rigorously controlled.
**Hardiness: US Zone 6, Canadian Zone 5.**

| | |
|---|---|
| *L. auratum* | w., red speck. July, 80cm (32in) |
| *L. candidum* | white, June, 1m (3ft) |
| *L. martagon** | brownish mauve, June, 1m (3ft) |
| *L. m.* var. *album*** | white, June–July, 1m (3ft) |
| *L. pumilum* | fiery red, July, 60cm (24in) |

*Lilium regale*

| | |
|---|---|
| *L. regale* | white with yellow centers, July, 1m (3ft) |
| *L. tigrinum* | orange red, speckles, July–Sept, 1.25m (4ft 2in) |

# Muscari

## GRAPE HYACINTH

Mistakenly, this is one of the favorite garden bulbs: the flowers are beautiful but the long-lasting foliage looks untidy. *M. armeniacum* and *M. botryoides* are two of the least expensive bulbs. Special offers of bulbs therefore contain a high proportion of grape hyacinths. *M.*

*Muscari azureum*

*latifolium** and *M. neglectum*** are among the most attractive species.
**Hardiness: US Zone 5-4, Canadian Zone 4-3.**

| | |
|---|---|
| *M. armeniacum* | blue, Mar–Apr, 20cm (8in) |
| *M. a.* 'Blue Spike' | blue (d), Apr–May, 20cm (8in) |
| *M. a.* 'Saffier'** | dark blue, Apr–May, 20cm (8in) |
| *M. azureum* | azure, Mar–Apr, 15cm (6in) |
| *M. a.* 'Album' | white, Mar–Apr, 15cm (6in) |
| *M. botryoides* 'Album' | white, Apr–May, 20cm (8in) |
| *M. comosum* | soft violet blue, May–July, 40cm (16in) |
| *M. c.* 'Plumosum' | violet blue, May–July, 40cm (16in) |
| *M. latifolium*!* | light blue and dark blue, Apr, 25cm (10in) |

# Narcissus

## DAFFODIL

*The Classified List and International Register of Daffodil Names* includes over 10,000 cultivars. Interested gardeners should try to obtain a copy of E.A. Bowles's *Handbook of Narcissus* (1934), a standard work that has been reprinted. The best daffodils for naturalizing belong to the *poeticus* division: 'Pheasant's Eye', 'Keats'**, and 'Actaea'; all of them are single, long-stemmed, pure white, and have a very small cup. They are also suitable for long grass. The hoop-petticoat *N. bulbocodium* ssp. *vulgaris* var. *conspicuus* is least like a daffodil; it is suitable for a sunny spot and soil that is not excessively dry. Most daffodils are suitable for containers.
**Hardiness: US Zone 7-5, Canadian Zone 6-4.**

*Narcissus triandus* 'Albus'

*Narcissus* 'Barrett Browning'

*Narcissus* 'Texas'

*Narcissus* 'Peeping Tom'

**Botanical narcissi:**

| | |
|---|---|
| *N. caniculatus* | wh., small yel. cup, 10cm (4in) |
| *N. minor* | yellow, Mar, 5cm (2in) |
| *N. nanus (N. lobularis)* | yellow, Mar, 20cm (8in) |
| *N. odorus* | bright yellow, Apr–May, 30cm (12in) |
| *N. poeticus* var. *recurvus* 'Pheasant's Eye'! | 40cm (16in) |
| *N. p.* 'Actaea'! | white, yellow cup, orange rim, 40cm (16in) |
| *N. p.* 'Keats'!** | white, delicate, yellow cup, orange margin, 40cm (16in) |
| *N. p.* 'Sinopel'* | white, green cup, yellow rim, 40cm (16in) |
| *N. triandus* 'Albus' | white, 20cm (8in) |
| *N. t.* 'Hawera' | yellow, 20cm (8in) |
| *N. t.* 'Thalia' | white, 40cm (16in) |
| *N.* 'W.P. Milner' | white and yellow, 20cm (8in) |

**Trumpet narcissi:**

| | |
|---|---|
| *N.* 'Golden Harvest' | yellow |
| *N.* 'King Alfred' | yellow |
| *N.* 'Mount Hood' | cream |

**Large-cupped narcissi:**

| | |
|---|---|
| *N.* 'Carlton' | yellow |
| *N.* 'Flower Record' | white, deep yellow cup |
| *N.* 'Fortune' | golden yellow, orange-red cup |
| *N.* 'Ice Follies' | light yellow, bright yellow cup |

**Small-cupped narcissi:**

| | |
|---|---|
| *N.* 'Barrett Browning' | white, orange cup |
| *N.* 'Quirinus' | lemon yellow, yellowish orange cup |
| *N.* 'Verger' | white, dark red cup |

**Double narcissi:**

| | |
|---|---|
| *N.* 'Dick Wilden' | yellow |
| *N.* 'Petit Four' | white and apricot |
| *N.* 'Texas'! | yellow and orange |
| *N.* 'White Lion' | white and soft yellow |

**Cyclamineus narcissi:**

| | |
|---|---|
| *N.* 'February Gold'! | bright yellow, 25cm (10in) |
| *N.* 'February Silver' | creamy white, 25cm (10in) |
| *N.* 'Jack Snipe' | white, yellow cup, 20cm (8in) |
| *N.* 'Peeping Tom' | deep yellow, 35cm (14in) |
| *N.* 'Tête-à-Tête' | yellow, darker cup, 20cm (8in) |

**Jonquils** (strong fragrance):

| | |
|---|---|
| *N.* 'Baby Moon' | soft yellow, 25cm (10in) |
| *N.* 'Bellsong'* | yellow, pink cup, 30cm (12in) |
| *N.* 'Sundial'! | dark yellow, green center, 25cm (10in) |

**Tazetta narcissi:**

| | |
|---|---|
| 'Cragford' | white, orange cup, 40cm (16in) |
| 'Geranium' | white, orange cup, 40cm (16in) |

## Nectarascordum

This bulb resembles an allium. The seed heads as well as the remarkable plants are attractive. Plant in a warm spot in well-drained soil. This plant was formerly called *Allium bulgaricum*.

*Nectarascordum siculum*

**Hardiness: US Zone 5, Canadian Zone 4.**

| | |
|---|---|
| *N. siculum* | green and mauve, white rim, June, 50cm (20in) |

## Nerine

Like the vallota and the zephyranthes, this plant should be treated like a container plant. Don't let it overwinter in less than 5°C (41°F); protect it from drying out. The most suitable species for the garden is *N. undulata*. Like cannas, they should be lifted in fall and not planted out again too early. The flowering season of this species depends greatly on the relevant summer temperature.
**Hardiness: US Zone 8, Canadian Zone 7.**

| | |
|---|---|
| *N. bowdenii* | pink, Sept–Oct, 50cm (20in) |
| *N. flexuosa* 'Alba' | white, Sept–Oct, 40cm (16in) |

## Ornithogalum

**STAR-OF-BETHLEHEM**

These rewarding bulbs for naturalizing are also, with the exception of *O. umbellatum,* good for cutting. Florists often display chincherinchees, *O. thyrsoides,* a non-hardy species from South Africa. Plant the following species in half-shade that is not too dry. *O. nutans*, the drooping star-of-Bethlehem, may also be planted in the shade.

**Hardiness: US Zone 8-5, Canadian Zone 7-4.**

| | |
|---|---|
| *O. arabicum* | white, May–June, 60cm (24in) |
| *O. balansae*** | wh./green, Mar–Apr, 15cm (6in) |
| *O. magnum*** | white, May–June, 60cm (24in) |
| *O. nutans*! | wh./sil. green, Apr, 30cm (12in) |
| *O. umbellatum* | white, Apr, 15cm (6in) |

*Ornithogalum arabicum*

*Nerine undulata*

## Oxalis

The hardy rock plant *O. adenophylla* comes from South America and flowers abundantly. Plant in soil that is not excessively moist to prevent rotting in winter. Covering the plant with a sheet of glass is beneficial. *O. deppei*, which is not hardy, is often sold as an indoor plant in spring. The other species are also suitable for a frost-free greenhouse.
**Hardiness: US Zone 6, Canadian Zone 5.**

*O. adenophylla*          pink, summer, 20cm (8in)

*Oxalis adenophylla*

## Puschkinia

It is difficult for beginners to distinguish between puschkinias and low-growing scillas and chionodoxas. Although there are of course botanical differences, a sense of color is likely to solve the problem. Conditions for growing puschkinias are the same as for the other genera.
**Hardiness: US Zone 5, Canadian Zone 4.**

*P. scilloides* var. *libanotica* china blue, Mar, 20cm (8in)
*P. s.* var. *libanotica* 'Alba' pure white, Mar, 20cm (8in)

*Puschkinia scilloides* var. *libanotica*

## Ranunculus

In my opinion, this old-fashioned garden plant is seen all too rarely nowadays. There is a difference between Turkish and Persian ranunculi. The former should be planted in November or December, and the latter in February or March; they should be covered with straw or peat dust. It is also possible to sow under glass in the second half of September. Although there are many cultivars, they are usually supplied as a mixture. They are unsuitable for heavy clay; mix that kind of soil with sharp sand and peat. Well-drained humus-rich sandy soil is ideal. Plant the clusters of tubers in March; the plants will flower from June until August, after which they should be lifted in fall.
**Hardiness: US Zone 9, Canadian Zone 8.**

**Turkish ranunculi:**
| | |
|---|---|
| *R.* 'Boule d'Or'* | golden yellow, early |
| *R.* 'Hercules' | white |
| *R.* 'Romano'* | red |
| *R.* 'Merveilleuse'* | coppery yellow |

**French ranunculi:**
| | |
|---|---|
| *R.* 'Mathilde Christina'* | white |
| *R.* 'Orange Queen'* | orange |
| *R.* 'Primrose Beauty'* | yellow |
| *R.* 'Veronica'* | red |

**Peony-flowered ranunculi:**
| | |
|---|---|
| *R.* 'Brilliant Star'* | red |
| *R.* 'Champagne' | light yellow |
| *R.* 'Flora'* | carmine, black center |
| *R.* 'Golden Ball'* | yellow |

**Persian ranunculi:**
| | |
|---|---|
| *R.* 'Barbaroux' | red |
| *R.* 'Fire Ball' | dark red |
| *R.* 'Jaune Suprême' | yellow |
| *R.* 'Pink Perfection' | pink |

Mixed ranunculi

# Scilla

## SIBERIAN SQUILL

A number of species formerly included in the genus *Scilla* are now classified under *Hyacinthoides*. It is best to plant them in moisture-retentive, limy and humus-poor sandy or clayey soils. *S. peruviana** is not fully hardy. *S. sibirica* (Siberian squill) is one of the best bulbs for naturalizing. Because of its early growing cycle, it is possible to start mowing again at a reasonable time.
**Hardiness: US Zone 6-5, Canadian Zone 6-4.**

| | |
|---|---|
| *S. bifolia* | gentian blue, Mar, 10cm (4in) |
| *S. mischtschenkoana* | very light blue, Feb–Mar, 10cm (4in) |
| *S. sibirica* | bright blue, Mar–Apr, 15cm (6in) |
| *S. s.* 'Alba' | white, Mar–Apr, 15cm (6in) |
| *S. s.* 'Spring Beauty' | dark blue, Mar–Apr, 20cm (8in) |

*Scilla bifolia* 'Rosea'

# Sternbergia

This is one of the few fall-flowering bulbs and also one of the best. Plant in a warm sunny spot.
**Hardiness: US Zone 6, Canadian Zone 5.**

| | |
|---|---|
| *S. lutea* | yellow, Sept–Nov, 15cm (6in) |

# Trillium

Trilliums are easily recognized by the three leaves at the top of a bare stem. Plant these natives in humus-rich soil in a half-shady spot such as a woodland corner of the garden.
**Hardiness: US Zone 6-5, Canadian Zone 5-4.**

| | |
|---|---|
| *T. cernuum*** | nodding, white, May, 30cm (12in) |
| *T. erectum* | brownish, purple, May, 30cm (12in) |
| *T. grandiflorum* | white, May, 30cm (12in) |
| *T. sessile* | brownish green, May–June, 20cm (8in) |
| *T. s.* 'Californicum' | brownish red, May–June, 20cm (8in) |

*Trillium sessile* 'Californicum'

# Triteleia

The leaves die away by the time this bulb comes into flower. It resembles the *Brodiaea*, a name often still given to the plant by growers. Plant in a sunny spot.
**Hardiness: US Zone 7, Canadian Zone 6.**

| | |
|---|---|
| *T. laxa* 'Queen Fabiola' | violet mauve, June, 50cm (20in) |

*Sternbergia lutea*

*Triteleia laxa* 'Queen Fabiola'

## Tritonia

This long-flowering bulbous plant for a cool but frost-free greenhouse may be planted out of doors in a very warm spot where it is well protected. The plants are only sold in mixtures of yellow and orange shades.
**Hardiness: US Zone 7, Canadian Zone 6.**

| | |
|---|---|
| *T. crocata* | mixed, June–July, 25cm (10in) |

*Tritonia crocata*

## Tulipa

### TULIP

What can I write about tulips? Even though this bulb would seem to be familiar enough, the botanical species, ideal for small city gardens and rock gardens, turn out to be inadequately represented in garden centers. They have received more attention in recent years, as have the old-fashioned striped tulips seen in seventeenth-century paintings. This trend is a recent one, with the result that such tulips are expensive, just as they were in the days of tulipomania. Never buy a mixture of large-flowered tulips: not only the colors, but also the differences in flowering seasons render mixtures less attractive. Blending them yourself and noting when they flower will make your garden unique!
**Hardiness: US Zone 7-5, Canadian Zone 6-4.**

Botanical tulips:

| | |
|---|---|
| *T. acuminata* | red/yellow, Apr, 50cm (20in) |
| *T. aucheriana* | deep pink, Apr, 5cm (2in) |
| *T. batalinii\** | yellow, Apr, 15cm (6in) |
| *T. biflora* | w./gr., Apr, 15–25cm (6–10in) |
| *T. celsiana\** | red, May, 10cm (4in) |
| *T. clusiana* | white/red, Apr–May, 30cm (12in) |
| *T. hageri* | red, Apr, 15cm (6in) |
| *T. kolpakowskiana* | y./gr., Apr, 15cm (6in) |
| *T. lanata\** | orange red, yellow margins, Apr, 25cm (10in) |
| *T. liniflora* | scarlet, Apr–May, 15cm (6in) |
| *T. marjolettii* | soft yellow, with pink margins, May, 50cm (20in) |
| *T. polychroma\** | white with yellow centers, Apr, 10cm (4in) |
| *T. praestans* | red, Apr, 25cm (10in) |
| *T. pulchella* var. *humilis* | viol./pink, Feb–Mar, 10cm (4in) |
| *T. saxatile* | pink and purplish pink, Mar–Apr, 30cm (12in) |
| *T. sylvestris* | yellow, Apr, 25cm (10in) |

*Tulipa hageri*

*Tulipa urumiensis*, Botanical tulip

*Tulipa* 'Lustige Witwe', Triumph tulip

| | |
|---|---|
| T. tarda | yel./white, Apr, 10cm (4in) |
| T. turkestanica | white, yellow centers, Mar, 25cm (10in) |
| T. urumiensis | golden yellow, red specks, Apr–May, 20cm (8in) |

*T. gregii, T. fosteriana, T. kaufmanniana* and their hybrids are not regarded as "botanical"; hybridization makes their origins uncertain. For hybrids, it is best to consult the latest growers' catalogs as it would be impossible to list a suitable selection. The assortment changes annually, and consists of thousands of cultivars. Make a selection from the following groups:

**Early-flowering tulips:**
single early
double early
**Mid-season-flowering tulips:**
Mendel tulips
Triumph tulips
Darwin hybrids
**Late-flowering tulips:**
Darwin tulips
lily-flowered tulips
cottage tulips (double late)
Rembrandt tulips
parrot tulips
peony-flowered tulips (double late)

*Tulipa* 'Brilliant Star': single and early

*Tulipa* 'Lilac Perfection': double, lily-flowered tulip

## Urginea

### CRUSADERS' SPEARS, SEA ONION, SEA SQUILL

This largest, though not loveliest, of bulbous plants, which grows up to 1.2m (4ft) tall, is frost-tender. Plant in a sunny spot in sandy soil, and water regularly during its growing period. Lift the plants at the same time as dahlias. The plant is also suitable for a large pot.

| | |
|---|---|
| U. maritima* | white, Aug–Sept, 1.2m (4ft) |

## Vallota

This plant with amaryllis-like flowers tolerates only a few degrees of frost. It will prefer it if you let it overwinter in a cool and frost-free place.

| | |
|---|---|
| V. speciosa | orange red, July, 50cm (20in) |

## Zephyranthes

### RAIN LILY, WIND FLOWER

Treat this plant like the vallota. Only Z. *candida* can be left out of doors in winter, provided it is well covered. The others should be stored frost-free at a minimum of 5°C (41°F).

*Vallota speciosa*

**Hardiness: US Zone 9, Canadian Zone 8.**

| | |
|---|---|
| Z. candida | white, Sept–Oct, 20cm (8in) |
| Z. grandiflora* | br. pink, May–June, 30cm (12in) |

*Zephyranthes grandiflora*

# 10. Water and marsh plants

*The assortment of water plants is infinitely greater than what is on offer at the average garden center. The great majority of plants are only available from specialized firms. Creating an attractive pond will therefore require some effort, although water plants will certainly become more popular now that so much interest is focused on ponds. It is essential to grow these plants at the right depth under water, and this is specified in the lists in this chapter (in centimeters, with the number of inches in brackets). The height of the plant above water is preceded by a + sign. The color of the flowers, the month in which they flower and, if relevant, the maximum height of the plant above the surface of the water follow.*

## Acorus

**SWEET FLAG, MYRTLE FLAG**
This plant grows to a maximum overall height of 1m (3ft); its flowers are unspectacular.
**Hardiness: US Zone 8-4, Canadian Zone 7-3.**

| | |
|---|---|
| *A. calamus* | 0–20cm (0–8in), white, June–Aug, 70cm (28in) |
| *A. c.* 'Variegatus' | 0–20cm (0–8in), yellow stripes, June–Aug, 70cm (28in) |
| *A. gramineus* | 10cm (4in), y. str., 30cm (12in) |

## Alisma

**WATER PLANTAIN**
The water plantain looks larger than the common plantain that is considered a weed. The flowers grow to a maximum height of 1.5m. (5ft)
**Hardiness: US Zone 4, Canadian Zone 3.**

| | |
|---|---|
| *A. natans* | float., wh., May–Aug, 40cm (16in) |
| *A. plantago-aquatica* | 30–+10cm (12–+4in), white, July–Aug, 70cm (28in) |

Left: *Sagittaria latifolia*

*Acorus calamus* 'Variegatus'

## Aponogeton

**CAPE PONDWEED, WATER HAWTHORN**
This floating plant is rooted in the bottom of the pond. This South African species should be planted deep enough to prevent the rootstock

*Alisma plantago-aquatica*

freezing in winter. The waxy flowers float on the surface of the water.
**Hardiness: US Zone 9, Canadian Zone 8.**

| | |
|---|---|
| *A. distachyos* | 30–50cm (12–20in), white, June–Oct, 5cm (2in) |

*Aponogeton distachyos*

## *Azolla*

**FAIRY MOSS, WATER FERN**
This attractive free-floating water fern is just as invasive as common duckweed but it is easier to remove. It also has a prettier shape and color.
**Hardiness: US Zone 8, Canadian Zone 7.**

| | |
|---|---|
| *A. caroliniana* | floating, green, brownish red |

*Azolla caroliniana*

## *Baldellia (Echinodorus)*

**SMALL WATER PLANTAIN**
The small water plantain is a marsh plant with grass-like leaves and small bright flowers. The species *Alisma, Luronium* and *Echinodorus* are sometimes referred to collectively as *Alisma* (water plantain), and this constantly changing

nomenclature causes considerable confusion.
**Hardiness: US Zone 6, Canadian Zone 5.**

| | |
|---|---|
| *B. ranunculoides* | 5–+5 (2–+2), white, June–Sept, 20cm (8in) |

*Baldellia ranunculoides*

## *Butomus*

**FLOWERING RUSH**
This plant requires a maximum water depth of 50cm (20in). Plant it in a sunny spot. Its umbels of pink flowers are at their best in July.
**Hardiness: US Zone 5, Canadian Zone 4.**

| | |
|---|---|
| *B. umbellatus* | 30–0cm (12–0in), pink, July–Aug, 1m (3ft) |

*Butomus umbellatus*

# Calla

## BOG ARUM

The bog arum is native to both North America and Europe and prefers semi-shade or shade.
**Hardiness: US Zone 4, Canadian Zone 3.**

| | |
|---|---|
| C. palustris | 15–0cm (6–0in), white, June–July, 20cm (8in) |

*Calla palustris*

# Caltha

## MARSH MARIGOLD, KINGCUP

In spring, marsh marigolds are striking marginal water plants, partly because other plants are still without leaves at that time and partly because of their large yellow flowers.
**Hardiness: US Zone 5, Canadian Zone 4.**

| | |
|---|---|
| C. palustris | 10–0cm (4–0in), golden yellow, Apr–May, 30cm (12in) |
| C. p. 'Alba'* | 10–0cm (4–0in), white, May–June, 20cm (8in) |

*Caltha palustris* 'Alba'

| | |
|---|---|
| C. p. 'Multiplex' | 10–0cm (4–0in), yellow (d), Apr–May, 30cm (12in) |
| C. polypetale*! | 10–0cm (4–0in), May–June, 60cm (24in) |

# Carex

## SEDGE

The attractive brown flower spikes constitute the main beauty of this marsh and marginal water plant, but being evergreen is more important.
**Hardiness: US Zone 6-3, Canadian Zone 5-2.**

*Carex pendula*

| | |
|---|---|
| C. paniculata | 10–0cm (4–0in), green, May–June, 1m (3ft) |
| C. pendula! | 10–0cm (4–0in), brown, June–July, 1.5m (5ft) |
| C. pseudocyperus | 20–0cm (8–0in), brown, June–July, 1m (3ft) |
| C. riparia | 10–+10cm (4–+4in), brown, June–July, 1m (3ft) |

*Ceratophyllum demersum*

## Ceratophyllum

**HORNWORT**
This good oxygenating plant is invasive and grows in soil or as a floating plant. Its flowers are insignificant.
**Hardiness: US Zone 5, Canadian Zone 4.**

| | |
|---|---|
| *C. demersum* | 1m–30cm (3ft–12in), gr., 0cm (0in) |

*Chrysoplenium alternifolium*

## Chrysoplenium

This small plant likes to grow in water. If the water flows gently, it will also grow under water.
**Hardiness: US Zone 5, Canadian Zone 4.**

| | |
|---|---|
| *C. alternifolium*** | 10–+10cm (4–+4in), yellow, July–Sept, 10cm (4in) |

*Cicuta virosa*

## Cicuta

**WATER HEMLOCK, COWBANE**
Water hemlock was used for Socrates' poisoned cup. The plant resembles some other umbelliferae (Apiaceae). It is extremely poisonous.
**Hardiness: US Zone 6, Canadian Zone 5.**

| | |
|---|---|
| *C. virosa*** | 10–0cm (4–0in), white, July–Sept, 1m (3ft) |

*Cladium mariscus*

## Cladium

**SAW SEDGE**
This sedge is native to western Europe, in pools, marshy woods and moist sand dune valleys.
**Hardiness: US Zone 5, Canadian Zone 4.**

| | |
|---|---|
| *C. mariscus*** | 30–10cm (12–4in), green, June–July, 1.5m (5ft) |

## Colocasia

This tropical aquatic plant is grown for its beautiful leaves, which are reminiscent of arrowhead.

| | |
|---|---|
| *C. esculenta*** | 50–20cm (20–8in), Aug–Nov, 1m (3ft) |

## Comarum

**MARSH CINQUEFOIL**
See: *Potentilla.*

*Colocasia esculenta*

## Cotula

**BRASS BUTTONS**
*Cotula squalida* (see: Perennials) is suitable for banks, particularly those of lined ponds, where the edge needs to be camouflaged. The cotula mentioned below will grow in the water; its flowers are more significant than those of the other species.
**Hardiness: US Zone 8, Canadian Zone 7.**

| | |
|---|---|
| *C. coronopifolia*\*\* | 5–0cm (2–0in), yellow, May–June, 20cm (8in) |

*Cyperus alternifolius*      right: *Dactylorhiza praetermissa*

## Cyperus

**GALINGALE**
Although many species are native to western Europe, those listed below come from elsewhere.
**Hardiness: US Zone 9, Canadian Zone 8.**

| | |
|---|---|
| *C. alternifolius* | 10–0cm (4–0in), light green, 70cm (28in) |
| *C. longus* | 20–0cm (8–0in), greenish brown, July–Sept, 1m (3ft) |

## Dactylorrhiza

Plant in poor, unfertilized, moist soil. In Europe, this plant easily becomes established on newly drained land.
**Hardiness: US Zone 6, Canadian Zone 5.**

| | |
|---|---|
| *D. praetermissa*\* | +5–+20cm (+2–+8in), flesh-col., May–June, 40cm (16in) |

## Echinodorus

**WATER PLANTAIN**
See: *Baldellia*.

## Egeria

These oxygenating submerged water plants can be rooted in the bottom of the pond or float freely. *E. densa* comes from Argentina and, like *Elodia*, which has a Canadian origin, the plant has become naturalized in parts of Europe. Its flowers are insignificant.

Hardiness: US Zone 8, Canadian Zone 7.

E. densa**                    1m–20cm (3ft–8in), green

## Eichhornia

**WATER HYACINTH**
See: Container plants and cool-green-house plants.

## Eleocharis

**NEEDLE SPIKE-RUSH**
This plant is suitable for a natural-looking pond. Its flower spikes are insignificant.
**Hardiness: US Zone 5, Canadian Zone 4.**

E. acicularis                30–0cm (12–0in), gr.,30cm (12in)
E. palustris                 0–+20cm (0–+8in), g., 30cm (12in)

## Elodia

This native invasive plant has now appeared in many European waterways. It is an excellent oxygenating plant, but should be thinned regularly. The plant floats in the water, but can also be rooted.
**Hardiness: US Zone 4, Canadian Zone 3.**

E. canadensis                1m–20cm (3ft–8in),gr., May–Aug

*Elodia canadensis*

## Epilobium

**WILLOW HERB, FIREWEED**
Epilobium is often regarded as an almost ineradicable weed and is only suitable for wild gardens.
**Hardiness: US Zone 3, Canadian Zone 2.**

E. angustifolium             0–+10cm (0–+4in), pink, July–Oct, 1m (3ft)
E. 'Album'**                 0–+10cm (0–+4in), white, July–Oct, 1m (3ft)
E. hirsutum                  0–+10cm (0–+4in), pink, July–Nov, 1.2m (4ft)

*Epilobium hirsutum*

## Epipactus

In nature, this orchid species grows in the same areas as *Dactylorhiza*: poor, moist, sandy, or loamy soil.
**Hardiness: US Zone 3, Canadian Zone 2.**

E. palustris**               +10cm (+4in), brown and white, June–Aug, 40cm (16in)

## Equisetum

**HORSETAIL**
E. fluviatile (water horsetail) and E. palustre (marsh horsetail) are acotyledons and do not bear flowers. Botanically, they have a low grading, and are always featured before ferns in floras.
**Hardiness: US Zone 6-1, Canadian Zone 5-1.**

E. hyemale                   30–+10cm (12–+4in), brownish 1.2m (4ft)
E. japonicum                 30–+10cm (12–+4in), brownish nodes, 80cm (32in)
E. scirpoides                10–0cm (4–0in), brown nodes, 20cm (8in)

## Eriophorum

**COTTON GRASS**
This grassy plant for a poor peat bog may grow just below the surface of the water. The pappi,

*Equisetum japonicum*

which remain on the plant for a long time, are its main decorative feature.
**Hardiness: US Zone 5-4, Canadian Zone 4-3.**

| | |
|---|---|
| *E. angustifolium*** | 0–+10cm (0–+4in), white seed heads, May–June, 30cm (12in) |
| *E. latifolium*** | 0–+10cm (0–+4in), white seed heads, Apr–May, 60cm (24in) |
| *E. vaginatum* | 0–+10cm (0–+4in), white seed heads, Apr–May, 40cm (16in) |

*Eriophorum vaginatum*

# Euphorbia

### MILKWEED, SPURGE

This native European marsh plant will also grow in water. It produces striking flowers, and turns a beautiful color in fall.
**Hardiness: US Zone 5, Canadian Zone 4.**

| | |
|---|---|
| *E. palustris* | 0–+10cm (0–+4in), yellow, May–June, 1.2m (4ft) |

# Filipendula

### MEADOWSWEET

This plant is suitable for moist banks. It thrives in sun and in semi-shade, but cannot survive in a sunless position. *F. vulgaris* (dropwort) looks attractive on a bank, but should have a drier position.
**Hardiness: US Zone 4, Canadian Zone 3.**

| | |
|---|---|
| *F. ulmaria* | 0–+10cm (0–+4in), cream, Aug–Sept, 80cm (32in) |
| *F. u.* 'Plena' | 0–+10c (0–+4in), white (d) July–Aug, 70cm (28in) |
| *F. u.* 'Variegata' | 0–+10cm (0–+4in), white varieg. leaves, July–Aug, 70cm (28in) |

*Filipendula vulgaris* 'Plena'

| | |
|---|---|
| *F. vulgaris* | +10–+20cm (+4–+8in), white, June–July, 50cm (20in) |
| *F. v.* 'Plena' | +10–+20cm (+4–+8in), white (d), June–July, 40cm (16in) |

## Glyceria

This plant grows like reeds: whole banks can be covered with it. It will tolerate a change in water level. Sometimes the plant will mutate back: remove the green leaves, as they become invasive.
**Hardiness: US Zone 5, Canadian Zone 4.**

G. maxima 'Variegata'     10–+10cm (4–+4in), July–Sept, 40cm (16in)

Glyceria maxima

## Groenlandia

Even the flower of this submerged water plant remains under water. It roots in the soil and is suitable for growing in shallow water. The genus *Groenlandia* has been separated from the genus *Potamogeton*.
**Hardiness: US Zone 6, Canadian Zone 5.**

G. densa**     10–40cm (4–16in), June–Sept

## Hippurus

The flowers of this invasive plant for semi-shade are unspectacular, but the ribbed stems resembling those of the horsetail are very attractive.
**Hardiness: US Zone 3, Canadian Zone 2.**

H. vulgaris     60–20cm (24–8in), g., 30cm (12in)

## Hottonia

The much-divided leaves of this water plant are partly submerged and partly above water. The plant is tolerant of half-shade.

**Hardiness: US Zone 6, Canadian Zone 5.**

H. palustris     80–10cm (32–4in), pink, May–June, 40cm (16in)

Hottonia palustris

## Houttuynia

See: Perennials.

## Hydrocharis

**FROG'S BIT**
This floating plant also roots in the soil and is suitable for shallow water.
**Hardiness: US Zone 4, Canadian Zone 3.**

H. morsus-ranae     floating plant, white, July–Aug, 5cm (2in)

Hippurus vulgaris

## Hydrocotyle

This European marsh plant for heathlands and sand dune soil is tolerant of a varying water level.
**Hardiness: US Zone 7, Canadian Zone 6.**

| | |
|---|---|
| *H. leucocephala* | 10–+10cm (4–+4in), white, June–Aug, 20cm (8in) |
| *H. vulgaris* | 20–+5cm (8–+2in), white to red, June–Sept, 10cm (4in) |

*Hydrocotyle vulgaris*

## Inula

See: Perennials.

## Iris

**FLAG**
An iris garden should include marshland and a pond if it is to simulate natural conditions. Pay special attention to the moisture of the soil (see also: Perennials).
**Hardiness: US Zone 5-3, Canadian Zone 5-3.**

| | |
|---|---|
| *I. laevigata* | 0–+10cm (0–+4in), blueish mauve, large, June–July, 80cm (32in) |
| *I. l.* 'Rose Queen' | bright lilac pink, June–July, 70cm (28in) |
| *I. l.* 'Snowdrift' | white, June–July, 70cm (28in) |
| *I. setosa* | |
| *I. pseudacorus* | 20–0cm (8–0in), yel, June, 1m (3ft) |
| *I. p.* 'Flore Pleno' | 20–0cm (8–0in), yellow (d), June, 1m (3ft) |
| *I. p.* 'Variegata' | 20–0cm (8–0in), yellow, leaves variegated, June, 80cm (32in) |
| *I. versicolor* | 0–+20cm (0–+8in), blueish mauve, May–June, 70cm (28in) |

## Juncus

**RUSH, CORKSCREW RUSH**
Rushes are suitable for ponds and also for botanical gardens simulating nature. They should be planted in the margins or in marshland.
**Hardiness: US Zone 5-3, Canadian Zone 4-3.**

| | |
|---|---|
| *J. effusus* | 10–0cm, (4–0in), brown, July–Aug, 60cm (24in) |
| *J. e.* 'Spiralis' | 10–0cm (4–0in), d.gr., 30cm (12in) |
| *J. ensifolius*** | 5–0cm (2–0in), dark brown, July–Aug, 20cm (8in) |

*Juncus effusus* 'Spiralis'

## Jussiaea

Jussiaeas have yellow flowers with a diameter of 5cm (2in) between dark green leaves. The plants float

*Iris versicolor*

from the margins to the center of the pond. They can be propagated by cuttings. It comes from S.E.Asia.
**Hardiness: US Zone 8, Canadian Zone 7.**

| | |
|---|---|
| *J. grandiflora*** | 50–30cm (20–12in), yellow, June, 30cm (12in) |

*Jussiaea grandiflora*

# Lemna

**IVY DUCKWEEK**
*Lemna gibba* is best kept out of a pond. Duckweed is often attached to plants introduced from elsewhere; even if you rinse it off thoroughly, there is always a chance of a few plants being left.
**Hardiness: US Zone 5, Canadian Zone 4.**

| | |
|---|---|
| *L. trisulca* | floating plant, green |

# Lobelia

**PERENNIAL LOBELIA, CARDINAL FLOWER**
Lobelias are suitable for positions similar to those of primroses, and the two plants form an attractive combination. *L. fulgens* has dark red leaves but is not entirely hardy; let the plant overwinter indoors in a frost-free place. In my opinion, the other species are therefore preferable.
**Hardiness: US Zone 9-3, Canadian Zone 8-2.**

| | |
|---|---|
| *L. cardinalis*! | 10–0cm (4–0in), red, July–Nov, 70cm (28in) |
| *L. fulgens* 'Queen Victoria' | 10–0cm (4–0in), red, July–Nov, 70cm (28in) |
| *L. sessifolia* | 10–0cm (4–0in), mauve, July–Nov, 70cm (28in) |
| *L. siphilitica*! | 10–+20cm (4–+8in), blue, Aug–Nov, 80cm (32in) |

# Lotus

Don't let the name of this plant make you think of a water lily. The sacred Lotus plant is

*Nelumbo nucifera* (see: Container plants and some cool-greenhouse plants). This is a rare native European plant which grows naturally in wet grasslands and sand-dune valleys. The plant has underground runners and requires full sun.
**Hardiness: US Zone 7, Canadian Zone 6.**

| | |
|---|---|
| *L. uliginosus*** | 0–+20cm (0–+8in), yellow, June–Aug, 20cm (8in) |

# Ludwigia

See: *Jussiaea*.

# Luronium

**FLOATING WATER PLANTAIN**
See: *Alisma natans*.

# Lysichiton

**SKUNK CABBAGE**
The photograph is misleading: the leaves are more interesting than the flowers! This somewhat expensive plant is rather frost-tender, but worth cultivating.
**Hardiness: US Zone 6-4, Canadian Zone 5-3.**

| | |
|---|---|
| *L. americanus* | 10–+10cm (4–+4in), yellow, Apr–May, 1m (3ft) |
| *L. camtschatcensis* | 10–+10cm (4–+4in), white, Apr–May, 1m (3ft) |

*Lobelia cardinalis*

*Lysichiton americanus*

## Lysimachia

**CREEPING JENNY, MONEYWORT**
Creeping Jenny makes good ground cover, and will also grow on dry land in moisture-retentive, humus-rich soil. It is an ideal marginal plant.
**Hardiness: US Zone 4, Canadian Zone 3.**

| | |
|---|---|
| *L. nummularia* | 5–+10cm (2–+4in), yellow, May–July, 5cm (2in) |
| *L. n.* 'Aurea' | 5–+10cm (2–+4in), yellow, May–July, 5cm (2in) |

*Lysimachia nummularia* 'Aurea'

## Lythrum

**PURPLE LOOSESTRIFE**
See: Perennials.

## Mentha

**WATER MINT**
The flowers are not impressive but the peppermint aroma released when the plant is touched makes up for this. The plant requires sun or semi-shade.
**Hardiness: US Zone 5, Canadian Zone 4.**

| | |
|---|---|
| *M. aquatica* | 10–0cm (4–0in), mauve, June Sept, 30cm (12in) |

*Mentha aquatica*

## Menyanthes

**BOG BEAN, BUCKBEAN**
The striking leaves resemble clover and are large, leathery, and blueish green. The waxy flowers look like chestnut blossom. The plant requires full sun.
**Hardiness: US Zone 4, Canadian Zone 3.**

| | |
|---|---|
| *M. trifoliata* | 30–0cm (12–0in), white, June–Sept, 20cm (8in) |

*Menyanthus trifoliata*

## Mimulus

**MONKEY MUSK**
Mimulus grows naturally in shallow running water, but may also have a slightly drier position. It requires full sun or semi-shade.

| M. guttatus | 5–+5cm (2–+2in), yellow, June–Nov, 20cm (8in) |
| M. luteus | 5–+5cm (2–+2in), orange yellow, June–Nov, 20cm (8in) |
| M. ringens | 5–+5cm (2–+2in), light mauve, June–Aug, 30cm (12in) |

*Mimulus guttatus*

## Molinia

For species related to this bog plant, see: Bamboos, grasses and ferns.
**Hardiness: US Zone 5, Canadian Zone 5.**

| M. altissima | +5–+10cm (+2–+4in), brown, July–Nov, 80cm (32in) |

## Myosotis

### WATER FORGET-ME-NOT
This undemanding water plant is suitable for the waterside amid other marginal plants. It flowers for a longer period than other forget-me-nots, if not as exuberantly.
**Hardiness: US Zone 5, Canadian Zone 4.**

| M. palustris | 5–+10cm (2–+4in), blue, May–July, 30cm (12in) |

## Myriophyllum

### PARROT'S FEATHER
The leaves of these submerged water plants resemble the underwater leaves of the water crowfoot *(Ranunculus aquatilis)*. These invasive plants overwinter on the bottom of the pond and begin to grow again as the light increases.
**Hardiness: US Zone 8-5, Canadian Zone 8-4.**

| M. aquaticum | 1m–30cm (3ft–12in), green, delicate foliage |
| M. spicatum** | 1m–30cm (3ft–12in), green, delicate foliage |

*Myriophyllum aquaticum*

| M. verticillatum** | 1m-30cm, green, fine foliage |

## Nasturtium

This plant provides luxuriant covering for a shallow pond or marsh.
**Hardiness: US Zone 5, Canadian Zone 4.**

| N. officinale! | 10–0cm (4–0in), white, May–Oct, 10cm (4in) |

*Nuphar pumila* 'Variegata'

# Nuphar

**BRANDY BOTTLE, YELLOW WATER LILY**

Nuphars look very much like large water lilies. The yellow flowers, however, appear to have remained in bud. This native plant is suitable for very large ponds, and can be invasive. *N. pumila* is more suitable for smaller ponds.
**Hardiness: US Zone 5, Canadian Zone 4.**

| | |
|---|---|
| *N. lutea* | 1m–50cm (3ft–20in), yellow, June–Sept, 20cm (8in) |
| *N. pumila* 'Variegata' | 80–40cm (32–16in), yellow, May–Aug, 10cm (4in) |

# Nymphaea

**WATER LILY**

Anyone intending to create a pond will think of water lilies. Which plants are suitable depends on the pond's dimensions: water lilies are available in all sizes as well as in every color. The

*Nymphaea* 'Attraction'

*Nymphaea* 'Laydekeri Purpurata'

depth of the water must be between 30cm (12in) and 1.5m (5ft). Only the common white water lily may be planted at a greater depth. Small water lilies are suitable for bowls and containers, provided they overwinter in a frost-free environment. The size of the plant may be deduced from the depths indicated below.
**Hardiness: US Zone 5, Canadian Zone 4.**

| | |
|---|---|
| *N. alba* | 2.5–1m (8–3ft), white |
| *N.* 'Atropurpurea' | 40cm (16in), dark carmine |
| *N.* 'Attraction' | 1.2m–60cm (4ft–24in), red/pink |
| *N.* 'Aurora' | 1.2m–60cm (4ft–24in), pink./or. |
| *N.* 'Cardinal' | 70cm (28in), red, lighter center |
| *N.* 'Charles de Meurville' | 80cm (32in), w. red, out.lighter |
| *N.* 'Chrysantha' | 30cm (12in), apricot |
| *N.* 'Colonel A.J. Welch' | 1.2m–60cm (4ft–24in), yellow |
| *N.* 'Colossea' | 70cm (28in), flesh–col./white |
| *N.* 'Comanche' | 50cm (20in), yel., darker later |
| *N.* 'Conqueror' | 60cm (24in), dark red |
| *N.* 'Ellisiana' | 60cm (24in), peach pink |
| *N.* 'Escarboucle' | 1.2m–60cm (4ft–24in), dark red |
| *N.* 'Gladstoniana' | 1m–50cm (3ft–20in), white |
| *N.* 'Gloriosa' | 60–40cm (24–16in), red center |
| *N.* 'Helvola' | 20cm (8in), sulfur yellow |
| *N.* 'Hermine' | 80–50cm (32–20in), w., tulip-sh. |
| *N.* 'James Bridon' | 1.2m–60cm (4ft–24in), red |
| *N.* 'King of the Blues' | 50–20cm (20–8in), lilac |
| *N.* 'Laydekeri Lilacea' | 60–30cm (24–12in), pink, red dots |
| *N.* 'Laydekeri Purpurata' | 60–30cm (24–12in), lilac pink |
| *N.* 'Mme Wilfron Gonnère' | 80–50cm (32–20in), pink (d) |
| *N.* 'Marliacea Albida' | 1m–60cm (3ft–24in), white. |
| *N.* 'Marleacea Carnea' | 1.2m–60cm (4ft–24in), pink |
| *N.* 'Marliacea Chromatella' | 1.2m–60cm (4ft–24in), yellow |
| *N.* 'Marleacea Rosea' | 1.2m–60cm (4ft–24in), br.pink |
| *N.* 'Maurice Laydeker' | 60–30cm (24–12in), or. to red |
| *N.* 'Moorei' | 1.2m–60cm (4ft–24in), y. leaves |
| *N.* 'Newton' | 60cm (24in), pink |
| *N.* 'Odorata Alba' | 50–30cm (20–12in), white |

| | |
|---|---|
| *N.* 'Paul Hariot' | 50–30cm (20–12in), flesh-col. |
| *N.* 'Pink Sensation' | 60cm (24in), pink |
| *N.* 'Princess Elizabeth' | 40–30cm (16–12in) |
| *N.* 'Pygmaea Alba' | 60–30cm (24–12in), white |
| *N.* 'Pygmaea Helvola' | 60–30cm (24–12in), light yellow |
| *N.* 'Pygmaea Rubra' | 60–30cm (24–12in), red |
| *N.* 'René Gérard' | 60–30cm (24–12in), soft pink with salmon pink |
| *N.* 'Richardsonii' | 1m–50cm (3ft–20in), white, |
| *N.* 'Rose Arey' | 60–30cm (24–12in), pink |
| *N.* 'Sioux' | 60–50cm (24–20in), flesh-colored |
| *N.* 'Sulfurea' | 1.2m–60cm (4ft–24in), light yellow |
| *N. tetragona* | 30–10cm (12–4in), white |

*Nymphaea tetragona*

## Nymphoides

**FRINGED WATER LILY, WATER FRINGE**
The yellow flowers resemble those of cucumbers, while the leaves are like those of a small water lily. The fact is, however, that this plant belongs to the gentian family. It grows rapidly and roots at the bottom of the pond, though it often floats.
**Hardiness: US Zone 5, Canadian Zone 4.**

| | |
|---|---|
| *N. peltata* | 80–20cm (32–8in), yellow, June–Aug, 10cm (4in) |

## Oenanthe

**FINE-LEAFED WATER DROPWART**
*O. aquatica* is a chervil-like plant which grows naturally in European drainage ditches and marshes. *O. f.* 'Flamingo' is the finest garden plant for an artificial pond.

**Hardiness: US Zone 7, Canadian Zone 6.**

| | |
|---|---|
| *O. fistulosa* | 10–0cm (4–0in), cream, June–Aug, 40cm (16in) |
| *O. f.* 'Flamingo' | 10–0cm (4–0in), pale pink, June–Aug, 40cm (16in) |

## Orontium

**GOLDEN CLUB**
This submerged water plant roots at the bottom; its bright yellow flower spikes emerge from the water. It tolerates some shade.
**Hardiness: US Zone 6, Canadian Zone 5.**

| | |
|---|---|
| *O. aquaticum*! | 20–0cm (8–0in), yel., May–Aug |

*Orontium aquaticum*

*Nymphoides peltata*

## Persicaria

See: *Polygonum*.

## Petasites

**BUTTERBUR**
See: Perennials.

## Phragmites

**REED**
The common reed is a very invasive plant in shallow water or moist soils due to its spreading rhizomes. Because of their aggressive nature, they are difficult to control in a garden setting, where they must be grown in a large container to control growth in shallow, natural ponds.
**Hardiness: US Zone 5, Canadian Zone 4.**

| | |
|---|---|
| *P. australis (communis)* | 30–+10cm (12–+4in), brown, Aug–Sept, 1.5m (5ft) |
| *P. a.* 'Variegatus'* | 20–+10cm (8–+4in), variegated leaves 1m (3ft) |

## Pistia

**WATER LETTUCE**
Take some of these small floating plants indoors in fall and return them to the outdoor pond from mid-May; they are frost-tender and require full sun.

| | |
|---|---|
| *P. stratiotes* | floating plant, light green |

*Pistia stratiotes*

## Polygonum

**KNOTWEED**
Like most polygonums, these marsh plants spread considerably. They have distinctive spikes of pink

flowers and require full sun or half-shade. The name *amphibium* refers to their appearance: the plant's leaves in the water differ from those grown on land.
**Hardiness: US Zone 5-4, Canadian Zone 4-3.**

| | |
|---|---|
| *P. amphibium* | 30–0cm (12–0in), pink, June–July, 5cm (2in) |
| *P. bistorta* | 0–+10cm (0–+4in), pink, May–July, 30cm (12in) |

*Polygonum amphibium*

## Pontederia!

**PICKEREL WEED**
No pond should be without the native pontederia's hyacinth-like flowers! It has the

*Pontederia lanceolata*

267

longest flowering season of all water plants but, as it is frost-tender, you should not grow it too high up on a bank. The leaves are attractive, and anyone familiar with the blue shade of the flowers should feel angry with the grower who first cultivated the white variant!
**Hardiness: US Zone 4, Canadian Zone 3.**

| | |
|---|---|
| P. cordata | 40–10cm (16–4in), gentian blue, June–Sept, 70cm (28in) |
| P. c. 'Alba' | 40–10cm (16–4in), white, June–Sept, 70cm (28in) |

## Potamogeton

**PONDWEED**
These submerged water plants are grown for their foliage. They root in the bottom of the pond and need clear water. *P. crispus* and *P. pectinatus* can grow in smaller ponds and tolerate shade. *P. natans* has brownish green flower spikes (the most common type) and leaves which float on the water.
**Hardiness: US Zone 6-4, Canadian Zone 5-3.**

*Potamogeton natans*

| | |
|---|---|
| P. crispus | 60cm (24in) |
| P. lucens | 2m (6ft) |
| P. natans | up to 1m (3ft) |
| P. pectinatus | up to 1.5m (5ft) |

## Potentilla

**MARSH CINQUEFOIL**
This is not a spectacular plant, although it is vigorous and suitable for shallow water.
**Hardiness: US Zone 4, Canadian Zone 3.**

| | |
|---|---|
| P. palustris | 5–+5cm (2–+2in), brown, June–Aug, 20cm (8in) |

## Ranunculus

**WATER CROWFOOT**
*R. aquaticus*, the water crowfoot, has two kinds of leaves: the submerged leaves are much divided, while those on the surface, or if the pond dries up, look like "ordinary" leaves. The leaves appear to float on the water. The other species are marginal plants and closely resemble buttercups.
**Hardiness: US Zone 5-4, Canadian Zone 4-3.**

| | |
|---|---|
| R. aquaticus | 1m–30cm (3ft–12in), white, June–July, 10cm (4in) |

*Ranunculus aquaticus*

| | |
|---|---|
| R. lingua | 20–0cm (8–0in), yellow, June–Aug, 50cm (20in) |
| R. l. 'Grandiflorus' | 20–0cm (8–0in), yellow |

## Rumex

**WATER SORREL**
The changing color of the leaves rather than the flowers is the main attraction of this species of sorrel. It requires sun or semi-shade.
**Hardiness: US Zone 6, Canadian Zone 5.**

| | |
|---|---|
| R. hydrolapathum | 40–10cm (16–4in), green, June–Aug, 1m (3ft) |

*Rumex hydrolapathum*

## Sagittaria

**ARROWHEAD**
*S. sagittifolia* is the common arrowhead. The arrow-shaped leaves emerge magnificently from the water. The indicated water depth need not be taken too literally.

*Sagittaria sagittifolia* 'Flore Pleno'

**Hardiness: US Zone 5-4, Canadian Zone 4-3.**

| | |
|---|---|
| S. latifolia | 50–10cm (20–4in), white, June–Aug, 70cm (28in) |
| S. sagittifolia | 60–10cm (24–4in), white, June–Aug, 50cm (20in) |
| S. s. 'Flore Pleno'! | 50–10cm (20–4in), white (d), June–Aug, 50cm (20in) |

## Salvinia

**WATER FERN**
Salvinias are rather like duckweed, but require

*Salvinia natans*

warmth. Winter frosts will kill the fern: let it overwinter indoors.

| | |
|---|---|
| S. natans | floating plant, green |

## Saururus

**LIZARD'S TAIL, SWAMP LILY, WATER DRAGON**
This plant has heart-shaped leaves and flowers in arching racemes. It spreads by rhizomes. The Chinese species requires winter protection.

*Saururus cernuus*

**Hardiness: US Zone 6-5, Canadian Zone 5.**

| | |
|---|---|
| S. cernuus* | 20–10cm (8–4in), white, July–Aug, 1.2m (4ft) |
| S. chinensis** | 10cm (4in), yellowish white, June–July, 40cm (16in) |

269

## Scirpus

### CLUB-RUSH

*S. lacustris* is the common rush for making chair seats. The other marginal plants are more interesting, particularly the striped and spotted rushes, which present a cheerful appearance on the bank.

*Scirpus tabernaemontani* 'Zebrinus'

**Hardiness: US Zone 5-4, Canadian Zone 4-3.**

| | |
|---|---|
| *S. lacustris* | 50–0cm (20–0in), brown, July–Aug, 1.2m (4ft) |
| *S. l.* 'Albescens' | 50–0cm (20–0in), striped leaves, 1m (3ft) |
| *S. maritimus* | 40–20cm (16–8in), brown, July–Aug, 80cm (32in) |
| *S. tabernaemontani* 'Zebrinus' | 40–0cm (16–0in), white spots, June–Aug, 1m (3ft) |

## Scutellaria

### SKULLCAP

This plant grows naturally on the banks of drainage ditches and in reedy marshland.
**Hardiness: US Zone 6, Canadian Zone 5.**

| | |
|---|---|
| *S. galericulata* | 10–0cm (4–0in), blueish mauve, June–Oct, 40cm (16in) |

## Solanum

### BITTERSWEET, WOODY NIGHTSHADE

Whereas the variegated variant thrives on dry land, the following species does quite well in a little water!
**Hardiness: US Zone 5, Canadian Zone 4.**

| | |
|---|---|
| *S. dulcamara* | 10–+10cm (4–+4in), mauve, June–Nov, up to 70cm (28in) |

*Solanum dulcamara*

## Sparganium

### BUR REED

This plant's burs are its main attraction. It is highly invasive and therefore only suitable for large ponds. Sparganium has a reed-like appearance and is unsuitable for lined ponds.
**Hardiness: US Zone 5, Canadian Zone 5.**

| | |
|---|---|
| *S. erectum* | 50–20cm (20–8in), white, June–Aug, 90cm (36in) |

*Scutellaria galericulata*

*Sparganium erectum*

## Stachys

This native plant attracts bees, and every nature garden should have one. It requires sun or half-shade.
**Hardiness: US Zone 5, Canadian Zone 4.**

| | |
|---|---|
| *S. palustris* | 20–0cm (8–0in), pink, June–Nov, 80cm (32in) |

*Stachys palustris*

## Stratiotes

**WATER SOLDIER**
These plants, which resemble bromelias, sink to the bottom in fall and drift to the surface again in spring. They require clear still water. Although they float, the pond must be deep enough. The white flowers project above the surface of the water.
**Hardiness: US Zone 5, Canadian Zone 5.**

| | |
|---|---|
| *S. aloifolia* | 1.5m–60cm (5ft–24in), white, May–July, 5cm (2in) |

## Symphytum

**COMMON COMFREY**
This vigorous species can also grow in drier conditions. It is an invasive plant for the margins of large ponds.
**Hardiness: US Zone 5, Canadian Zone 4.**

| | |
|---|---|
| *S. officinale* | 0–+20cm (0–+8in), w. red., or mauve, June–Aug, 80cm (32in) |

## Thelypteris

**MARSH BUCKLER FERN**
This is a fern for wet pond margins. It tolerates sun or shade, needing an acid soil.
**Hardiness: US Zone 4, Canadian Zone 3.**

| | |
|---|---|
| *T. palustris* | 0–+10cm (0–+4in), green, 20–30cm (8–12in) |

*Thelypteris palustris*

*Stratiotes aloifolia*

## Trapa

**JESUIT'S NUT, WATER CHESTNUT**
This fragile floating plant roots in the bottom of the pond. It has a fine fall color, requires a sunny pond, and needs protection against ducks and other water birds.
**Hardiness: US Zone 6, Canadian Zone 5.**

| | |
|---|---|
| *T. natans*\*\* | fl. plant, w. July–Sept, 5cm (2in) |

*Trapa natans*

## Typha

**CATTAIL**
These are the familiar reed-like plants with broad leaves and brown seed heads instead of plumes. Always plant the lesser reedmace (*T. angustifolia*) in ponds, as it is less rampant and therefore requires less maintenance.
**Hardiness: US Zone 6-3, Canadian Zone 5-2.**

*Typha minima*

| | |
|---|---|
| *T. angustifolia* | 50–20cm (20–8in), brown, July–Nov, 1.5m (5ft) |
| *T. latifolia* | 50–20cm (20–8in), brown, July–Nov, 2m (6ft) |
| *T. l.* 'Variegata' | 50–20cm (20–8in), striped leaves, 1.8m (5ft 8in) |
| *T. minima* | 30–10cm (12–4in), brown, May–Nov, 70cm (28in) |

## Valeriana

**VALERIAN**
The roots of this valerian are used to produce tranquilizers. The plant is suitable for the sides of a large pond or for damp areas.
**Hardiness: US Zone 4, Canadian Zone 3.**

| | |
|---|---|
| *V. officinalis* | 0–+20cm (0–+8in), pale pink, May–July, 1m (3ft) |

*Valeriana officinalis*

## Veronica

This plant has fleshy leaves and blue flowers resembling forget-me-nots. It is suitable for moist and shady positions, but can also grow in water.
**Hardiness: US Zone 5, Canadian Zone 5.**

| | |
|---|---|
| *V. beccabunga* | 10–+10cm (4–+4in), blue, May–Nov, 20cm (8in) |

# 11. Annuals and biennials

Annuals, also referred to as bedding plants, can be planted in perennial borders or individual flower beds during intervals in flowering seasons, and can provide cut flowers and dried flowers. Growers often fail to adhere to the correct nomenclature when referring to annuals and biennials: the official name for Alyssum, for instance, has been Lobularia for the past twenty-five years at least, but the old name is still found in seed catalogs. This causes confusion with perennial Alyssum. Growers of trees and perennials use uniform names for cultivars; seed firms often make a hash of things. Annuals have been attracting a lot of interest in recent years, and the assortment is consequently subject to change. Even so, the traditional "bedding plants" are unlikely to be abandoned, since they are already in flower when they appear on the market in mid-May. Most special annuals begin to flower a month later. Many visitors to garden centers consequently fail to realize what they are missing!

Seed catalogs often refer to **F1 Hybrids**, hybrids which have been created by cross-fertilization with inbred plants. Seed from these plants must always be newly obtained by cross-fertilization, and is therefore more expensive than that of "ordinary" cultivars, as the latter produce seed which can be sown without the plant's characteristics changing to any marked degree. You can collect the seeds of many plants yourself; store them in a cool, dark and dry place and sow them the following spring. Seeds are often supplied in "seed protective packaging," which for most plants means that it will be possible to sow them during a second spring, provided they have been stored properly. Most seeds germinate in the dark; place a newspaper on top of a sheet of glass above the planted seeds and remove it when they have germinated. Plant seed mixtures, sometimes selected by color, are marketed in packets with names such as "Field Mixture", "Garden Bouquet", "Japanese Flowering Carpet" and so on.

If there is no mention of a flowering season in the lists, this means that the plants will flower all summer, that is from mid-May until the end of October. They all require full sun, unless there is a note to the contrary. Their height is given in centimeters, followed, in brackets, by the approximate equivalent in feet or inches.

## Adonis

This plant produces small red flowers between delicate foliage, and looks well mixed with perennials in a border. It is a classic annual and may be sown directly where it is to flower.

| | |
|---|---|
| A. aestivalis | blood red, July–Sept, 1m (3ft) |

## Ageratum

**FLOSS FLOWER**
The genus *Ageratum* includes low-growing bedding plants and tall ones for cut flowers. Its former name *A. mexicanum* is indicative of its origin. The shorter cultivars are suitable for edging purposes, the tall ones for borders.

| | |
|---|---|
| A. houstonianum | |
| A.h. 'Blue Horizon' | blue, 45cm (18in) |
| A. h. 'Blue Mink' | light blue, 20cm (8in) |

| A.h. 'Pink Powder Puff' | bright pink, 15cm (6in) |
| A.h. 'Hawaii Hybrids' | mix blue, white, 20cm (8in) |

| A. r. 'Pleniflora' | mixed (d), July–Sept, 1.75m (5ft) |

*Ageratum houstoniatum* 'Pink Powder Puff'

*Alcea rosea* 'Nigra'

# Agrostemma

## CORN COCKLE

Like poppies, cornflowers and cinquefoils, this plant grows wild in European cornfields. It is highly suitable for an annual "flowering meadow" and will naturalize. Sow directly in fairly dry soil where it is to flower. The seeds are toxic.

| A. gracilis | mauvish pink, June–July, 80cm (32in) |

*Agrostemma gracilis*

# Alcea

## HOLLYHOCK

Always use canes to support these old-fashioned biennials, or else plant them against a wall, protected from the wind. Although they are biennials, they often behave like perennials in well-drained soil with some protection against frost. Sow in July; plant out in late summer.

| A. rosea 'Nigra' | d. red (s), July–Sept, 1.75m (5ft) |

# Alonsoa

These stiff, medium-sized, bushy plants may be kept through the winter in a frost-free position. Alonsoas are old-fashioned plants, with a long flowering season starting in June, and should be grown more often. Plant in a warm and sunny spot.

| A. linearis | tomato red, 40cm (16in) |

*Alonsoa meridionalis*

| | |
|---|---|
| A. meridionalis* | apricot, 70cm (28in) |
| A. scutifolia | bright red, 70cm (28in) |
| A. warscewicsii | scarlet, 70cm (28in) |

## Althaea

**HOLLYHOCK**

See: *Alcea* and Perennials.

## Alyssum

See: *Lobularia*.

## Amaranthus

**LOVE–LIES–BLEEDING, PRINCE'S FEATHER**

Sow these plants *in situ* and don't let them dry out; they are particularly suitable for sandy soil. Not only the panicles of flowers, but also the leaf colors are interesting. They are good flowers for cutting and for drying.

| | |
|---|---|
| A. caudatus | green, pendulous, July–Sept, 1m (3ft) |
| A. paniculatus | erect, July–Sept |
| A. p. 'Monarch' | bronzy brown, 1m (3ft) |
| A. p. 'Pigmy Torch' | blood red, 40cm (16in) |
| A. p. 'Pigmy Green' | green, 40cm (16in) |
| A. p. 'Ticolor' | crimson, gold leaves, 1m (3ft) |

*Amaranthus caudatus*

## Ammobium

Sow *in situ* in full sun in the cut-flower section of your garden; the plant is less suitable for a border. The flowers are also good for dried flower arrangements.

| | |
|---|---|
| A. alatum | white, July–Aug, 80cm (32in) |

*Ammobium alatum*

## Antirrhinum

**SNAPDRAGON**

Choose the taller cultivars for cutting, and the shorter ones for bedding purposes. Seeds are usually supplied mixed: it is preferable to buy single colors and blend toning shades if you

*Antirrhinum majus* 'Black Prince'

wish. The plant can be forced, but sowing *in situ* is also possible. The flowering season is from July to August.

| A. *majus* 'Black Prince' | deep wine red, 50cm (20in) |
| A.*m.* 'Butterfly Hybrids' | mix double, 80cm (32in) |
| A. *m.* 'Orchid Monarch' | lilac pink, 50cm (20in) |
| A. *m.* 'The Rose' | soft pink, 80cm (32in) |

## *Arctotis*

You can tell by its grayish-green leaves that the plant needs full sun. The large flowers only open in a sunny and fairly dry position.

| A. *grandis* | pinkish blue, May–Oct, 60cm (24in) |

*Arctotis grandis*

## *Argyranthemum*

**MARGUERITE**

See: Container plants and some cool-greenhouse plants.

## *Balsamina*

**BALSAM**

See: *Impatiens balsamina*.

## *Begonia*

It is preferable to buy young plants, as sowing is only successful at a high temperature (over 20°C/68°F). The plants are in full bloom as early as May. Begonias are suitable for edging purposes, for flower beds, and for hanging baskets. It is also possible to choose between green and brown foliage for flowers in every shade.

| B. *semperflorens* | red, pink or white, 20cm (8in) |

*Begonia semperflorens*

## *Bellis*

**DAISY**

These biennial daisies are on sale as young plants in early spring. Usually they are the large-flowered double variant; the small-flowered 'Pomponettes' look rather more natural. Remove them from the garden in good time to prevent seeding: the double daisies will degenerate and come up again as ordinary ones all over the lawn. *B. rotundifolia* can be grown as an annual, but will survive a mild winter.

*Bellis perennis*

| B. perennis | red, white or pink, 15cm (6in) |
| B. rotundifolia | soft lilac, 10cm (4in) |

## *Borago*

**BORAGE**

This culinary herb looks attractive in among flowers in a border. It self-seeds spontaneously every year; simply remove surplus plants. You can also sow borage directly *in situ* (see also: Perennials).

| B. officinalis | blue, May–Sept, 80cm (32in) |

## *Brassica*

**ORNAMENTAL CABBAGE**

*Borago officinalis*

Most florists sell brassicas in fall; they are convenient for filling empty flower beds or containers. They can also be used to "dress" a bare kitchen garden. Brassicas are generally frost-hardy.

| B. oleracea 'King' | crinkled leaves, mixed, 30cm (12in) |
| B.o. 'Nagoya Hybrids' | lacy leaves, red, white, 20cm (8in) |
| B.o. 'Tokyo Hybrids' | crinkled leaves, mixed, 30cm (12in) |

## *Browallia*

**BUSH VIOLET**

This is a compact plant with campanula-like flowers. Until recently, it was cultivated only as an indoor plant; now it is also grown for bedding purposes. It is suitable for edging, containers, and hanging baskets. Sow in a heated greenhouse.

| B. speciosa | blueish lilac, 50 cm (20in) |
| B. viscosa | violet/white, 40cm (16in) |

*Brassica oleracea* 'King'

## *Calceolaria*

The golden yellow flowers are smaller than those of the indoor plant. Calceolarias should be sown in fall; in spring, it is more convenient to buy young plants.

| C. biflora | |
| 'Goldcrest' | yellow, 20cm (8in) |

*Browallia speciosa*

*Calceolaria integrifolia* 'Goldwinner'

## Calendula

**POT MARIGOLD**

It is said of these plants that they dispel ants. Marigolds are old-fashioned plants grown for edging purposes or for flower arrangements. The flowers are usually single or double in shades of orange or yellow. Cultivars with more delicate colors are listed below. Sow marigolds *in situ*.

*C. officinalis*
| | |
|---|---|
| 'Apricot Bon Bon' | apricot |
| *C. o.* 'Lemon Beauty' | lemon yellow |
| *C.o* 'Radio' | orange |

*Calendula officinalis*

## Callistephus

**CHINA ASTER**

China asters require well-drained rich soil and full sun. Grow the shorter plants in flower beds and the taller ones for cutting, the single cultivars being most suitable for that purpose. They are cultivated in a rapidly changing range of colors. Don't grow them in the same place for too many years.

*C. chinensis*  all colors, Aug–Sept, 40–80cm
  (16–32in)

*Callistephus chinensis*

## Campanula

**CANTERBURY BELL**

Canterbury bells have amazingly large flowers on stems which sometimes grow up to 1m (3ft) tall. The flowers can be either pink, blue or white. Sow in June for flowering the following year. You

*Campanula medium*

should cover the plants lightly in winter.

| | |
|---|---|
| C. medium | lilac, 75cm (30in) |
| C. m. 'Alba' | white, June, 75cm (30in) |
| C. m. 'Plena' | double, June, 90cm (36in) |
| C.m. 'Russian Pink' | pink, June, 90cm (36in) |

## Celosia

Celosias add bright, reflecting color to unnatural-looking plants. Yet they are unpainted. The colors are difficult to combine with those of other plants: put them in a bed by themselves. There are two shapes: cockscombs and plumes. Keep them moist after planting; they should have less water later on.

| | |
|---|---|
| C. argentea 'Cristata' | cockscomb-shaped, 75cm (30in) |
| C. a. 'Globosa' | full plume, 75cm (30in) |
| C. a. 'Plumosa' | torch-shaped, 70cm (28in) |

Celosia argentea 'Cristata'

## Centaurea

### CORNFLOWER

Cornflowers are usually supplied in mixtures of single or double flowers. Try to buy individual colors: they are available in blue, pink, white, yellow, and mauve. The plant is suitable for the wild-flower meadow, but can also be used to fill gaps in borders.

| | |
|---|---|
| C. cyanus 'Black Ball' | blackish mauve, 60cm (24in) |
| C. c. 'Snowball' | white (d), 25cm (10in) |

## Cheiranthus

### WALLFLOWER

Wallflowers are biennials and are supplied in orange, red, purple, yellow, but usually brownish shades. Sow in June to herald spring with a blaze of color. They will sometimes live for a further year, but then become very woody.

| | |
|---|---|
| C. cheiri | mixed, Apr–May, 30–60cm (12–24in) |

Cheiranthus cheiri

## Chrysanthemum

### ANNUAL CHRYSANTHEMUM

*Chrysanthemum segetum* also grows wild in Europe. *C. frutescens* (syn. *Argyranthemum frutescens*) is sold as a plant in spring. The others are undemanding bedding plants; the taller ones are suitable for cutting. Give these rewarding summer-flowering plants full sun and soil that is not excessively moist.

| | |
|---|---|
| C. carinatum | yellow or white, dark center, 60cm (24in) |
| C. frutescens | white, yellow center, 40cm (16in) |

Centaurea cyanus

| *C. multicaule* | buttercup yellow, 20cm (8in) |
| *C. segetum* | yellow, 60cm (24in) |

*Chrysanthemum segetum*

## Cineraria

See: *Senecio*.

## Clarkia

Sow clarkias where they are to flower. The seed is nearly always supplied in mixtures, but the dark red, pink, violet, and white colors blend well together. This flower is good for cutting and suitable for growing in cultivated as well as wild gardens.

| *C. elegans* | mixed, July–Sept, 60cm (24in) |
| *C. e.* 'Apple Blossom' | soft pink, 60cm (24in) |

*Clarkia elegans*

## Cleome!

### SPIDER FLOWER

Scatter spider flowers throughout the border to blur less successful combinations. The plants are usually supplied in mixed colors or in pink, but there are other colors for more fastidious gardeners. The plant does best in warm summers, but try again if you are unsuccessful!

| *C. hasslerana* (syn. *C. spinosa*) | pink, 1.2m (4ft) |
| *C. h.* 'Cherry Queen' | carmine pink, 1.2m (4ft) |
| *C. h.* 'Pink Queen' | soft pink, 1.2m (4ft) |
| *C. h.* 'Purple Queen' | lilac mauve, 1.2m (4ft) |
| *C. h.* 'Violet Queen' | deep mauve, 1.2m (4ft) |
| *C. h.* 'White Queen' | white, 1.2m (4ft) |
| *C. serrulata* | pinkish lilac, 60cm–1.2m (24in–4ft) |

*Cleome hasslerana* 'Pink Queen'

## Cobaea

### CUP-AND-SAUCER VINE

This twining climber bears campanula-like, bell-shaped flowers. The seeds need to be sown early, and planted out after mid-May. Cobaeas need a warm spot; allow for the fact that the plants do not grow well in a cool summer. It is a wonderful plant to fill a small greenhouse with in summer.

| *C. scandens* | dark violet, July-Sept, 2m (6ft) |

## Coleus

This foliage plant can be sown or grown from cuttings indoors. The leaves rather than the flowers are the plant's main decorative feature. It looks well in between annuals, but also when grown as an indoor plant. Pinch out the top shoots in good time to achieve a bushy shape. Sow as early as February–March.

*Cobaea scandens*

*Convolvulus tricolor*

| C. blumei-hybrids | red, brown, and green leaves, 50cm (20in) |
|---|---|

*Coleus blumei*-hybrid

## Convolvulus

This climbing annual can also trail along the ground or be grown in hanging baskets. The flowers open during the day and close again in late afternoon.

| C. tricolor | blue, white, and yellow, July–Oct, 2m (6ft) |
|---|---|

## Cosmos!

### COSMEA

Cosmeas can be sown *in situ*, but it is advisable to sow them earlier under cover, so that they flower sooner. They are usually supplied in mixtures, but it is preferable to buy separate colors.

| C. bipinnatus 'Dazzler' | carmine red, 1m (3ft) |
|---|---|
| C. b. 'Gloria' | deep pink, red ring, 1m (3ft) |
| C. b. 'Purity' | white, 1.2m (4ft) |
| C. b. 'Radiance' | pale pink, 1m (3ft) |
| C. sulphureus 'Diablo' | bright red, 80cm (32in) |

*Cosmos bipinnatus*

## Cucurbita

### ORNAMENTAL GOURD

There are ornamental gourds in all kinds of shapes and colors: green, yellow, orange; speckled or striped; smooth or with warts or pimples; apple-, pear- or banana-shaped. In short, it is impossible to tell beforehand what the seeds will produce. Sow each seed separately in a pot indoors in April, and put them out of doors

281

in mid-May. Give them plenty of space: the plants trail across the ground and therefore need a large area. This plant can be grown by the compost heap. Look out for snails: check regularly. The flowers are edible.

| | |
|---|---|
| *C. pepo* | yellow flowers, trailing, 8m (26ft) |

*Cucurbita pepo*

*Cuphaea miniata* 'Purpurea'

## *Cuphaea*

It is best to sow cupheas in a warm greenhouse, but they are also available as young plants. They are low-growing and compact, and bear small red tubular flowers with yellow rims which make them look like matchsticks. The plants are suitable for flower beds or rock gardens, and continue flowering until the first frost.

| | |
|---|---|
| *C. miniata* 'Purpurea' | reddish white, 50m (20in) |

## *Cynoglossum*

### HOUND'S TONGUE

The seed can be sown directly in a warm place out of doors. Cut back in August as the flowers fade, and they will flower again later on. The plant is suitable for a limy border in full sun.

| | |
|---|---|
| *C. amabile* | blue, June–Sept, 50cm (20in) |
| *C. a.* 'Firmament' | blue, more compact |
| *C.a.* 'Mystery Rose' | pinkish white, 45cm (18in) |

*Cynoglossum amabile* 'Firmament'

## *Dahlia*

The low-growing species may be sown; this should be done as early as the month of February. The tubers developing in the summer should be lifted in the fall. See also: Bulbs and tuberous plants.

## Delphinium

### LARKSPUR

Larkspurs are good flowers for cutting and drying, and are also suitable for perennial borders to extend the flowering season. *D. consolida* in particular is often used for dried-flower arrangements. Seeds are also available by color and should be sown directly in the spot where they are to flower.

| | |
|---|---|
| *D. ajacis* | low-growing, mixed (d), 50cm (20in) |
| *D. ajacis* | tall, mixed (d), 1m (3ft) |
| *D. consolida* | various colors, 1m (3ft) |

*Delphinium ajacis*

## Dianthus

### SWEET WILLIAM, INDIAN PINK

Sow biennial sweet Williams in a seed bed in June, and plant them out where they are to flower in October. It is all right to buy mixed seed as the various colors blend well together. *D. chinensis* is an annual plant and should be sown under glass.

| | |
|---|---|
| *D. barbatus* | mixed, May–June, 30–50cm (12–20in) |
| *D. chinensis* | red, white or pink, May–June, 30cm (12in) |

## Digitalis

### FOXGLOVE

Foxglove is a biennial and should be sown in June. The seed will come up well in humus-rich soil, but not in heavy clay. The plant needs sun or shade and moisture-retentive soil, which helps the leaves to retain their beauty.

| | |
|---|---|
| *D. purpureus* 'Alba'! | white, 1.2m (4ft) |
| *D. p.* 'Gloxinaeflora' | distorted flower, 1.2m (4ft) |
| *D.p.* 'The Shirley' | pink shades, 150cm (5ft) |
| *D. p.* 'Sutton's Apricot' | apricot, 1.2m (4ft) |

*Digitalis purpureus*

## Dipsacus

### TEASEL

This biennial plant may be sown *in situ* in July–August; it will flower exactly a year later. Teasels are suitable for cutting and drying.

| | |
|---|---|
| *D. sativus* | lilac purple, July-Aug, 1.5m (5ft) |

*Dianthus chinensis*

*Dipsacus sativus*

## Dorotheanthus

These plants are usually still referred to as *Mesembryanthemum*, a generic name still used for other succulents. They require afternoon sun. The flowers do not open on a sunless day. Plant in a dry warm spot in sandy, well-drained soil. Remove dead heads regularly to extend their flowering period.

| | |
|---|---|
| *D. bellidiformis* | all colors, 10cm (4in) |
| *D. oculatus* | all colors, 10cm (4in) |

*Dorotheanthus bellidiformis*

## Eccremocarpus

**CHILEAN GLORY FLOWER**

There are not so many annual climbers and this warmth-loving plant is a welcome addition to the range. Early sowing in a greenhouse is to be recommended, though directly out of doors is also possible; in that case, the glory vine will flower later. Sow by a warm south-facing wall in well-fertilized, humus-rich soil.

| | |
|---|---|
| *E. scaber* | red, July–Sept, 3m (10ft) |

*Eccremocarpus scaber*

## Echium

Echium is particularly suitable for poor dry sandy soil, although it will also do well elsewhere. It is a good plant for attracting bees and may be planted directly where it is to flower.

| | |
|---|---|
| *E. plantagineum* | blue, June–Aug, 35cm (14in) |

## Eschscholzia

The botanical name is rarely spelt correctly. This small plant turns the deserts of California and Chile into flowering wildernesses. Let the children sow the seeds: it is virtually impossible for anything to go wrong. There are also yellow and double cultivars.

*Echium plantagineum*

| | |
|---|---|
| *E. caespitosa* 'Sundew' | lemon yellow, scented, 15cm (6in) |
| *E. californica* | orange, July–Sept, 30cm (12in) |
| *E. c.* 'Flore Plena' | (d), 30cm (12in) |

*Eschscholzia californica* 'Flore Plena'

## Felicia

**BLUE MARGUERITE**

This slender plant is suitable for edges, borders, and containers. You can sow it yourself, but it will not flower until late in the season. It is therefore preferable to buy young plants in May. Let them overwinter in a frost-free position, in a warm sunny spot in the garden.

| | |
|---|---|
| *F. amelloides* | blue, June–Oct, 40cm (16in) |

*Felicia amelloides*

## Gazania

These plants love sun and warmth. Mixed colors are not a drawback: the shade of bronze, orange, and yellow go very well together. Gazanias are suitable for rock gardens and require a warm spot with as much sun as possible.

| | |
|---|---|
| *G. rigens* | mixed, June–Sept, 20cm (8in) |

*Ganzania rigens*

## Godetia

This old-fashioned bushy plant produces flowers somewhat resembling azaleas. They are good for cutting and keep well. Sow under glass at 20°C (68°F). The temperature for growing them on may also be high: 15°C (59°F). Put them in a sunny spot in the garden. The following cultivars are low-growing and single-flowered.

| | |
|---|---|
| *G. bottae* 'Amethyst Glow' | pinkish white, 35cm (15in) |

*G. grandiflora*
| | |
|---|---|
| *G.g.* 'Catteya' | sal. pink, 35cm (14in) |
| *G. g.* 'Firelight' | red, 35cm (14in) |
| *G. g.* 'White Giant' | white, 35cm (14in) |

*Godetia grandiflora*

## Gypsophila

This annual has larger flowers than the perennial species. It is suitable for borders or a cut-flower corner of the garden. Sow *in situ* and thin if necessary. Try filling up all the empty spaces in a border with this plant. The effect is sensational.

| | |
|---|---|
| *G. elegans* | white and pale pink, July–Aug, 60cm (24in) |

*Gypsophila elegans*

## Helianthus

### SUNFLOWER

To grow the very tallest sunflowers, just remove a few seeds from a packet of bird's food as sold by pet shops. Sunflowers are ideal plants for children's competitions. The winner is the one who grows the tallest plant. If you want handsome cut flowers, choose one of the following cultivars:

| | |
|---|---|
| *H. annuus* | yellow, black center, 2.5m (8ft) |
| *H.a.* 'Chianti' | blood red, 1.5m (5ft) |
| *H. a.* 'Moonwalker' | soft yellow, 2m (6ft) |
| *H.a.* 'Pastiche' | yellow, red, buff, 2m (6ft) |
| *H. a.* 'Sunbeam' | gold., yellow center, 2m (6ft) |
| *H. a.* 'Sunbright' | yellow, black center, 2m (6ft) |
| *H. a.* 'Sungold' | yellow (d), 2m (6ft) |
| *H.a.* 'Sunset' | red and gold, 90cm (3ft) |

*Helianthus annuus*

## Helichrysum

### EVERLASTING FLOWER, STRAWFLOWER

Although strawflowers are perennials, they behave like annuals in some parts of Europe. The plant itself has little appeal, and is therefore only suitable for the dried-flower section of the garden. The stems often become weak after they have been dried, and the flowers may need to be wired.

| | |
|---|---|
| *H. bracteatum* | mixed, July–Aug, 80cm (32in) |
| *H. monstrosum* 'Nanum' | mixed, 30cm (12in) |

## Heliotropium

### HELIOTROPE

The plant is usually grown as an annual, but can survive the winter. Growing it like a fuchsia on a

*Helichrysum monstrosum* 'Nanum'

short stem is possible. Heliotropes may be planted in borders, in flower beds, or in a warm spot in a butterfly garden. Try again after a cold rainy summer!

H. arborescens          reflecting violet, 40cm (16in)

*Heliotropium peruvianum*

## Helipterum

This attractive flower for dried-flower arrangements looks quite well in a wild garden. It is still often referred to as *Rhodanthe* in the dried-flower trade. If you want to dry the flowers, cut them off before they have come out. Plant in a warm and sunny spot.

H. humboldtiana     yellow, July–Aug, 40cm (16in)
H. manglesii        pink/w., July–Aug, 30cm (12in)

*Helipterum manglesii*

## Heracleum

**COW PARSLEY**

Although this plant is regarded as a biennial, a non-flowering specimen will survive for many

*Heracleum mantegazzianum*

years. Keep it in check by not allowing the seeds to ripen. A single specimen in a garden looks magnificent, but a garden with rampant cow parsley is hideous. The leaves may cause an unpleasant inflammation; if you have touched one, you may still avoid burns by moving out of the sun immediately. The plant is unsuitable for gardens where children play in the summer and generally should not be grown!

| | |
|---|---|
| H. mantegazzianum | white, June–July, 4m (13ft) |

## *Hesperis*

### DAME'S VIOLET, SWEET ROCKET

This undemanding biennial "cottage-garden" plant is suitable for a shady position. It self-seeds or behaves like a perennial. Hesperis will flower twice if it is cut back after its first flowering. Sow *in situ* in June for flowering a year later.

| | |
|---|---|
| H. matronalis | white or pink, June, 1m (3ft) |

*Hesperis matronalis*

## *Humulus*

### HOP

This hop can be used to camouflage an unattractive area quickly. Contrary to the perennial plant, it does not produce "hops," but the leaves are more beautiful. A warm spot is to be recommended if you want the plant to grow really tall. If you sow under cover at an earlier date, the plants will grow taller than the heights given below.

| | |
|---|---|
| H. scandens | green, deeply lobed leaves, 4m (13ft) |
| H. s. 'Variegatus' | white-spotted leaves, 3m (10ft) |

## *Impatiens*

### BUSY LIZZIE, BALSAM

*I. wallerana*, Busy Lizzie, is, like fuchsias, among the few annuals to prefer a position in semi-shade when used for edging, as a container plant, and so on. The white or pale pink Busy Lizzies usually grow taller than those which produce red, deep pink, or mauve flowers, but dwarf strains can be obtained in all shades. The old-fashioned *I. balsamina*, balsam, is an attractive bushy plant for the border, with both single- and double-flowered cultivars. *I. glandulifera*, spring balsam, is usually appreciated only by people who admire cow parsley. Bear in mind that it self-seeds freely!

| | |
|---|---|
| I. balsamina | mixed Jun–Sep, 30–40cm (12–16in) |
| I. glandulifera | pink/red, June-Oct, 2.5m (8ft) |
| I. wallerana | mixed, May-Nov, 40cm (16in) |

*Impatiens wallerana*

*Humulus scandens*

## Ipomoea

### MORNING GLORY

This annual climber for a warm spot or greenhouse will twine itself round canes or wires fixed to (south-facing) walls. Seeds require pre-soaking. Germination is also encouraged by "chipping" the seeds with a file.

| | |
|---|---|
| *I. tricolor* 'Heavenly Blue' | sky blue, 2.5m (8ft) |
| *I.t.* 'Pearly Gates' | white, 2.5m (8ft) |

*Ipomoea tricolor* 'Wedding Bells'

| | |
|---|---|
| *I. t.* 'Wedding Bells' | lilac to pink, 2.5m (8ft) |

## Kochia

This plant is often for sale at florists in fall. It is a bad buy: the first night frost will kill it, and it is not suitable as an indoor plant either. Buy a small plant in spring, or sow it yourself under glass: the pale green "conifer" will grow and turn a beautiful shade of red toward fall.

*Kochia heterophylla* 'Trichophylla'

| | |
|---|---|
| *Kochia heterophylla* 'Acapulco Silver' | cream-colored young leaves, 90cm (36in) |
| *K. h.* 'Childsii' | lime green, 90cm (36in) |
| *K. h.* 'Trichophylla' | red, 90cm (36in) |

## Lagurus

### HARE'S-TAIL GRASS

This is the best-known grass for dried-flower arrangements and can be grown either in the garden section for cut flowers or in a border. Find a sunny spot with dry, well-drained soil.

| | |
|---|---|
| *L. ovatus* | light green-cream, 30cm (12in) |
| *L. o.* 'Nanus' | light green-cream, smaller |

*Lagurus ovatus*

## Lathyrus

### SWEET PEA

This climber has flowers suitable for cutting and can be sown where it is to flower. If you want a lot of flowers, sowing at a temperature over 15°C (59°F) is required, after which they can be grown on at a lower temperature. There are tall, short

*Lathyrus odoratus*

and long-stemmed cultivars. They are sold either mixed or by color.

| L. odoratus | all colors, 80cm–2m (32in–6ft) |

## Lavatera!

### TREE MALLOW

This plant is splendid for filling gaps in a border: it is strong, long-flowering, and also good for cutting. It thrives in fairly dry soil in full sun.

| L. trimestris | |
| 'Mont Blanc' | white, 50cm (20in) |
| L. t. 'Mont Rose' | bright pink, sturdy, 50cm (20in) |
| L. t. 'Pink Beauty' | soft pink, 70cm (28in) |
| L. t. 'Ruby Regis' | deep pink, 50cm (20in) |
| L. t. 'Silvercup' | salmon pink, large, 50cm (20in) |

*Lavatera trimestris* 'Silvercup'

## Limnanthes

### MEADOW FOAM, POACHED-EGG FLOWER

Meadow Foam has cheerful low-growing flowers and is suitable for edging, as a rockplant, or as underplanting. Sow directly *in situ*; the seed will often come up again the following year.

| L. douglasii | yellow and white, Aug–Oct, 20cm (8in) |

## Limonium

### SEA LAVENDER

Sea lavender is a good flower for cutting, and is usually grown in greenhouses for drying. Remember to hang the bunches of flowers upside down when drying them. In hot summers you will have a rich harvest.

| L. perezii! | d. blue, Sept–Nov, 75cm (30in) |
| L. sinuatum | var. col., June–Oct, 80cm (32in) |
| L. suworowii | pink, July–Aug, 60cm (24in) |

*Limonium sinuata*

## Lobelia

Trailing lobelias (*Pendula* hybrids) are usually distinguishable from the compact plants by their white eyes (with the exception of *L.* 'Rosamund'). Plant them close to the edges of containers. These easy-to-grow plants are also essential for hanging baskets and for adding interest to rock gardens.

**L. erinus – *Compacta* hybrids:**

| L. e. 'Cambridge Blue' | l. blue, green-leafed, 20cm (8in) |
| L. e. 'Emperor William' | gentian blue, 10cm (4in) |
| L. e. 'Marine' | medium blue, 10cm (4in) |
| L. e. 'Rosamund' | pink, white eyes, 10cm (4in) |
| L. e. 'White Lady' | green-leafed, 20cm (4in) |

*Limnanthes douglasii*

**L. erinus – Pendula** hybrids:

| | |
|---|---|
| L. p. 'Blue Cascade' | bright blue, 60cm (24in) long |
| L. p. 'Lilac Fountain' | soft lilac, 60cm (24in) long |
| L. speciosum | |
|   'Fan Cinnabar Rose' | salmon pink, 90cm (36in) |
| L. s. 'Fan Deep Red' | bright red, 90cm (36in) |

Lobelia erinus

# Lobularia

## SWEET ALYSSUM

Sow lobularias directly *in situ*, but not too densely. They are good edging plants which often come up again the following year; they are also suitable for hanging baskets. The plants thrive in any soil, even in dry positions.

| | |
|---|---|
| L. maritima 'Carpet of Snow' | white, Apr–Oct, 10cm (4in) |
| L. m. 'Oriental Nights' | violet purple, 5cm (2in) |
| L. m. 'Rosario' | bright pink, 10cm (4in) |
| L. m. 'Rosy O'Day' | deep pink, 10cm (4in) |
| L. m. 'Royal Carpet' | violet purple, 5cm (2in) |
| L. m. 'Wonderland' | pinkish red, 5cm (2in) |

Lobularia maritima 'Carpet of Snow'

# Lunaria

## HONESTY

You should sow this white or pinkish mauve biennial in June; it may be planted out even before the winter. The flowers are exuberant in May, but the flat round seed pods give the plant its greatest appeal. Honesty requires sun or half-shade.

| | |
|---|---|
| L. biennis 'Alba' | white, May–June, 1m (3ft) |
| L. b. 'Violet' | violet, May–June, 1m (3ft) |

Lunaria biennis 'Violet'

# Lupinus

## LUPIN

The yellow *L. luteus* is used as a green fertilizer in agriculture. The others are usually supplied in mixed colors. Lupin seeds can easily be sown directly where they are to flower.

| | |
|---|---|
| L. luteus | yellow, Aug–Sept, 60cm (24in) |
| L. 'Nanus' | |

Lupinus nanus

## *Lycopersicon*

**CHERRY TOMATO**

Unlike ordinary tomatoes, cherry tomatoes look very well either in a perennial border, or in pots or flower beds. The plants grow up to 2m (6ft) tall, need staking, and should be pinched out like ordinary tomatoes. Sowing is easy: under glass in April.

| *L. esculentum* | |
|---|---|
| 'Gardener's Delight' | red, 2m (6ft) |
| *L. e.* 'Husky Gold' | yellow, 1.2m (4ft) |

## *Matthiola*

**STOCK**

There are annual and biennial stocks. The annuals listed below are the most convenient species for filling bare spaces in a border. You should sow them in May. Stocks in every imaginable soft shade are available from specialists.

| *M. bicornis* | lilac and white, June–Sept, 40cm (16in) |
|---|---|
| *M. incana* | mixed, July–Sept, 70cm (28in) |

*Matthiola incana*

## *Mesembryanthemum*

**ICEPLANT, LIVINGSTONE DAISY**

See: *Dorotheanthus*.

## *Mirabilis*

**FOUR O'CLOCK FLOWER, MARVEL OF PERU**

Like the *Celosia*, this plant has alarmingly bright colors which are impossible to combine with any others. Perhaps they should be planted in a separate flower bed in a warm and sunny spot? The flowers do not open until afternoon and then give out a wonderful fragrance until evening, hence the name 'Tea Time' for a group of cultivars sold in individual colors. The other cultivars are only supplied mixed. You can, if you like, lift the rootstocks to let them overwinter.

| *M. jalapa* | mix., July–Sept, 90cm (36in) |
|---|---|

*Mirabilis jalapa*

## *Myosotis*

**FORGET-ME-NOT**

Forget-me-nots are available not only in shades of blue, but also in pink and white. They are biennials and should be sown in July in order to flower the following spring. Like pansies, they are suitable for planting in a bulb bed, as their flowering season coincides with that of late tulips.

| *M. alpestris* 'Blue Ball' | blue, Apr–June, 15cm (6in) |
|---|---|
| *M.a.* 'Victoria Alba' | white, 20cm (8in) |

*Myosotis alpestris* 'Blue Ball'

# Nemesia

Nemesias produce flowers in all kinds of bright colors. The plants can be sown where they are to flower. One disadvantage is that they finish flowering quite early in the summer, particularly if they are growing in too dry a position. They do, however, need full sun.

| | |
|---|---|
| N. strumonia | mixed, 20cm (8in) |
| N. s. 'Carnival Mix' | dark red and white, 20cm (8in) |

Nemesia strumonia

## Nicandra

**APPLE OF PERU, SHOOFLY**

This is not an attractive plant, but its remarkable fruits make it worth a try. The shoofly has an unpleasant odor – don't plant it close to a patio. It is suitable for dried-flower arrangements.

| | |
|---|---|
| N. physaloides | light mauve, July–Aug, 1m (3ft) |
| N. p. 'Black Pod' | deep violet, July–Aug, 1m (3ft) |

## Nicotiana

**TOBACCO FLOWER**

You can easily sow this annual yourself, but nowadays you can also buy plants, often still called *N. alata*. They look well in between perennials in a border, but also as solitary plants. Give them plenty of fertilizer. The cultivar 'Only the Lonely' has remarkable tubular flowers and may well be grown by itself.

| | |
|---|---|
| N. langsdorffii<br>  'Lime Green' | greenish yellow, July-Sept,<br>1.5m (5ft) |

| | |
|---|---|
| N. suaveolens | white, July–Oct,<br>60cm (24in) |
| N. sylvestris | white, July–Sept, 2m (6ft) |
| N. s. 'Only the Lonely' | white, July–Sept, 1.5m (5ft) |

Nicotiana sylvestris

## Nigella

**LOVE-IN-A-MIST**

This delicate-looking plant with its attractive flowers and graceful seed pods, is the easiest of all annuals to sow, and is useful in borders as well as for cutting and drying. *N. hispanica* and *N. orientalis* have remarkable seed pods. The plant is suitable for any kind of soil, preferably in a sunny position. It is an excellent plant for children as it is so easy to sow.

Nigella damascena

| | |
|---|---|
| N. *damascena* 'Albion' | white, 60cm (24in) |
| N. *d.* 'Miss Jekyll' | pink, d. seed pods, 40cm (16in) |
| N. *d.* 'Mulberry Rose' | pink, 60cm (24in) |
| N. *d.* 'Oxford Blue' | deep blue, 75cm (28in) |
| N. *hispanica* | deep mauvish blue, 45cm (18in) |
| N. *orientalis* 'Transformer' | yellow, 50cm (20in) |
| N. *sativa* | pale blue |

## Papaver

**POPPY**

The field poppy, *P. rhoeas*, is suitable for wild gardens, especially for flowering meadows. *P. nudicaule* (Iceland poppy) is a tidy plant for a cultivated garden. Allow for considerable self-seeding. *P. somniferum* (opium poppy) is a plant for the cut-flower section and brings additional color to a border. It can be used to create beautiful color combinations. All poppies prefer sun and rather dry soil. Even poor unfertilized soil is excellent.

| | |
|---|---|
| *P. nudicaule* | yellow or orange, June–Oct, 30cm (12in) |
| *P. rhoas* | red or orange, June–Aug, 40cm (16in) |
| *P. somniferum*! | many colors, July–Sept, 1m (3ft) |

*Papaver somniferum*

## Pelargonium

**GERANIUM**

The botanical name *Geranium* refers to perennials; the *Pelargonium* is a bedding or pot plant ' which is also suitable for tubs and containers. Propagation is by seed or cuttings: seedlings are less expensive to buy than cuttings, which often have larger flowers and whose bottom leaves do not turn yellow after they have been planted out. People with "green fingers" keep them through the winter in a light and dry position. If you buy new plants every year, you will have containers full of flowers at an earlier date. The various groups of pelargoniums are listed below.

| | |
|---|---|
| *P. grandiflorum* | regal geranium |
| *P. peltatum* | ivy-leafed trailing geranium |
| *P. zonale* | common geranium |

*Pelargonium grandiflorum*

## Perilla

Like the coleus, this plant is cultivated only for its remarkable brownish red leaves. It looks splendid in flower beds with brightly colored flowers. The following have very dark leaves.

| | |
|---|---|
| *P. frutescens* | |
|   'Atropurpurea' | dark leaves, 60cm (24in) |
| *P. nankinensis* | |
|   'Atropurpurea Laciniata' | lobed leaves, 60cm (24in) |

## Petunia

Petunias have been popular for years, which is why growers have long been engaged in improving them. Cultivars change every year, depending on fashion. One major breakthrough occurred when "self-cleansing" cultivars were introduced; the dead flowers, brown and conspicuous, were no longer left hanging on the plant but were overgrown by new flowers. Whether the two-color cultivars and double variants are an improvement is a moot point. There is little purpose in listing the cultivars: it is best to see what seeds or plants are on offer in any particular year.

*Perilla frutescens*

*Phacaelia tanacetifolia*

## Phacaelia

This plant is easy to sow and attracts bees. It is therefore best to sow at intervals up to June to prolong the flowering season. It is ideal for filling bare spaces in the garden.

| | |
|---|---|
| P. campanularia* | gentian blue, July–Aug, 25cm (10in) |
| P. congesta* | lavender blue, July–Sept, 30cm (12in) |
| P. tanacetifolia | blue, July–Oct, 1m (3ft) |
| P. viscida* | sky blue, July–Sept, 60cm (24in) |

## Phalaris

**CANARY GRASS**

Phalaris is grown as an agricultural crop, but also looks elegant in a cut-flower section of the garden. The name of the species mentioned below indicates that canaries like the seed. Sow this kind of grass in a sunny position in spring.

| | |
|---|---|
| P. canariensis | soft green, 70cm (28in) |

## Phlox

Low-growing phloxes are suitable for edging and flower beds; taller cultivars look better in borders or cut-flower corners of the garden. Sow phlox seed under glass. Phloxes are often for sale as small plants.

*Phlox drummondii*

*Petunia* hybrid 'Flore Plena'

| P. drummondii | all colors except yellow, JulySept |
| P. d. 'Blue Beauty'! | lavender blue, 20cm (8in) |
| P. d. 'Brilliant' | pink, 40cm (16in) |
| P. d. 'Promise Pink' | pink double, 40cm (16in) |

## Polygonum

### KNOTWEED

This genus includes climbers, perennials and weeds. Annual polygonums are ideal for edging or rock gardens, but also look well trailing over the sides of containers.

| P. capitatum | pink, May–Oct, 10cm (4in) |
| P. orientale! | carmine red, July–Oct, 1.5m (5ft) |

Polygonum orientale

## Portulaca

### SUN PLANT

The bright colors of these flowers remind one of iceplants, and, like them, they only open when it is sunny. They are suitable for rock gardens and edges. Plant in poor, sandy, well-drained soil in full sun.

| P. grandiflora | all colors, June–Oct, 10cm (4in) |

## Reseda

### MIGNONETTE

This plant attracts bees, and it is advisable to extend its flowering season by not sowing all the seeds at once. It needs nutritious limy soil. The flowers are not striking, but their scent fully compensates for that.

| R. odorata | white, all summer, 45cm (18in) |

Reseda odorata

Portulaca grandiflora

## Ricinus

### CASTOR-OIL PLANT

The castor-oil plant is suitable for a warm position. The large bean-like seeds are highly poisonous! It is a handsome plant for growing in the center of a flower bed, but it cannot tolerate drought. Water it daily if it is grown in a tub.

| | |
|---|---|
| *R. communis* | green leaves, 2m (6ft) |
| *R. c.* 'Impala' | bronze-colored leaves, 1.5m (5ft) |
| *R.c.* 'Sanguineus' | red color leaves, 1.5m (5ft) |

*Ricinus communis*

## Salpiglossis

This plant requires limy soil in full sun and produces excellent flowers for cutting. Who would have thought it: like the petunia, salpiglossis is related to the potato. The colors are not glaring and sowing a mixture will produce satisfactory results. Grow salpiglossis in a sunny spot and, in view of its height, out of the wind. The seeds can be sown *in situ*, but the seedlings will need thinning. There are tall and low-growing mixtures.

| | |
|---|---|
| *S. sinuata* | mixed, July–Sept, 80cm (32in) |

| | |
|---|---|
| *S. s.* 'Casino' | violet bl., July–Sept, 45cm (18in) |

## Salvia

### SAGE

*S. coccinea*, which resembles the common *S. splendens* but is more beautiful, has some new cultivars. They are available from many growers as annuals. *S. farinacea* has spikes of flowers in reflecting shades of blue. In the case of *S. viridis* (syn. *S. horminum*), the bracts are more decorative than the flowers, even up until late fall. This species can be grown as an annual or a biennial. *S. patens*, which has the finest blue flowers, can survive the winter. It is actually a perennial, though it is not suitable as such for all climates. *S. splendens* is the red salvia for Victorian flower beds. Unfortunately, the genuine shade of red is now rarely on offer, and has usually been replaced by orange red (see also: Container plants and some cool-greenhouse plants).

| | |
|---|---|
| *S. coccinea* 'Lady in Red' | scarlet, 25cm (10in) |
| *S. c.* 'Coral Nymph'! | soft pink, 30cm (12in) |
| *S. farinacea* | dark blue, June–Oct, 70cm (28in) |
| *S. f.* 'Blue Bedder'! | deep blue, 70cm (28in) |
| *S. f.* 'Victoria'! | deep blue, 40cm (16in) |

*Salpiglossis sinuata*

| *S. patens* | br. blue, June–Sept, 60cm (24in) |
| *S. sclarea* | light blue, July–Aug, 80cm (32in) |
| *S. splendens* | bright red, June–Oct, 25cm (10in) |
| *S. viridis* 'Oxford Blue' | dark blue, July–Oct, 60cm (24in) |
| *S. v.* 'Pink Gem' | bright pink, 50cm (20in) |
| *S. v.* 'White Swan' | white, 50cm (20in) |

## *Sanvitalia*

At one time, this compact plant was popular but, unfortunately, it has been relegated to the background. The small flowers have black centers. Plant in humus-rich soil; the leaves look dreary when splashed with loose earth.

| *S. procumbens* | yellow, June–Oct, 15cm (6in) |

*Sanvitalia procumbens*

## *Senecio*

Don't confuse this senecio with the indoor plant called cineraria. The species mentioned below refers to a small gray-leafed plant, commonly called Dusty Miller which is suitable for edging and filling bare spaces. It can be kept through a mild winter and will then produce small yellow flowers the following year. It requires full sun. The plant's previous names were *S. cineraria, S. maritima*, and *Cineraria maritima*.

| *S. bicolor* ssp. *cineraria* 'Silverdust' | gray leaves, 20cm (8in) |

## *Statice*

See: *Limonium*.

## *Tagetes*

### AFRICAN MARIGOLD

African marigolds have added value in that they combat disease. Poor growth among roses planted in the same area may be due to eelworms such as *Pratylenchus Vulnus*. You can prevent such deterioration by planting African marigolds between the rose bushes every few years. If the color combinations do not appeal to you, just remove the flowers from the marigolds (or the roses!). The small flowered marigold (*T. tenuifolia*) is most suitable for this purpose.

| *T. erecta* | tall or low-growing, large flowers |
| *T. patula* | low-growing |
| *T. tenuifolia* | low-growing, small flowers |

*Tagetes erecta*

*Senecio bicolor* ssp. *cineraria* 'Silverdust'

# Thunbergia

### BLACK-EYED SUSAN

Sow thunbergias in March at room temperature. They are suitable for growing in pots in a warm position. Let them twine around canes placed in the pot beforehand.

T. alata                 or. yellow, black eyes, 1m (3ft)

*Thunbergia alata*

# Tropaeolum

### NASTURTIUM

The flowers of *T. majus* and the tubers of *T. tuberosum*\*\* are edible. The largest nasturtium is *T. majus*, of which there are many hybrids: low-growing and non-twining, tall, single, and double – all in shades of red, yellow, and orange. Unfortunately the packets of seed often contain mixtures, and it is worthwhile trying to buy them in single colors. Nasturtiums often self-seed. Give tall cultivars an opportunity to climb up against something. This is essential for *T. peregrinum* (canary creeper), which needs a warm summer to look its best.

T. majus                 var. col, tall or low-growing
T. peregrinum            yellow, July–Sept, 2m (6ft)

# Verbascum

### MULLEIN

Verbascums are biennial, but several species behave like perennials. The slender spikes of flowers make them suitable for planting in solitary positions, especially in cobbled areas of the garden. Some self-seed extensively. They require limy, rather dry soil in full sun.

V. blattaria            yellow, June–July, 1m (3ft)
V. bombyciferum         yellow, June–Aug, 1.5m (5ft)
V. chaixii 'Album'      white, July–Aug, 1m (3ft)
V. densiflorum          yellow, July–Sept, 1m (3ft)
V. nigrum               yellow, July–Sept, 1.5m (5ft)
V. olympicum            yellow, July–Sept, 1.7m (5ft 4in)

*Verbascum chaixii* 'Album'

*Tropaeolum peregrinum*

## Verbena

The four popular species listed below are totally different in appearance. *V. aubletia* is excellent as an edging plant clambering over a low wall, and is also best for hanging baskets. *V. bonariensis* (formerly: *V. patagonica*) is a tall slender plant, excellent for adding to a perennial border. It is actually a perennial itself, but is usually grown as an annual in cool regions. *V. rigida* usually has soft colors which blend harmoniously, whereas those of *V. x hybrida*, a suitable plant for edges and flower beds, are rather hard. Buy them as young plants; they need to be sown under glass.

| | |
|---|---|
| *V. aubletia***! | lilac, pink or white, June–Nov, 40cm (16in) |
| *V. bonariensis* | mauve, July–Oct, 1.5m (5ft) |
| *V. x hybrida* | various colors, May–Oct, 30cm (12in) |
| *V. rigida* (*V. venosa*) | orange, various colors, June–Oct, 40cm (16in) |

*Verbena x hybrida*

## Viola

### VIOLET

Sow this biennial plant early in July to produce flowers from fall, and early in August for flowers in spring. At one time there were only cultivars in the 'Aalsmeer Giants' and 'Swiss Giants' series, but small-flowered cultivars in the most delicate shades are now in vogue. There are innumerable cultivars; growers have even been guilty of cultivating pink and bright red pansies!

*V. tricolor*

## Zea

### SWEET MAIZE, ORNAMENTAL MAIZE

Maize does not look very attractive in ornamental gardens, but shows up well in a section for cut flowers. It is also marvelous for children to sow a plant which is always successful. The male flowers are superior; the female ones develop into edible cobs.

| | |
|---|---|
| *Z. mays* | green, 1.5m (5ft) |
| *Z. m. 'Strawberry'*! | red strawberry-shaped cobs, 80cm (32in) |

*Zea mays 'Strawberry'*

## Zinnia

This annual produces flowers suitable for flower arrangements. The low-growing cultivars are suitable for flower gardens; the taller ones for cut-flower sections. There are single- and double-flowered, dahlia- and pompon-flowered cultivars. It is advisable to sow the seeds under glass: the best temperature for germination is 20°C (68°F).

| | |
|---|---|
| *Z. haageana* | often mixed colors |

*Zinnia haageana*

# 12. Container plants and some cool-greenhouse plants

The assortment of available container plants changes constantly, as so many plants are affected by fashion. There are also many new ways of keeping them through the winter. At one time, people took their container plants indoors; except for living-rooms, houses were unheated. Then, following the introduction of central heating, many plants, including those grown in containers, were forgotten as indoor temperatures rose and were no longer suitable for them. There were, however, many opportunities for houseplants. Now, with ever-increasing prosperity, and with cool- and hot-greenhouses as well as conservatories coming on to the market, there are new opportunities for container plants. The concept of container plant has become more flexible: at one time it merely included plants grown in an orangery, whereas it now means any plant that is frost-tender and can be grown in a container outside in summer but still requires bringing indoors in winter. The bulbs belonging to this category are easiest: most of them can be kept in a cool dark place. Remember that most container plants that withstand a few degrees of frost when planted in a cool- greenhouse, cannot do so if they remain in a pot! Having their roots frozen solid is often just too much for them.

In this chapter, the most important aspect of the plant is mentioned first. That is, in this case, the temperature at which they should be kept during the winter. This is followed by the month in which they flower and their height. Methods of propagation are not mentioned as special facilities for this are required. A temperature of 25°C (77°F) are often required for seeds and cuttings and propagating tables giving full details should be consulted. Only "classic" plants are mentioned here; real enthusiasts can refer to specialized literature.

## Agapanthus

**AFRICAN LILY**
See: Bulbs and tuberous plants.

## Agave

Agaves originated in North America, but have become naturalized in most of the world's tropical and subtropical regions. Some species are used as cattle feed; others provide fibers for

*Agave americana*

ropes (sisal). The plant is frost-tender, though older plants are likely to survive an occasional night frost. Propagate simply by removing offsets from the mother plant during repotting. When placed in a large container, an old agave may start producing flower stems up to 3m (10ft) tall. Do not water the plants in winter.

| A. americana | 5°C (41°F), gray. green, 1m (3ft) |
| A. a. 'Marginata' | gray. green, yel. margins, 1m (3ft) |
| A. filifera | 5°C (41°F), stiff, very sharp, 50cm (20in) |

## Ampelopsis

This vigorous climber bears blue berries after a hot summer. The plant is deciduous. This hardy garden vine can be grown in pots where the details given here apply.

| A. brevipedunculata | 0–5°C (32–41°F), green leaves 4m (13ft) |
| A. b. 'Elegans' | 0–5°C (32–41°F), white- and pink-spotted leaves, 2m (6ft) |

*Ampelopsis brevipedunculata* 'Elegans'

## Arbutus

### STRAWBERRY TREE

In southern Europe, an arbutus will grow into a tall tree; further north it will never be more than a large shrub. The plant has leathery oblong leaves; flowers and the previous year's fruits are often on the tree simultaneously. Temperature

for overwintering: 3–5°C (37–41°F), although the plant will withstand a few degrees of frost.

| A. unedo | white, 3–5°C (37–41°F), white, Sept–Nov, 3m (10ft) |

*Arbutus unedo*

## Argyranthemum

### MARGUERITE

This plant is often sold as an annual in spring and can quite well be kept through the winter. It is also possible to grow argyranthemums on short stems. Long flowering season.

| A. frutescens | 5°C (41°F), white, yellow center, May–Oct, 70cm (28in) |

*Argyranthemum frutescens*

## Brugmansia

There are several different species: the species with the upright flowers is an annual and bears the botanical name *Datura*; the one with the pendent flowers is called *Brugmansia* and can be kept through the winter. Both species require a minimum temperature of 5°C (41°F).

| | |
|---|---|
| *B. suaveolens* | 5°C (41°F), many colors, July–Sept, 2m (6ft) |

*Brugmansia suaveolens*

## Camellia

The most famous camellia is in Pullnitz (Saxony, Germany). It is 200 years old and 6m (20ft) tall; a mobile glasshouse is placed over it every fall. Nowadays there are hardier cultivars (minimum temperature -15°C/5°F). It is better to grow the plants in tubs or containers which are filled with acid, humus-rich soil; they can then overwinter in a frost-free position. A cool-greenhouse is also suitable for these plants, provided the roots are in open soil. *C. sinensis* requires a warmer position.

| | |
|---|---|
| *C. japonica* | -5–5°C (23–41°F), pink, Apr–May, 3m (10ft) |

## Canna

Cannas should be treated in much the same way as dahlias. The winter temperature needs to be higher: 15°C (59°F) is ideal, as rot will occur at lower temperatures. The flowering season is from August to October.

| | |
|---|---|
| *C. indica* 'Alberich' | salmon pink, 1.5m (5ft) |
| *C. i.* 'Lucifer' | 15°C (59°F), red/yel., 1m (3ft) |
| *C. i.* 'Perkeo' | red, 1.5m (5ft) |
| *C. i.* 'Puck' | yellow, 1.5m (5ft) |

*Canna indica* 'Lucifer'

*Camellia japonica*

## Chamaerops

Some palms will stand a few degrees of frost. This palm has no trunk; the leaves appear to emerge from the soil. Find the sunniest possible position for this plant.

C. humilis                    -2–10°C (28–50°F), 80cm (32in)

Chamaerops humilis

## Choisia

MEXICAN ORANGE BLOSSOM

The choisya is an acid-loving evergreen plant for humus-rich soil (a lot of garden peat). Its flowers resemble those of the orange, to which it is related. The plant flowers at an early age and will tolerate a few degrees of frost when it is older.

C. ternata            -5–10°C (23–50°F), white,
                      April, 2m (6ft)
C. t. 'Sundance'      -5–10°C (23–50°F), white,
                      yellowish green leaves

## Chrysanthemum

MARGUERITE

See: Argyranthemum.

## Citrus

LEMON, ORANGE

This is the ancient container plant *par excellence*.

Louis XIV imprisoned his Minister of Finance because he was jealous that Foquet's garden was more beautiful than his own. All the orange trees from Foquet's garden at the Château de Vaux-le-Vicomte were taken to Versailles. Citrus trees – which include all the lemon, orange, mandarin, and grapefruit trees – can be kept in a very cool place in winter. It is true that you can grow pretty little trees from a pip, but you cannot be sure whether the plant will be true to species. Don't worry if the orange pip subsequently produces sour lemons. The winter temperature for lemons and mandarins may be slightly lower.

Citrus                10–15°C (50–59°F), white,
                      May–Oct, 3m (10ft)
C. aurantiifolia      lime

Citrus aurantium

Choisia ternata

| C. aurantium | bitter orange |
|---|---|
| C. limon | lemon |
| C. x paradisi | grapefruit |
| C. reticulata | mandarin |
| C. sinensis | orange |

## Clivia

Clivias were often grown as indoor plants by our grandmothers, but we prefer them as container plants. Put them out of doors in the shade in summer, and in a cool room in winter; the ideal temperature is 18°C (64°F). Treated in this way, the plants will flower twice: once in late summer and once in early spring. Pollination out of doors will result in green berries, which will turn red a year later. Excessive watering during rest periods will prevent the flower stems from developing.

| C. miniata | 8–15°C (46–59°F), orange, red |
|---|---|
| C. m. 'Citrina' | 8–15°C (46–59°F), cream |
| C. m. 'Striata' | 8–15°C (46–59°F), striped leaves |
| C.n. 'Yellow Hybrids' | 8–15°C (46–59°F), yellow |
| C. nobilis | 8–15°C (46–59°F), red, more pendulous |

*Clivia miniata*

## Cordyline

### NEW ZEALAND CABBAGE PALM

Cordylines are ideal in the center of Victorian summer flower beds. The plant has narrow leaves produced on a straight stem. Do not prune the plant. Overwinter in a frost-free position – will tolerate minimum temperatures of -5°C (23°F). In Australia, cordylines develop into single- or multi-stemmed trees.

| C. australis | 0–10°C (32–50°F), green, 2m (6ft) |
|---|---|

*Cordyline australis*

## Corokia

### WIRE-NETTING BUSH

This attractive shrub for a pot or the open ground of a cool greenhouse has small star-shaped flowers. Tolerate some frost.

| C. cotoneaster | 4–10°C (39–50°F), white, Apr–May, 2m (6ft) |
|---|---|

*Corokia cotoneaster*

# Crinum

See: Bulbs and tuberous plants.

# Cupressus

Cypresses cannot survive the winter out of doors in many parts of North America, even though temperatures as low as -5°C (23°F) are not a problem. This means that this conifer will have to overwinter in a cool greenhouse. It is a suitable plant for introducing some "height" in a greenhouse, as there is often a dearth of tall evergreen plants.

C. sempervirens      -5–10°C, (23–50°F), blueish
green, columnar, 5m (16ft)

# Cycas

**SAGO PALM**

This plant is often referred to incorrectly as a "palm," even though it belongs the *Cycadaceae* rather than the *Palmae* family. Fierce sunlight causes yellow leaf burn. The plants can quite well overwinter in a living-room or cooler area. They will tolerate a few degrees of frost, but not for too long.

C. revoluta      5–15°C (41–59°F), broad, 60cm
(24in)

*Cycas revoluta*

# Datura

Daturas are annuals with dull green leaves and erect white flowers. They grow on old manure heaps, in neglected gardens, and so on. The plants are highly poisonous. See also *Brugmansia*.

D. stramonium      white, June–Sept, 1m (3ft)

# Dicksonia

**TREE FERN**

By far the most tree ferns are tropical plants. *D. antarctica* is the only one that will tolerate a few degrees of frost. The plant is suitable for a cool-greenhouse which can be slightly heated during severe frost. This tree fern can also be grown as a container plant. It is very expensive.

D. antarctica      5–10°C (41–50°F), 3m (10ft)
wide, 4m (13ft) tall

*Dicksonia antarctica*

*Datura stramonium*

## Eichhornia

**WATER HYACINTH**

This water plant can best overwinter in the living-room in very wet potting compost. In summer it prefers to float in water in a warm sunny spot. It is very suitable for a pond in a greenhouse. In spite of many failures, this plant continues to appeal because of its exceptionally beautiful hyacinth-like flowers.

| | |
|---|---|
| *E. crassipes* | 15°C (59°F), floating plant, blueish mauve, 20cm (8in) |

*Eichhornia crassipes*

## Eucalyptus

In southern U.S.A many species can grow out of doors, but in many areas of the U.S.A. even a moderate frost will kill them. The plant is suitable for growing in a (high) cool-greenhouse or as a container plant in a large pot. The listed species will tolerate a few degrees of frost; others are not worth trying, even in patio gardens.

| | |
|---|---|
| *E. gunnii* | 0–10°C (32–50°F), blueish green (when young), 10m (33ft) |
| *E. niphophila* | 0–10°C (32–50°F), grayish green (when young), 10m (33ft) |

## Eucomis

**PINEAPPLE FLOWER**

See: Bulbs and tuberous plants.

## Fatsia

Formerly an indoor plant, the fatsia has now been "downgraded" to container plant. It will tolerate a few degrees of frost: in Southern U.S.A. the shrub can overwinter out of doors. Put them in full or partial shade. It seems inconceivable that this large-leafed plant is closely related to *Hedera* (ivy). There is even a hybrid: x *Fatshedera lizei*, an indoor plant.

| | |
|---|---|
| *F. japonica* | 4–8°C (39–46°F), green, 2m (6ft) |

*Fatsia japonica*

## Fuchsia

Currently over 2,000 cultivars are grown in a small country like Holland. It is best for enthusiasts to join a fuchsia society. Amateurs usually grow them as annuals; enthusiasts dig them in (an old box freezer filled with peat dust

*Eucalyptus* (species)

is suitable) and unearth them again in April. It is amazing to see how they will grow again! Of course, it is also possible to let them overwinter in a slightly heated greenhouse.

*Fuchsia*

## Galtonia

See: Bulbs and tuberous plants.

## Grevillea

This Australian tree with delicately pinnate leaves will briefly tolerate a few degrees of frost. It requires slightly acid soil. Planted in a greehouse, the evergreen plant will grow into a tall tree, but it will remain much smaller in a container.

| | |
|---|---|
| *G. robusta* | 4–10°C (39–50°F), whitish yellow, all year round, 5m (16ft) |

*Grevillea robusta*

## Griselinia

This evergreen plant with round leathery light green leaves will tolerate a few degrees of frost. It may be planted in a cool-greenhouse, or in a container on a sheltered patio. The flowers are insignificant: male and female flowers are on different plants.

| | |
|---|---|
| *G. litoralis\** | -5–5°F (23–41°F), white, summer, 4m (13ft) |

*Griselinia litoralis*

## Hebe

Evergreen hebes can overwinter in a very sheltered position out of doors; a cool-greenhouse is better. Note that plants rooted in open ground will tolerate more frost than those in pots. Hebes prefer acid soil: add one-third garden peat to the potting compost. *H. armstrongii* and *H. cupressoides* have a bushy

*Hebe armstrongii*

growth rather like conifers; the others have "ordinary" leaves. Only the commonest species are listed here. The number of hebe cultivars is almost limitless and is still increasing. The species will tolerate considerably more frost than the hybrids.

| | |
|---|---|
| H. albicans | white, July–Aug |
| H. a. 'Andersonii' | blue, Aug–Sept |
| H. a. 'Autumn Glory' | mauve, Sept–Oct |
| H. a. 'Blue Clouds' | light blue, July |
| H. a. 'Midsummer Beauty' | lilac pink, Sept |
| H. armstrongii | white |
| H. buxifolia | white |
| H. cupressoides | white, June–July |
| H. kirkii | white, Aug–Sept |
| H. pinguifolia | white, June–Aug |
| H. salicifolia | lilac, Aug–Sept |

## Heliotropium

### HELIOTROPE

See: Annuals and biennials.

## Jasminum

### JASMINE

Jasmine is a frost-tender vine suitable for a slightly heated cool-greenhouse. It can grow very tall, but will stay much shorter in a pot (see also: Vines and wall plants). *J. mesnyi* and *J. polyanthum* will tolerate a slight frost.

| | |
|---|---|
| J. mesnyi* | 0–10°C (32–50°F), bright yellow, Mar–May, 4m (13ft) |

Jasminum mesnyi

| | |
|---|---|
| J. officinale | 5–10°C (41–50°F), white, June–Aug, 8m (26ft) |
| J. o. 'Affine' | 5–10°C (41–50°F), white, touch of pink, 8m (26ft) |
| J. polyanthum* | 5–12°C (41–53°F), May–Sept, 7m (23ft) |
| J. sambac* | 10–15°C (50–59°F), white (d), summer, 3m (10ft) |

## Lantana

In the event of a few degrees of night frost, lantanas will lose their leaves, but these will sprout again. The rounded flower heads, followed by berries (only after pollination, if they are grown out of doors), are the plant's main beauty. It may overwinter in the dark.

| | |
|---|---|
| L. camara | 5–10°C (41–50°F), red and yellowish, June–Sept, 2m (6ft) |

Lantana camara

## Laurus

### BAY LAUREL, SWEET BAY

We often find this evergreen shrub clipped, or grown in a globular shape on a rootstock. The plant will tolerate a night frost but prefers to overwinter at a higher temperature. If there is no frost, the bay tree may remain out of doors, and it should be put out of doors in a sheltered position early in the spring. This prevents its being seriously affected by cottony maple scale.

| L. azorica** | 5–10°C (41–50°F), green, 1.5m (5ft) |
| L. nobilis | -5–10°C (23–50°F) |

*Laurus nobilis*

## Lavandula

**LAVENDER**

This is the most attractive lavender for growing in a container (see also: Perennials).

| L. stoechas* | 0–5°C (32–41°F), pinkish mauve, June–Sept, 50cm (20in) |

*Lavandula stoechas*

## Leptospermum!

**'NEW ZEALAND TEA TREE'**

The New Zealand tea tree is not recommended as either an indoor or a container plant. If you forget to water it a single time, it will die. It would be far better to plant the tree in a cool-greenhouse, where the soil is guaranteed to remain moist. It will tolerate a few degrees of frost.

| L. scoparium | white, May–June, 2m (6ft) |
| L. s. 'Album Plenum' | white (d), 1.5m (5ft) |
| L. s. 'Crimson Sentry' | red, May–June, 1.5m (5ft) |
| L. s. 'Kea' | pink, low, May–June, 1m (3ft) |
| L. s. 'Kiwi' | deep pink, low, May–June, 1.5m (5ft) |
| L. s. 'Kotuki' | pink, low, May–June, 1m (3ft) |
| L. s. 'Nanum' | pink, May–June, 30cm (12in) |
| L. s. 'Nichollsii' | crimson, June–July, 1.5m (5ft) |
| L. s. 'Red Damask' | dark red (d), June–July, 1.5m (5ft) |
| L. s. 'Ruby Glow' | wine red (d), June–July, 1.5m (5ft) |

*Leptospermum scoparium*

## Liriope

See: Perennials.

## Magnolia grandiflora

See: Vines and wall plants.

## Malvaviscus

### SLEEPY MALLOW

This shrub is something in between a hibiscus and an abutilon. You can tell by the winter temperature that the sleepy mallow should be taken indoors in early fall. Like all members of the mallow family, the plant tends to be affected by whitefly.

| | |
|---|---|
| M. arboreus | 10–12°C (50–53°F), bright red, July–Sept, 1m (3ft) |

*Malvaviscus arboreus*

## Myrtus

### MYRTLE

This one-time indoor plant requires acid soil. It is frost-tender and needs to be kept moist. It is therefore better to grow myrtle in semi-shade, though full sun is possible.

| | |
|---|---|
| M. communis** | 5–10°C (41–50°F), white, July–Sept, 2m (6ft) |

*Myrtus communis*

## Nelumbo

### LOTUS

The word lotus has a magical ring to it – perhaps because it was cultivated by the ancient Egyptians? In zones colder than 5, it is difficult to winter this small water lily in a pond. Enthusiasts cultivate them in barrels which are placed in the warmest part of the garden in summer. When the plant dies down, it may overwinter more or less dry in not too cool a place. Do not confuse the English word lotus with the botanical name *Lotus* (see: Water plants).

| | |
|---|---|
| N. nucifera** | 15°C (59°F), pink or white, July–Sept |

*Nelumbo nucifera*

## Nerium

### OLEANDER

This genus includes many different-colored

*Nerium oleander*

cultivars, with either single or double flowers. To encourage an abundance of flowers, don't let them overwinter in too warm a place. The plants are usually supplied by color rather than by cultivar. The oleander is poisonous!

| | |
|---|---|
| *N. oleander* | 5–10°C (41–50°F), all colors, July–Sept, 2m (6ft) |

## Olea

### OLIVE

Regular pruning will give this old-fashioned evergreen container plant a handsome shape. It will tolerate a minimum temperature of -2°C (28°F); let the plant overwinter indoors in a cool place. Its flowers are not spectacular.

| | |
|---|---|
| *O. europaea* | 0–10°C (32–50°F), white, 2m (6ft) |

## Olearia

### DAISY BUSH

This evergreen shrub for very sheltered court-yards looks better when planted in the ground in a cool-greenhouse. It will tolerate temperatures as low as -5°C (23°F). The other species are less suitable for regions with cold winters.

| | |
|---|---|
| *O. haastii* | -5–5°C (23–41°F), white, July–Aug, 2m (6ft) |

*Olearia haastii*

## Passiflora

### PASSION FLOWER

In cold areas there are far greater opportunities for growing passion flowers in cool- or heated greenhouses than there are out of doors. If they are grown in pots, they can all go out of doors in summer. *P. edulis* has edible fruits. Several other species are hard to obtain. *P. caerulea* also has some new cultivars (see also: Vines and wall plants).

| | |
|---|---|
| *P. caerulea* 'Constance Elliott' | 5–10°C (41–50°F), white, June–Oct, 3m (10ft) |
| *P. edulis*** | 5–10°C (41–50°F), purplish white, July–Sept, 3m (10ft) |

*Passiflora caerulea*

## Phoenix

### DATE PALM

The familiar Canary Island date palm is often on sale in florists. Most of them die of excessive heat in winter. They also suffer from scale insects. Beware of leaf burn when you put the plant out of doors in May: keep it in the shade at first.

*Phoenix canariensis*

| | |
|---|---|
| _P. canariensis_ | 5–10°C (41–50°F), coarse, 3m (10ft) |
| _P. roebelenii_ | 8–10°C (46–50°F), delicate, 3m (10ft) |

## Phormium

**NEW ZEALAND FLAX**

This grass-like plant does not flower readily in some European climates, but its leaves are its main decorative feature. Give the plant a moist, or even a wet position. The indicated height is exclusive of flowers. This container plant can over-winter in a cool – but not frost-free greenhouse. If it is covered, New Zealand flax can remain out of doors; the leaves will then freeze off and it will be July before the plant's beauty is restored.

| | |
|---|---|
| _P. colensoi_ | 0–5°C (32–41°F), dk. g., 1m (3ft) |
| _P. tenax_ | -5–5°C (23–41°F), g. leaves, 1.5m (5ft) |
| _P. t._ 'Bronze' | -5–5°C (23–41°F), brown leaves 50cm (20in) |
| _P. t._ 'Variegata' | -5–5°C (23–41°F), yel. striped 1.5m (5ft) |

_Phormium tenax_ 'Purpureum'

## Pittosporum

Some species of this evergreen shrub with fragrant white flowers tolerate a degree or so of frost, but it is better to let them all overwinter at 5°C (41°F). Put them out of doors in not too sunny a spot in summer.

| | |
|---|---|
| _P. crassifolium_ | -2–10°C (28–50°F), purple, June–July, 3m (10ft) |
| _P. tenuifolium_ | 5–10°C (41–50°F), w., 3m (10ft) |
| _P. tobira_ | 0–10°C (32–50°F), brownish purple, May–June, 3m (10ft) |
| _P. t._ 'Variegatum' | 0–10°C (32–50°F), brownish purple, May–June, 3m (10ft) |
| _P. undulatum_ | 0–10°C, (32–50°F), white, May–July, 2m (6ft) |
| _P. u._ 'Variegatum' | 0–10°C (32–50°F), silvery variegations, May–July, 2m (6ft) |

_Pittosporum undulatum_

## Plumbago

**CAPE LEADWORT**

This plant is more or less evergreen, depending on the winter temperature. It will tolerate a minimum temperature of -2°C (28°F). If planted in the ground in a greenhouse, plumbago will grow to 3.5m (11ft). Cutting back the plant before removing it for the winter will simplify transportation. The name _P. capensis_ is outdated.

_Plumbago auriculata_ 'Alba'

| P. auriculata | 5–10°C (41–50°F), light blue, June–Oct, 2m (6ft) |
| P. a. 'Alba' | 5–10°C (41–50°F), white, June–Oct, 2m (6ft) |

## Punica

### POMEGRANATE

The pomegranate is a classic container plant. Let it overwinter at 5°C (41°F), and stand it in a sunny spot in summer. It should have humus-rich loamy soil with some sharp sand added. The height is based on large pots; in Mediterranean countries the plants will grow to 8m (26ft).

| P. granatum | 0–10°C (32–50°F), red, June–Aug, 3m (10ft) |
| P. g. 'Nana' | 0–10°C, (32–50°F), red, June–Aug, 1m (3ft) |

Punica granatum

## Rhodochiton

This annual climber can also be grown as a container plant, which should then be sown in spring (don't use old seed). The plant may be cut back in fall. Plants grown from seed will remain shorter for the first year, and will flower later.

| R. atrosanguineum | 4–12°C (39–53°F), d.p., June–Oct, 2m (6ft) |

## Rosa

### ROSE

The following scented small-flowered roses can be trained along the top of an unheated greenhouse. They can be grown outdoors in Zone 7 (Canadian). Pruning is unnecessary. These roses are only available from specialists. Exceptionally, they flower on three-year-old wood. If severely pruned, the rose will therefore not flower for two years in succession.

| R. banksiae var. banksiae* | -2–5°C (28–41°F), white, June–July, 10m (33ft) |
| R. b. var. lutea*! | -2–5°C (28–41°F), creamy yellow (d), June–July, 10m (33ft) |
| R. b. 'Alba Plena' | -2–5°C (28–41°F), yellow, single, June–July, 10m (33ft) |
| R. b. 'Lutescens' | -2–5°C (28–41°F), yellow, single, June–July, 10m (33ft) |

Rosa banksiae

Rhodochiton atrosanguinea

## Rosmarinus

### ROSEMARY

This herb is too tender to remain out of doors in areas subject to severe winters: it is better to grow it in a pot that can be brought indoors in winter. It can also be planted in the soil in a cool-greenhouse where the temperature cannot fall below -4°C (25°F).

| | |
|---|---|
| R. officinalis | 0–5°C (32–41°F), blue, Mar–Apr, 50cm (20in) |

## Salvia

### SAGE

Although they are not container plants, these species of sage cannot be regarded as annuals either. They are all frost tender and should overwinter indoors or in a cool-greenhouse. They can be planted in well-drained soil out of doors again in April, but are not so suitable for cultivating in pots.

| | |
|---|---|
| S. coccinea | blood red, 50cm (20in) |
| S. discolor | dark blue |
| S. guaranitica | cornflower blue |
| S. involucrata | pinkish red, 80cm (32in) |
| S. patens! | blue, 60cm (24in) |
| S. scabra | light blue |

Salvia patens

## Solanum

Some species are annuals, others are vines; they should all overwinter in a cool frost-free environment. The later are herbaceous with strong upright stems and large lancet-shaped leaves. The others are slender vines.

| | |
|---|---|
| S. crispum 'Glasnevin'* | 0–5°C (32–41°F), blue, June–Sept, 3m (10ft) |
| S. jasminoides | -5–5°C (23–41°F), light blue, June–Oct, 3m (10ft) |
| S. j. 'Album' | -5–5°C (23–41°F), white, June–Oct, 3m (10ft) |
| S. laciniatum** | 5–10°C (41–50°F), violet, July–Sept, 4m (13ft) |
| S. rantonettii** | 5–10°C (41–50°F) violet blue, July–Sept, 3m (10ft) |
| S. wendlandii** | 5–10°C (41–50°F), lilac blue, July–Sept, 3m (10ft) |

Solanum wendlandii

## Sparmannia

### AFRICAN HEMP

Like the arum lily and the clivia, this indoor plant had to make way for the central heating. Cut it back after it has flowered and put it out of doors in semi-shade in not too windy a spot.

| | |
|---|---|
| S. africana** | 8–12°C (46–53°F), white, Feb–Apr, 3m (10ft) |

## Tibouchina

### GLORY BUSH

The leaves feel velvety and the flowers look velvety. Compared with other container plants,

*Sparmannia africana*

*Viburnum tinus*

the glory bush should overwinter in a relatively warm position. Prune in early spring.

| | |
|---|---|
| *T. urvilleana*! | 10–15°C (50–59°F), mauvish blue, Sept–Oct, 2m (6ft) |

*Tibouchina urvilleana*

## Viburnum

### LAURUSTINUS

It takes the flower buds a long time to open. The white heads of flowers are followed in summer by black berries. It can perhaps remain out of doors on a sheltered patio, but it is better to let the plant overwinter in a cool-greenhouse.

| | |
|---|---|
| *V. tinus* | -5–5°C (23–41°F), white, Oct–Apr, 1.5m (5ft) |

## Washingtonia

### DESERT FAN PALM, THREAD PALM

Put this palm out of doors in summer and in a cool place in winter: a living-room is too warm. At one time, palms adorned parlors and drawing-rooms, but then they were not heated to such high temperatures. The palms will tolerate a few degrees of frost, but it is better not to take any risks.

| | |
|---|---|
| *W. filifera* | 5–10°C (41–50°F), green, 2m (6ft) |
| *W. robusta* | 8–12°C (46–53°F), green, 2m (6ft) |

*Washingtonia filifera*

# Index

# Acknowledgments

*The publishers and authors wish to thank all the following individuals, businesses, and organizations for their kind co-operation. This book could not have been produced without their help.*

**Perennials**
Rob de Boer, Frederiksoord
Decker-Jacobs bv, Heythuysen
Ploeger, De Bilt
J. de Jong en Zonen, Aalsmeer
Gebr. Koetsier, Boskoop
Rijnbeek en Zoon, Boskoop
De Kleine Plantage, Eenrum
Afien Torringa
Robert Adams

**Tree Nurseries**
De Bonte Hoek, Glimmen

**Bulbs and tuberous plants**
Kwekerij P.C. Nijssen, Heemstede
Bloembollen- en zaadhandel Van Tubergen, Heemstede

**Container Plants**
De Eglantier, Paterswolde

**Rose Growers**
Van Wanroy Rozen, Haps
Tuincentrum Vroom Dorkwerd, Groningen

**Seeds**
Cruydt-Hoeck, Groningen
Hamer Bloemzaden, Hendrik-Ido-Ambacht
Van Hemert & Co, Waddinxveen

**Bamboos**
Oosterwijck, Gilze
Jos van der Palen, *Groei en Bloei*

# Picture credits

G. Bierma, Voorst: pp. 114–130

Internationaal Bloembollencentrum, Hillegom: pp. 227, 228, 229 top and bottom left, 230 top and bottom left, 231–237, 238 right and bottom, 239, 240 bottom, 241–245, 246 top and bottom right, 247, 248 center and bottom, 249 top, bottom right, 250, 251

Fleurmerc, Wormerveer: pp. 35, 36 left, 39 top, 40 top, bottom left, 43 right, 56 top, 58 bottom left, 136 right, 143–160, 161 left and centre right, 162 left and right, 163–174, 175 left and right, 176–185, 186 bottom, 187–197, 198 bottom, 199–201, 202 top and bottom left, centre, 203–205, 206 top and bottom right, 207–209, 210 top and bottom left, 211, 212, 213 top, 214, 215, 216 top and bottom left, 217 bottom, 218–224, 225 top left, 226, 229 right, 230 bottom right, 238 top left, 240 bottom, 246 top left, 248 top, 249 bottom left, 252–258, 259 top left and right, 260–272, 274 bottom right, 277 top right, 279 top right, 280 bottom left, 281 top left, 282 right, 284 top left and right, 285 top left, 286 bottom left, 287 top right, 288 bottom right, 290 bottom right, 294 top, 295 top left and right, 296 top right, 298 bottom right, 299 left and top right, 300 top right, 302 left, 304 left and bottom right, 305 right, 306, 308 top right, 309 left, 310 bottom left, 311 top left, 314 bottom right, 315 left, 316 bottom left and right

A.H. Hekkelman, Bennekom: front cover: bottom center, top center, top left

R. Houtman, Boskoop: pp. 17 top left, 26 top left, 28 top right, 30 center, 33, 39 bottom, 52 bottom, 57 top, 60 top, 72 bottom, 74 bottom left, 82 right, 102 right, 103 right, 105 right, 106 top, 107 top, 108 top, 132 left and bottom, 137 top, 142 top left, 175 bottom, 186 top, 198 top, 202 bottom right, 206 left, 210 bottom

right, 259 bottom left, 278 bottom left, 313 left

F. Meijer, Landgraaf: front cover: center left and right, bottom left and right, back cover: top left and right, p. 3

J. Mol, Rijswijk: pp. 10–16, 17 top and bottom right, 18–25, 26 top and bottom right, 27, 28 top and bottom left, 29, 30 top and bottom, 31, 32, 34, 36 right, 37, 38, 40 bottom right, 41, 42, 43 left and bottom, 44, 45–51, 52 left and top, 53–55, 56 bottom, 57 bottom, 58 top, bottom right, 59, 60 bottom, 61–71, 72 top, 73, 74 top, bottom right, 75–81, 82 left, 83–101, 102 left, 103 left and bottom, 104, 105 left, 106 bottom, 107 bottom, 108 bottom, 109–113, 131, 132 right, 133–135, 136 left, 137 center and bottom, 138–141, 142 center and bottom, 161 bottom, 162 bottom, 213 bottom, 216 top right, 217 left and top, 225 top and bottom right, 274 left and top right, 275, 276, 277 left and bottom right, 279 left and bottom right, 280 top left and right, 281 bottom left and right, 282 top left and bottom, 283, 284 bottom left, 285 bottom left and right, 286 top left and right, 287 left and bottom right, 288 left and top right, 289, 290 left and top right, 291, 292 left and top right, 293, 294 bottom, 295 bottom left and right, 296 left and bottom right, 297, 298 left and top right, 299 bottom right, 300 left and bottom right, 301, 302 top right, 303, 304 top right, 305 left, 307, 308 top left and bottom right, 309 right, 310 right, 311 bottom right, 312 left and top right, 313 right, 314 left and top right, 315 right, 316 top left and top right

G.M. Otter, IJsselstein: pp. 302 bottom right, 308 bottom left, 310 top left, 311 bottom left and top right, 312 bottom right

S.W.T. Tolboom, Didam: front cover: top right, back cover: top center, p. 1